M000233874

THE ANTHROPOLOGY OF CLIMATE CHANGE

In addressing the urgent questions raised by climate change, this book provides a comprehensive overview of the anthropology of climate change, guided by a critical political ecological framework. It examines the emergence and slow maturation of the anthropology of climate change, reviews the historic foundations for this work in the archaeology of climate change, and presents three alternative contemporary theoretical perspectives in the anthropology of climate change.

This second edition is fully updated to include the most recent literature published since the first edition in 2014. It also examines a number of new topics, including an analysis of the 2014 American Anthropological Association's Global Climate Change Task Force report, a new case study on responses to climate change in developed societies, and reference to the stance of the Trump administration on climate change.

Not only does this book provide a valuable overview of the field and the key literature, but it also gives researchers and students in Environmental Anthropology, Climate Change, Human Geography, Sociology, and Political Science a novel framework for understanding climate change that emphasizes human socioecological interactions.

Hans A. Baer is Principal Honorary Research Fellow, School of Social and Political Sciences, University of Melbourne, Australia.

Merrill Singer is Professor at the Departments of Anthropology and Community Medicine, University of Connecticut, USA.

Routledge Advances in Climate Change Research

Adapting Infrastructure to Climate Change
Advancing Decision-Making Under Conditions of Uncertainty
Todd Schenk

Local Action on Climate Change
Opportunities and Constraints
Edited by Susie Moloney, Hartmut Fuenfgeld and Mikael Granberg

Pricing Carbon in Australia
Contestation, The State and Market Failure
Rebecca Pearse

The Paris Framework for Climate Change Capacity Building
Mizan R. Khan, J. Timmons Roberts, Saleemul Huq and Victoria Hoffmeister

The Anthropology of Climate Change
An Integrated Critical Perspective
Hans A. Baer and Merrill Singer

EU Climate Diplomacy
Politics, Law and Negotiations
Edited by Stephen Minas and Vassilis Ntousas

The Global Climate Regime and Transitional Justice
Sonja Klinsky and Jasmina Brankovic

Climate Justice and the Economy
Social Mobilization, Knowledge and the Political
Edited by Stefan Gaarsmand Jacobsen

A Critical Approach to Climate Change Adaptation
Discourses, Policies and Practices
Edited by: Silja Klepp and Libertad Chavez-Rodriguez

(Series page: https://www.routledge.com/Routledge-Advances-in-Climate-Change-Research/book-series/RACCR)

THE ANTHROPOLOGY OF CLIMATE CHANGE

An Integrated Critical Perspective

Second Edition

Hans A. Baer and Merrill Singer

LONDON AND NEW YORK

from Routledge

Second edition published 2018
by Routledge
2 Park Square, Milton Park, Abingdon, Oxon, OX14 4RN

and by Routledge
711 Third Avenue, New York, NY 10017

Routledge is an imprint of the Taylor & Francis Group, an informa business

First edition published by Routledge 2014

British Library Cataloguing in Publication Data
A catalogue record for this book is available from the British Library

Library of Congress Cataloging-in-Publication Data
Names: Baer, Hans A., 1944- author. | Singer, Merrill, author.
Title: The anthropology of climate change : an integrated critical
perspective / Hans A. Baer and Merrill Singer.
Description: Second edition. | New York : Routledge is an imprint
of the Taylor & Francis Group, an Informa Business, 2018. |
Series: Routledge advances in climate change research | Includes
bibliographical references and index.
Identifiers: LCCN 2017055882 (print) | LCCN 2018005594 (ebook) |
ISBN 9781351273121 (eBook) | ISBN 9781138574823 (Hardback) |
ISBN 9781138574847 (Paperback)
Subjects: LCSH: Human beings—Effect of climate on. | Climatic changes.
Classification: LCC GF71 (ebook) | LCC GF71. B34 2018 (print) |
DDC 304.2/5—dc23
LC record available at https://lccn.loc.gov/2017055882

ISBN: 978-1-138-57482-3 (hbk)
ISBN: 978-1-138-57484-7 (pbk)
ISBN: 978-1-351-27312-1 (ebk)

Typeset in Bembo
by Keystroke, Neville Lodge, Tettenhall, Wolverhampton

CONTENTS

ILLUSTRATIONS

Figures

Table

ACKNOWLEDGMENTS

Our scholarly interest in climate change or global warming began in the hot summer of 2005 while we were working on the first edition of *Introducing Medical Anthropology* (AltaMira Press, 2007). In Chapter 7, "Health and the Environment," of our text-book we included a section on "The Impact of Global Warming on Health." Indirectly, this small effort led to a book titled *Global Warming and the Political Ecology of Health* (Left Coast Press, 2009). Upon arriving at the University of Melbourne in January 2006, Hans Baer quickly touched base with fellow academics as well as students who share an interest in climate change. They include Peter Christoff, Liam Cooper, Peter Dwyer, Jim Falk, James Goodman, Jonathan Marshall, Monica Minnegal, Thomas Reuter, and Ariel Salleh. Hans joined forces with Verity Burgmann, a political scientist at the University of Melbourne, in the writing of *Climate Politics and the Climate Movement in Australia* (Melbourne University Press, 2012). He also collaborated with anthropologists interested in climate change at various other universities and institutions. These include Marcus Barber, Megan Jennaway, and Kay Milton (University of Auckland). Hans records his apprecia-tion to the University of Melbourne for granting him a six-month study leave in 2009 to conduct research on Australian climate politics and the climate movement.

Merrill Singer would like to acknowledge support from a University of Connecticut Provost's General Education Course Development Grant that led to the development of the course Global Climate Change and Human Societies and helped advance his understanding of climate change from an anthropological perspective. Merrill would also like to acknowledge colleagues at the University of Connecticut with whom he has had many climate change discussions, including Michael Willig and Peter Gunther.

INTRODUCTION

Even more so than the first edition, the second edition of *The Anthropology of Climate Change* provides the first comprehensive overview of the anthropology of climate change, an endeavor which has been in the making for the past 25 years. It highlights why anthropologists must significantly expand their focus on climate change and their contributions to responding to climate change as a grave risk to humanity. It has become increasingly apparent that climate change constitutes a major threat to human well-being and even survival. The overwhelming majority of climate scientists conclude that the warming of the planet and the associated climatic events that the planet has been experiencing are largely anthropogenic or the result of human activities, particularly since the Industrial Revolution. Climate change will have serious political-economic, sociocultural, and health impacts on human societies which have never faced an environmental problem on this scale and complexity in such a compressed time frame before. Numerous natural science disciplines from climatology to oceanography and from geophysics to biogeography have become involved in climate change research and its effects. Climate science maintains that a global average temperature increase of 2°C (3.6°F) constitutes a tipping point with respect to climate change. Some climate scientists place the tipping point lower, at around 1.5°C (2.7°F). Reportedly, 566 billion metric tons of CO_2 emissions have been added to the atmosphere since 1750 as a result of fossil fuel consumption and land cover change due to increased agricultural production and deforestation. Human societies have never faced an environmental problem on the scale of climate change before. While climate scientists have debated for a long time whether recent climate change is primarily a natural phenomenon rather than an anthropogenic one, the vast majority of them now agree that it has been largely created by the emission of various greenhouse gases, particularly carbon dioxide, nitrous oxide, and methane, which have increased, in the case of carbon dioxide, from 280 parts per million (ppm) at the time of the Industrial

Revolution to 406ppm in 2017. The Industrial Revolution, an important milestone in the development of global capitalism, was highly dependent on fossil fuels, initially coal and later petroleum and natural gas. Particularly after World War II, global capitalism began to place even more emphasis on the consumption of a seemingly endless array of products, a process that has increasingly diffused from the developed countries to the developing countries. As Renee Hetherington and Robert Reid (2010: 269) astutely observe: "Our growing obsession with, and economic dependency on fossil fuels, combined with our penchant for consumerism, has resulted in humans becoming a climate-change mechanism."

Ironically, about the same time that the first edition of this book appeared, Michael R. Dove (2014) published an anthology also titled *The Anthropology of Climate Change* with a different subtitle. He sought to compile key selections on what he terms "canonical works in the history of the anthropological study of climate and society" which include ones from "early anthropological works, recent ones, and those in between" (Dove 2014: xi). Achieving such a task in a single volume constitutes a daunting task, even in a relatively new subfield of anthropology that has emerged and rapidly grown over the course of the past 25 years or so. Dove's anthology does not constitute the first one in anthropology of climate change. That distinction belongs to Susan A. Crate and Mark Nuttall (2009a), who edited *Anthropology and Climate Change: From Encounters to Actions*, a book that appeared shortly after our *Global Warming and the Political Ecology* was released, also by Left Coast Press (Baer and Singer 2009). Yet another anthology in the rapidly burgeoning literature in the anthropology of climate change is *Climate Cultures: Anthropological Perspectives on Climate Change*, edited by Jessica Barnes and Michael R. Dove (2015a). While they acknowledge that many disciplines and scholars, including anthropologists, have turned their attention to climate change and assert that anthropology has much to offer to the examination of the "nexus of nature, culture, politics, and belief that constitutes climate change," they may be incorrect in their assertion that there exist "few books that represent the range of anthropological perspectives on climate change" (Barnes and Dove 2015c: vii). We certainly feel that the first edition of this book achieved this objective, and believe that the second edition does so even more. Conversely, Barnes and Dove (2015b: 9) are correct in asserting that anthropological perspectives on climate change are informed by ethnographic research, historically contextualize present-day anthropogenic climate change, and offer holistic views of the relationship between society and the environment.

More recently, Crate and Nuttall (2016b) published a second edition of their anthology which they assert boldly does not replace or make obsolete their first edition, but builds upon it as a "stand-alone volume that can be used in tandem" with it (Crate and Nuttall 2016a: 19). At any rate, the appearance of the above-mentioned books testifies to the fact that the anthropology of climate change has quickly become a vibrant subfield within anthropology, and more specifically within ecological or environmental anthropology.

In sum, the combined work of scholars spanning multiple disciplines has demonstrated that Earth is steadily warming; human activities are the dominant driver of this process; the pace and effects of warming have been increasing; and climate-based changes in the world we inhabit threaten significant if not severe consequences for human well-being on the planet. Yet, despite increasing recognition of the seriousness of these developments on the part of the governments around the world, they, as a whole, have been slow to respond effectively, beyond lofty pronouncements, to this pending threat, as seen in the failure of a series of international climate conferences designed to generate such a response. At the same time, while manufacturing and agro-business producers of greenhouse gases have developed a public discourse of Green Capitalism in recent years, continued emphasis on unceasing growth inherent in this initiative contradicts assertions that the current world economic system can achieve sustainability. Further, complicating the potentially confusing messages about the seriousness of our climate situation, a corporate-supported global warming denial campaign has succeeded in lowering public concern about climate change in the face of ever-mounting scientific evidence that anthropogenic climate change is a real and pressing fact.

How seriously should anthropologists take the claims of climate science in light of the fact that mainstream or conventional science has proven to be wrong at various times in the past on various assertions? Peter Doran and Maggie Kendall Zimmerman (2009) conducted a survey in which they found that 97.4 percent of the climatologists and 82 percent of the Earth scientists in their sample maintain that human-related activities are a significant factor in increasing global temperatures. They argue that the "debate on the authenticity of global warming and the role played by human activity is largely nonexistent among those who understand the nuances and scientific bases of long-term climate processes" (Doran and Zimmerman 2009: 23). This unprecedented level of agreement among natural scientists, supported by a growing body of observations by social scientists on the existing impacts of climate change, suggests that climate change should be taken very seriously indeed, far more seriously than has thus far been the case within and beyond anthropology.

All of these events have produced a significant challenge for anthropological relevance and for Sidney Mintz's (1985: xxviii) vision of crafting an *anthropology of the present*. In what fashion have anthropologists responded to climate change as a powerful force shaping the lives of the people they study? Does climate change constitute another instance of anthropology "missing the revolution" or, unlike other emergencies, such as the AIDS pandemic (to which anthropologists were somewhat slow to react), has anthropology been nimble in realizing the significance of climate change to human communities around the world and acting accordingly? Moreover, what does anthropology have to teach us about climate change and how we might move toward a human course that does not lead to self-destruction? These are questions that we address in this book

Moreover, it is appropriate to ask: What can a distinctly anthropological approach offer to the understanding of and social response to climate change? Jessica Barnes *et al.* (2013) suggest several general answers that will be explored more fully on the pages to follow: (1) the discipline's long tradition of carrying out in-depth field research gives anthropologists the tools needed to develop insight into the cultural values and political relations that structure the creation and flow of climate-related knowledge; (2) a concern with diversity and with local populations positions anthropologists to witness many on-the-ground adverse consequences of climate change, as well as the wide range of human responses to it that are unfolding around the world; (3) anthropological work on development projects like dam- or road-building efforts provides a foundation for assessing the unforeseen consequences of mitigation efforts; and (4) anthropology's holistic view of society unveils the complex interactions across sectors that it will be necessary to understand in implementing successful public policies concerning climate change.

In addressing these issues and the urgent questions raised by climate change, this book has the following purposes. First, we aim to document and assess the developmental status of the anthropology of climate change. Second, we seek to promote the rapid further development of this field in light of the world-changing implications of climate change. Third, we hope to demonstrate the useful contributions of the critical socioecological framework that guides our assessment. Finally, based on our review, we propose an orientation to a course of action that we believe is needed to avoid calamity.

In order to document and consolidate awareness of initial efforts in climate change anthropology and thereby provide a foundation for the further development of the field, this book provides an overview of the following anthropological approaches to climate change or global warming: (1) precursors to the anthropology of climate change, starting with Margaret Mead's pioneering interest in the topic; (2) archaeological approaches to past and current evidence of climate changes and their effects on and responses of human communities; (3) cultural ecological approaches; (4) cultural interpretive or phenomenological approaches; (5) the critical anthropological approaches; and (6) applied anthropological approaches. Over the past several years, we have been developing a critical anthropology of climate change, one that is derived from our work in critical medical anthropology and the relationship between health and the environment. This effort expanded into an understanding of anthropogenic climate change as yet another glaring contradiction of the capitalist world system, and the need to transcend it with an alternative world system based upon social equity and justice and environmental sustainability (Baer and Singer 2009).

This book is structured as follows.

Chapter 1, "Climate turmoil: introducing a socioecological model of human action, environmental impact, and mounting vulnerability," provides a framework for understanding the impacts of anthropogenic climate change induced by various greenhouse gases, particularly carbon dioxide, methane, and nitrous oxide. This framework provides an approach for understanding the impact of climate change in interaction with other anthropogenic ecological crises on human societies, particularly settlement patterns, subsistence and food security, and health.

In Chapter 2, "The emergence and maturation of the anthropology of climate change," we chronicle the work of various precursors of the anthropology of climate change, including Margaret Mead and archaeologist Brian Fagan. Despite the work of these scholars, anthropologists have been hesitant in their response to climate change although there appears now to be a slow maturation of the anthropology of climate change commencing with the publication of the American Anthropological Association's Anthropology Newsletter Forum on climate change in December 2007 and the publication of the first two anthropological books on climate change, *Global Warming and the Political Ecology of Health* (Baer and Singer 2009) and *Anthropology and Climate Change* (Crate and Nuttall 2009a).

Chapter 3, "The archaeology of climate change," explores the long-term role of climate change in human evolution as has been considered by human paleontologists, archaeologists, and other scholars. This chapter provides an overview of the role of primarily natural climate change (largely independent of human activity) in the biocultural evolution of humans in Africa and their subsequent dispersal to Eurasia, Australia, and the Americas. Climate change appears to have played a prominent role in the formation of various civilizations, the occupation or abandonment of regions over time, and the collapse of other civilizations. Rates of change, it is shown, have become ever more dramatic with the Industrial Revolution and with more recent patterns of globalism and deforestation.

In Chapter 4, "Theoretical perspectives in the anthropology of climate change," we provide an overview of three theoretical perspectives—cultural ecology, cultural phenomenology, and critical political ecology—that have emerged in the anthropology of climate change, which seek to grapple with various aspects of the human–climate change interface over the course of the past century or so.

In Chapter 5, "Case studies in the anthropology of climate change," we note that while there exist distinct theoretical perspectives employed by anthropologists seeking to comprehend climate change, in reality working on climate change may lead to a blending of these perspectives through eclectic approaches in a particular locale and how a local population perceives and respond to it. Bearing this in mind, this chapter presents several case studies that examine the research of various anthropologists who have worked on climate change issues in regions impacted by climate change or on specific topics related to climate change: The case studies that we present in this chapter are: (1) the Arctic and sub-Arctic region; (2) low-lying islands in the South Pacific; (3) Bangladesh; (4) high mountainous areas—the Andes, Himalayas, and the Alps; (5) dry places—sub-Saharan Africa and Australia; (6) the indigenous US Southwest; (7) responses to climate change in developed societies; and (8) the scientists of climate science and the anti-scientists of climate change.

In Chapter 6, "Applications of anthropological research on climate change," we note that proponents of the various anthropological perspectives tend to acknowledge that their research has an applied component, both for specific groups or societies that constitute the focus of their research and for the future of humanity in general. In this chapter, we review the applied work of anthropologists at four broad and quite distinct levels: (1) teaching about climate change in the anthropology curriculum; (2) climate policy; (3) working with local communities on climate change issues; and (4) working with and within the climate movement, both nationally and internationally. We maintain that anthropologists need to become involved as observers and engaged scholars in applied initiatives seeking to respond to climate change at the local, regional, national, and global levels. This requires that anthropologists be part of larger collective efforts to mitigate and, when necessary, adapt to climate change, whether it is on the part of international climate regimes, national and state or provincial governments, non-governmental organizations (NGOs), or climate action and sustainability groups.

Chapter 7, "What other social scientists are saying about climate change," maintains that climate change, especially anthropogenic climate change, is a topic that is inherently multidisciplinary and interdisciplinary. In this chapter, we provide a broad overview of the contributions that sociologists, political scientists, and human geographers.

In Chapter 8, "Conclusion: toward a critical integrated social science of climate change," we conclude that anthropology focuses upon the holistic study of human societies from their very beginning and into the future and in all parts of the world, and that it has a unique contribution to make to the study of the impact of climate change on human societies and how human activities have contributed to climate change, particularly since the Industrial Revolution. At the same time, it is important that anthropologists studying climate change remain conversant with the work of physical scientists, particularly climate scientists, as well as other social scientists and even scholars in the humanities.

1

CLIMATE TURMOIL

Introducing a socioecological model of human action, environmental impact, and mounting vulnerability

Human societies began to make the transition from small foraging or hunting-and-gathering bands to larger horticultural village groupings at least 12,000 years ago, and the transition to comparatively enormous stratified states about 6,000 years thereafter, starting initially in Mesopotamia and continuing somewhat later in Egypt, the Indus Valley, and China, and even a little later in the Americas and sub-Saharan Africa. These transitions have occurred in the context of what geologists call the Holocene, a geological era generally believed to be an interglacial period characterized globally by only minor shifts in climate, such as the Medieval Warm Period (AD 950–1250) and the Little Ice Age (AD 1300–1850). In local environments, however, there is geological and archeological evidence of marked climatic change during the Holocene. Climate change, although primarily driven at the time by natural forces rather than anthropogenic or human-created ones, appears to have played a role in shaping human societies over the centuries, including contributing to the collapse of some ancient civilizations, such as the Classic Maya in the ninth century AD (Kennett *et al.* 2012), and in the settlement or abandonment of various regions over time. In this sense, climate has always been a significant although often disputed factor influencing life on Earth, including the lifeways and behaviors of humans. For example, evidence suggests that "the climate controlled desiccation and expansion of the Saharan desert since the mid-Holocene may ultimately be considered a motor of Africa's [cultural] evolution up to modern times" (Kuper and Kröpelin 2006: 807).

Perspectives on the nature of the human/climate nexus, at times reflecting an environmental determinist or climate determinist stance, have passed through three broad phases. In the first, dating to ancient times, the celebrated Greek philosopher Hippocrates wrote a treatise titled "Airs, Waters, Places" in which he attributed cultural or dispositional differences to environmental factors. Similarly, polymath scholar/philosophers such as Ibn Khaldûn, credited by some as the father of the social sciences and historiography, explained the cross-cultural differences of which he was aware in terms of the determinant influence of the local physical environment, including habitat and climate (Gates 1967). By the second decade of the twentieth century, however, the power of environmental determinism as an intellectual current was in decline.

In anthropology, a field that has long grappled with the notion that each habitat presses for the development of a distinctive mode of cultural life or adaptive social pattern, researchers were moved away from determinist thinking under the influence of the detailed and particularist ethnographic focus on individual cases originated by Franz Boas and Bronislaw Malinowsi. At the heart of this turn was the realization that two groups in reasonably similar environments might develop differing and unique responses leading to differing cultural outcomes, or, conversely, that similar cultural traits might develop under divergent climatic and environmental conditions. Consequently, as Dean (2000: 89) indicates, "Scientific perspectives on the relationship of human societies to the natural environment have ranged from doctrinaire environmental determinism to the contention that environment has minimal impact on human societies." Beginning in the 1950s, with the insightful work of Julian Steward (1955), a new ecological perspective emerged in anthropology that once again began to give serious consideration to the role of the environment as an important influence—although certainly not a narrow and overwhelming determinant one—on human ways of life. In this new approach to the human relationship to the rest of nature, environmental determinism is tempered by an expanded awareness of the extensive impact of human action on other domains of the world. Humans do not adapt to existing environmental niches, they cope with existing challenges and exploit cultural opportunities, while re-shaping other components of the world to address culturally rooted needs and desires.

More recently, within the shadow of Steward, in what has come to be called environmental anthropology, "the [applied] study of the human–environmental relationship [has been] driven largely by environmental concern" about climate change, natural disasters, loss of biological diversity and related issues of sustainability (Shoreman-Ouimet and Kopnina 2011: 1). This same concern, strongly propelled by the seeking of answers to fundamental questions about "who owns the Earth [and who] owns the global atmosphere being polluted by the heat-trapping gases" (Chomsky 2013) and what we are to do meaningfully in a time of consequential global warming, motivates this volume. In answering these questions from the perspective of anthropology, with its core embrace of the rights and dignity of all people on the planet and with its recognition of the significance of human/environment interaction, we arrive at similar conclusions to those of Foster et al. (2010: 107): that "nothing less than an ecological revolution—a fundamental reordering of relations of production and reproduction to generate a more sustainable society—is required to prevent a planetary disaster." Like other critical social scientists, we believe that anthropology has been somewhat slow in addressing the destructive environmental trends triggered by earlier human actions and significantly magnified by contemporary neoliberal capitalism, especially "the expansion of human populations and consumption habits in the context of industrial and economic development" within the world economic system (Kopnina and Shoreman-Ouimet 2017: 4).

Increasingly, however, some anthropologists have turned their lenses to the issue of contemporary climate change, seeking to ground it both in an understanding of the human/climate interface through time and within the contexts of living communities encountering and responding both to marked changes in their local environments and to the science of climate change and denials of the validity of such science. As the size of this literature has grown at an increasing pace, there is value in consolidating this body of work, assessing its primary features and scope, noting gaps in efforts to date, suggesting a model for thinking about climate change anthropologically, and calling attention to a pathway of needed praxis and change in light of the exigent nature of our assessment.

It is evident to researchers of various disciplines that climate on Earth has never been static. Sixty-five million years ago, for example, when dinosaurs were a dominant life form, much of the planet was tropical, with palm trees growing in what we now call Antarctica and crocodiles living in Greenland. In the contemporary period, however, of far greater importance than the natural sources (e.g., volcanoes, solar variation) that were the primary engines of climate change in the past are those driven by intentional human activities and technologies. For the past 10,000 years, Earth's overall temperature has been "remarkably mild and stable—nicknamed a 'sweet spot' by climate scientist Robert Correll—not increasing or decreasing more than 0.5°C [0.9°F]" (Aitken 2010: 129). Human impact, however, has destabilized Earth's climate in ways never before believed to be possible. Driven by a global dependence on fossil fuels, the level of carbon dioxide in the atmosphere passed 400 parts per million in 2013, the highest level since the Pleistocene, and it continues a relentless rise, as seen in the record increase of 1.4 percent to 31.6 gigatons of CO_2 emissions in 2012. There is now direct observational evidence of atmospheric CO_2 levels and surface temperature on Earth (Kahn *et al.* 2016). As a result of this heating trend, we now face a planetary emergency that demands a sea change in our understandings and actions.

Conceptualizing anthropogenic climate change

At first blush, talking about a distinct anthropological take on climate change, which entails a global set of physical processes, may appear out of character or at least illusive for a social science field like anthropology that made its name based on intensely focused small-scale studies of particular peoples living out varying cultural lives in local settings around the planet. In fact, in the latter part of the twentieth century and continuing since, anthropology has undergone dramatic change as the forces of neoliberal globalization and development have reconfigured human life everywhere. While often carried out, at least in part, in provincial settings, anthropological research today focuses on the consequential engagement of local worlds with global processes and structures. As Eriksen (2001: 2) stresses:

It has been common to regard its traditional focus on small-scale non-industrial societies as a distinguishing feature of anthropology. . . . However, because of changes in the world and in the discipline itself, this is no longer an accurate description.

Today, anthropologists often study big issues in small places, as well as carrying out multisited studies across multiple physical settings and structural locations in hierarchical social systems. This has entailed the development of approaches for the study of entwined social and environmental/climatic complexity.

Local worlds, we realize, are not made only on the ground, but are reflections of historic and ongoing connections and impacts that occur across levels and as a result of cross-cutting processes like power or dynamic global impacts such as climate change (Wolf 1982). Today, anthropological research is pitched at various scales, and especially at points of intersection and flow between the local and the global or among levels in between. It is in this context that an anthropology of climate change has come into being, stressing "the importance of inserting anthropological arguments into debates on climate change" (Hirsch *et al.* 2011: 267).

Our model

This chapter introduces our human "climate/environment/society" or socio-ecological framework comprised of three linked concepts—"anthropogenic climate turmoil," "ecocrisis or pluralea interactions," and "environmental unpredictability" and the associated concepts of "perceived precarity" and "vulnerability"—that guides our discussion of the human/climate change interface in this volume, as illustrated in Figure 1.1.

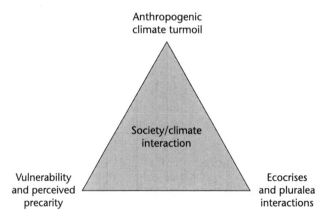

FIGURE 1.1 Socioecological framework for the anthropological study of climate change

Underlying our model is the recognition that Earth as an ecological system has limits and that human technologies now have the capacity to overtax *"planetary boundaries"* and "trigger abrupt or irreversible environmental changes that would be deleterious or even catastrophic for human beings" (Rockström et al. 2009). By "planetary boundaries," Johan Rockström of the Stockholm Resilience Centre at Stockholm University and his multinational team of fellow authors stress the importance of biophysical processes that shape the self-regulating capacities of the planet. This approach draws attention to immutable thresholds and tipping points, the crossing of which, for prolonged periods, can set in motion non-linear changes that put in jeopardy "the safe operating space for humanity" on the planet (Rockström et al. 2009). This understanding builds on the *limits-to-growth* (LtG) analyses that began in 1972 at the Massachusetts Institute of Technology (Meadows et al. 1972) and have sought, based on repeat reviews of available information, to link the world economy with the state of the environment. This work has involved the development of increasingly sophisticated models of the planetary consequences of unchecked economic and population growth. Although the LtG perspective has been dismissed by advocates of unfettered growth as leading to unsupported doomsday predictions, several years ago Graham Turner (2008), an applied physicist, carefully assessed the past 30 years of lived reality in light of the predictions made in 1972 and in subsequent LtG reports (e.g., Meadows et al. 1992, 2004). He concluded that the expansion of industrial production, the spread of high-tech agriculture, and the resulting generation of expanding quantities of pollution and greenhouse gases are consistent with LtG predictions of ecological, economic, and societal collapse during the twenty-first century. Turner (2008: 38) observes that existing evidence "lends support to the conclusion of the LtG that the global system is on an unsustainable trajectory." In a subsequent 40-year review of LtG predictions, Turner (2014), concluded that "a challenging lesson of the LtG analysis is that global environmental issues are typically intertwined and should not be treated as isolated challenges." Moreover, he stresses that:

> the alignment of data trends with the LtG dynamics indicates that the early stages of collapse could occur within a decade, or might even be underway. This suggests, from a rational risk-based perspective, that we have squandered the past decades, and that preparing for a collapsing global system could be even more important than trying to avoid collapse.
>
> *Turner 2014: 16*

Further, with regard to the growing size and environmental demands of the human population, Giorgio Nebbia (2012: 86) asks the following question:

> The population of the world has increased almost fivefold, which has entailed a tenfold increase in the demand for food, energy, metals, space, housing, and water. There has also been a tenfold increase in the number of people living in urban agglomerations. How long can this last?

At first glance, given its ultimate goal of human survival, embedded in the planetary boundaries framework there appears to be some degree of what has been called *anthropocentric environmentalism*. This term refers to efforts to justify the protection of nature primarily as a necessity of human survival. In its most explicit forms, anthropocentric environmentalism draws a sharp divide between humans and the environment. This distinction has deep roots in mainstream Western thought, from the Judeo-Christian tradition to Cartesian thinking to sectors of contemporary environmentalism, and has led to the development of "binary oppositions [such as] human beings versus animals, and nature versus culture" (Koensler and Papa 2013: 286). As Williams (2003: 5) observes:

> It is a deeply rooted myth in the Western psyche and its culture that nature is a passive, harmonious, God-given backdrop against which the drama of human life is played out; the "sound and fury" of human existence contrasting with the notion that "earth abides."

Within the planetary boundaries model, and within our own perspective as expressed in this book, however, there is keen recognition that nature is not a backdrop to the important events that unfold on the stage of human activity. Rather, there is a multidirectional aspect to the human interaction with the rest of nature based on an ever-ongoing "interrelatedness of human actions and biogeophysical processes" (Dearing 2007: 27). Further, there is recognition of the distortions and dangers of anthropocentrism, no less than those of ethnocentrism, as both these reductionist orientations fail to comprehend broader structures and processes characterized by deep entwinement, be it people with other sectors of nature or the various human ethnocultural groups dispersed around the planet with each other (LeVine and Campbell 1972; Taylor 1986). Uniting critiques of both of these fraught lenses on "people in the world," we seek to develop a model founded on a view of humans and their cultures as being within and not separate from nature, and an assessment of the ways power, a productivist ethic of endless economic expansion, and social injustice, environmentally expressed and experienced, can push ecological systems beyond the coping capacity of species, including our own. From the standpoint of living systems, human and otherwise, we face a form of destruction from within, a set of circumstances that "can be called, without hyperbole, threatened apocalypse" (Foster *et al.* 2010: 109). Given the demonstrated ability of life forms to thrive under an extremely wide range of ecological conditions, what is at stake is not life or even the planet, but life as we know it, including the historic life of our species and that of many other faunal and floral inhabitants of Earth.

A starting point for our approach lies in the recognition that while the terms "climate change" and "global warming" are in common use to label the significant climatic changes occurring on Earth in the contemporary period and projected into the future, neither of these terms quite captures what is happening in the world around us. Certainly, climate is changing, but what is important is not change itself, but the distinctive overall trend toward warming. Within this trend, moreover, there are changes, such as ocean acidification and black carbon build-up, which are not quite obvious from the term "climate change."

Similarly, while "global warming" is the behind-the-scenes engine driving an array of climate changes, it too does not express the erratic nature of what is occurring, nor does it seem to cover the sudden and even more frequent appearance of extreme storms like Hurricane Sandy of 2012 or Typhoon Haiyan in 2013.

Additionally, while human activity, such as massive industrial increases in the release of greenhouse gases, is the engine driving changes in climate patterns, there are a number of important environmental feedback mechanisms—outside of direct human causation—that also are at play. Thus the melting of sea ice by rising planetary temperature exposes dark water (which, unlike ice, absorbs rather than reflects solar energy), increasing the temperature of the oceans. Warming of arctic areas accelerates the release of carbon dioxide from permafrost, adding to the green-house blanket. Similarly, heat waves, droughts, and storms impede plant growth, weakening a major safeguard against increases in the level of CO_2 in the atmosphere. Plants withdraw from the air a significant amount of the CO_2 that is produced through the burning of fossil fuels. Droughts and heat waves, as well as extreme storms that destroy forest biomass, can lead to measurable increases in atmospheric CO_2. Additionally, increasing CO_2 levels in the atmosphere may create turbulence, especially over the North Atlantic, over which 600 airplane flights occur every day. To get around this turbulence—and save passengers from feeling as though their plane is going to crash—aircraft are having to fly further, using more fuel, and generating more CO_2 in an ongoing upward spiral. Many climatic feedback mechanisms are of grave importance because once a threshold is passed triggering their activation, they can drive planetary heating without additional anthropogenic inputs.

Climate turmoil

In light of these challenges, in this book we argue for the alternative labeling of "climate turmoil"—to encompass global warming, weather extremes, diverse and even seemingly contradictory expressions of climate change, and mounting erraticism. The use of the term "turmoil" in this context has its roots in the volume *Gaia in Turmoil* (Crist and Rinker 2010). Gaian theory, first articulated by James Lovelock and Lynn Margulis (1974), rests on the anti-anthropocentric view that Earth's physical and biological processes are inextricably bound together to form a self-regulating system that helps sustain the conditions that allow life to flourish on the planet. Notably, as part of this theory, the greenhouse gas CO_2, and the activities of living organisms in the carbon cycle, are seen as playing critical roles in the maintenance of Earth's surface temperature within the limits of habitability. While carbon monoxide is a potentially lethal toxin, the addition of a second oxygen atom to form carbon dioxide makes the molecule harmless to life. Carbon dioxide is not even an environmental pollutant. In fact, without CO_2 in the atmosphere holding in some of the Sun's radiation, Earth would be an ice planet devoid of life.

Atmospheric CO_2 and other greenhouse gases such as methane and nitrous oxide are transformed into threats at the point at which their density holds in so much solar energy that they cause temperature destabilization. By analogy, warm water in a shower is pleasant and cleansing, but above a certain temperature, hot water becomes scalding and dangerous.

As a result of the voluminous and growing human release of greenhouse gases, our world has begun to reach that perilous threshold separating the temperature comfort zone of the last 10,000 years and the beginning of a new climatic era characterized by far less stability. The disruption of climatic patterns through the heating up of the planet results in the onset not only of generally rising temperatures, but increased frequency and intensity of severe storms, deadly summer heat waves, persistent and withering droughts, rising oceans that threaten low-lying islands and coastal areas, devastating flooding, and ocean acidification, among other dramatic changes. In other words, climate change in the form of global warming is the superstructure and hence only part of what is shifting in our world. In their attempt to call attention to the diverse, and even seemingly contradictory, aspects of the new climate instability (e.g., droughts in some places, flooding in others), the journalists and climate scientists at Climate Central, a non-partisan science and journalism organization, chose the quirky title *Global Weirdness* (Elert and Lemonick 2012) for their public education audiobook detailing the diverse impacts of contemporary anthropogenic climate change.

We opt for the alternative of "climate turmoil" to underline the mayhem and disorder caused by superstorms like Hurricane Sandy of 2012, which was gargantuan in size and carried an unusual amount of moisture. Much of the warming from climate change occurs in the ocean, and in 2012 sea surface temperatures were well above normal. September 2012 saw the second highest ocean temperatures on record globally. During its formation, Hurricane Sandy spent significant time over uncommonly warm seas, boosting the amount of moisture available to rain down on the Northeast United States (Fischetti 2012). Moreover, Hurricane Sandy encountered a weather "traffic jam" in the North Atlantic, a phenomenon known as a "block" to meteorologists. This block did not allow Sandy to track out to sea like most northeast storms. Meanwhile, a storm associated with very cold air over the Midwest also ran into this Atlantic traffic jam, resulting in an unusual "hybrid" storm that devastated portions of the Caribbean and the Mid-Atlantic and Northeastern United States. The storm caused damage worth at least $75 billion and killed 285 people. Importantly, recent research has shown that these blocking events and Fall cold outbreaks are related to sea ice loss in the Arctic, a recognized product of global warming. Thus, in an op-ed published in the *Washington Post* after Hurricane Sandy, James Hansen (2012a), formerly of NASA's Goddard Institute for Space Studies, wrote:

> Our analysis shows that it is no longer enough to say that global warming will increase the likelihood of extreme weather and to repeat the caveat that no individual weather event can be directly linked to climate change. To the

contrary, our analysis shows that, for the extreme hot weather of the recent past, there is virtually no explanation other than climate change.

Hansen added that the Russian heat wave of 2010 and the catastrophic droughts that hit Texas and Oklahoma in 2011 could all be attributed to climate change based on existing research. Further, he noted that: "The odds that natural variability created these extremes are minuscule, vanishingly small. To count on those odds would be like quitting your job and playing the lottery every morning to pay the bills." The same applies to Typhoon Haiyan, perhaps the largest typhoon to make landfall in recorded history, where a warmer ocean may well have contributed to the size and force of this lethal example of extreme weather.

Similarly, global warming has increased fivefold the risk that Australians will suffer record hot summers, according to new research by climate scientists Sophie Lewis and David Karoly (2013) of the University of Melbourne. During the summer of 2013, Australia experienced the hottest summer ever recorded, which Lewis and Karoly concluded was very likely (with a greater than 90 percent confidence level) a consequence of anthropogenic climate change. At the same time, in places like the American West and in Europe, forest fires are occurring more often during longer fire seasons, wildfires are larger and hotter, and they are causing more damage, all as a result of drying conditions produced by climate change (Moritz et al. 2012). In short, we have entered into an era of climate turmoil in which, in Hansen's words (2012a), diverse extreme weather events "will become even more frequent and more severe," changing the human experience of life on Earth.

The magnitude of the changes we are seeing led Dutch atmospheric chemist Paul Crutzen (Crutzen and Stoermer 2000) to suggest that the geographic age of Earth in which we now live should be renamed the Anthropocene (Age of People). His argument is that for the last 150 years, more so than natural forces, it is human activity that has had the most impact on shaping the bio-geological environments of the planet and its climate. In fact, as far back as 1870, the Italian geologist Antonio Stoppani proposed the term anthropozoic, for precisely the same reason, although Stoppani's proposal was ignored. Now, however, the extent of the human footprint on the planet is so much more obvious than in Stoppani's day. Already, the human biomass, for example, is 100 times greater than any other large animal species that ever lived on Earth, dinosaurs included, according to calculations done by noted biologist and ecologist Edward O. Wilson (Kolbert 2011).

In Crutzen's view, the start of the Anthropocene can be dated to the latter part of the eighteenth century, when analyses of air trapped in polar ice showed the beginning of growing global concentrations of carbon dioxide and methane. This date also coincides with James Watt's design of the steam engine in 1784. The extent of the human impact on the planet took a sizeable jump after the Second World War, when the human population doubled, going from three billion in 1950 to six billion in 2000, and the scale of industrial production, consumerism (which might better now be called hyper-consumption), and globalism accelerated rapidly. Today, in Crutzen's terms (Crutzen and Schwägerl 2011), Earth "is being anthroposized at high speed."

Reflecting on the first of the Grand Challenge Symposia organized by the Smithsonian Institution in 2012, anthropologist Shirley Fiske (2012c) emphasized that "the meaning of the Anthropocene is ethical and moral—how do we want the future to look and what can we do with the knowledge we have?" Whatever human intentions may be, however, it is clear that, barring a global catastrophe (e.g., a major meteor impact, all-out nuclear war, an unstoppable infectious disease pandemic, or worst-case global warming), humankind likely will remain a major environmental force for the foreseeable future. Already, some, like Bill McKibben (2010: 2), have suggested that:

> The world hasn't ended, but the world as we know it has—even if we don't quite know it yet. We imagine we still live back on that old planet, that the disturbances we see around us are the old random freakish kind. But they are not. It's a different place. A different planet.

Pluralea interactions

Beyond the myriad impacts of climate change expressed in the concept of climate turmoil, we stress that it is critical to recognize that radical changes happening on Earth are not happening in isolation solely as a result of greenhouse gas emissions. Rather, many of the most threatening changes are a product of anthropogenic climatic interactions with other human-wrought ecocrises such as deforestation, coral reef loss, mangrove loss, wetlands loss, air pollution, and water pollution. These anthropogenic climate/environment interfaces, as explained below, have been termed in the anthropological literature "pluralea interactions," and they suggest the unintended ways combined human actions and their effects are ominously reshaping Earth (Singer 2009b, 2010a).

This component of our model emphasizes the need not to see the various environmental calamities that we have helped to create—from oceans rapidly losing important components of their biodiversity to air over the world's cities that is toxic to breathe—as standalone threats to human well-being. To do so produces a narrow and siloed outlook on contemporary ecocrises that leads to fragmented and even competing mitigation responses. Rather, adverse human impacts on the environment intersect in consequential ways, and the resulting interactions significantly exacerbate the overall consequences for humans, as well as for other animals and plants, creating potentially catastrophic outcomes (Rees 2003).

The term "pluralea interactions" is derived from the Latin words *plur*, meaning "many," and *alea*, meaning risks or hazards. What is of importance here is not just the number of risks we have created, but the ways they are mutually magnifying in their impact. Central to the pluralea perspective is the development of an understanding of the pathways and mechanisms through which two or more ecocrises interact to produce synergistic, magnified environmental and human impacts. A case in point is that respiratory health has been growing worse "because of interaction between heavier pollen loads and increased air pollution; thunderstorms and extreme precipitation events; worsening heat-related ground-level ozone pollution; increased ambient air pollution from natural and anthropogenic sources; and air pollution related to wildfires" (Shea *et al.* 2008: 445). This conclusion, based on a review of various studies, is supported by high-resolution climate/air pollution computer modeling (Noyes *et al.* 2008; Ren *et al.* 2008). The specific linkages between global warming, air pollution, and respiratory health include: (1) the deleterious effects of toxins produced by motor vehicles, industrial power plants, and industrial chemicals, such as environmentally released pesticides, as a result of expanded environmental discharge and increasing planetary temperatures; (2) forest fires that release ever-greater quantities of hazardous particulate matter, carbon monoxide, and polyaromatic hydrocarbons as a result of global warming and drier environmental conditions; (3) noxious mold exposure facilitated by changes in precipitation patterns, farm land restructuring, and more frequent flooding and water intrusion in buildings associated with climate turmoil; and (4) expansions in both the range and quantity of pollen from ragweed and other allergy-linked flora produced by global warming (Ontario Lung Association 2008).

These kinds of complex sets of interactions between global warming and various anthropogenic impairments to clean air can be seen as well in other planetary ecozones. Forests, for example, are being cut down at an alarming pace, removing a vital "carbon sink" that stores CO_2. It is estimated that one-fifth of the world's tropical rainforest was destroyed between 1960 and 1990 (Mongillo and Zierdt-Warshaw 2000). Deforestation releases stored carbon into the atmosphere, enhancing the greenhouse blanket and accelerating global warming. Warming, in turn, creates droughts, as have begun occurring in the Amazon, that are killing sections of forests.

The size of the continental United States, the Amazon holds 20 percent of Earth's fresh water and generates a fifth of its oxygen. With the planet's climate increasingly threatened by anthropogenic carbon emissions, the Amazon has been one of the few forces (the oceans being another) keeping global warming in check. The rainforest absorbs two billion tons of atmospheric CO_2 annually. Climate researchers report, however, that billions of trees died in record droughts that hit the Amazon in 2005 and 2010 (Lewis *et al.* 2011). An area in the Amazon twice the size of California experienced what scientists have called "megadroughts" during these periods. Satellite and ground data show an increase in wildfires and tree die-offs following both the 2005 and 2010 droughts. These findings support others indicating that the Amazon is receiving less and less rainfall per year. All the tree deaths caused by these droughts contribute to the forest transforming from a carbon sink into an emission source of CO_2, leading to an enhancing process of further warming and further droughts, and threatening the entire region and all regions that benefit from the oxygen, hydraulic, and carbon-sequestering environmental services of the Amazon. Magnifying the intensity of this crisis is a massive level of intentional deforestation to create pasture lands for cattle and clear acreage for mono-crop agricultural production of soy or biofuels, especially for export to wealthy countries (Williams 2003).

Another pluralea interaction of consequence for human populations involves the multiple ways human activities are contributing to the loss of coral reefs around the planet. An analysis titled *Reefs at Risk* undertaken by the World Resources Institute and 25 other research organizations (Burke *et al.* 2012) concludes that currently three-quarters of the world's coral reefs are at risk and that by 2050 virtually all such systems will be in danger. Already, the Great Barrier Reef in Australia has lost more than half of its coral cover since 1985, with two-thirds of this loss occurring since 1998 (De'ath *et al.* 2012). The consequences for countries in what has been called the Coral Triangle, which includes Indonesia, Malaysia, Papua New Guinea, the Philippines, Solomon Islands, and Timor-Leste, as well as in the Caribbean and elsewhere, that depend for food on the fish and other animals attracted by coral reefs, is projected to be severe. It is estimated that 275 million people around the world live near (i.e., within 30km of) coral reefs, and many people in these areas depend on reefs for a livelihood (Burke *et al.* 2012). Coral reefs are also vital as a barrier protecting coast lands and islands from erosion, storm surges, flooding damage, and salinization of crop lands and fresh water sources (Wilkinson 2008). The anthropogenic threat to coral reefs has several sources. Climate change, by raising the temperature of the oceans, is leading to coral bleaching, which is a stress response to rising ocean temperatures. As the ocean waters around reefs heat up, zooxanthellae, the tiny organisms that provide coral reefs with their brilliant colors, emigrate from their hosts in massive numbers, killing both themselves and the coral they leave behind. Additionally, greenhouse gas emissions are increasing the carbon dioxide in the ocean, altering ocean chemistry (by making it more acidic), resulting in a slowing of coral growth and a weakening of coral structures. Additionally, in many environments, corals compete for space with seaweed. Seaweed grows much faster than coral, giving it a modest competitive advantage. Humans, however, have helped to tip this balance strongly in favor of seaweed by over-harvesting the fish and other herbivores that keep seaweed under control. Additionally, the dumping of human sewage into the oceans has provided nutrients for rapid seaweed and algae growth, to the disadvantage of corals. The interaction of climate change and ocean acidification, sewage dumping, and overfishing in the demise of coral reefs affirms the significance of pluralea interactions as a risk factor in a time of global warming.

Another important example of pluralea interaction involves black carbon. The term "black carbon" refers to a climate change-forcing agent better known outside of climate science as soot, which is a form of particulate matter with its own adverse impacts on living organisms that breathe oxygen. It is formed anthropogenically as a result of the incomplete combustion of fossil fuels and biofuels and the intentional burning of biomass (e.g., to clear land), as well as through wildfires. When black carbon lands on snow or ice-covered areas, such as the Arctic, glaciers, and high mountains, it causes Earth to absorb more sunlight, rather than reflecting it back into the atmosphere as uncovered snow does, a process called albedo. After greenhouse gases, black carbon is the second biggest human cause of global warming. It is estimated that black carbon, the climate change impact of which has been significantly unstudied until recently, is responsible for a quarter of observed global warming (Bond *et al.* 2013).

Black carbon is unevenly distributed around the planet, with "hot spots" being close to emission sources on the ground (e.g., parts of Asia or the city of Chicago). Black carbon is now known to be a significant contributor to Arctic ice-melt, and all that results from it such as sea ocean rise. Unlike CO_2, black carbon is an anthropogenic pollutant that is toxic to humans and, simultaneously, has the effect of a greenhouse gas in that it promotes global warming.

One type of pluralea interaction that has been posited involves the effects of what has been called "peak oil" on global warming. In 1974, M. King Hubbert, a geoscientist who worked at the Shell research laboratory in Houston, Texas, asserted that, given levels of extraction and in-ground availability, global oil production would peak in 1995. As early as 1956, in fact, he argued that "we can assume with complete assurance that the industrial exploration of the fossil fuels will consist in the progressive exhaustion of an initially fixed supply" (Hubbert 1956: 4). While this prediction proved inaccurate in the time frame proposed by Hubbert, various analysts have written a series of papers and books expressing similar expectations about the potential consequences of passing the point of peak global oil production. In *Peak Oil and the Second Great Depression (2010–2030)*, Kenneth Worth (2010), for example, argues that reductions in oil availability will drive up costs and lead to mass unemployment far beyond the recession of the first decade of the twenty-first century. Some, however, have seen the arrival of peak oil as an opportunity for a social shift to renewable and sustainable energy sources, while others have worried about the pressure peak oil would create for an expansion of nuclear energy development and the environmental threats that it introduces.

In the short run, it is now evident that we have not reached peak oil, as levels of oil production continue to rise, as have those of natural gas. In retrospect, it is clear that peak oil theorists did not anticipate rapid developments in technology that are now driving production increases in new or previously abandoned locations. The result is that oil production will continue to be high for some (indeterminate) period of time, and hence the availability of oil will not be a factor driving efforts to cut greenhouse gas emission. On the contrary, oil availability (and hence profitability), even at rising prices, is likely to be a continued force contributing to a warming planet.

In sum, beyond climate turmoil, climate change is a vital component of a broad array of adverse climate/environment interactions that reveal both the true depth of the human footprint on the planet and the extent of the mounting, interconnected threats before us.

Unpredictability, perceived precarity, and vulnerability

Finally, the third component of our model emphasizes the fact that climate turmoil and pluralea interactions profoundly magnify climate/environment unpredictability, people's sense of precarity, and vulnerability in a world of enormous population densities, already existing global food and water shortages, deep social inequalities, and fragile and conflicted social structures.

Human abilities to depend on environmental resources and conditions, feel safe in environmental settings, and plan for the future are threatened by the gradual changes and sudden ruptures of climate turmoil and pluralea interactions. This kind of essential unpredictability is manifest at various scales, impacting nations, communities, households, and individuals. At the national level, growing unpredictability destabilizes already fragile national structures, as seen in anthropogenic climate/environment impacts on what have been called failed states. In such nations, there is an erosion of legitimate authority to make collective decisions and an inability of the government to provide needed public services. As Brown (2011) notes: "One reason for government breakdowns that has become more relevant recently is the inability to provide food security—not necessarily because the government is less competent but because obtaining enough food is becoming more difficult." Notably, climate change, drought, and desertification, in interaction with adverse human land use practices and unequal access to land and water, threaten global food production and food availability and contribute to malnutrition and starvation.

By the end of the twenty-first century, it is predicted with high probability (over 90 percent) by climate scientists that average temperatures during growing seasons will be higher than ever before in recorded history across a big swath of the planet. High temperatures cause crops like corn, wheat, and rice to grow faster, but reduce plant fertility and grain production. Worldwide, the impacts will fall most heavily on impoverished subsistence farmers, of whom there are hundreds of millions in the world. Already, many developing countries have average temperatures that are near or above crop tolerance levels; these countries are predicted to suffer an average 10 to 25 percent decline in agricultural productivity by the 2080s (Center for Global Development 2007). Thus a report titled *Climate Change, Agriculture, and Food Security: Impacts and Costs of Adaptation to 2050*, issued by the International Food Policy Research Institute (2009), a Washington, DC-based anti-hunger organization, estimates that 25 million more (than would otherwise be expected) children will be malnourished in 2050 because of the impact of climate change on global agriculture. The hardest-hit areas will be the tropics and subtropics, Africa, the southern United States, and much of India, China, and Central and South America.

Research by the Center for Global Development (2012) suggests that because of global warming, Mexico stands to lose between a quarter and a third of its agricultural production by 2080, the most for any country beside India. Similarly, Central America will see agricultural output shrink between 12 and 24 percent, according to the Center's research, a loss somewhat cushioned by the region's average rainfall of some 6mm per day, compared with Mexico's 2mm per day. One outcome will be the displacement through the region of large numbers of "climate refugees" within and across international borders seeking food and means of livelihood. Analyses by Feng *et al.* (2010), for example, suggest that by approximately the year 2080, climate change will induce 1.4 to 6.7 million adult Mexicans (or 2–10 percent of the current population aged 15–65 years) to seek to emigrate to the United States because of climate-driven declines in agricultural productivity. This migration is likely to exacerbate a range of problems, including further deterioration of ecosystems, loss of human and political rights, and increased international conflicts and border fortifications.

As this discussion suggests, anthropogenic climate/environment changes will significantly amplify the vulnerability of human communities while lowering people's sense of everyday and future security, disproportionately among those that are already poor, and especially the very poorest households in all communities. Populations will be pushed out of their home areas by droughts and food insecurity, be overwhelmed by rising oceans and flooding, be battered by increasingly frequent extreme weather and superstorms, suffer from the spread of infectious diseases because rising temperatures allow vectors like mosquitoes and ticks to inhabit new areas, be stricken as well by diseases caused by fungal spores blown because of drying into the air and into human bodies, and be pushed into greater tension with other populations for limited resources. Moreover, because of the stress of perceived precarity and the emotional traumas of catastrophic events, there are serious mental health burdens of climate turmoil, as seen among the survivors of Hurricane Katrina.

As a result of all of these factors, the adaptive capacity and resiliency of human groups will be severely challenged and their vulnerability to multiple threats to their health and well-being enhanced. The environment and life itself will become less predictable and far more precarious as people feel more exposed to sequential and overlapping environmental adversities. Lived experience increasingly will reflect a sense of environmental precarity, resulting in a diminishment of social dependability and support.

Without doubt, throughout human history, relatively isolated human communities have faced deepening and often entwined and anthropologically influenced environmental challenges. At times, these worsening conditions have so increased the experience of precarity and so extensively destabilized vital socioeconomic systems that the result has been societal collapse. What is different today? In the past, when local societies collapsed their relative isolation from other regions blocked any extensive outward flow of social disruptions to more distant geographic zones. By contrast, as stressed by Costanza *et al.* (2007: 3) of the Integrated History and Future of People on Earth (IHOPE) project, in the modern world people everywhere on the planet "live in an increasingly global system in which our most critical problems span national borders, cover continents, or are truly global." As a result, substantial social failure in one region may threaten to destabilize the entire world system. This raises critical questions:

> Can the current global civilization adapt and survive the accumulating, highly interconnected problems it now faces? Or will it collapse like Easter Island, the Classic Maya, the Roman Empire, and other past civilizations, but on a larger scale?
>
> *Costanza* et al. *2007: 3*

As defined by Charles Edwards (2009: 18), resilience is the "capacity of an individual, community or system to adapt in order to sustain an acceptable level of function, structure, and identity." The notion of community resilience refers specifically to the ability of a group of people to mobilize their collective skills, knowledge, and resources to prepare for and handle the consequence of emergencies and other threats (Baker 2013). From an anthropological standpoint, an essential element of resilience in the face of climatic/environmental change is the "means by which societies accumulate, store, and retrieve information about the environment and variable responses to environmental variation" (Dean 2000: 89). In part, the capacity of a society to respond effectively to novel environmental change reflects information gained and culturally stored (in the memories of elders, narratives, rituals, texts, or other devices) during past group encounters with environmental transitions mediated by experience and cultural beliefs and values.

In this regard, anthropologist Robert Weller (2006) has introduced the concept of "environmental consciousness." It has been a presumption of environmental studies that people only come to develop concerns about the environment if their basic subsistence needs are being met (Inglehart 1990). Weller (2006: 157), based on his research in rural China, questioned this perspective, arguing that people in the rural Chinese communities he studied expressed concern "about environmental effects on the health of their children and their crops." What they lack, he noted, was a concern for the environment issues that might provoke the sensitivities of political and intellectual elites who speak the various global languages of modern environmentalism. In other words, environmental consciousness needs to be assessed, Weller argues, in terms of locally held views of the environment and differential cultural ways of valuing it. Based on her own ethnographic research in China, Anna Lora-Wainwright (2013) adds that local environmental consciousness is constrained by political factors, including configurations of dependency and power as well as the nature of available opportunity structures. She reports that:

> Uncertainty about the evidence of environmental health harm and its potential to obtain redress is just as telling of villagers' understanding of the complexity of science and inherent uncertainty as it is of their skepticism that local officials would really protect their interests, that the industry would really listen, and that doctors would really disclose their illnesses and make suggestions about their causes.
>
> *Lora-Wainwright 2013: 13–15*

The experience of powerlessness, in short, bodes against elite-style environmental consciousness. At the same time, also writing on perceptions of environmental risk in China, Bryan Tilt (2010: 103) argues that:

> industrial workers' and managers' narratives about pollution display a form of "strategic risk repression," since it allows them to persist in manufacturing industrial products and profits while compromising their own health as well as the environmental quality of the community and the region at large.

Folded into prevailing global, national, and regional hierarchical social structures are various discursive mechanisms that differentiate valued and expendable bodies. These built-in and usually not fully articulated (at least publicly) ways of thinking, cast some people—based on their social standing, wealth, race, or similar criteria—as valued and deserving and others as undeserving, and even disposable. The latter may be thought of in elite circles or portrayed in the media as social dead weight that holds back the progress and health of the larger social body. Often included in the expendable category are indigenous populations, ethnic minorities, and the poorest social strata in society. The sentiments are activates across social issues from welfare to climate change damage relief and from housing to health care.

Medical anthropologists have engaged this topic by examining health-related deservingness. This is defined as the manner in which "some social groups, but not others, are deemed worthy of attention, investment, and care" (Yarris and Castañeda 2015, Holmes and Castañeda 2016; Willen 2014). This differentiation is fundamental because it shapes how social goods, including climate change preparedness and disaster recovery resources, are distributed in society, despite official legal discourses concerning social equality (Willen 2012). Underlying meanings of validated citizenship and non-citizenship are made visible in who can and who cannot claim effective and recognized membership in community and the benefits that ensue from such inclusion. These meanings are also revealed in the treatment of people throughout the institutions and social settings of any society.

The concept of deservedness has a long history. Dominant understandings about who comprise the deserving poor and who do not date to sixteenth-century Europe, where they were shaped by an emergent capitalist system that developed an expanding need for low-wage workers (Piven and Cloward 1993; Wagner 2005). Since the eighteenth century, the provision of relief for the poor has been decided by those with wealth, influence, and power. The elite social strata had the social authority to decide who was deserving and not deserving of assistance in any situation.

Commonly, deservedness has been racialized (Katznelson 2005b; Neubeck and Cazenave 2001). For example, during the New Deal in the US, the Social Security Act specifically excluded farm laborers, domestic workers, and personal service workers, a set of socially devalued jobs commonly filled by people of color (Katznelson 2005a). Historically, in the US, Black bodies have been considered of limited value, expendable, and readily replaceable. This attitude traces to the Western regime of African slavery, including the willingness to sacrifice the lives of tens of millions of Africans during the forced voyage to slave markets and the development of a slave labor plantation system that, in addition to being forced, was often brutal and refused to recognize familial relationships. After slavery ended, the expendability of Black people continued unabated, as seen, for example, in the use by the United States Public Health Service of Black men to monitor the effects of untreated syphilis in the Tuskegee Syphilis Study in 1932–1972.

In the arena of environmental exposures, there has been a long pattern of siting landfills, polluting factories, and other toxin-generating facilities near poor communities, including Black neighborhoods (Singer 2011b). Further evidence of environment-related expression of expendability was seen in 2005 during and after Hurricane Katrina in New Orleans, where 1,300 people died, most of them residents of the poor, impoverished, and predominantly Black Orleans Parish. Moreover, survivors reported multiple cases of discrimination in access to rescue, relief, and recovery resources (Lavell 2006).

A very explicit expression of lacking deservedness and the embrace of a disposability stance were voiced by President Donald Trump with regard to the hurricane-ravaged island of Puerto Rico in 2017. During a presidential visit to the US territory, where residents are US citizens, Trump said that the relief needs of the territory were disrupting the US economy. He proceeded to add that the federal government's emergency responders cannot provide badly needed hurricane relief on an ongoing basis. In his comments, Trump blamed the crisis on the island as "largely of [Puerto Rican] making," adding that Puerto Rico's infrastructure was a disaster before the hurricane. Minimizing the rising death toll and widespread suffering, Trump compared the hurricanes that slammed Puerto Rico to Hurricane Katrina, based on the number of people who died, saying what was occurring in Puerto Rico did not rate as a real disaster. Upon being told by Puerto Rico's governor that sixteen people had been reported dead so far, Trump praised federal and local emergency officials and downplayed the hurricane's damage, indicating that it was not "a real catastrophe like Katrina" (quoted in Frej and Fang 2017). As Frej and Fang observe,

> While Trump bragged about the official number of dead, the final death toll will likely turn out to be higher. Poor communication services have hindered reporting, and current living conditions on the island could jeopardize more lives, especially those of the sick and elderly.
>
> *Frej and Fang 2017*

Trump never voiced any such sentiments with reference to the hurricanes that flooded Houston and other southern coastal areas just weeks prior to Puerto Rico's catastrophe, never raised the issue of the significant recovery costs for hurricane damage on the US mainland or the record-setting wildfires burning through Northern California at the time, and offered nothing but praise for hurricane victims and his own performance in the mainland disasters (Campbell 2017; Landler 2017). The vulnerability felt by marginalized populations in a time of climate turmoil is directly tied to elite practices regarding disposable underserving bodies, affirming the very sociopolitical nature of human environment/climate relationship.

Enhancing resilience

Of note, at the national and international levels, there is growing emphasis, especially in the worlds of global health services and humanitarian aid, on developing methodologies for enhancing community resilience, including the ability to prepare both for natural or other shocks and for enhanced capacity for so-called "bounce-backability" after adverse events occur. In a world of multiple, increasingly intense, overlapping, mutually enhancing, and frequent shocks, however, community resiliency itself is at risk. Speaking of communities in sub-Saharan Africa, for example, Rajiv Shah, as head of the United States Agency for International Development, and an expert who affirmed that climate change contributed to the severity of the humanitarian crisis that brought over 13 million people to the brink of hunger and starvation and killed 50,000 in East Africa in 2011, observed: "There's no question that hotter and drier growing conditions in sub-Saharan Africa have reduced the resiliency of these communities" (Hirsch *et al.* 2011). Similarly, the lead humanitarian relief official of the United Nations, Valerie Amos, pointed to the role of climate change during a tour of a refugee camp of drought victims in Somalia, saying: "We have to take the impact of climate change more seriously. . . . Everything I've heard has said that we used to have drought every ten years, then it became every five years and now it's every two years" (Hirsch *et al.* 2011). Reduction in community resiliency as a consequence of climate change and pluralea interactions will be a likely growing contributor to worsening humanitarian disasters. Moreover, while local resilience in a time of global warming is contingent on the ability to retrieve and use cultural knowledge about the environment, that knowledge is shaped at every turn by wider political factors, and hence resilience itself is a product of social relations and structures of inequality. Importantly, vulnerability, like resilience, in human groups is conditioned not only by anthropogenic climate and environment factors, but by social structures and inequitable social distributions of power and resources. One critical environmental/climatic expression of the global architecture of inequality is the externalization of key costs of capitalist industrial production onto vulnerable populations in the forms of pollution, hazardous dumping, and greenhouse gas release into the atmosphere. While corporations must consider the cost of technology, labor, land, marketing, and resources, the costs of safely limiting or controlling the toxic by-products of production are often not calculated because they are simply released into the environment. Because the inherent inequalities of capitalism infiltrate every aspect of social and moral life, they are necessarily embodied in society's and the economy's relationship to the natural world (Harvey 1997). For over 50 years, however, environmental activists and scholars have pointed out that one way in which inequality is expressed and routinely reproduced is through the targeted handling and mishandling of natural resources (United Church of Christ's Committee on Racial Justice 1987). Central to this pattern is the treatment of the environment as an open trash receptacle with limited associated cost. But, as climate turmoil affirms, there are limits and grave costs to the externalizing strategies of polluting industries, and these are borne disproportionately by the most vulnerable groups in society (Singer and Hodge 2016).

In the face of mounting environmental challenges, household and community social systems may begin to break down, further enhancing the process of vulnerability and immiseration. How this plays out in local, regional, and in broader and even global contexts, including identification of facilitators of resilience and vulnerability, constitutes critical work on the agenda of the anthropology of climate change.

In sum, the socioecological approach guiding this book, involving the three components described above, is a distinctly anthropological model that recognizes the significance of dynamic interactions of humans with their environments (best phrased as humans with the rest of nature), of anthropogenic climatic factors with anthropogenic environmental factors, and of humans with each other in social structures embedded within climate/environmental contexts. Only by holistically including all of these interacting elements in the model can we confront the undeniable complexities of the new human condition in the time of climate change.

Constructing an anthropology of climate change

With the understanding of key factors expressed in our socioecological model, in the following chapters this book has the following purposes: (1) to document and assess the developmental status of the anthropology of climate change; (2) to review the kinds of insights gained by anthropological framing; (3) to promote the rapid further development of this field in light of the world-changing implications of climate change; and (4) to demonstrate the useful contributions of a critical political ecological framework in guiding this work.

In order to begin the process of documenting and consolidating awareness of initial efforts in climate change anthropology and thereby provide a foundation for the further development of the field, the following chapter provides an overview of the precursors to the anthropology of climate change, including Margaret Mead's pioneering consideration of the topic.

2

THE EMERGENCE AND MATURATION OF THE ANTHROPOLOGY OF CLIMATE CHANGE

Precursors of the anthropology of climate change

Early voices in anthropology

While Margaret Mead was a Visiting Scholar at the Fogarty International Center, given her interest in interactions between "world society and its planetary environment," she used her persuasive skills in prompting the Center to sponsor a conference which would explore ways to contribute to a healthy atmospheric environment. For many years the public face and voice of anthropology, Mead's views on this issue had been articulated five years earlier when she spoke at the first Earth Day, an event designed to heighten public awareness of the world's environmental problems, on April 22, 1970 (History.com 1996). Mead is often quoted for her plain and direct statement: "We won't have a society if we destroy the environment" (St. Peter 2010: 213).

The climate conference, titled *The Atmosphere: Endangered and Endangering*, took place at the National Institute of Environmental Health Sciences, Research Triangle Park, North Carolina in April 1975. Mead appears to have been the only anthropologist at the conference, and perhaps the only social scientist as well, in a meeting that was largely attended by physical and natural scientists and public health experts. Mead, along with William W. Kellogg, a scientist at the National Center for Atmospheric Research in Boulder, Colorado, edited the conference proceedings (Kellogg and Mead 1980). In the Preface to the volume, Mead (1980: xxi) noted that "responsible scientists" need to develop "ways in which farsightedness can become a habit of the citizenry of the diverse peoples on the planet" and that "natural scientists need to develop ways of making their statements on the present danger credible to each other" in order to "make them credible to social scientists, politicians, and the citizenry." While Mead did not make profound anthropological observations about the anthropogenic sources of climate change or other forms of environmental degradation, or their impact on human societies, she indirectly voiced the precautionary principle with respect to adopting policies to address the environmental and atmospheric crises by noting that the "time interval required before we begin to see clear evidence of a particular manmade effect on the environment may be long compared to the time in which society has to act" (Thompson 1980: 68). Despite the fact that Mead did not encourage her fellow anthropologists to work on climate change per se, her involvement in the conference foreshadowed the beginning of the anthropology of climate change.

Steve Rayner has also functioned as a key precursor to the anthropology of climate change and continues to work on climate change policy issues. Rayner and Elizabeth Malone (1998a) edited a four-volume work titled *Human Choice and Climate Change: An International Assessment*. These volumes brought together almost a hundred authors and contributors from around the globe. In their introductory essay to Volume 1, Rayner and Malone (1998b: xvii) present a research agenda for the anthropology of climate change relative to the theme human choice. The research agenda posed by Rayner and Malone is one which different anthropological perspectives have been grappling with over the course of the past 20 years, albeit in different ways and with different emphases. Adherents of the cultural interpretive perspective observe that the "topic of 'climate change' encompasses people's perceptions and behavior based on the threat (or, in a few cases, the promise) of such change, as well as the causes, processes, and prospective impacts of the change itself" (Rayner and Malone 1998b: xix).

In Volume 1, a chapter by anthropologist Mary Douglas *et al.* (1998: 196) "pin[s] responsibility for massive greenhouse gas emissions on human efforts to satisfy their wants." While they note the concern on the part of some environmentalists that "insatiable consumption habits" are contributing to "depletion of the globe's resources, including capacity to absorb atmospheric carbon," Douglas and her colleagues make no direct mention of the roots of consumerism in global capitalism. The implication is that unquenchable consumptive desires are inherent rather than cultural and a product of a particular political economy. However, the authors do refer to the distinction that Agarwal and Narain (1991) made between *survival emissions* and *luxury emissions*.

While Douglas *et al.* (1998: 201) recognize that the "theory of wants will one day come to terms with the theory of society," they evade the issue that in the modern world, capitalism plays a major role in shaping people's wants, with nonstop, multimedia, ubiquitous advertising serving as one influential link between the production and consumption processes. Douglas *et al.* (1998: 202) do recognize that the societal achievement of a clean environment will require that people "change their laws, and changing these will change the pattern of wealth and income distribution, and this will change the flows of goods and people on birthdays, anniversaries and weddings, retirements, funerals, sick visiting, and ordinary Sunday family gatherings." They employ the notion of *sustainable development* proposed by the World Commission on Environment and Development, perhaps better known as the Brundtland Commission, as providing a guideline for constructing a "theory of human needs" that could be used to determine "how the burden of reducing greenhouse gas emissions could be distributed in order to meet 'the needs of the present without compromising the ability of future generations to meet their own needs'" (Douglas et al. 1998: 204). However, the concept of sustainable development presupposes a complementarity between ongoing economic expansion and environmental sustainability, an assumption that has come under increasing scrutiny from a growing number of theorists, not only political ecologists or eco-Marxists, but also environmental thinkers such as James Gustave Speth (2008), who has held positions as Chairman of the Council on Environmental Quality in the Executive Office of the US President, Administrator of the United Nations Development Program, and dean of the Yale School of Forestry and Environmental Studies.

Various archaeologists, whose work is cited in Chapter 3, have also served as precursors of the anthropology of climate change (Henry 1989; McGovern 1994; Potts 1996; Ambrose 1998; Dincauze 2000). Harvey Weiss, for example, organized a symposium held on April 18, 1993 at the annual Society of American Archaeologists meeting in St. Louis which led to an international conference of paleoanthropologists and archaeologists titled the *Third Millennium BC Climate Change and the Old World Social Collapse* in Kerner, Turkey (Nuzhet Dalfes et al. 1994). The period around 5000 to 3000 BP ("before present") reportedly was one characterized by particularly unstable climatic events in many parts of the world. Around 4000 BP, urban civilizations in Mesopotamia, Egypt, and India collapsed as a result of climatic changes. Among the proceedings emanating from the conference were essays that examined the relationship between Nile floods and political disorder in early Egypt, climate and the eclipse of the ancient cities of India, environmental and climatic changes between three and five thousand years ago in southeastern Ukraine, the third-millennium climate in the Near East, mid-Holocene climatic change in Anatolia and adjacent regions, middle and Late Holocene vegetarian and climate changes in Italy, climate change at Lake Van in Turkey, and late third-millennium abrupt climate change and social collapse in West Asia and Egypt.

Another conference, titled *Climate and Culture at 3000 BC*, focusing on the mid-Holocene from about 9,000 to 5,000 years ago, was convened in October 1998 at the University of Maine (Anderson et al. 2007). Brian Fagan has been especially prominent in developing the archaeology of climate change which is part and parcel of the encompassing anthropology. For over a decade, he has been grappling with the impact of climate change, primarily natural in origin, but also anthropogenic, on human societies. The first book in which he addressed the impact of global warming and climatic-related events is *Floods, Famines, and Emperors* (Fagan 1999). He observes that humans have experienced "constant and dramatic swings in global climate over the past 730,000 years," a period that has included at least nine glacial episodes interspersed with warm interglacial periods (Fagan 1999: 76). Fagan discusses the impact of El Niño events and associated droughts and floods on ancient Egypt, the Moche civilization of coastal Peru, the Mayan civilization, the Anasazi of the American Southwest, and the peoples of the Sahel. He also discusses the impact of the Little Ice Age on the Norse colonies in Greenland and North America as well as on Europe, issues that will be examined in Chapter 3.

In his first book about climate change, Fagan appears to waver on the question of whether climate change in recent historical times is primarily natural or anthropogenic. In noting that some scientists maintain that Earth is due for another glacial period in several thousand years, he maintains that this does not take into account the "new spoiler on the climatic block—fossil-fuel-using industrial humanity" that "could precipitate dramatic, and premature, climatic change within a few centuries," if not much sooner (Fagan 1999: 76). Later on in the book, he observes that the Little Ice Age ended in the 1850s during the height of the Industrial Revolution and states that the "world entered a new era of warmer temperatures and less extreme climatic swings, apparently triggered by entirely natural causes" which he does not explicitly identify, but then adds a qualifier in which he acknowledges that "Some experts do wonder whether the higher levels of carbon dioxide released into the atmosphere by the growing forces of the Industrial Revolution contributed to the warm-up" (Fagan 1999: 200–201).

By 2007, in the assessment of the Intergovernmental Panel on Climate Change, the evidence for the anthropogenic origin of climate change was unequivocal. Among climate scientists, at least, that debate had ended.

In his subsequent book, *The Little Ice Age*, Fagan (2000: xv) argues that scholars have tended to ignore the impact of climate change over time on human societies. Whereas Fagan tends to view the climatic changes during the Little Ice Age as primarily due to natural causes, he comments upon the impact of the Industrial Revolution, which was in full swing by the time that the Little Ice Age ended around 1850. He observes:

> The pioneer agricultural explosion, fueled by large-scale emigration, railroads, and ocean steamships, was the first human activity that genuinely altered the global environment. The second came from coal, already a significant air polluter in large cities.
>
> *Fagan 2000: 204*

Historic ecology

Some of the work done in historical ecology also has served as a precursor to the anthropology of climate change. The School of American Research (now known as the School of Advanced Research) in Santa Fe held an advanced seminar on historical ecology in October 1990. Several of the chapters in the book *Historical Ecology* that resulted from the seminar touch on topics related to climate change. Archaeologist Carol Crumley (1994: 7), for example, defines historical ecology as the "practice of globally relevant archaeology, ethnohistory, ethnography, and related disciplines." She refers to global warming along with pollution, species extinctions, and massive disruptions of critical ecosystems as manifestations of environmental change that is "arguably the most pressing and potentially disastrous problem facing the global community" (Crumley 1994: 1). Further, Crumley (1994: 8) maintains that historical ecology has the potential to address several questions related to needed global action on the global ecological crisis, including climate change. Based on ethnohistorical research on late prehistoric and early historic Europe, Crumley proposes an interesting hypothesis about the relationship between social structures and climate change:

> Periods of stable climate (whether hot or cold, wet or dry, or even consistently unpredictable) allow humans the opportunity to experiment and convey the results to succeeding generations in the form of successful strategies given to a particular set of conditions. . . . Periods of unpredictable climate require much greater flexibility on the part of human populations in their utilization of resources: also required is a much larger store of potentially useful information.
>
> *Crumley 1994: 192*

First emergence of an explicit anthropology of climate change

Perhaps the earliest example of an explicitly cultural interpretive analysis of climate change was a component of a study done by Willet Kempton (1991) and later Kempton *et al.* (1995). The latter research examined US environmental values by conducting semi-structured interviews with 43 informants (20 laypeople, 21 environmental specialists, and two pilot subjects) as well as surveys of 142 respondents (30 Earth First members, 27 Sierra Club members, 29 sawmill workers) from New Jersey and Maine (Kempton *et al.* 1995). The researchers investigated their informants' perceptions of three major local environmental changes, namely ozone depletion, species extinctions, and global warming. Many laypeople, they found, confounded global warming as a subset or a consequence of ozone depletion.

Celeste Ray (2002) wrote perhaps what constitutes the first relatively broad overview of the anthropology of climate change, reflecting a particularly multi-disciplinary anthropological approach that includes contributions from a geologist, an atmospheric physicist, two ecologists, an economist, and a political scientist. In terms of anthropology, she notes that archaeology, ecological anthropology, ethnohistory, and historical ecology, all contain the potential to contribute to the anthropology of climate change. Ray utilizes a cultural interpretive approach to climate change, noting the importance of "cultural models" in terms of shaping human responses to environmental crises. She asserts that cultural models of the environment "change over time with environmental changes, with population dynamics, with religious beliefs, and with new technologies" (Ray 2002: 85), which is surely not an exhaustive list of factors that shape cultural models. In terms of climate change mitigation, Ray (2002: 98) argues that effective approaches will "draw support from those of different cultural perspectives, socioeconomic classes, and educational and religious backgrounds." However, what she fails to acknowledge in her pluralist framework is that some players, such as the higher social classes and corporations, have much greater input into climate policies than people from the lower social classes or a wide diversity of subaltern groups, such as indigenous people. Moreover, various sectors of the richest social classes, those who in the early years of the twenty-first century have come to be known as the 1 percent, may have vested economic interests in particular carbon-emitting industries, a fiscal commitment to ever-expanded production, and a desire to keep using the environment as a free waste bin for the by-products and wastes of the industrial production process.

A small group of climate anthropologists have also functioned as precursors of the anthropology of climate change. Brown (1999) published an article on *climate anthropology* in which she argued that this subfield includes an examination of the impact of global warming on human societies. Several articles delineating various aspects of climate change appeared in a symposium, *Practicing Anthropology*, in Fall 2000. In their introductory contribution, Roncoli and Magistro (2000) argued that anthropologists need to examine global climate change as part and parcel of the anthropology of climate variability, a phenomenon that includes droughts, hurricanes, and other instances of erratic weather. Other articles in the symposium discuss the emergence of climate anthropology in northeast Brazil (Nelson and Finan 2000), climatic shocks and pastoral risk management in northern Kenya (Mahmoud and Little 2000), and variation in coping with El Niño droughts in northern Costa Rica (Otterstrom 2000).

Roncoli and Magistro draw attention to the need for anthropologists to address climate change in the introduction to a special issue of *Climate Research* emanating from two sessions that focused on "Social Science Dimensions and Policy Contributions to Climate Change Research" at the 1999 meeting of the Society for Applied Anthropology. They highlight the need for "attempting to bridge global analyses on climate change with locally identifiable processes of community response and perception on climate" (Magistro and Roncoli 2001: 91). While anthropologists contributed to all of the essays in the collection, most of the essays were interdisciplinary in that they included scholars from other fields of study.

Turning to a major work in climate anthropology, in the introduction to their anthology *Weather, Climate, Culture*, Sarah Strauss and Ben Orlove (2003: 10–11) refer to "climate change" only in passing, and none of the essays included in their volume focuses specifically on global warming. In other publications, however, Orlove, along with various colleagues, has examined several local climatic events related to climate change, especially El Niño in the Andean area and in Southern Uganda (Orlove 2003; Orlove *et al.* 2000, 2002; Orlove and Kabugo 2005).

As this review suggests, the anthropology of climate change has its roots in the scattered initiatives of various researchers inside and outside of anthropology who began, in the shadow of earlier discounted attempts to consider the role of climate in society, to link social action, climate change, and social consequence. On one level, this development was to be expected as the direct experience of the adverse effects of a warming and polluted planet began to mount and as climate scientists advanced and broadcast their understanding of the notable extent and effects of climate change across the ecological systems of the planet.

The maturation of the anthropology of climate change

Perhaps the first indicator that the anthropology of climate change had come into its own as a distinct field occurred in December 2007 when the *Anthropology Newsletter* of the American Anthropological Association published a series of short articles on climate change research guest-edited by Myanna Lahsen. In her article, Lahsen (2007a: 9) observes that a good starting point for the anthropology of climate change is to examine the controversies surrounding knowledge of environmental changes, including those occurring "'upstream,' at the sites at which scientific knowledge is produced and adjudicated," such the UK Tyndall Centre for Climate Change Research. In another article, Kathleen A. Galvin (2007) observed that there is a need for anthropologists to enter into interdisciplinary efforts in order to contribute to global environmental change research.

Virtually on the other side of the globe from the United States, various anthropologists situated in Australia also had commenced working on the anthropology of climate change. Climate change had become frequent front-page news in Australia by beginning of the twenty-first century, not only because of rising temperatures, but also due to severe droughts, particularly in southeastern Australia, and severe cyclones or hurricanes in northeastern Australia. Inspired in part by the panel on climate change at the 2007 Australian Anthropological Society conference convened by Hans Baer and Megan Jennaway, the *Australian Journal of Anthropology* published a Soapbox Forum in its first issue of 2008 on "Anthropological Perspectives on Climate Change" guest-edited by Kay Milton, who had been spending time in Australia as a visiting research fellow from Queen's University in Belfast. In his essay in the Forum, Hans Baer posited that global warming in many ways constitutes yet another contradiction of the capitalist world system with its treadmill of production and consumption and heavy reliance on fossil fuels (Baer 2008). Monica Minnegal and Peter Dwyer (2008) discuss the response of fishermen in Gippsland (Victoria) to the uncertainties in their environment, and Deborah Bird Rose (2008) and Sandy Toussaint (2008) discuss the contemporary experiences of Aboriginal communities whose immediate everyday preoccupations do not include climate change, but whose futures might ultimately be shaped by it.

The year 2009 may well have been the turning point in the emergence of the anthropology of climate change. Left Coast Press published two anthropology books on climate change that year. The first one was authored by Hans Baer and Merrill Singer and titled *Global Warming and the Political Ecology of Health* (Baer and Singer 2009). It constituted an expansion of our earlier work on the relationship between health and the environment which previously had appeared in several sources (Baer *et al.* 1997, 2003, 2013; Singer and Baer 2007; Singer 1995). The book makes a case for a critical anthropology and a critical medical anthropology of climate change which is discussed in greater detail in Chapter 6. Suffice it to say for the moment that the critical anthropology of climate change regards anthropogenic climate change, particularly since the Industrial Revolution, as having its roots in global capitalism with its emphasis on profit-making, continual economic expansion, a treadmill of production and consumption, and heavy reliance on fossil fuels to energize the entire economic system. Our book examined the impact of climate change on settlement patterns and subsistence, including people's access to water and food. We also explored how global warming contributes to mounting frequency of heat stress, pollutants, environmental diseases, and the spread of waterborne and vector-borne infections. As part and parcel of creating a healthy world, we examined the inadequacies of existing climate regimes and "green" capitalism and suggested the creation of a democratic eco-socialist world system, an idea that we also proposed in *Medical Anthropology and the World System*, a health anthropology textbook that we co-authored with Ida Susser (Baer *et al.* 2003). While the first (1997) and second (2003) editions of this textbook made no mention of climate change, reflecting our own inattention at the time to mounting knowledge about our warming planet, the third edition included a focused chapter on it (Baer *et al.* 2013). Singer meanwhile began to develop two relevant concepts for the anthropology of climate change. The first of these was *ecosyndemic* (Singer 2009c; Singer 2010c), which refers to socially influenced and environmentally mediated adverse interactions among diseases that increase the health burden of populations. In his publications on ecosyndemics, for example, Singer (2013) discusses various physical interactions between anthropogenic global warming and air pollution in the exacerbation and increasing frequency of global respiratory diseases such as asthma. The second of these concepts was *pluralea interaction*, discussed in Chapter 1, which, as noted, refers to the fact that global warming and the multiple risks it entails are only part of a far larger environmental crisis involving a set of convergent and potentially interacting anthropogenic threats to the environment and to human health. In a related article, Singer (2010b) explored the question: Are the planet-unfriendly features of capitalism barriers to the sustainability of contemporary patterns of social life?

The second book to appear in 2009 was *Anthropology and Climate Change*, a significant addition to the still emerging anthropology of climate change. As the editors of that volume, Susan Crate and Mark Nuttall (2009a), observe, with a few notable exceptions, anthropologists only began to take note of recent climatic changes in recent years. By bringing together the work of multiple anthropological authors on climate change working around the globe, this book helped to establish this arena of anthropological research. Part One of the book, titled "Climate and Culture," comprises four chapters which seek to develop a framework for the remainder of the volume by exploring the relationship between climate change (both historically and more recently) and sociocultural systems, while making a case for anthropology's unique ability to examine this crucial relationship. Most of the subsequent chapters in the volume focus on the impact of climate change on various local populations and their perception of it and efforts to adapt to it. Of note, the concept of cultural adaptation has been challenged from a critical perspective on the grounds that while all societies must engage the threats and opportunities in their environment, it is far from clear that the biological notion of "adaptation" well explains systems that to varying degrees restructure and degrade natural environments in light of culturally constituted understandings (and misunderstandings), techno-logical capacities, and modes of production (Singer 1996). Part Two of the book consists of 11 case studies that focus on how specific populations are being impacted by and have been adapting to climate change. These include studies by Susan Crate on the Sakha, horse and cattle breeders in northeastern Siberia; Anne Henshaw on the Inuit of the eastern Canadian Arctic; Sarah Strauss on a village in the Swiss Alps; Timothy Finan on peoples living in southwestern Bangladesh; Benedict Colombi on the Nez Perce in the Columbia River Basin; Jerry Jacka on the inhabitants of the Porgera region of Papua New Guinea; Elizabeth Marino and Peter Schweitzer on the Inupiat and other indigenous groups in northwestern Alaska; Donna Green on Indigenous Australians; Inge Bolin on the Quechua people of the Peruvian Andes; Heather Lazrus on Tuvaluans in the South Pacific; and Robert Hitchcock on the Kalahari San. Some of these chapters are discussed in greater detail in later chapters in this book. Part Three of *Anthropology and Climate Change*, "Anthropological Actions," consists of nine chapters which explore what anthropologists are doing and can or need to do in their field research settings, the larger anthropological community, and public policy decision-making in terms of both adapting to and mitigating climate change.

In their epilogue, Crate and Nuttall (2009b) recommend an interdisciplinary approach to studying and seeking to address climate change. While *Anthropology and Culture Change* provides a relatively comprehensive overview of many of the kinds of studies that anthropologists investigating climate change and society are doing, the book lacks a clear-cut recognition of the critical anthropology of climate change. While the editors *of Anthropology and Climate Change* and most of its contributors tend to interpret climate change from either a phenomenological or a cultural ecological perspective, or a combination of both of these, they do not fully assess whether climate change represents a dangerous contradiction of the capitalist world system. Nevertheless, Crate and Nuttall (2009c: 11) at some level are conversant with a critical anthropological perspective on climate change. For example, in the introduction to their book they observe that the "effects of climate change are the indirect costs of imperialism and colonization."

Baer published *Global Capitalism and Climate Change* (2012). This book consti-tutes an effort to develop a critical social science of climate change, one which posits its roots in the capitalist world system with its powerful engine of production and consumption, heavy reliance on fossil fuels, and commitment to ongoing economic expansion. Further, this book explored the systemic changes, both long-term and transitional, necessary to create a more socially just and sustainable world system that would possibly start to move humanity toward a safer climate and the role of a burgeoning climate movement in this effort, issues discussed in Chapters 6 and 8.

Since 2009, the anthropology of climate change has undergone a significant growth spurt as it has become increasingly clear that climate change is already having dramatic impacts upon many of the peoples, including foragers, horticulturists, pastoralists, and peasants, as well as coastal and city dwellers, that anthropologists have been studying for over a century. Small-scale indigenous communities, for example, are finding themselves threatened by sea-level rise, loss of fresh water supplies due to increased aridity, or loss of food supplies as familiar native species are lost due to climate change. Indeed, for societies of all kinds, especially poorer communities, climate change is having and will continue to have a grim impact on subsistence and water supply, settlement patterns, and human health. However, it is not sufficient to merely examine the impact of climate change on human societies or to assess how they are conceiving it and responding to it. It is imperative as well that anthropologists identify the social origins of the multiplicity of anthropogenic sources of climate change, many of which, we argue, are part and parcel of the existing global economy or the capitalist world system, a political economy that is committed to profit-making and unequal distribution of wealth, and continual resource-depleting and waste-producing economic expansion. Even more important, however, is anthropological participant-observation in applied initiatives seeking to respond to climate change at the local, regional, national, and global scales. This requires that anthropologists be part of larger collective efforts to mitigate climate change, whether it is on the part of international climate regimes, national and state or provincial governments, NGOs, communities, and/or climate action and sustainability groups. Thus, as argued in subsequent chapters, anthropologists must engage in the public policy and decision-making arenas, and even seek pathways to become involved as collaborative agents of social change in climate change mitigation and climate justice movements.

In the contemporary moment

Perhaps symbolic of the maturation of the anthropology of climate change is the fact that in late 2011 the Executive Board of the American Anthropological Association (AAA) created the Task Force on Climate Change (American Anthropological Association 2011: 1). The then AAA president, Virginia R. Dominguez, appointed Shirley J. Fiske to chair the task force and appointed as members Susan A. Crate, Heather Lazrus, George Luber, Lisa Lucero, Anthony Oliver-Smith, Ben S. Orlove, Sarah Strauss, and Richard Wilk. Task force members rapidly developed a series, published in various media (the *Huffington Post*, *CounterPunch*), titled "Why Climate Matters," which consists of short editorials on climate-relevant anthropological perspectives. Additionally, the task force initiated a listserv to enhance communication among climate-interested anthropologists and a regular column in the online monthly edition of *Anthropology News*, the newsletter of the American Anthropological Association. The task force used the column to introduce anthropologists working on climate change issues and the types of work they are engaged in. Additionally, the task force began promoting the organization of various kinds of sessions on climate change at American Anthropology Association meetings.

The report of the AAA Global Climate Change Task Force was released in December 2014, shortly after the publication of the first edition of this book. The report contains five foci:

- "human causes and contributions to climate change and the problematizing of human drivers";
- "the identification of lessons learned about human adaptation, survival and change over long periods";
- "the critique of central concepts used in climate policy on global, state, and local levels (adaptation, vulnerability, and resilience)";
- "the importance of the local and community engagement";
- "interdisciplinary strengths and opportunities, and research priorities for the future of anthropology and global environmental change" (Fiske *et al.* 2014: 5).

The Task Force report adopts an idealist perspective rather than a materialist perspective, as we do, on the primary source of climate change, arguing that "Ultimately all drivers of climate change have roots in human cultural values," such as the culture of consumption (Fiske *et al.* 2014: 5). The Task Force report questions the validity of existing top-down climate policies such as those framed by the Intergovernmental Panel on Climate Change and Framework Convention on Climate Change because they fail to consider the socioeconomic factors that shape vulnerability to climate change, such as poverty, marginality, lack of education and information, and loss of control over basic resources. The Task Force report reviews various community-centered approaches to climate change impacts, including (1) place-based ones, such as communities situated along coastlines and islands; and (2) path-dependent ones, such as present vulnerability to climate change based upon socioeconomic, demographic, gender, race and other variables. From a climate justice perspective, the Task Force advocates "empowering affected communities by facilitating a community's agency to self-identify adaptation possibilities, preferences and priorities" (Fiske *et al.* 2014: 53). It also suggests that anthropologists collaborate with local and scientific experts, in essence serving as "cultural brokers" between communities impacted by climate change and policy-makers. The Task Force encourages anthropologists to participate in interdisciplinary research on climate change, not only with natural scientists, but also with other social science scholars, including economists, political scientists, sociologists, and psychologists (Fiske *et al.* 2014: 57). This is an issue that we touch upon in Chapters 8 and 9. The Task Force report identifies two key elements of anthropology within interdisciplinary activities: (1) ethnography and local knowledge and (2) integration of the human and natural systems. It delineates the following nine anthropological research frontiers, starting "with those most directly participating in involved in the major international climate change frameworks, moving next to those that engage more critically with the politics of such frameworks, and closing with those that question the assumptions of the same frameworks" (Fiske *et al.* 2014: 65).

The Task Force proposes the following nine anthropological research frontiers:

- Frontier 1—global and regional models making projections about future climate scenarios;
- Frontier 2—development of a resiliency framework based primarily on ecological constructs;
- Frontier 3—fostering the notion of adaptation to climate change as a process that is influenced by many sectors of society alongside scientific and policy experts;
- Frontier 4—incorporating scientific, political and cultural concepts of habitability into anthropological research;
- Frontier 5—engaging with the cultural politics of decarbonization;
- Frontier 6—identifying alternative consumption patterns, such as eco-villages, slow cities, transition towns, local currencies, vegetarianism, simple living, food sovereignty, the Occupy movement, different forms of environmentalism, and collaborating with researchers in other disciplines who are conducting work on various topics, such as the degrowth movement, the sharing economy, alternative energy sources, and anti-consumerism;
- Frontier 7—conducting research on and engaging with mitigation and adaptation frameworks in policy circles, such as REDD (Reducing Emissions from Deforestation and Degradation);
- Frontier 8—continuing a dialogue with Science and Technology Studies (STS) in terms of studying natural scientists, such as those working within the umbrella of the Intergovernmental Panel on Climate Change (IPCC);
- Frontier 9—engaging with the ontological turn within anthropology that is grappling with the radical differences between modern Western science and other knowledge systems, particularly on climate change-related issues.

Based upon the recommendations made by the Task Force to the AAA, the latter passed a *Statement on Humanity and Climate Change*, which opens with the following paragraph:

> Climate change creates global threats that affect all aspects of human life, including our health, homes, livelihoods, and cultures, as well as our physical environment. Threats of this magnitude affect our stability—our sense of cultural identity, our well-being, and our security. As the discipline most clearly devoted to the human condition over time and space, anthropology offers important insights that can help create workable solutions to mitigate the impacts of climate change.
>
> *American Anthropological Association 2015*

The statement delineates eight points for comprehending the impacts of climate change on human populations from an anthropological perspective:

1. "Climate change is a *present reality* that alters our physical environment and impacts human cultures around the globe";
2. "Climate change *intensifies underlying problems*—poverty and economic disparities, food and water security, and armed conflict – heightening these issues to the point of widespread crisis";
3. "We can expect to see *widespread impacts on communities* as they face dislocation and pressure to migrate";
4. "While climate change affects all of Earth's inhabitants, *the impacts will fall unevenly* and with particular weight on those already affected by existing vulnerabilities, including children, the elderly, and those who live with handicaps and restrictive health conditions, and those who do not have sufficient means to move or change their lives";
5. "Specific human actors and choices drive climate change by emphasizing fossil fuel as the primary energy source, creating a *culture of consumerism*, and favoring land practices that undermine ecological resilience";
6. "The archaeological record reveals diverse human adaptations and innovations to climate stresses occurring over millennia, providing evidence that is *relevant to contemporary human experience*";
7. "Climate change is a global problem with local and regional impacts that *require local and regional solutions*";
8. "Focusing solely on reducing carbon emissions will not be sufficient to address climate change—that will not address the systemic causes. Climate change is rooted in social institutions and cultural habits. *Real solutions will require knowledge and insight from the social sciences* and humanities, not only from the natural sciences."

As our overview of the anthropology of climate change in this book indicates, anthropologists have been addressing over the past few decades many of the points delineated in the *AAA Statement on Humanity and Climate Change* from a number of theoretical perspectives in sociocultural anthropology as well as the archaeology. As proponents of a critical anthropology of climate change informed by political economy and political ecology, we feel that anthropologists, along with other social and behavioral scientists and humanities scholars, need to examine more closely the systemic causes of climate change, which we argue is nothing less nor nothing more in the current era than global capitalism or the capitalist world system. Perhaps more important is the need for the anthropology of climate change to grapple with the anthropology of the future. At least in the case of a critical anthropology of the future, the commitment is to ultimately transcend the existing global political economy to an alternative world system based upon social justice, democratic processes, environmental sustainability, and safe climate for all of the peoples living on our fragile planet.

As contrast with 1990, the year when the Intergovernmental Panel on Climate Change issued its First Assessment Report—affirming the existence of a greenhouse gas effect, asserting with confidence that CO_2 has been the primary source of global warming, and stressing that warming will have adverse effects such as ocean level rise—there has now emerged an anthropology of climate change. Now having coming of age but still growing, this field is beginning to define issues of concern, identify specific contributions of the discipline to climate change research and response, and formulate theoretical perspectives for understanding climate change and the human condition. These and related aspects of this new arena of anthropological initiative are explored in the subsequent chapters of this book, as is the authors' vision of vital directions in the development of the anthropology of climate change.

3

THE ARCHAEOLOGY OF CLIMATE CHANGE

Climate in the making of society and society in the making of climate

A central theme of this chapter is that humans, biologically and socially, have been shaped in part by the changing climates of the natural environments they have inhabited. At the same time, the inverse is true as well. Humans have long had the ability to have local impacts on climate and, with the evolution of advanced industrial technologies, to significantly shape the very climates at ever higher scales with which they must cope. Based on an examination of the writings of archaeologists, those working on the reconstruction of human ways of life at specific research sites, as well as those carrying out temporal or regional analyses, this chapter assesses the nature of the human–climate interaction through the sweep of archaeological time. Ironically, it was historical geographers, like Carl Sauer (1941), rather than archaeologists, who examined the anthropogenic impact of humans on the environment and climate. Archaeologists became to turn their attention to these topics around 2000 (Redman 1999; Redman, James, *et al.* 2007; Contreras 2016). As a cautionary note, given that we are sociocultural anthropologists, our overview of the archaeology is by no means comprehensive. Therefore, readers who wish to pursue the field more may wish to consult various archaeological journals, such as *American Antiquity, Journal of Archaeological Science, Geoarchaeology, and Environmental Archaeology* (also see Sandweiss and Kelley 2012).

Changing climate and human dispersal over time

When one contemplates time in terms of the age of the universe (estimated to be about 15 billion years) or even the age of Earth (estimated to be about 5 billion years old), it becomes quickly obvious that human existence has been so far, and probably ultimately will constitute, a quick blip in cosmic time. Gareth Morgan and John McCrystal (2009: 85–86) delineate a geological memory lane for Earth consisting of the following distinctive stages:

- Snowball Earth—the planet is covered in ice, making it virtually uninhabitable until around 635 million BP.
- Greenhouse Earth—the planet is tropical even at the poles. During this period, which included the Age of the Dinosaurs, global temperatures were 4–6°C (7.2–10.8°F), perhaps 10°C (18°F), warmer than today. Furthermore, CO_2 concentrations were at times six times greater than today. This era lasted until about 70 million BP.
- Icehouse Earth—a period consisting of glacial–interglacial oscillations beginning around 34 million BP. Over the course of the last 2.6 million years of this era, ice sheets formed over the Eurasian and North American land masses, pulsing about every 40,000 years. The last phase of icehouse Earth is known to science as the Pleistocene, a period from 1.8 million BP until 11,550 BP.
- The Holocene interglacial—commencing at the end of the Pleistocene, it is the contemporary era, although, as noted in Chapter 1, there has been a movement to use the term Anthropocene to label the segment of most dramatic human impact on the planet.

Figure 3.1 displays the various geographic ages identified by the environmental sciences that match up with Morgan and McCrystal's climatic world model. These ages are dated to have occurred within particular geological and climatic epochs in Earth's history.

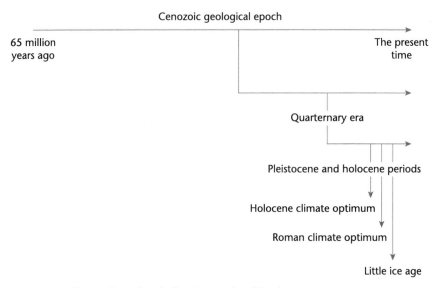

FIGURE 3.1 The geological and climatic epochs of Earth

Figure 3.1 includes a number of different systems of periodization, including both climatic and geological timescales, as clarified below:

- **Glacial periods** are named intervals of time (in thousands of years) within an ice age, marked by cooling temperatures and the growth of glaciers around the planet. Interglacials, in turn, are named warmer periods within an ice age that occur between cooler glacial periods. A stadial (such as the Older Dryas, the Younger Dryas, and the Little Ice Age) is a period of lower pressure during an interglacial of insufficient duration (less than 10,000 years) to be classified as a glacial period. There have been at least five major ice ages in Earth's history, outside of which Earth seems to have been ice-free even in high latitudes.
- **Thermals** are named climate events, including the Holocene Climate Optimum (a warm interval from 8,000 to 5,000 years ago) and the Roman Climatic Optimum or Medieval Warm Period (a mild climatic period from 1,060 to 900 years ago prior to the Little Ice Age).
- **The Cenozoic** (meaning "new life") is a *geological epoch* of time that stretches from 65 million years ago, marked by the extinction of most dinosaur species, to the present. It is subdivided into three *eras*, the Quaternary (2.5 million years ago to the present), the Neogene, and the Paleogene. Of importance to human history and activity on the planet are the two time *periods* that comprise the Quaternary: the Holocene (12,000 years ago to the present) and before it the Pleistocene (2.5 million to about 12,000 years ago).

Climatically, as this discussion suggests, Earth has seen periods of both relative stability and dramatic change.

As seen in the various studies cited in this chapter, archaeologists and paleontologists use several different dating schemes, including "kyr" (thousand years before present), BCE (years before the contemporary or common era), BP (years before present), and BC/AD (before Christ and Anno Domini, "in the year of the Lord."). We mention these here to avoid confusion in the review below.

This chapter scans times and places that "climate change" played a role in human dispersal across the planet. In the course of the evolutionary history of our species, different patterns of climate change occurred in different eras and in different locations (across a spectrum of heating and cooling ranges). Throughout the sweep of time, climate conditions have interacted with the tendency of life forms (in this case, our pre-human and human ancestors) toward biological dispersal across local environments. Such movement tends to be constrained by dispersal barriers, such as climate, that can make some places hard to colonize at particular points in time. In the case of our species, the expanding capacity of the human brain, other bodily changes, and the emergence of culture allowed a particularly flexible response to quite diverse environmental challenges and opportunities.

Children of the ice

Between 8 and 5 million years ago, Earth underwent a long-term drying and cooling period. The reason this development is of importance, as Wood (2005: 75–76) observes, is that:

> Hominin [or hominid] evolution began in Africa at the times of these climatic changes. Due to the increasing dryness, the dense forests were gradually replaced with open woodland. Tracts of grasslands began to appear between large patches of trees. We tend to think that the grass-adapted animals we associate with the modern-day African savannahs, such as the antelopes and zebra, have always been there. But they and the savannah they inhabit are relatively recent phenomena. The common ancestor of modern humans and living chimpanzees probably lived in the dense forest. Some of its descendants, though, began to adapt to life on the ground in more open conditions.

The particular epoch of our 5–6 million years or so on the planet has led to humans being described by some as the "children of the ice" (Behringer 2010: 39). In all, Earth has experienced ten major and 40 minor episodes of glaciations over the past million years (Farley 2008). Milankovitch cycles, during which the tilt of the Earth's axis fluctuates between 22° and 24.5°, occur about every 41,000 years. This shift in the axis of the planet causes the beginning and ending of ice ages. Other natural forces that can affect climate include (1) changes in the Sun's energy output; (2) variations in the distance of the Earth from the Sun; (3) changes in the atmospheric and oceanic circulation systems; (4) changes in the absorption or radiations of energy by the Earth's surface, related to the extent of cloud cover and the nature of the planet surface; and (5) volcanic eruptions (Farley 2008; Officer and Page 2009). The climate for the better part of the past 110,000 years has fluctuated between "warm" states resembling the present time and prolonged "cold" states marked by glacial advances and temperatures of 8°C (14.4°F) or more below the present average, with the Last Glacial Maximum having occurred about 20,000 years ago (Kennedy 2006). Atmospheric CO_2 hovered between 180 and 300 ppm over the course of the 650,000 years prior to recent times (Maslin 2009: 8). Most recently it has begun to rise, but not because of natural factors.

Despite the emphasis that some archaeologists, such as Brian Fagan, give to climatic factors in the rise and fall of civilizations, many archaeologists, as well as historians, ignore or downplay the role of environmental and climatic change in shaping social evolution as a reaction to the strong environmental determinism earlier posited by V. Gordon Childe (1928/1954). Some archaeologists, in fact, believe that scholars who write books like the one you are reading have fallen prey to what Butzer (2011: 1) terms the "popular 'new' environmental determinism centered on civilizational collapse in response to 'abrupt' climate climatic change" and in relation to which he calls for "strong voices of caution." He objects to the work of people like Jared Diamond (2005) who argue that various ancient societies, including Classic Mayan civilization, collapsed as a result of overexploiting their environments. Butzer (2011: 13) asserts:

> Most of the more popular claims that climate has impacted history are deductive and based on data that are inadequate or misrepresented. Social resilience and adaptation are not considered, ignoring case studies of the ways in which people have confronted short- or long-term crises in the past.

Conversely, Ferri A. Hassan (2009: 60) argues that while historically human societies have often "adapted" to multi-decadal fluctuations, they are "not immune from experiencing environmental stresses caused by unanticipated, multicentennial and millennial severe, abrupt climatic events." Paleoanthropologist Ian Tattersall (2012: 3) also recognizes the role of climate change in the human evolutionary trajectory:

> The earliest representatives of our own group lived at the end of the Miocene and at the beginning of the following Pliocene epoch, each between about six and 4.5 million years ago. And they appear just as the arrival of many new open-country mammal genera in the fossil record signals another climatic change. Oceanic cooling affected rainfall and temperatures on continents worldwide. . . . [I]n Africa it inaugurated a trend toward the breakup of forest masses and the formation of woodlands into which grasslands intruded locally. This episode of climatic deterioration furnished the larger ecological stage on which the earliest known hominids made their debut.

Controversies of this sort are not unusual in the sciences. The passage of time, new data, new ways of understanding older data and of seeing the world, and the arrival of a new generation of scholars often helps to sort out such disagreements. Increasingly, in the work of younger scholars especially, acceptance of the significant impact of climate change is becoming apparent.

Climate and the global spread of prehistoric foraging societies

The precise role played by climate change in the pathway of human evolution has been considered by human paleontologists, archaeologists, and other scholars. Fagan (2009b: 11) observes:

> The seesawing Ice Age created extraordinary challenges and opportunities for the humans and animals that inhabited the Pleistocene world . . . When the Ice Age began, somewhat ape-like hominins were the only humans on earth. They walked upright, made and used tools, foraged in small bands and were well adapted to the more open country of cooler, drier times. At first, humans were purely African mammals, but around 1.8 to 1.7 million years ago people suddenly appeared in Eurasia and Asia, living as far north as 40 degrees. By this time, we were no longer purely tropical animals.

Steven M. Stanley, a geologist, presents a highly provocative theory that Homo, as opposed to the earlier australopithecines, is the true "child of the Ice Age." He maintains that the modern Ice Age contributed to the evolution from Australopithecus to Homo by suddenly altering the African landscape, and leading ultimately to the extinction of the australopithecines (Stanley 1996: 4). Australopithecus, despite being bipedal, was a relatively good tree climber, which allowed it to find refuge from predators in the vast tropical forests. But climate change shrank the African rain forest in the middle of the Pliocene epoch around the time of the onset of the Ice Age (Stanley 1996: 111). Paleoanthropologist Rick Potts (1996: 42) argues that "Protohominids became more terrestrial as the spreading savanna inspired greater reliance on tools and meat." *Ardipithecus ramidus*, a species that appeared about 4.4 mya (million years ago) in Ethiopia, appears to have been bipedal, but had a large, flexible toe allowing it to effectively climb trees, making it well adapted to the humid woodland that it inhabited (Potts 2012: 156–157). *Australopithecus afarensis* of "Lucy fame", dating back to 3.8–3.5 mya at the Laetoli and Hadar sites in Ethiopia, "shows the loss of some of the arboreal adaptations evident in *Ardipithecus*, the environmental evidence from *Au. Afarensis* sites suggests similar habitat diversity over time and space" (Potts 2012: 157). *Australopithecus afarensis* disappeared from East Africa around 3 mya as the climate became drier. Several lines of hominins, particularly *Australopithecus africanus*, a gracile form, and *Australopithecus robustus*, a stockier form, emerged afterwards and were also found in South Africa.

As the forest contracted with the onset of the Ice Age, the australopithecines could no longer easily escape predators, such as saber-toothed and leopard-type cats, crocodiles, and hyenas, whereas chimpanzees and gorillas, which were nimble in terms of retreating to the trees, were able to do so. Thus, the bones of our ancient ancestors discovered by paleontologists and archaeologists often show signs of having been gnawed by carnivores. Under conditions of erratic instability, environmental and climatic pressures contributed to the evolution of a larger brain (a near doubling of cranial capacity as well as a change in the size of the frontal lobes of the brain) among some australopithecines around 2.4 million years ago that enabled a new genus, namely Homo, to evolve and to survive by developing stone-tipped weapons that allowed it to defend itself against various carnivores (Stanley 1996: 59). Potts (2010: 48) adds: "Although early hominins may have been relatively defenseless from a physical standpoint, part of their primate heritage included impressive defenses against predators, including being social and vocal." As opposed to Australopithecus, or more precisely *Australopithecus africanus*, Paranthropus or *Australopithecus robustus* survived longer into the Ice Age, eventually becoming extinct about a million years ago. Stanley maintains that the latter's powerful jaws and large molars provided it with a broader diet that included foodstuffs such as tubers and roots—a factor in its longer persistence. In reality, the fossil record on australopithecines is much more complex than the existence of a simple distinction between *Australopithecus africanus* and *Australopithecus robustus*, a point that Potts (1996: 216) admits in his observation that somewhere between eight and 13 distinct species of bipedal hominids, including *Homo habilis* and *Homo erectus*, existed at one time or other over the course of the past 4 million years. Since this observation, paleoanthropologists have identified and debated over several new categories of proto-hominids and early hominids, as well as added new named members of the hominid family to our branch-rich family tree, a discussion that falls outside the purview of this book.

Potts (1998) has proposed what he terms a variability selection hypothesis, which asserts that specific adaptations that appeared among early human ancestors were not narrowly shaped by any particular habitat. Rather, the key to human evolution was environmental instability. Hominins did not become physically limited by diet or other factors to a single type of environment, as is seen in some species, but, because of continued exposure to a changing environment/climate, developed as generalists capable of surviving in many different kinds of habitats. Indeed, the "survival conditions of human evolution were continually revised as climate oscillated between arid and moist and between cold and warm" as supported by environmental records on shifting conditions from around the world (Potts 2010: 50). Over the course of human evolution, hominins increased their physical and cultural coping skills, allowing them to invade new and ecological quite different physical environments.

Prior to 2 million years ago, the African climate had been temperate and humid, but became colder and more arid after about 1.9 million BP (Hetherington and Reid 2010). The first hominids may have moved out of Africa about 2 million years ago, with *Homo erectus* populations living in the region we today known as Pakistan about this time and arriving in Java by 1.5 million years ago, possibly as early as 1.9 million years ago, and in Jordan by around 1.5 million years ago. It is at this time that Earth underwent another warming, leading to an expansion once again of the African forests (Hetherington and Reid 2010). Around 1.3 million years BP, the climate chilled again, resulting in increased grasslands in Africa. *Homo erectus* appeared in Europe around 900,000 years ago, a period of warming and rising of sea levels. As Hetherington and Reid (2010: 87) observe:

> During the early Pleistocene, glaciations were generally low amplitude and high frequency, occurring about every 41,000 years. In the middle Pleistocene, after about 800,000 years ago, glaciations were of higher amplitude and reducing frequency, occurring about every 100,000 years. . . . Transitions between glacial and interglacial conditions were more pronounced, resulting in greater latitudinal shifts in fauna and flora. Beginning 1.2 million years ago, a series of mainly mammalian dispersals began in Asia. By about 800,000 years ago, more than 25 species of mammals had left Asia and relocated in central and Western Europe. These dispersals are believed to be related to climate change. It is possible that early hominins were part of this major mammalian dispersal out of Asia.

Potts (1996) maintains that in the period between 500,000 and 200,000 years ago there was a continual process of human diversification. Some scientists, he notes, believe all of the hominids that lived during this period were members of a single evolving evolutionary line that connected *Homo erectus* to modern *Homo sapiens*. Other researchers, by contrast, view the paleontological record as being comprised of four different species of humans during this era, with *Homo erectus* living in eastern Asia, *Homo heidelbergensis* dwelling in Europe, some poorly known populations of archaic *Homo sapiens* occupying Africa, and toward the end of this time range, the Neanderthals, who had evolved in Europe and western Asia, living in Africa.

In John Hoffecker's (2009) reading of the paleontological and archaeological records, the Asian counterparts of *Homo heidelbergensis* vacated northern Asia during glaciations. The Neanderthals followed in the wake of *Homo erectus* and *Homo heidelbergensis* in Europe. Many scholars view the Classic Neanderthals, with their big bodies, as an adaptation to intense cold in Europe and Eurasia. While many physical anthropologists have argued that the Neanderthals were more or less in direct line with modern humans, and have been designated as *Homo sapiens neanderthalensis*, others, like Fagan (2010), view them as having been a sideline that fell outside the genetic range of modern humans, a group that could not compete with the more modern Cro-Magnon types who filtered into Europe from western Asia around 45,000 years ago. However, genetic studies indicate that Neanderthal genes are still found in human populations, so some interbreeding clearly occurred, thus substantially supporting an argument posited by some paleoanthropologists in the past (Stringer 2012).

In contrast to the Neanderthals, who "survived by moving into sheltered valleys and slightly warmer environments in Italy and south of the Pyrenees," the Cro-Magnons with their more elaborate tool kits refined hunting techniques in a wide array of landscapes, ranging from tundras to the margins of coniferous forests (Fagan 2010: 156–157). Fagan (2010: 157) boldly asserts that the "diverse Cro-Magnon societies of the Last Glacial Maximum were an exemplar of later arctic hunter-gather societies." Eurasia's population possibly fluctuated between the stadials and interstadials of the Upper Paleolithic (Fagan 2010: 140). The climate in Europe suddenly became warmer with the Boelling oscillation that set in about 14,500 BP, lasting about 1,500 years (Fagan 2010: 226).

One study based upon a database of 499 archaeological collections from 332 European sites indicates that the Neanderthal tool kit only began to diversify during the Fourth Glacial, suggesting technological stagnation during the long duration of the Middle Paleolithic, a period of 200,000–250,000 years, with a high degree of climatic variability (Bocquet-Appel and Tuffreau 2009). In contrast, modern humans during the Upper Paleolithic developed a wide variety of more sophisticated tools, indicating a higher cognitive capacity.

Fagan (1999: 68) argues that oceans and deserts have repeatedly proven to be "powerful engines in human affairs." The Sahara Desert, for example, functions as a pump which is driven by atmospheric changes and global climatic shifts (Fagan 1999: 68). The area had more precipitation some 130,000 years ago and contained shallow lakes and semi-arid grasslands. When the Sahara dried up as glaciers advanced in more northerly environments, it became a barrier between tropical Africa and the Mediterranean area, but not before modern humans or *Homo sapiens* emerged in Africa and radiated out to Eurasia (Stanley 1996: 208–211). Thus, Hassan (2009: 47–48) argues:

> Human dispersal out of Africa took place between 130 and 90kyr . . . and may have coincided with the global climatic changes associated with the last major glaciation. Modern humans appeared in Palestine ca. 90kyr, and remains of early humans in Southeast Asia date to *c*.75kyr. . . . This suggests that this phase of dispersal may have been associated with warmer interstadials that cluster in the period *c*.85–75kyr.

Lake Chad has been a climatological barometer of the ancient Sahara. Present-day Lake Chad is miniscule compared with the Lake Chad of 120,000 years ago, which filled a vast basin larger than the Caspian Sea. The Sahara began to dry up sometime before 2,700 BP for reasons that are still not understood. The Sahel became an undulating grassy steppe fluctuating between 200 and 400km in length, bordered on the north by the Sahara and to the south by forests. The Sahel has experienced a climate characterized by irregular and sometimes severe droughts for the past 2,500 years.

Between 1 million and 10,000 years ago, a period that more or less corresponded with the Fourth Glacial, humans made their way to Eurasia, Australia, and the Americas (Burroughs 2005). Hassan (2009: 48) identifies dispersals into southwest Asia at about 50,000–40,000 years ago and into northern Europe around 40,000 years ago which apparently were "triggered by very severe cold conditions 50kyr," to Australia around 38,000 to 30,000 years ago, which "coincided with a period of frequent millennial changes in climate starting before 40kyr until 36kyr," to northeastern Siberia around 20,000 years ago, "during the Last Glacial Maximum (LGM), perhaps in response to episodic amelioration in climate during that cold phase," and across the Bering Strait to the Americas possibly "during the Younger Dryas 13,000 to 11,600 years ago." According to Hoffecker (2009: 127), a "wave of innovation and change ensued between 30,000 years ago, when the Neanderthals disappeared, and the maximum cold of the last glacial period about 23,000–21,000 years ago." Technological innovations that occurred during this period included large settlements in northern Eurasia and large dwelling units with multiple fireplaces in south Siberia, at sites near Lake Baikal, as well as kilns used to fire ceramics in parts of northern Eurasia.

As this discussion indicates, in the end, the Neanderthals joined many other branches of the diverse evolutionary tree of hominids and became extinct. Notes Potts (2010: 52):

> Over the past three million years in particular, powerful climate swings would have led to large fluctuations in supplies of crucial resources, contributing to occasional crashes in population size. All of these factors can influence the survival or extinction of species.

A lesson of the hominid fossil record is that extinction related to climate change is as familiar to our own ancestral line as it is to other species. The critical question, of course, is how it will figure in the hominid future.

As the foregoing review indicates, the progressive interaction of our biology with climate/environments in conjunction with human interaction led us on a biosocial course of brain capacity expansion and cultural production, which, in turn, allowed our full dispersal to most ecological zones on the planet. We have become the beings we now see in the mirror through our interactions with shifting climate/environments, and, as the capacities born of this interface grew, especially the cultural capacities, we have, in turn, shaped the world around us. When carried further, however, with the continued development of the transformative capacity of culture (particularly of technology), there has emerged an ability for humans to not only adapt to varied environments, but to adversely impact and degrade the climate/environment at the peril of our own extinction.

Alluding to the disappearance of various species of mega-fauna (i.e., large animal species) in the Americas and Australia at the end of the Pleistocene, Potts (1996: 216) maintains:

> it has always been difficult to separate the effects of climate and of human predation on the extinction episodes of that time. The splurge of human hunters over new landscapes occurred against a background of major climate change, a time of ecological trauma in some places, such as Australia, and of ecological recovery from glacial conditions in others, such as North America.

Over the course of the past 10,000 years or so, generally referred to as the Holocene and viewed by many as essentially the Fourth Interglacial, Earth's climate, as noted in Chapter 1, has been relatively stable (although hardly rigid and unchanging). Indeed, it would be appropriate to refer to much of the Holocene as a period of constrained but shifting stability. Anthropogenic climate change in very recent times, however, has begun to play havoc with this relative stability. This is not an entirely new set of circumstance for our species. Certainly, prior to the Holocene, humanity, over the course of the last glacial, was in a climatically precarious situation. Stanley Ambrose (1998: 623) refers to the Late Pleistocene as an era of "bottlenecks and releases" during which many humans perished but some survived in large tropical refuges, such as in equatorial Africa. He maintains that the Fourth Glacial was preceded by 1,000 years of the coldest temperatures of the Later Pleistocene (c. 71,000–70,000 years ago) which may have been caused by the eruption of the Toba volcano in Sumatra, resulting in the decimation of most modern human populations of the day.

Lower sea levels proved to be beneficial for some sectors of humanity, in that they facilitated the movement of populations that had to migrate in order to gradually accommodate their increasing numbers. According to Burroughs (2005: 102):

In particular, in the Persian Gulf, around India, and most of all, down through southeast Asia and Indonesia, the linking of many of the islands (which we now call Sundaland) greatly assisted human mobility. The drop in sea level after 85kya, and the low level between 67 and 61kya may have played a crucial part in the movement out of Africa and the early arrival of humans in Australia, although they still had to overcome the considerable challenge of sailing across the much reduced Timor Sea. The same pattern applies to the land bridge that formed between northeastern Asia and Alaska (termed Beringia), which is regarded to be the only feasible route for modern humans to reach North America.

The retreat of ice sheets allowed humans to penetrate North America and Scandinavia (Hoffecker 2009). The subsequent rise of the sea levels, however, eradicated the Bering Land Bridge between Siberia and Alaska possibly by 11,000 years ago (Hoffecker 2009). In the case of North America, a corridor developed between the eastern and western ice sheets that allowed humans to penetrate into the interior of North America and eventually make their way to South America.

A sea level drop of some 90m exposed a 300m-wide relatively flat section of the continental shelf, the now submarine plain bordering the continent, which allowed humans to penetrate the western coast of North America.

Climate change continued to be somewhat erratic at the end of the Fourth Glacial, but overall the climate was warmer, facilitating the peopling of the New World from Canada to the tip of South America, and from the Atlantic to the Pacific coasts.

In retrospect, it appears that while fluctuations in climate nearly wiped out the entire hominid line at certain points in time, these shifts also allowed the dispersal of humans to new geographic zones, a dissemination that probably played a role in the survival of our species despite devastating local climate/environmental upheavals.

Climate impacts on the Neolithic

Intensive food production began in the Near East toward the end of the Fourth Glacial, or more specifically the Younger Dryas (a renowned cold spike that began about 12,700 years ago in various locations around the globe) and the beginning of the Holocene, which facilitated significant population growth (Dincauze 2000; Hetherington and Reid 2010). Various scholars suggest that both climate change and population growth contributed to the emergence of agriculture in several parts of the world (Christian 2011; Hetherington 2012). Joy McCorriston and Frank Hole (1991: 46) argue that plant domestication in the near East was driven by the "synergistic effect of climate change, anthropogenic environmental change, and social innovation." These kinds of interaction are reflected as well in the "oasis theory" developed in 1951 by Childe, who:

> suggested that a colder, dryer climate forced humans and animals to retreat to where the best sources of water remained and where hunting and

> gathering continued to be good. These localized groups then developed agriculture to feed the newly concentrated populations—perhaps some refugees fleeing areas of drought or destruction brought with them knowledge of upland wild cereals and stocks of their seeds. The growing population provided the labor necessary to seed, tend, irrigate, and harvest the crops. Society necessarily became stratified to organize the effort, and so began the rise of civilization.
>
> *Hetherington 2012: 74*

In a similar vein, Fagan (2013: 40) argues that the drought cycle that contributed to a shift from a reliance on nuts and wild grasses to the domestication of plants and animals in the Middle East led to the rapid spread of farming settlements throughout the region as well as the eastern Mediterranean coast as the "cold snap and accompanying droughts eased."

Climatic factors also have played an important role in human relations with the seas. Archaeologist Lewis Binford (1968) asserted that global change in sea level in the post-Pleistocene era contributed to greater reliance on fish and other aquatic resources, which in turn led to sedentarization in areas rich in marine resources and to rapid population growth in certain regions based on stable, protein-rich diets. Conversely, population pressures in these regions forced some populations into more marginal environments where they shifted to food production as a means of retaining or replicating standards of living in richer environments.

In a somewhat alternative perspective, Donald O. Henry (1989) argues that environmental changes prompted by global climatic oscillations forced human populations to gradually shift to farming near the end of the Fourth Glacial, some 10,000–13,000 years ago. According to Ian Whyte (2008: 56), the:

> onset of the drier conditions that characterized the Younger Dryas period may have forced the later Natufians [the name given to the sedentary hunter-gatherers living in the Eastern Mediterranean between about 12,500 and 10,200 years ago] to switch from harvesting wild cereals to the deliberate cultivation of these same crops in the Fertile Crescent.

Climate change appears to have placed pressure on the peoples of Mesopotamia to relocate from the densely populated villages of the Hilly Flanks (an area curving around the Tigris, Euphrates, and Jordan valleys of the Near East) to congregate in cities in which elites coordinated elaborate irrigation systems (Morris 2011). As Hoffecker (2009) observes, archaeologists speculate that the brief cold phase known as the Younger Dryas forced changes in human subsistence economies that led to the rapid emergence of village farming. Within a few millennia, the Near East witnessed a sizeable enlargement of agricultural areas, the appearance of cities, and the development of pre-modern civilizations, a pattern repeated in other parts of the world as well.

Hassan describes the possible relationship between climate change and the movements of Saharan populations between 7,800 and 6,800 BP, a period characterized by frequent climatic oscillations and droughts. Climatic conditions became progressively drier and led to the onset of severe aridity by 5,500–5,300 BP, signaling the desertification of much of North Africa. The succession of wet and dry episodes seems to have encouraged the adoption of pastoralism and the successive movements of cattle and then ovicaprids (i.e., sheep and/or goats) westward following the better-watered range and basin areas associated with the Saharan highlands (Hassan 2009). In the case of Central Africa, a team of archaeologists maintain that climate change-induced expansion of savannahs in the Sanaga-Mbam confluence region around 4,000–3,500 BP contributed to the large-scale settlement of Bantu-speakers into Central Africa, later accompanied by the development of cereal crop farming and metallurgy around 2,500 BP (Bostoen *et al.* 2015).

Ancient civilizations and later tribal societies

Based upon a Dahlem Workshop on the "Integrated History and Future of People on the Earth" in Berlin in 2005, several archaeologists and other scholars identified at least six global or at least semiglobal periods during which the amplitude of change in precipitation, temperature, and wind was somewhat higher than before the Holocene (Redman, Crumley, *et al.* 2007). They concurred that there were two eras in climate history that underwent notable global scale climate change, namely the 4.2K (kiloyear) event, a drier and much cooler period lasting from 2200 to 1800 BC and the seventh- to tenth-century episode. The 4.2K event induced some sedentary farmers in northern Mesopotamia to abandon their settlements in a move to more dispersed villages, but also witnessed the collapse of the Old Kingdom in Egypt, cooler and drier conditions in much of China, and the renaissance of the Harappan civilization in the Indus Valley due to the high flow of water from melting Himalayan glaciers that was used for irrigation. Hassan (1994: 1) maintains that the "collapse of centralized [Egyptian] government about 2200 BC . . . coincides with the reduced Nile flood discharge, invasion of the Nile Valley by dune sand, and possible degradation of the Delta floodplain." The seventh- to tenth-century event, which witnessed an increase in solar emissions and sea level rises higher than the present day, contributed to the emergence of the High Middle Ages in Europe, the fall of the Bal He Kuk Kingdom in Korea, the collapse of the Maya civilization, and the fluorescence of the Hohokam culture in what is today called Arizona (Redman, Crumley, *et al.* 2007).

Based upon their selected case studies, Redman, Crumley, *et al.* (2007: 143) conclude:

> It is clear that even within relatively uniform global climatic events, societies respond in both parallel and diverse ways. Moreover, the same society at one point in time may respond in a positive direction to the input and at another point negatively.

Fagan (2011: 134) describes Mesopotamia as a "world of climatic extremes and violent floods, of torrential rains and steaming-hot summers, a place where political rivalries always simmered." Archaeologist William R. Thompson (2007: 168) has described the role of climate change in the Near East prior and after the fourth century BC in the follow terms:

> The availability of water initially encouraged the expansion of human populations in the region, particularly in the river valleys. When precipitation and river levels declined, subsequent water scarcities prompted the development of new adaptive strategies leading to the accelerated emergence of nomadic-sedentary divergence, urbanization, writing, government, religion, and state-making. Climate change did not determine what transpired. There were a host of possible responses, many of which were pursued. The most successful strategies, however, involved the development of cities and states. . . . But climate change accelerated the development of multiple, interactive process to new levels of intensity.

Thompson (2007: 168–169) develops five working hypotheses that could be used to interpret the impact of climate change on ancient civilizations, with the understanding that similar climate–society interactions also occur in other regions of the world:

H1—Periods of economic decline in the ancient world were systematically associated with periods of deteriorating climate and diminished water supply.

H2—Periods of trade collapse in the ancient world were systematically associated with periods of deteriorating climate and diminished water supply.

H3—Regime transitions in the ancient world were systematically associated with periods of deteriorating climate and diminished water supply.

H4—The most significant center–hinterland conflicts in the ancient world were systematically associated with periods of deteriorating climate and water supply.

H5—The conjunction of significant political and economic crises in the ancient world were systematically associated with periods of deteriorating climate and diminished water supply.

These hypotheses are reflected in our socioecological model introduced in Chapter 1. With climate change and its symptoms of climate turmoil (e.g., droughts, severe storms), environments became less predictable, populations became more vulnerable, and ultimately their resiliency began to deteriorate, as expressed in the economic and political breakdowns Thompson mentions.

Renowned archaeologist Joseph Tainter (1988: 1) argues that civilizations are "fragile, impermanent things" which are sooner or later subject to collapse. He delineates 11 major themes in the collapse of civilizations:

1. Depletion or cessation of a vital resource or resources on which the society depends.

2. The establishment of a new resource base which alleviates social inequities and leads to a reversion to a simpler society.
3. The occurrence of some insurmountable catastrophe.
4. Insufficient response to circumstances.
5. Presence of other complex societies.
6. Intruders.
7. Class conflict, societal contradictions, elite mismanagement or self-serving behavior.
8. Social dysfunctions that contribute to societal disintegration.
9. Mystical factors such as societal decadence or loss of social vitality.
10. Chance concatenation of events such as invasion by warrior tribal societies or the coming to power of ineffectual rulers.
11. Economic factors.

Tainter notes that there is considerable overlap in the factors listed above. He argues that two major explanations for the collapse of civilizations are subsumed under the theme of resource depletion, namely "the gradual deterioration or depletion of a resource base (usually agriculture), often due to human mismanagement, and the more rapid loss of resources due to an environmental fluctuation or climatic shift" (Tainter 1988: 44). Various scholars have sought to link climate and resource depletion with the collapse of civilizations. Below is a brief review of the connection between climate and resource depletion in selected places cited by Tainter.

The American Southwest:

> Climatic change is the most common explanation for the collapse of horticultural settlements, and of social complexity, in various areas of the Southwest. . . . The most frequent resource depletion arguments postulate such things as drought, erosion, shifts in rainfall seasonality, lower temperatures, overhunting of game, and depletion or increasing alkalinity of cultivable soils.
>
> *Tainter 1988: 46*

Eastern North America:

> The collapse of northern Hopewell was ascribed by James B. Griffin to a slightly cooler climatic phase in the upper Mississippi Valley.
>
> *Tainter 1988: 47*

On Egypt, Tainter comments:

> Karl Butzer has argued in a number of studies . . . that the collapse of the Old Kingdom, and other political catastrophes of Egyptian history, can be traced at least in part to variations in Nile flood levels, and thus to precipitation patterns in the interior of Africa. . . . [He] sees Nile fluctuations

as a contributory rather than a causal agent, acting in concert with political weakness.

Tainter 1988: 47

On the Mycenaean civilization, in 1966, Tainter (1988: 49) reports, Rhys Carpenter "developed an elegantly written argument for the collapse of Mycenaean civilization: that it, and other thirteenth-century BC upheavals in the Mediterranean, were due to climatic change leading to famine, depopulations, and migration."

The societal collapses that have occurred through history, as Tainter's account suggests, reflect the interplay of climatic factors, pluralea interactions (e.g., over-hunting of game, anthropogenic alkalinization of cultivable soils), and vulnerability (e.g., political weakness), the complex entwinement of climate/environment/society factors incorporated in our model.

More recently, Tainter (2014) has argued that while the Roman and Mayan civilizations exhibited many differences, they also followed similar paths of socio-cultural evolution and developed similar vulnerabilities. He seeks to highlight the following seven lessons from the Roman and Mayan cases in terms of comprehending environmental sustainability challenges in modern industrialized societies, particularly the United States:

1. funding retirements for the baby-boom generation;
2. continuing increases in the cost of health care;
3. replacing decaying infrastructure;
4. adapting to climate change and repairing environmental damage;
5. developing new sources of energy;
6. continuing high military costs;
7. continued need to innovate (Tainter 2014: 210).

Tainter is not highly optimistic about the capacity of industrialized societies to effectively address these problems. Efforts to more or less maintain the status quo in terms of the complexity and high material standard of living may result in "serious consequences" and "political discontent as incomes stagnate and shrink." In our concluding chapter, we explore alternatives to not merely adapting to climate change, but mitigating it by shifting to an alternative world system.

The human hand in historically relevant climate change

Climatic changes prior to at least 10,000 years ago can be safely assumed to have been due to the natural forces delineated above. At some point, however, slowly but increasingly, humans became a contributing agent to climate change. William Ruddiman (2005: 5) contends that CO_2 emissions began to slowly increase as humans began to clear the land in their shift from foraging to farming about 8,000 years ago in places such as China, India, and Europe. Starting about this time, the burning of peat for heating and cooking and of limestone to produce lime for mortar and plaster also added to CO_2 emissions. According to Dincauze (2000), the massive deforestation that has occurred in various regions of the world for several millennia has contributed to climate change. Ruddiman contends that methane emissions began to increase around 5,000 years ago as various populations started to irrigate for rice production and to raise livestock. Livestock produces methane from both manure and gaseous belches. The clearing of forests and burning of grasslands also produced methane, as did human waste. Of course, as these human-driven transformations of the environment were taking place, people were unaware of the larger impacts on the planet. Had human technologies remained at these levels, those impacts would have been limited. This is not what occurred, however.

Collapse of the great civilizations

The great civilizations of history were all ultimately impacted by climate. In Mesopotomia, the Sumerians built the world's first civilization "when sea levels stabilized and short-term drought cycles related to the Southern Oscillation and periodic monsoon failures became a reality of life in Egypt and southern Iraq" (Fagan 1999: 92). Sumerian civilization existed in a fragile environment subjected to cycles of floods and droughts.

Egypt underwent frequent arid spells around 7,800 to 6,800 BP, inducing many Saharan inhabitants to settle on the banks of the Nile (Hassan 2009). According to Hassan (2009: 54), between 5,800 and 5,300 BP, "Egyptian farming communities made a transition to a state society." He maintains that a "global climatic cold event" (Hassan 2009: 54) contributed to a reduction of Nile floods, and political unification followed, driven by a need to ensure collective protection against crop failures. As this suggests, climate factors were critical to the emergence of ancient Egyptian civilization, a societal fluorescence that had historical cultural impact on subsequent developments in the Near East, Europe and the Americas.

The Roman Empire developed in northwestern Europe in the last two centuries BC and the first century AD during a warm, dry period called the Roman Warm Period or Roman Climatic Optimum (Tainter and Crumley 2007). Just as the Empire underwent a series of crises during the third century, the Roman Warm Period ended, resulting in lower agricultural yields. Rulers responded to these crises by beefing up the state's administrative apparatus and military, a costly endeavor sustained by higher taxes, which negatively impacted the productivity of the peasants, further exacerbating a tense situation and eventually leading to social collapse.

The Mayan civilization in Mesoamerica, which came into existence around AD 250, suddenly collapsed in the tenth century (Fagan 1999: 140). A number of archaeologists who ascribe the collapse of Mayan civilization primarily to a series of devastating droughts during the eighth and ninth centuries (Gill 2000; Ford and Nigh 2014; Beach 2016). As a result of the inability of the Mayan elite to fulfill their social obligation to ensure the flow of water, village farmers fled, dispersing into smaller communities that permitted them to survive. Vernon L. Scarborough

(2007), however, contends that in the light of the environmental and societal resilience of the Mayan civilization, political, economic, and ideological factors internal to the composition of that society may have been of greatest significance. Nevertheless, along with these factors, he, along with Lisa J. Lucero and Joel D. Gunn, argues that the Mayan royal rulers who managed the supply of water for farming public ceremonies, games, festivals, feasts and other socially integrative activities by means of an elaborate system of reservoirs in the interior of their kingdom lost their legitimacy as the water supply seriously diminished as a result of a series of droughts during the Terminal Classic period (c. AD 800–950) (Lucero et al. 2011).

Farther south, the Moche civilization flourished along the arid north coast of Peru between AD 100 and 800 (Fagan 1999). This state society relied upon an elaborate agricultural system that captured water from the Andes and fed a complex irrigation system. The Moche also consumed anchovy and other fresh fish that they extracted from the Pacific Ocean. Ultimately, however, El Niño contributed to the collapse of yet another ecologically fragile empire that existed in a generally parched environment (Fagan 1999). There had been droughts between AD 534 and AD 540 and again between AD 563 and AD 594. In addition, El Niño produced devastating floods that polluted springs and streams, strained sanitation systems, and eroded fertile fields (Fagan 1999). These multiple climate-related assaults eventually overwhelmed local resiliency, leading to household, community and societal collapse.

Climate change also appears to have been a factor in the collapse of the Anasazi culture of the American Southwest. Due to droughts and El Niño events, the Anasazi abandoned sites such as Mesa Verde in southwest Colorado and Chaco Canyon in northwest New Mexico in the twelfth century (Fagan 1999). Today the Pueblos Indians, descendants of the Anasazi, live in a series of villages scattered about the Rio Grande Valley of New Mexico, three mesas in northeast Arizona (in the case of the Hopi), and the villages of Laguna and Acoma in western New Mexico. As has occurred in multiple times and places, as complex social systems lose their resiliency and collapse under pressure from climate/environment changes, people, often less densely gathered together and in simpler social arrangements, manage to survive in the shadow of fallen hierarchical social structures. The lesson of this repeated pattern is difficult to gauge because the megacities of today are far greater than anything seen in human history. It is hard to imagine societal collapse of globally connected nation states in the contemporary era that would not lead to a significant drop in the surviving populations.

The Medieval Warm Period (c. AD 900–1200) or the Medieval Climatic Optimum has been the topic of much scholarly discussion. Apparently, actual warming varied regionally during this period, with some places, such as Scandinavia, Greenland, China, the Sierra Nevada Mountains in California, the Canadian Rockies, and Tasmania experiencing warming, and other places, such as the US Southwest, southern Europe along the Mediterranean, and parts of South America, not experiencing warming (Hassan 2009). The Vikings took their long boats to

Iceland, Greenland, and Vinland (North America) during the Medieval Warm Period. The population in northern Europe probably doubled between AD 1100 and 1300 during the Medieval Warm Period (Morris 2011: 363). Conversely, the Medieval Warm Period adversely impacted the Islamic core, where population size may have declined by 10 percent (Morris 2011: 364). By contrast, some areas of North Africa flourished during this period.

The Little Ice Age commenced around AD 1250 and lasted until around the mid-nineteenth century. While McGovern (1994: 141) acknowledges that climate change played a major role in the extinction of the Norse colonies in Greenland, he does not believe it was the only factor involved, noting that they "had failed to make full use of resources locally available, while continuing to deform the subsistence economy to produce inedible prestige goods for export." McGovern (1994: 154) further argues that the fate of the Norse colonies serves as a lesson for large portions of humanity which are "pursuing limited, but intensive strategies of exploitation requiring precarious balancing of distant resource zones and markets," processes that are inherent in the capitalist world system. The Low Countries were buffeted by storm surges during the fourteenth and fifteenth centuries, and a seven-year period of heavy summer rains devastated farming, resulting in the deaths of some 1.5 million people (Fagan 2009a). According to Fagan (2009a: 204):

> The climax of the Little Ice Age came in the late 17th century, during the Maunder Minimum, a period of reduced sunspot activity. This was when the Thames froze and fairs thrived on the ice. . . . The cooler and unsettled centuries saw major fluctuations in Alpine glaciers, as well as a revolution in agriculture that first took hold in the Netherlands, then Britain. The incidence of famine was reduced, except in much of France, where bread shortages, caused in part by poor harvests, contributed to the unrest of the French Revolution.

The Little Ice Age ended in the 1850s as the Industrial Revolution was well under way and already dependent on coal as an energy and warming source (Fagan 1999). Generally, the world entered a new era of warmer temperatures and less dramatic climatic swings, although occasional cold spells occurred, including three severe winters between 1939 and 1942 which interfered with Nazi invasions in France and the Soviet Union (Fagan 1999). Behringer (2010: 174) argues that if was not for rapid industrialization, which contributed significantly to global warming, the "Little Ice Age was heading for another 'cold maximum', all the more intense because of the volcanic eruption on Krakatoa in Indonesia."

The lessons of history

Karen Holmgren and Helena Oberg (2007: 130) propose several generalizations that shed light on some possible impacts of climate change on human societies over time:

1. Societal changes often coincide with climatic changes.
2. Climatic changes do not always result in societal changes—a stable and resilient society can survive severe climate conditions.
3. Climatic change is a common external trigger in societies suffering from internal instability. When periods of climate change coincide with periods of socioeconomic and political instability, this may result either in societal catastrophes or in new social developments.
4. Climatic conditions that are favorable for agricultural or pastoral production have been an important factor in the rise of new and powerful centers of wealth accumulation.
5. From the historical data, we can observe that adaptational or resiliency strategies include:

    a. flexibility in short- and long-term mobility and in the relocation of centers;
    b. flexibility in agricultural practices and in types of staple crops; and
    c. the possibility of controlling external trade.

Comparative sociologist Sing C. Chew (2001, 2007) has discussed in detail the idea of Dark Ages which various civilizations, including the Mesopotamian, ancient Egyptian, Harappan in northwestern India, and Mycenaean Greece, as well as the vast Roman Empire, historically encountered in the wake of periods of rapid climatic, ecological, and social upheaval. However, these Dark Ages, such as the one during the Middle Ages in western Europe when socioeconomic activities broke down, allowed for the rejuvenation of the environment. Thus, "In certain ways, the Dark Age of Antiquity was a rebalancing of Nature–Culture relations following centuries of anthropogenic stress of the landscape" (Chew 2007: 165). In the past, climatic and ecological crises often prompted populations to disperse to new locations which had previously been either uninhabited or sparsely populated by human beings. In contrast, catastrophic climate change in the present world may not leave many options for adversely affected populations to relocate to uninhabited areas. As Chew (2007: 181) so eloquently argues:

> At this stage of the globalization process, planet Earth is fully encompassed, and thus if ecological collapse (Dark Age) occurs there are few replacement areas for system expansion. Besides this, the level of connectivity of the world system in terms of production and reproduction processes means that the collapse will be felt globally, unlike previous Dark Ages in which not all the peripheral areas were impacted by the collapse.

In the present, societal collapse, expressed as failed states, economic crises, mass migrations of populations, and intense humanitarian crises, is not likely to be solely a consequence of climate change, but rather the multiple blows of climate-induced turmoil in interactions with diverse anthropogenic ecocrises that overwhelm the ability of states, communities, and households to adapt. Indeed, Tattersall (2012:

230) somberly reminds us that "behaviors that a resilient environment could simply absorb when *Homo sapiens* was thin on the ground became hugely damaging to human populations when there are seven billion of us around." However, it is important to note that the more affluent sectors of the world, particularly in the developed countries, but increasingly among the rising super-rich and middle classes of the developing world, are having a more drastic destructive impact on the planet than the billions of indigenous peoples, peasants, and poor urbanites who struggle for their existence from day to day. These are the conditions of our world today, a world that anthropologists among and with others are struggling to understand and to develop meaningful responses.

Towards a climate change archaeology

Robert van de Noort (2013) has made the first explicit effort to create a climate change archaeology, largely by examining how communities in the past have adjusted and today are adjusting with sea level variations, particularly sea level rise related to climate change, largely natural in the past, but mainly anthropogenic in the present era. Even though he notes that archaeologists have been examining past climate change and its impacts for at least 150 years (see Trigger 2006), he laments that "studies of how societies adapted to climate change and its environmental impacts in the past have made no contribution to the debates on the ways in which humanity will need to adapt to climate change in the future" (Van de Noort 2013: 2).

Van de Noort, however, maintains that archaeological research theoretically provides visions of adaptive pathways that can assist communities in their efforts to respond to climate change. In his book, he focuses on four diverse coastal regions, namely the North Sea basin, the Sundarbans in the Bay of Bengal, Florida's wetlands in the Gulf of Mexico, and the Al-Ahwar/Iraqi Marshlands in the Persian Gulf. Van de Noort (2013: 227) chose these landscapes, which have all adapted to fluctuating sea levels in the past and will have to in the future, because the people who live in them "are amongst the first that will be affected significantly by climate change–sea level rise." Whereas in the North Sea basin, policy-makers have adopted an integrated approach to coastal zone management, which includes building sea walls, such an effective coastal zone management plan has not been implemented in part due to an on-going dispute between Bangladesh and the Indian state of West Bengal over the Farakka Barrage constructed between 1961 and 1975, thus putting communities at risk from flooding and erosion. What Van de Noort does not consider is differential access to resources to adapt to sea level rises in, on the one hand, developed countries bordering the North Sea basin and the United States in the case of Florida's wetlands, and, on the other hand, developing countries, such as Bangladesh in the case of the Sundarbans and Iraq in the case of the Persian Gulf wetlands. His ambitions for a climate change archaeology are modest and do not seek large-scale solutions that will be required as a result of rising sea levels and climate change as a whole. In a similar vein to Van de Noort, Jeneva Wright (2016) asserts that maritime archaeology is "uniquely positioned to support climate change research and the understanding of the past human adaptations to climate change." Furthermore, archaeologists associated with the IHOPE-Maya Project believe that Maya archaeology is well positioned to "contribute to broader, more current debates concerning climate change, population limits, urban forms, landscape modifications, and degrees of stability" (Chase and Scarborough 2014: 5).

However, what is needed is a more critical climate change archaeology, one that engages with critical social science perspectives that we discuss in subsequent chapters and touches upon not only adaptation to climate change, but also mitigation strategies for addressing climate change. A possible step in this direction is a paper titled "The possibility of collapse from a marxist perspective: Marx, Luxemburg and Benjamin" presented by Miguel Fuentes, a PhD student at the Institute of Archaeology, University College London, at the multidisciplinary conference on *Climate Change, Archaeology and History* in December 2016.

4

THEORETICAL PERSPECTIVES IN THE ANTHROPOLOGY OF CLIMATE CHANGE

Theory in the anthropology of climate change

In this chapter, we examine the three most commonly used theoretical perspectives that have emerged in the anthropology of climate change. The alternative perspectives seek to provide a framework for understanding various aspects of the human–climate change interface over the course of the past century or so. As noted in Chapter 1, these are: (1) the cultural ecological, (2) the cultural interpretive, and (3) the critical anthropological perspectives of climate change. In some ways, the anthropology of climate change may be viewed as a subfield of ecological anthropology or environmental anthropology which examines the historic and current human–environment interactions (Kopnina and Shoreman-Ouimet 2017). Even prior to the emergence of the anthropology of climate change as a subfield of ecological anthropology, the latter subsumed concerns such as primate ecology, paleoecology, cultural ecology, ethno-ecology, ethno-ornithology, historical ecology, spiritual ecology, human behavioral ecology, and evolutionary ecology. While some anthropologists working on climate change draw heavily upon cultural ecology, others draw heavily upon political ecology.

In his effort to explore the issue of explanation in science, philosopher Karl Popper (2002: 37) defined theories as "universal statements" about the nature of the world we live in. Anthropology, especially the subfield of cultural anthropology, lacks an overarching and unifying theory on the order of Darwinian evolution and natural selection in biology and related sciences. Instead, the field has tended to construct often contested alternative explanatory frameworks that draw attention to certain issues, focus work on answering particular questions, and assist anthropologists in explaining or interpreting their research findings. In writing up the findings of research, the theoretical frameworks in use by anthropologists may be stated explicitly or they may be implied by the types of questions addressed as well as the types of questions not addressed by the researcher. While some of the debate over theory in anthropology is the product of the fact that different theoretical frameworks raise different questions, and lead to answers that may be deemed unsatisfactory to those who see other questions as being of equal or greater importance, disagreement also arises from different understandings of what anthropology is and its role among the disciplines and within society. While the anthropology of climate change has not as yet generated intense internal theoretical debates, it has embraced contrasting and potentially conflicted understandings of the human condition and the human dimension in climate change, as discussed below.

The cultural ecological perspective on climate change

Cultural ecology or ecological anthropology examines human–environment relations and has a long history in anthropology, dating back to the work of Julian Steward (1955). It also draws from the field of human ecology, and while denying the simplistic environmental determinism of an earlier era, recognizes that environments play a vital role in shaping cultures and providing possibilities and setting constraints on what they are likely to do. For example, irrigation agriculture is much more likely to develop in areas with flowing rivers than in arid environments without immediate water sources (although intensive and expensive hydraulic systems are used in some places to move water to dry regions to support agricultural production). There is a strong tendency in cultural ecology to see culture as an adaptive mechanism, although certainly many cultural ecologists recognize that culture can exhibit environmentally maladaptive dimensions as well. Moreover, cultural ecology views each individual cultural system as having evolved in and adapted to specific eco-niches, such as savannahs, tropical rainforests, or arctic tundra environments. In other words, the cultural ecological perspective tends to view culture and its various techno-economic, social structural, ideological, and attitudinal components as expressing collective human engagement with challenges and opportunities in local environments and to ask questions directed at expanding understanding of the adaptive process. According to Milton (1996: 59), the "ecosystem approach developed by ecologists in the 1940s and 1950s, and adopted into anthropology in the 1960s, held no place for an understanding of culture in its narrower sense—people's thoughts, feelings and knowledge about the world." As this statement suggests, the framework of cultural ecology does not easily lend itself to asking questions—questions some anthropologists might see as important— like how people's attitudes about the world shape their engagement with it, or the ways knowledge about the environment is structured within a cultural system or dispersed within a society across gender or other social divisions.

Cultural ecologists generally have been somewhat slow in fully coming to grips with the far-reaching impact of climate change on human societies. Although in their *Introduction to Cultural Ecology*, Mark Q. Sutton and E. N. Anderson (2004: xiii) assert that "One of the goals of most cultural ecological work is to use the knowledge in an effort to stem global catastrophe," they only briefly mention global warming in passing, in their observation that: "deforestation releases massive amounts of greenhouse gases as the trees are burned or allowed to decay. These gases have been a factor in global warming, although fossil fuels are a far more serious cause" (Sutton and Anderson 2004: 298).

As emphasized in Chapter 1, in our view, a more comprehensive approach involves assessment of pluralea interaction between anthropogenic deforestation and fossil fuel emission, as both of these human activities are changing the planet, often in tandem.

Within the anthropology of climate change, there are various anthropologists who are asking the questions raised by a cultural ecological understanding. As part of their extensive Arctic Climate Impact Assessment project, for example, Nuttall *et al.* examined the impact of climate change on subsistence patterns and adaptive strategies of indigenous Arctic peoples in the past and present. They argue that "as the climate changes, the indigenous peoples of the Arctic are facing special challenges and their abilities to harvest wildlife and food resources are already being tested" (Nuttall *et al.* 2004: 685). As this statement suggests, in questions about human–environment inter-action, attention must be paid not only to changing human behaviors (e.g., adoption of new adaptive strategies), but to changing environments as well. In other words, human communities are not merely adapting to existing environment niches; the environment itself is a dynamic arena, and humans are increasingly critical players in forcing the directions of environmental change.

Ben Orlove (2005) examines climate variability in three frequently mentioned historical cases, namely the Mayan civilization of Mesoamerica, the Norse settlements in Greenland, and the US Dust Bowl. He asserts that while these three societies were remarkably different from each other, they all experienced climatic conditions that threatened their basic subsistence patterns. Orlove (2005: 596) seeks to blend the sociology of the future with comparative historical analysis: "The former offers broad concepts, particularly adaptation and mitigation, which can contribute to the urgent debates of the present. The latter permits us to trace the complex interactions of different elements within each society."

Orlove believes that the possibility of migration provides a bridge between the sociology of the future and the comparative history of the past. While apparently the Norse in Greenland did not opt to return to Iceland or elsewhere in Scandinavia, by and large many Mayan Indians opted to move from various urban centers to surrounding hinterlands in order to survive, and the victims of the Dust Bowl in southern Kansas, western Oklahoma and nearby sections of Colorado, Texas, and New Mexico opted to move to California, a saga that novelist John Steinbeck poignantly chronicled for posterity in *The Grapes of Wrath*.

Orlove, who is based at Columbia University, along with Arun Agrawal, Maria Lemos, and Jesse Ribot, created the Initiative on Climate Adaptation Research and Understanding through the Social Sciences (ICARUS), a body that seeks "to bring together researchers and practitioners to address the growing need for social-scientific contributions to address climate change" (Agrawal *et al.* 2012: 330). Focusing on three primary research areas: (a) theorizing key concepts like vulnerability, adaptation, adaptive capacity and resilience; (b) understanding the causal structures of vulnerability, effects of adaptation, and the empirical referents of both adaptation and vulnerability at various scales; and (c) understanding and informing adaptation policy, ICARUS has organized a series of major conferences as well as smaller seminars (which they call writeshops), and related network-building activities. To date, ICARUS's founders argue, social scientists have made significant contributions to thinking about climate change. Included in these contributions are "integrated assessments of risks and costs; theorizing about vulnerability, adaptation, and mitigation; institutional analyses of climate mitigation at different scales; and the extent to which climate change and responses are likely to be equitable, just, or ethically acceptable" (Agrawal *et al.* 2012: 329).

Emilio F. Moran, one of the few anthropologists to have served on the Intergovernmental Panel on Climate Change, refers to climate change in various places in his book *People and Nature* (Moran 2006). He stresses that the growing amount of CO_2 in the atmosphere threatens the climate system, coral reefs, and the Antarctic ice sheets (Moran 2006: 1). Moran (2006: 3) argues that both the North, or developed countries, and the South, or developing countries, have had a significant impact on nature, the former largely due to a high level of consumption, and the latter due to high population growth. Moran mentions as well the role of climate change in the spread of various vector-borne diseases, plant growth, and animal migration, and poses a critical question:

> Once we begin to operate well above any recorded levels [of greenhouse gas emissions] not just for one but more many measureable parameters, the question has to be asked if we have begun to play a reckless game with the survival of our species on planet Earth. Do we recognize that business-as-usual threatens the end of life as we know it?
>
> *Moran 2006: 21 and 23*

Moran argues that while the vast majority of Americans view themselves as "environmentalists" of one sort or another, most do not see a conflict between this identity and their heavy reliance upon automobiles, which act as symbols of individualized freedom to go anywhere at a fast pace (Moran 2006: 45). Needless to say, the private motor vehicle constitutes a major simultaneous source of not only air pollution, but also greenhouse gas emissions, not only in the United States, but around the world, and increasingly so as "car culture" (the belief that cars are a necessary form of transport and self-expression in the modern world) spreads globally. While not citing climate change per se, Moran's proscription for attending to environmental problems blends individual and collective solutions:

> The solution [to environmental problems] must begin with the individual and a commitment to resist the forces of global consumerism in favor of a concern with the planet as our home. . . . But the individual alone cannot adequately win this battle with the well-organized interests that have since

World War II led us in an unsustainable path. . . . Individuals and organizations must come together to bring about institutional change through changes in priorities, in how we set prices and assign value, and in building a society where trust and community are more important than having a larger vehicle or a larger home.

Moran 2006: 166

Moran views our "global economy" in its present form as unsustainable and destructive of the "planet's future productive capacity" because it is exhausting Earth's "fisheries, its water, its soils, and a host of other resources" (Moran 2006: 171). More recently, he has argued that:

The exploitation of the huge amounts of fossil fuel materials stowed away for geological periods of time in sub-terrestrial sinks and the launching of the by-products from their use into the biosphere kicked off biogeochemical changes in the atmosphere that took a couple centuries to be felt and which now threaten our planet.

Moran 2010: 64

Another environmentally oriented anthropologist, John Bodley, in his book *Anthropology and Contemporary Human Problems* (2014), refers only in passing to global climate change, despite the fact that he discusses in great depth the contemporary global environmental crisis. Nevertheless, he is quite cognizant of the link between capitalist economic growth and climate change, as is evident in his assertion that fossil fuels made the Great Acceleration, namely the "elite-directed push for economic growth and globalization" which "contributed greatly to the sudden increase in atmospheric carbon dioxide and climate change" (Bodley 2014: 108).

McElroy and Townsend (2009: 116–118), two anthropologists well known for their work in applying ecological models in medical anthropology, view the "traditional ecological knowledge" of the Inuit as an adaptive mechanism for reducing vulnerability to climate change which has impacted very dramatically upon their culture over the past several decades. Townsend (2011: 191) asserts that the:

strongest contribution of anthropology to the study of global climate change is likely to be its patient accumulation of hundreds of local level small-scale studies, both prehistoric and contemporary, of how human populations have adapted, or failed to adapt, to drastic changes in climate from melting polar ice to encroaching desert edge.

These types of studies, based on ethnographic climate change response research, now constitute a dominant segment of the growing literature on the anthropology of climate change.

While utilizing the concept of adaptation in her own work on the Viluni Sakha, horse and cattle breeders in the Viliui regions of northeastern Siberia, Susan A. Crate

(2008: 571) critiques what has become an excessive reliance on the concept in "boardrooms, living rooms, and government offices, often as a substitute for mitigation of the human-induced effects of global climate change" as well in international forums and even within the corridors and publications of the Intergovernmental Panel on Climate Change. Elsewhere, Nicole Peterson and Kenneth Broad (2009) argue that climate change discourse should give mitigation as much consideration as adaptation strategies. Crate and Nuttall (2009a: 9) observe that while much of the discourse on climate change treats adaptation as both a research and policy priority, but query whether the "frames of adaptive capacity and resilience . . . are sufficient," in that the "ability to respond to climate change is severely constrained for many people around the globe." They go on to argue:

> Resilience, both social and ecological, is a crucial aspect of the sustainability of local livelihoods and resource utilization, but we lack sufficient understandings of how societies build adaptive capacity in the face of change. Furthermore, we suspect that environmental and cultural change, far beyond the reach of restoration, is occurring. Combined with institutional and legal barriers to adaptation, the ability to respond to climate change is severely constrained for many people around the globe. Some of us feel we are in an emergency state as field researchers and struggle to design conceptual architecture sturdy enough to withstand the storminess of the intellectual and practical challenges before us.
>
> *Crate and Nuttall 2009a: 10–11*

As Wijkman and Rockström (2011: 42) aptly observe: "No one knows with any certainty how long Earth's capacity for resilience with regard to greenhouse gases will last" and when the climate system will reach tipping points that are irreversible.

These perspectives lend support to the tripartite model introduced in Chapter 1, underlining the growing threat to resiliency facing many of the communities traditionally studied by anthropologists. As Crate (2009: 147) aptly observes: "we need not be overly confident in our research partners' capacity to adapt." One of the reasons for the threat to resiliency wrought by climate change that Crate points out is potential to cause relocation, which can result in a breakdown of locally situated environmental knowledge. As she emphasizes:

> climate change is forcing not just community adaptation and resilience, but also relocation of human, animal, and plant populations. Lost with those relocations are the intimate human–environment relationships that not only ground and substantiate indigenous worldviews but also work to maintain and steward local landscapes. In some cases, moves also result in the loss of mythological symbols, meteorological orientation, and even the very totem and mainstay plants and animals that ground a culture.
>
> *Crate 2009: 147*

Stripped of this kind of cultural grounding, climate change refugees may suffer "the disorientation, alienation, and loss of meaning in life that happens when any people are removed from their environment of origin," whatever the cause (Crate 2009: 147–148). The results may include a breakdown of resiliency and a failure to adapt.

Various other anthropologists who have adopted a cultural ecological perspective also employ the notions of "risk" and "resilience" in their analysis of climate change, concepts discussed in Chapter 1. Mark Nuttall (2009: 298), in his work on the Greenland Inuit, argues that these indigenous people exhibit ecological resilience which has allowed them over time to "adjust to climate variation and change, to move around, and to see and seize opportunities in the environment." Kirsten Hastrup edited a volume titled *The Question of Resilience: Social Responses to Climate Change* (Hastrup 2009b), derived from a symposium on a collaborative research project titled "Waterworlds, Natural Environmental Disaster, and Social Resilience in Anthropological Perspective" that occurred at the University of Copenhagen. The Waterworlds project focused on climate change/water-related threats, namely "the melting ice, the rising seas, and the drying lands, emanating to communities around the world" (Hastrup 2009b: 9). In the opening chapter, Hastrup (2009c: 15) observes that the risks related to climate change are unevenly distributed around the world, leading to "new patterns of regional migration, political unrest, economic vulnerability, shifting resource bases, and a profound sense of risk affecting everyday life in many parts of the world." She argues that "Resilience . . . is not simply a question of systemic (social or cultural) adaptation to external factors, but a constitutive element of any working society" (Hastrup 2009c: 28). Indeed, it is culture that bestows a high degree of resilience on societies, but it cannot be assumed that this capacity is limitless any more than the capacity of Earth to absorb anthropogenic disruptions is limitless. In Chapter 2 of *The Question of Resilience*, Orlove and Caton (2009: 34) observe that water issues are linked to concerns about Earth's atmosphere or "airworlds," which started with concerns about air pollution in the 1960s and 1970s and continued with concerns about acid rain in the 1970s and 1980s, and subsequently concerns about climate change and ocean acidification. Both the airworlds and the waterworlds of Earth are subject to the entwined and adverse effects of human activity, an interaction that threatens the resilience of impacted communities.

A few medical anthropologists who adopt a biocultural or medical ecological perspective have engaged the issue of climate change. Armelagos and Harper (2010: 303) observe that various infectious vector-borne diseases, such as dengue and chikungunya, are on the rise, in part due to global warming. They maintain that humanity is in the throes of a "third epidemiological transition in which we have the re-emergence of diseases thought to be near extinction" (e.g., tuberculosis) that is "occurring in an era of globalization, unprecedented urbanization, and global warming as we are approaching the end of an antibiotic era" (Armelagos and Harper 2010: 304).

Overall, the cultural ecological perspective in the anthropology of climate change makes its mark in studies designed to answer questions about sociocultural responses to the challenges presented by the climatic chaos of a warming planet. The perspective draws attention to the ways people collectively react and use their cultural system to cope with new threats and develop new options in the face of climate change adversity.

The cultural interpretive perspective of climate change

Environmental anthropologists who employ a cultural interpretive perspective view culture as a set of "perceptions as well as interpretations" that situate humans within the environment (Milton 1996: 63). Most cultural interpretive or phenomenological examinations of climate change tend to focus on perceptions on the part of diverse peoples or "local knowledge" about climate change. Carla Roncoli *et al.* (2009: 95), key figures in climate anthropology, for example, observe that anthropologists have begun to explore the relation between "local knowledge and climate phenomena." This perspective may have become the predominant one in the anthropology of climate change, given that it flows naturally from prior work that cultural anthropologists have done on small-scale societies or local communities where they tend to gather data on people's "emic" (insider) views, information that can be grouped under the rubric of *local knowledge*. Ironically, while local knowledge may recognize the reality of climate change, for larger segments of people in modern societies, culture may also serve to downplay or even deny that it is occurring. As Milton (1996: 138) observes:

> Our understanding of past climatic changes, in which successive ice ages have given way to warmer periods, helps to insulate us, to some extent, from the fear that we might ultimately be responsible for irreversibly changing the Earth's climate. The changes provoked by human activities seem less alarming when set in the context of the larger, "natural" pattern.

More broadly, anthropologists who embrace the cultural interpretive perspective seek to help "make the experiences of one place/time/people intelligible to those who inhabit different life worlds" (Strauss 2009: 166). Based on her work in Leukerbad in the Swiss Alps, Strauss (2009) asks what it means to people that because of climate change their glaciers, storage banks of water needed throughout the year, are disappearing. In her research, she found that people felt they were capable of handing the environmental contingencies they face, that ultimately what will happen is God's will, but that some people, despite these attitudes, are beginning to be fearful of what the future holds. Inherent in these attitudes is a fatalistic sense people have that "nothing preventative can be done" (Strauss 2009: 172).

One of the concerns of the body of work we see as fitting a cultural interpretive perspective is that large-scale social and technological responses to climate change must be sensitive to local sociocultural configurations and local understandings of the environment. Celeste Ray (2002: 90), for example, argues that policies about climate change "must employ cross-cultural knowledge of benign environmental practices while maintaining consciousness of traditional family and community structures, labor division, and localized subsistence strategies."

In practice, anthropologists do not necessarily draw immutable theoretical boundaries, but may draw on different theoretical perspectives to address different problems. Although, as discussed earlier, Crate adopts a cultural ecological perspective in some of her work on climate change, she also utilizes a cultural interpretive perspective. Guided by her research on the Viliui Sakha, she argues:

> that global climate change—its causes, effects, and amelioration—is intimately and ultimately about culture. It is caused by the multiple drivers of Western consumer culture, it transforms symbolic and subsistence cultures (represented by the Viliui Sakha case here), and it will only be forestalled via a cultural transformation from degenerative to regenerative consumer behaviour. Accordingly, anthropologists are strategically well-placed to interpret, facilitate, translate, communicate, advocate, and act both in the field and at home in response to the cultural implications of unprecedented climate change.
>
> *Crate 2008: 570*

Elsewhere, Crate (2008: 574) asserts that anthropologists need to "listen, share, and accommodate our research partner's way of knowing and observing and construct cultural models of how they perceive the local effects of global climate change on their world and worldview." She views this effort as part of an applied agenda, in that "Once their perceptions are accounted for in whatever ways our research partners see fit, we can reframe and inform them to encourage positive change" (Crate 2008: 574).

Crate's assertion that Western consumer culture is the driving force behind climate, while a useful starting point, does not fully address what might be termed "upstream questions," namely questions about the social location and determinants of consumer culture. A perusal of the arch of human history affirms that an obsessive focus on ever-expanding desire and consumption is not an inherent or automatic feature of the human condition or of human nature. Rather, contemporary modes of insatiable consumption are part and parcel of the larger system of global capitalism, an economic system that in its impulse for profit-making requires ongoing accumulation and non-stop expansion. Global capitalism fosters a worldwide, energy-gobbling machine. This global political economy ensures wealth and profits for the richest sectors of society, but in the process, because they are rated of lesser importance than profit-making, sacrifices basic human needs for large sectors of humanity as well as environmental sustainability. In order to survive, capitalism must generate an artificial need—namely, the need to unceasingly consume a wide array of commodities, even potentially dangerous and lethal ones (Singer and Baer 2009). Consumerism has provided an ideological rationale for capitalism. For example, the tobacco industry has expended billions of dollars promoting tobacco consumption. In the wake of recognition of the absolutely deadly nature of this behavior, other sectors of the capitalist economy have promoted the consumption of pharmaceutical drugs containing bupropion hydrochloride to treat tobacco addiction, nicotine replacement gums, nicotine lozenges, nicotine patches, and nicotine inhalers, as well as non-tobacco electronic cigarettes that simulate smoking. There is profit, in short, to be gained from making people ill and treating the consequent illness. A similar pattern is beginning with efforts to promote seeing pollution and greenhouse gases as potential arenas for profit-making.

Kay Milton (2008), a well-known environmental anthropologist, has sought to delineate a culture theory of climate change by drawing upon the work of Mary Douglas. Douglas delineates two key variables of human social organization which she calls respectively "grid" and "group." Grid "measures the freedom of choice people exercise," and group "measures their degree of collective allegiance" (Milton 2008: 40). Put otherwise, "grid" refers to the extent to which people's actions are constrained, and "group" refers to the extent to which people act for themselves as individuals or for the groups to which they belong. The relationship between grid and group results in a matrix depicted in Figure 4.1, which in turn produces different cultural orientations.

A hierarchical perspective within society occurs when "group allegiance is high and people's actions are relatively constrained" (Milton 2008: 40). An egalitarian perspective entails a "low level of constraint together with a high degree of group allegiance . . . in which social justice and common interests are valued" (Milton 2008: 40). An entrepreneurial perspective entails a "low level of constraint combined with a low degree of group allegiance" which contributes to individualistic ambitions such as is promoted in market economies (Milton 2008: 40). A fatalistic perspective occurs in a situation where "actions are tightly constrained and group allegiance is low," prompting people to feel powerless in the face of adversity. In terms of perspectives about nature, Milton reconfigures the grid–group model as depicted in Figure 4.2.

Milton (2008: 45) asserts that, in terms of global warming, multinational corporations and Western governments, which have tended to operate with the

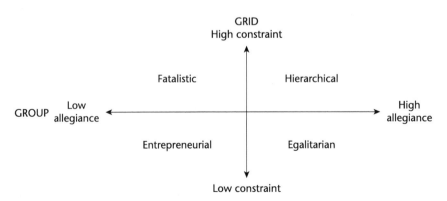

FIGURE 4.1 Douglas's grid–group model

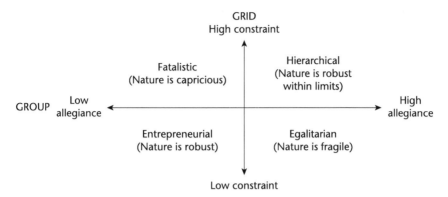

FIGURE 4.2   The grid–group model with respect to views of nature

entrepreneurial perspective, have had to admit that nature is not as robust as they have believed to be the case (a belief that has rationalized an enormous level of environmental release of industrial toxins and greenhouse gases), meaning that "increasing numbers of people are adopting the view that nature is fragile." A growing understanding of climate science and climate change has made growing numbers of people aware that their lifestyles are contributing to a historic ecological crisis. While many people adopt a fatalistic attitude about global warming, or deny its reality, or at least the role that human activities play in creating it, Milton argues for an "expansive egalitarianism," one which attempts to merge egalitarianism and green values to "include future generations and/or non-human nature" (Milton 2008: 48). She argues that the debate around global warming has renewed the left/right divide. Milton (2008: 49), however, eschews the tendency on the part of leftist groups and commentators to "argue that a radical reorganization of [the global economy], and a fundamental change in the distribution of wealth, provide the best way forward." She asserts that egalitarians are not bringing about needed social change, and puts her faith in an entrepreneurial perspective which rewards people for making the sorts of technological innovations that will reduce greenhouse gas emissions and hierarchical structures that will facilitate "quick decisive action" needed to mitigate global warming. Milton (2008: 50) asserts that "some national governments, international organizations and commercial companies are beginning to take global warming seriously; whether they are doing so soon enough to be effective remains to be seen."

Anthropologist David Lipset (2011) presents a nuanced relationship between masculinity and climate change among the Murik, a coast people in Papua New Guinea. Lipset uses the notion of *chronotrope* in referring to contested images of manliness in space and time. He defines a chronotrope as a "category or unit of analysis that constitutes and organizes the meaningful ordering of events in the space and time of narrative texts" (Lipset 2011: 21). Murik villages are situated at sea level on very narrow beaches that separate the Pacific Ocean from shallow lagoons and mangrove forests and that have been eroded by about 0.8–1.2km or even more.

In their responses to the particularly high tides of 2007, some people viewed them as resulting from global warming which threatened males in carrying out traditional subsistence activities. Conversely, some men spoke about the history of rising sea levels and tsunami events in terms of the chronotrope of *timit* associated with a male cult complex which required appeasing angry sea-spirits by throwing food into the ocean. The spirits have sought retribution on Murik men who have emasculated themselves by shifting from a traditional lifestyle in which they maneuvered out-rigger canoes to a modern one in which they "steer dinghies powered by outboard motors" (Lipset 2011: 39–40).

Kirsten Hastrup (2015) coined the term "climate worlds," which captures the reality in the modern world that people's knowledge about climate change is not simply situated in their local setting, but draws upon information they derive from the larger world. She asserts that:

> while . . . cultures were seen as self-contained and rather fixed in the early days, today we realise that all worldviews are plastic and continuously incorporating—and *locating*—knowledge coming from elsewhere, along with new patterns of weather and wind, for instance.
>
> *Hastrup 2015: 8*

Based upon her ethnographic research in the High Arctic, Hastrup contends that the Inuit climate world is not particularly more traditional or local than people elsewhere, and given the attention paid to climate change in the Arctic, they are highly concerned about its implications for their future. In making a case for a comparative study of climate worlds, she argues:

> It is one of the challenges facing anthropologists to show how located knowledge practices other than western science may move and affect not only present concerns but also future solutions. Anthropology can contribute vitally to the perception of humans, not only as destroyers but also creators of new possibilities, precisely because the burgeoning anthropological studies of how people deal with climate change shows how all people are capable of integrating diverse forms of knowledge.
>
> *Hastrup 2015: 151*

Indeed, since June 2010 a Climate Worlds research team based in the Institute of Advanced Studies in Essen and the Bielefeld Graduate School in History and Sociology has been conducting interdisciplinary ethnographic research on the impact of climate change and how it is culturally framed in various parts of the world (Greschke 2015). The team has focused primarily on coastal areas, such as Ameland, a West Frisian island in the Netherlands; Churchill on Hudson's Bay in Manitoba, and Cape Verde in the North Atlantic, and is committed to long-term fieldwork, approximately 20 months, in its various research sites.

There is considerable evidence that indigenous peoples have been "particularly vocal about climate change as a threat to their traditional ways life represented in their cosmovision or traditional worldview," translating often into demands, particularly on the part of their leaders and representatives, that developed countries and the United Nations recognize the seriousness of climate change and adopt drastic climate change mitigation efforts (Eisenstadt and West 2017: 41). For example, a national survey of Ecuadorians revealed that respondents who subscribe to an indigenous cosmovision are more likely to acknowledge the threats posed by climate change, particularly evident in Andean countries which are experiencing rapidly diminishing glaciers, than those respondents who do not subscribe to an indigenous cosmovision. Indeed, the Ecuadorian constitution is the only constitution in the world that recognizes the "rights of nature," or grants that Mother Nature has rights just as do humans. Unfortunately, the Correa government decided in 2013 to discontinue its pledge to protect the bio-diverse rainforest in Yasuni National Park by not allowing the drilling of oil on the condition that international donors, who contribute only about $1 million, compensate Ecuador for oil revenues, by leaving it in the ground (Eisenstadt and West 2017: 43).

From the cultural interpretive perspective, the questions that are raised concern how people culturally construct a meaningful world of nature and society, including their perceptions and understandings of the changing environment around them. Answering such questions will provide insight about how to best work with various peoples, both in responding to climate change and in the development of culturally grounded climate change policies. Failure to recognize that people are not blank slates, but have their own understandings of the world and of changes that are occurring within it, can lead to failed efforts to impose climate change adaptations that conflict with local cultural knowledge. This type of failure is not new, but in fact has long been a feature of externally initiated development or health promotion programs. Given the stakes, interpretively oriented anthropologists argue it is vital that we do not repeat old errors.

Conversely, it is important to recognize the limitations of ethnographic fieldwork which focuses on local perceptions of climate change. As Alf Hornborg (2013: 54) observes, some anthropologists miss the forest because of the trees by immersing themselves in "obscure representations of exotic, local particularities of experience," thus downplaying the macroscopic forces driving anthropogenic climate change in the modern era, a central concern of the critical anthropology of climate that we discuss next, and one to which we adhere.

The critical anthropology of climate change

The critical anthropology perspective on climate change is guided by an ecosocial perspective that is informed by three theoretical currents in and beyond anthropology: world system theory, and its particular application within an ethnographically informed anthropology; political ecology theory, with its understanding of the politicized nature of human interaction with the environment; and critical medical anthropology, and its focus on the social determinants of health inequalities, experiences, and behaviors.

In the contemporary period, the first of these is a perspective on the features of capitalism as a particular kind of economic and social system that transcends national boundaries and ties regions and countries together around the privatization of the means of production, a market-based distribution of goods and services, and the control of labor based on the buying and selling of it as a commodity. These features of capitalism, world systems theory argues, create two interlocked hierarchies. First, there is hierarchical ordering of relationships among the countries of the world involving a tripartite division into economically dominant (and greatest greenhouse gas-producing) core countries, developing but subordinate semi-periphery countries (that rapidly become important greenhouse gas emitters as they drive for economic development), and the periphery countries with relatively weak (and potentially failing) governments and local economies focused on extracting and exporting raw materials from nature to core nations (and often receiving back the waste products of industrial production for local environmental disposal). It is people living in the peripheral zones of the world that produce the least amount of greenhouse gases but are beginning to suffer the most from its impact on global warming. The second hierarchy involves labor and the construction of social classes. As Wolf (1982: 354) observes, a market economy "creates a fiction that this buying and selling [of labor] is a symmetrical exchange between partners, but in fact the market transaction underwrites asymmetrical relationship between classes." Consequently, in ways that parallel the climate change features of the world economic system, wealthier (labor-buying) classes most benefit from the processes that lead to the environmental emission of greenhouse gases (i.e., expanding production, growing markets), while the poorest laboring classes, through structures of environmental injustice and limited protective resources, suffer disproportionate harm from global warming. World systems theory has tended to generate the asking of macro-level questions like: To what degree do core countries need the periphery to remain underdeveloped? Or what causes the world system to change? In its uptake within anthropology, and the field's focus on on-the-ground sociocultural arrangements around the world and cross-cultural human subjectivity, research questions have been directed at the nature of the relationship of macro-level forces and structures and more micro-level social realities and actions, including issues of resistance, resilience, and emergent cultural heterogeneity in the face of the homogenizing influences of globalism.

Second, political ecology theory is a multidisciplinary perspective that developed out of the study of societies in environmental context, especially the cultural ecology initiative discussed above (e.g., Cole and Wolf 1974; Wolf 1972). This perspective draws attention to the fundamental importance of the interplay among political, economic, and environmental factors (Foster 1994; Roberts and Grimes 2002). In particular, political ecology moves beyond the cultural ecological approach by drawing attention to questions about the role of power in the unequal distribution of the costs and benefits of environmental change (e.g., across class, ethnic, or other social divisions), the ways this unequal distribution reinforces (or, in particular contexts, reduces) existing social and economic inequalities in society, and the political consequences of environmental changes.

Finally, critical health anthropology is a theoretical perspective on the nature and causes of human health and treatment systems. During the early years of medical anthropology's formation, explanations within the discipline tended to be narrowly focused on accounting for the nature of health-related beliefs and behaviors at the local level in terms of specific ecological conditions, cultural configurations, or psychological factors. While increasing the sum of knowledge about the nature and function of local medical models, the original perspectives in the field overlooked the wider causes and determinants of human decision-making and health-related behavior. Questioning the values of explanations that are limited to accounting for health-related issues in terms of the influence of human personalities, culturally constituted motivations and understandings, or even local ecological relationships, medical anthropologists beginning in the 1980s pointed to the importance of under-studied "vertical links" that connect the local social group to larger and cross-cutting regional, national, and global processes (e.g., commodification and the capitalist market, the globalization of production and restructuring of labor forces, the spread of biomedicine as a reflection of the penetration of capitalism globally). Since it emerged, what came to be called critical medical anthropology has drawn attention to questions about the social origins of illness, such as the way poverty, discrimination, violence, and exposure to stress and violence create and sustain disease. Critical medical anthropology is also concerned with the origins of dominant cultural constructions in health and with the role of social inequality in the structuring of health care practices and delivery. More recently, critical medical anthropology has focused increasingly on environmentally mediated inequalities in health, such as the role of polluting industries in causing disease and creating disparities of health across social classes, genders, or ethnic populations (Baer 2009; Singer 2011b).

Integrating components of these approaches, the critical anthropology of climate change asks questions about the relationship of the capitalist mode of production and planet sustainability, the role of power in the production and control (or non-control) of greenhouse gases and industrial pollution, the social origins and social impact of the climate change denier movement, the unequal and unjust distribution of health and other climate change effects, the contradictions of green capitalism, and local and wider social movements that have emerged in opposition to business-as-usual corporate environmental degradation. In short, the critical anthropology of climate change seeks to develop integrative understanding of the interface of power and social hierarchy in the anthropogenic making of climate change and other environmental disruptions, and the unequal health and social consequences, differential experiences, and responses that occur as a result of climate change turmoil.

The critical anthropology of climate change seeks to be conversant with archaeological, cultural ecological, and cultural interpretive approaches to climate change, while emphasizing the limitations of analyses that fail to consider how local patterns connect to the world system and to the distribution and direct and hegemonic roles of power in society locally, regionally, and globally. Like critical anthropology in general, the critical anthropology of climate change is committed to an activist/scholar notion of praxis or the merger of theory and social action in which the two arenas of work feed each other. Thus, like many others involved in the anthropology of climate change, regardless of whether they adopt an archaeological, cultural ecological, or cultural interpretive approach, the critical anthropology of climate change promotes an applied anthropology of climate change involving collaboration with local communities and other subordinated populations and social movements of climate change response. The critical anthropology of climate change asserts:

1. Social systems do not last forever, whether at the local, regional, or global level.
2. The capitalist world system or global capitalism has been around for about 500 years, but has come to embody so many inherent contradictions that it must be transcended to ensure the survival of humanity and animal and plant life on a sustained basis.
3. There is a need for an alternative global system, one that is committed to meeting people's basic needs, social equity and justice, democracy, and environmental sustainability. Proposals for such an alternative system have come under various terms, including *global democracy*, *Earth democracy*, *economic democracy*, *eco-anarchism*, and *eco-socialism*.
4. Anthropologists and other progressive social scientists are too small a group to act as a vanguard in the struggle against global warming and capitalism. They must form links with anti-systemic movements, including the labor, anti-corporate globalization or social justice, peace, indigenous and ethnic rights, and environmental movements, women's movements, and a growing climate or anti-global warming movement (Baer and Singer 2009).

In keeping with point four above, Laura Nader (2013: 230) asserts that anthropologists who operate with a *longue durée* perception recognize that "not all civilizations last."

In sum, the critical anthropology of climate change posits the roots of recent climate change largely within the context of the capitalist world system as a political economy committed to continual growth and expansion, heavy reliance on greenhouse gas-emitting fossil fuels, and global social inequality within and across nations.

Even conventional economists such as Nicholas Stern (2007) and Ross Garnaut (2008) in Australia, who have expressed alarm about the potential ravages of climate change and the need to take measures to mitigate against it, accept the premise that the global economy must continue to grow and that humans have an inherent need to consume, to acquire more and more things. Panic sets in when retail sales diminish, particularly during the mad Christmas shopping season. In the modern world, regardless of whether we are speaking of a developed country such as the United States or Australia, or a developing country such as China or India, capitalist hegemonic ideology has diffused itself throughout supposedly common-sense thinking that humans have an innate need to acquire more and more things, whether they need them or not.

Human nature is highly malleable. If we live in a capitalist society, most people around us will be highly acquisitive, one might even say greedy—impulses which are stimulated by massive numbers of advertisements wherever we may look. In such a society, based on the analysis of Antonio Gramsci, people are influenced by a *cultural hegemony of consumerism*. As discussed earlier in this chapter, cultural hegemony involves the social diffusion through the dominant institutions of society of a set of ideas, norms, and values that have their origin in the dominant social class, but come to be perceived as natural and inevitable by all classes in society. But is consumerism natural, an inherent characteristic of human nature? As numerous ethnographic studies on indigenous or tribal peoples, particularly foraging or hunting and gathering societies, have shown, most people in these societies emphasize sharing and reciprocity, and not the accumulation of material goods or the assessment of achievement or self-worth in terms of material possessions or other acquirable commodities (e.g., purchased access to activities and experiences).

Within the world created by global capitalism, there are more than a billion people who go without many of the basic necessities of life, while at the same time there are many who consume much more than they need and end up storing unused possessions in increasingly larger dwelling units, even multiple dwelling units, as well as storage facilities. Unfortunately, not only are such high-level consumption patterns depleting natural resources and degrading the natural environment as a result of the process of producing them, they are generating greenhouse gas emissions which in turn result in climate change.

It is evident that, as noted earlier, anthropogenic climate change has been inducing and will continue to induce severe economic, social, political, military, and health consequences as the twenty-first century unfolds. Ongoing global warming and associated climatic and other anthropogenic environmental changes raise the question of how long humanity can thrive, at least in its present numbers and occupying much of its present-day place of habitation, into and beyond 2100. Thus, perhaps more than any other environmental crisis, anthropogenic climate change forces us to examine whether global capitalism needs to be transcended and humanity needs to begin to develop an alternative—or, as some would see it, a democratic eco-socialist—world system.

From the critical perspective, climate change constitutes one of the most important social issues, perhaps the most important issue, in that it is related to numerous other environmental challenges of the twenty-first century. The capitalist world system exhibits numerous contradictions, including: (1) its emphasis on profit-making, economic expansion, and the treadmill of production and consumption; (2) the growing socioeconomic gap between rich and poor both within nation-states and between nation-states; (3) the depletion of natural resources and environmental degradation, the most profound form of which is climate change; (4) population growth, which in large part is stimulated by ongoing poverty; and (5) the resource wars waged by various developed countries, particularly the United States, United Kingdom, and Australia, in promoting the interests of multinational corporations. Climate change perhaps more than any other environmental crisis illustrates the unsustainability of the capitalist world system, but, as stressed in Chapter 1, its impact does not occur in a vacuum, but rather is magnified by inter-actions with other ecocrises. Singer (2013), for example, observes that respiratory risks to human health, as exemplified by rises in diseases like asthma around the globe, are a product of the combined effects of anthropogenic air pollution and cli-mate change. An important cause of this increase in respiratory disease is interaction between heavier pollen loads, noxious molds, wildfires, thunderstorms and extreme precipitation events (related to climate warming), and diminished air quality due to industrial, vehicular, chemical, and other sources of air pollution. Singer (2013: 98) notes that, while various ecocrises are a grave hazard:

> because the respiratory system is a primary body nexus for diverse environ-mental threats to cluster, intermingle, and multiply their adverse impacts (e.g., diesel fuel droplets and bacteria, allergens and infectious agents), there is a second set of threats to respiratory health also being ushered in by global warming.

While it is inevitable that over the short run humanity must adapt to climate change (in that it has been ongoing for some time and its erratic effects are already being felt by people around the globe), from the perspective of the critical anthrop-ology of climate change, the more crucial longer-term issue is that of *mitigation*— that is, addressing the causes of greenhouse gas build-up in order to ensure the survival of humanity as well as preserving biodiversity. Since the late 1980s, climate regimes have emerged at the international, regional, provincial or state, and even local levels. The vast majority of climate regimes function within the parameters of green capitalism, a notion that capitalism, by adopting emissions trading schemes, various technological innovations, energy efficiency, recycling, and other practices, can be environmentally sustainable. In seeking to mitigate both environmental damage and climate change, a growing number of corporations, politicians, policy-makers, research scientists and academics have become advocates of green capitalism, even climate capitalism—the idea that embracing efficiency and renewables, the curbing of waste, carbon markets, new technologies, and sustainable business plans is not only good for the planet, but can be very profitable. While historically cor-porations have been resistant to the assertion on the part of environmental activists that many of their practices are environmentally destructive and also contribute to climate change, a growing number of corporations have begun to assert that they can achieve sustainable development while reducing their greenhouse gas emissions by engaging in a process of ecological modernization. Technological innovations, such as renewable sources of energy and energy efficiency, have an important role to play in climate change mitigation, but even they cannot contain climate change over the long run as long as they accept the capitalist imperative of continual economic growth. Consequently, the critical anthropology of climate change argues that green capitalism as well as climate capitalism exhibits essential limitations in terms of mitigating climate change.

As a result, climate change compels us to engage in a serious assessment of alternatives to global capitalism. The critical anthropology of climate explores various social justice initiatives which, while not seeking to transcend global capitalism per se, attempt to make it both more socially just and environmentally sustainable, including in terms of climate change. The critical anthropology of climate change maintains that that it is imperative to think outside of the socially allowable box and construct an alternative to global capitalism as the ultimate climate change mitigation strategy. Despite historic emphasis in many capitalist nations on individual freedoms, there has often been little tolerance for truly critical thought, as some ideas are rapidly dismissed as illegitimate and not worthy of serious consideration. This mechanism of social control is woven deeply into the fabric of capitalist society, finding expression overtly or more covertly across social institutions. For example, one of the ways researchers have brought to light subtle academic forms of hierarchicalization and legitimization is through the analysis of what is known as the politics of citation. In this form of academic politics, authors tend to be cited based on their relative status in a field of study or the stature of their home institutions, while texts that question reigning social mythologies about the capitalist world system are delegitimized (through academic snubbing). This pattern can even be seen, for example, in the emergent anthropology of climate change and its growing literature, in the failure in much of that literature to recognize the body of work done within a critical anthropology of climate change framework.

The effort to examine the impact of climate change on humanity and how to mitigate it has to be an interdisciplinary one that involves collaboration among natural and social scientists, public health people, policy analysts, and humanists who are willing to collaborate with the climate justice movement and other anti-systemic movements. Going from the present capitalist world system, which has created and continues to generate anthropogenic climate change, to an alternative global political economy, however it is defined, will require much effort, and there are no guarantees that we will be able to create a more socially equitable and environmentally sustainable world. But do we really have any other meaningful choice than an ongoing downward spiral and the destruction of much of humanity and other forms of life, and further environmental degradation, including climate change?

In building a critical anthropology of climate change, Myanna Lahsen (2005a), an Associate Researcher in the Earth System Science Center at the Brazilian Institute for Space Research, has done critical ethnographic research on how climate models and atmospheric scientists deal with issues of certainty and uncertainty associated with general circular computerized models that seek to project possible global climatic changes emanating from greenhouse gas emissions. She has also written about US climate politics and discussed the role that "conservative and financial elites" have played in supporting campaigns to counter growing concerns among Americans about climate change (Lahsen 2005b) as well as how Northern countries dominate the framing of science, including climate science, that underpins international environmental and climate negotiations (Lahsen 2007b). In her commentary on Crate's (2008) seminal article, which, as noted earlier, asserts that anthropologists are strategically well situated to interpret the impact of climate change on local populations, communicate information about this process, and even respond to climate change both in the field and at home as advisors to climate policy decision-makers and as advocates for the people they study, Lahsen (2008a: 587) astutely observes:

> To truly enhance our effectiveness and overcome our marginality in scholar-ship and policy arenas related to global change research, we need to study all types of relevant "locals" and especially those populating institutions of power. That means overcoming our abated but continued aversion to study power brokers such as scientists, government decision makers, industry leaders, journalists, and financial elites, all of whom are much more important in shaping climate change and associated knowledge and policies than are the marginal populations we are accustomed to studying.

In keeping with Laura Nader's (1972) admonition over four decades ago, Baer participated in a collaborative effort with political scientist Verity Burgmann to examine Australian climate politics at three levels: "from above," "in the middle," and "from below" (Burgmann and Baer 2012). Part I of the book concerns itself with climate politics from above, namely the corporations and their peak parties and federal and state governments. In terms of climate politics in the middle, we looked at the Australian Greens; the major environmental non-government organizations; academic research centers; think tanks; public intellectuals; and the trade union movement. Actors in the middle frequently reach out to the burgeoning move-ment from below and participate in ground-level climate movement activities, and occasionally have formal and informal input into the very top level of climate politics, for example in official consultations or off-the-record conversations with relevant ministers or public servants. Finally, in terms of climate politics from below, we examined the grassroots climate movement: the many and varied local, regional, and nationwide climate movement groups and networks, and far-left groups for whom climate change confirms their worst suspicions about global capitalism.

Another anthropologist working with a critical climate change perspective is Raminder Kaur (2011) in her examination of how Indian elites are promoting a nuclear state as a mechanism for responding to climate change. India is not the only country where certain parties are promoting nuclear energy. Such moves are being made in places such as the United Kingdom, the United States, and even Australia. Fortunately, as Kaur (2011: 277) comments, "critics continue to dispute the hijacking of environmentalism of the states and argue that if climate change is the problem, then nuclear power is by no means a solution."

Richard Wilk (2009) also alludes to a critical anthropology of climate change understanding in his critique of the notion of individual overconsumption as the cause of climate change. Rather, he observes that many consumption choices are made by "governments, regulatory agencies, and businesses" (Wilk 2009: 266). Anthropology and the other social sciences, he maintains, have "provided only fleeting and partial answers to questions of why have human beings become so insatiable" (Wilk 2009: 269). While an anthropology of consumption does indeed remain in its infancy, such an endeavor must start from the recognition that global capitalism spends billions of dollars marketing the commodities that it produces and creating a strong sense that people need many items, indeed a continuing array of new things, to lead full, meaningful, and enjoyable lives, to be liked by others, to succeed in relationships and careers, to remove all pain and discomforts, and to mark personal achievement. Wilk (2009: 266) observes that most non-renewable resources, such as copper, iron, and coal, are still in abundant supply, while various theoretically renewable resources, such as timber and fish, are in danger of being depleted due to overconsumption and population growth. Ultimately, Wilk contends that what he terms the "consumer economy," or what we would call global capitalism, is being driven by the generally luxurious lifestyles of rich, developed countries and the narrow concentration of global wealth in an elite strata of super-rich individuals and families.

Consumer capitalism began to take off in a profound way beginning in the 1950s, when households in developed societies were flooded with energy-intensive appliances and devices, including electric cookers, washing and drying machines, refrigerators, toasters, electric irons, microwave ovens, electric toothbrushes, electric razors, television sets, record players, cassette players, video recorders, computers, printers, electric tools, power lawnmowers, electric hedge cutters, leaf blowers, elaborate lighting systems, and so forth. Capitalism, with its predilection for built-in obsolescence, encourages people to update older models with new ones, such as the latest plasma televisions, CD, DVD and Blu-Ray players, mobile phones, iPods and iPads, and many other devices. Sociologist Zygmunt Bauman (2011: 24) reports that "Europe and the United States spend 17 billion dollars each year on pet food, while according to some experts, just 19 billion dollars is needed to save the world's population from hunger." Although developed societies constitute the leading cultures of consumption, various rapidly developing societies, such as China and India, are quickly joining the pack. Many of the refrigerators, air conditioners, washing machines, televisions, and computers manufactured in China are exported, yet growing numbers of them are being sold to the members of the new Chinese middle class as well as to the elites of Chinese society.

Linda Connor argues that "Climate change is a cultural crisis of life worlds that begs critical anthropological analysis" (Connor 2010: 1). She found in her interviews with religious believers in the Hunter Valley of New South Wales that almost all of her interviewees "linked CC [climate change] to the threat of an ending, although there was a variety of 'end' scenarios, dominated by humanistic rather than apocalyptic views." Pentecostals, however, tend to deny climate science's assertions about the reality of climate change, but even if climate change is occurring, faith in the Apocalypse assures them of another life. For Connor (2010: 12–13), consumer capitalism functions as an ersatz "immortality system" in which "consumerism engenders and sustains feelings of pleasure and future security though linking self-identity with values and practices of acquisition, affluence, endless exploitation of nature, novelty, and perpetual renewal."

Adding to the literature on the critical anthropology of climate change is James Trostle's (2010) identification of a contradiction between the World Bank's statements and actions on climate issues. The World Bank is an international financial institution that provides loans to developing countries for capital programs and has a history of pressuring countries to adopt structural adjustment and market-based reforms. Trostle notes that the *World Development Report 2010: Development and Climate Change* (World Bank 2010: xx–xxi) states that:

- efforts must continue to reduce poverty and sustain development, especially because climate change will make this even more difficult;
- addressing climate change is critical because it threatens all countries, and especially poor ones;
- economic growth alone is not the answer to resolving climate change;
- a global climate deal is urgently needed;
- behavior and public opinion must be changed so that new policies can be developed and implemented at all levels, local, regional, national, and international.

Trostle observes that while many World Bank-sponsored development projects in developing countries, such as large-scale fossil fuel power plants, are contributing to greenhouse gas emissions, the Bank's report fails to acknowledge its role in increased emissions.

In sum, while the critical anthropology of climate change recognizes with ecological approaches the importance of the human–environment interface, and with interpretive approaches the need to understand local views of and attitudes about climate change, central to the perspective is a concern with the ways that structures of social inequality and power impact how humans engage and interact with ecological systems.

Since the release of the *World Development Report 2010*, physician-anthropologist and health activist Jim Yong Kim has been elevated to the prestigious position of the Presidency of the World Bank, an organization he once proposed should be abolished. Co-founder of Partners in Health, he previously served as Chair of the Department of Global Health and Social Medicine at Harvard Medical School and as President of Dartmouth College. In a development that historically is highly unusual for an anthropologist, Kim was propelled into the international limelight in March 2012 when President Barack Obama nominated him to head the World Bank. Kim's nomination met with stormy opposition, not only from parties in the developing countries, but also from neoliberal economists. His involvement as the lead co-editor of an anthology titled *Dying for Growth* (Kim *et al.* 2000) prompted some economists to assert that he is "anti-growth." In its various chapters, the book explores the linkages between neoliberalism and health problems among the poor in various countries. Despite its significant contributions in revealing how the emphasis on economic growth has led to worsening poverty for many people around the world, a shortcoming of *Dying for Growth* is its failure to provide readers with a vision that goes beyond simply ameliorating the worst effects of global capitalism on the health of poor. Consistent with the critical medical perspective, this vision would entail the creation of a capacity for health and all that entails, constructing an alternative global political economy oriented toward meeting social needs rather than to profit-making—a vision we will discuss in the final chapter. Perhaps this omission in *Dying for Growth* provided Kim with the wiggle room he may have needed when, during his nomination process for the presidency of the World Bank, many questions were asked about whether, as some presumed from his role as lead editor of the book, he was anti-growth or anti-capitalist. In a BBC interview, he replied to these questions by stating: "I'm very much for capitalist market-based growth, which will create jobs and at the same time, lift people out of poverty" (BBC News 2012). In his role as President of the World Bank, which he assumed on July 1, 2012, Kim joined the climate change policy debate. In the foreword to the World Bank's 2012 report *4°: Turn Down the Heat—Why a 4°C World Must Be Avoided*, a document which takes the findings of climate science on the impact of climate of changes on the environment and human societies seriously, he states: "The lack of action on climate change not only risks putting prosperity out of reach of millions of people in the developing world, it threatens to roll back decades of sustainable development" (Kim 2012: ix). From a critical anthropological perspective, however, the notion of *sustainable capitalist development* is problematic in that it tends to imply the possibility of a complementarity between economic expansion and environmental sustainability. Kim (2012: x) goes on to argue:

> The World Bank Group will continue to be a strong advocate for international and regional agreements and increasing climate financing. We will redouble our efforts to support fast growing national initiatives to mitigate carbon emissions and to build adaptive capacity as well as support inclusive green growth and climate smart development. Our work on inclusive green growth has shown that—though more efficiency and smarter use of energy and natural resources—many opportunities exist to drastically reduce the climate impact of development, without slowing down poverty alleviation and economic growth.

Further, in an opinion editorial titled "Make climate change a priority" that appeared in the *Washington Post* on January 24, 2013, Kim states that the World Bank is committed to preventing a climate catastrophe through its $7 billion-plus Climate Investment Fund which purportedly is "managing forests, spreading solar energy and promoting green expansion for all cities, all with the goal of stopping global warming" (Kim 2013a). At the G20 Meeting in Moscow on February 16, 2013, Kim (2013b) added:

> At the World Bank Group we are stepping up our mitigation, adaptation and disaster risk management work. I would welcome more attention from the G20 on what we need to do to face climate change, which is a very real and present danger.

Kim's perspective was further confirmed in an interview with the *Guardian*, during which, according to Larry Elliott (2013), Kim claimed that:

> reducing poverty . . . was impossible without growth, and 90% of new jobs would be created by thriving private sectors. But he said growth on its own was not enough, and governments needed to adopt policies that made growth more inclusive.

Despite his deep concern with effectively addressing the issue of poverty, Kim appears to be overlooking the increasing number of scholars and activists who are challenging the growth paradigm associated with the capitalist world system, especially in light of the mounting evidence that the fossil fuel-driven treadmill of production and consumption is not only contributing to increasing social inequality around the world, but also the depletion of natural resources and worsening climate/ environmental crises. Kim and the World Bank are proponents of ecological modernization, a perspective popular not only in certain corporate and govern-mental circles, but also among many social scientists, as we will show in Chapter 7. Proponents of ecological modernization believe that climate change can be sufficiently mitigated through the adoption of various technological innovations, such as greater development of renewable sources of energy, enhanced energy efficiency, expanded use of public transit, adoption of electric cars, and other related "tech-fix" approaches. While Kim and the World Bank call for the eradication of global poverty, they nowhere assert that this might be achieved by increasing social equality or by creating a level economic playing field where most wealth is no longer concentrated in few hands. Additionally, there is no consideration of whether long-term sustainability might only be achieved by transcending global capitalism.

Conclusion

As discussed in this chapter, the anthropology of climate change has produced three alternative perspectives, and with them differing sets of questions that anthropological researchers bring to their encounter with climate change issues. While we ourselves tend to favor a critical perspective which draws upon world systems theory, we acknowledge that this approach, as Orr *et al.* (2015: 161) assert, may be "overdrawn because it seemed to local all agency at the level of global actors and none at the level of local communities." It is for this reason that we believe critical anthropologists need to closely examine the climate movement and other localized responses to climate change, as well as global capitalism and social inequality, around the world (Cassidy 2012).

While alternative perspectives can lead to debate and disagreement, this is not an inherently negative occurrence, as even heated discussion can lead to new insights, raise new questions, and result in productive synergies. It is precisely to the issue of synthesis that the next chapter turns, by presenting several case studies.

5

CASE STUDIES IN THE ANTHROPOLOGY OF CLIMATE CHANGE

Blending perspectives

While in the previous chapter we delineated and described distinct theoretical perspectives employed by anthropologists seeking to comprehend climate change—namely the cultural ecological, the cultural interpretive, and the critical—in their day-to-day work anthropologists involved in climate change research often blend these perspectives by being eclectic in their approach. For example, while Crate and Nuttall mix cultural ecological and cultural interpretive approaches, at times their observations also are conversant with the critical anthropology of climate change. The notion introduced by Crate and Nuttall of *environmental colonialism*—the idea that industrial societies and greenhouse gas-emitting and polluting industries have used the planet as a dumping ground for the by-products and waste products of production, packaging, and commodity obsolescence—is particularly apt from a critical perspective. The parallels to the earlier era of colonial regimes treating the peoples, lands, and natural resources of the world as their own to take and control with little regard for indigenous ways of life are unmistakable. The environmental ethic invoked by colonialism, which Harvey (2003) refers to as "accumulation through dispossession," involved the amassing of capital through forced entry, legal manipulation, and the privatization of what had been collective wealth. In this light, the environmental ethic embedded in contemporary anthropogenic greenhouse gas emissions involves an inverse dynamic that might be labeled the "apportioning of waste," involving the environmental release and dumping of toxic and other by-products of production, causing collective harm rather than private harm among accumulating classes. Crate specifically comments on the need to integrate the cultural ecological and cultural interpretive perspectives, noting that while anthropologists have begun to investigate how climate change undermines people's capacity to adapt to their local environments, they also are exploring "their cultural orientations and symbolic frameworks that ground their specific adaptations" (Crate 2011a: 179).

Similarly, Thomas Reuter (2010) seeks to blend the cultural interpretive and critical anthropological perspectives in his effort to comprehend the cultural causes of resistance to addressing the climate change problem. While he recognizes that the "modern economic system of mass consumption and associated cultures of consumerism and ideologies of capitalism are responsible for the current [climate] crisis," he asserts that "they will not lend themselves to empowering fundamental changes that would negate their own core principles" (Reuter 2010: 15). Thus, Reuter argues that the prolific reliance on fossil fuels which emit carbon dioxide has become an inherent component of a Western cultural system that embraces a "crude oil cosmology" (Reuter 2010: 14).

Rather than turn to the terminology of individual psychopathology to talk about social patterns, environmental anthropologists have used the term "mode of production resilience" to discuss the ability of a social system and its mode of subsistence/production to respond to threats and challenges encountered in the environment. Often this has been found to entail changing just enough so as to enable a continuation of the core features of a cultural way of life. A case in point is the Anasazi people discussed in Chapter 3. To build the roofs of their multi-level, multi-family dwellings, as well as to meet the other needs they had for wood, the Anasazi used locally harvested pinyon pine and juniper from forests surrounding their multi-story community dwellings. As their populations grew, forests that were near to settlements were depleted, but this did not lead to new types of housing construction; it led to a switch to other kinds of wood to retain their basic social system (a short-term resilience, at best, allowing a few more generations of the older cultural pattern). The concept of mode of production resilience is contrasted with the notion of stabilized rigidity. While a resilient system can absorb disturbances and undergo some degree of change to respond to them, a stabilized or rigid system is one that is fixed and resistant to adaptive change. Instead of changing to new cultural forms, people invest ever greater amounts of effort and suffer rising levels of deprivation (e.g., eating lower-quality diets) to try to maintain existing cultural patterns. The most dangerous form of stabilization is known as "the rigidity trap." Rigidity traps occur in social/environmental systems when institutions become highly interconnected, self-reinforcing, and increasingly inflexible (Gunderson and Holling 2002). Cultural systems that strongly resist change despite increases in human disease, suffering, and death can be said to be locked in such a rigidity trap (Goodman et al. 1980). These systems, resistant to core system change and committed to retaining familiar sociocultural patterns despite the rising costs of doing so, are slowly increasing their risk of social collapse. This narrative may well explain what happened to the Anasazi or other Southwestern groups like the Hohokam, who left behind their structures and earthworks as ruins to be discovered by later visitors and settlers in the areas where they had lived.

Questions have been raised as to whether the capitalist world system is caught in an ever-enhanced, production-geared, consumption-oriented, and fossil fuel-driven rigidity trap. In this regard, Reuter (2010: 22) suggests that secularization and a drift from a "recognition for the sacredness of the whole" in Western culture has contributed to a view that humans can exploit nature, thus contributing to a "metabolic rift" between capitalism and the ecosystem (Foster *et al.* 2010), as will be discussed in Chapter 7.

One of the engines driving multidisciplinary work on climate change is large research centers that bring together investigators from across multiple disciplines. The Centre for International Climate and Environmental Research is an independent research center associated with the University of Oslo, for example, which views climate change as one of the gravest threats facing humanity today. Central to the Centre's mission is recognition that cooperation must take place across both scientific disciplines and national borders. Disciplines represented at the Centre include anthropology, atmospheric chemistry, meteorology, geophysics, human geography, sociology, biology, chemistry, political science, and economics. Similarly, the Stockholm Resilience Centre seeks to advance the understanding of complex social-ecological systems and generate new insights and development to improve ecosystem management and long-term sustainability. A focus on resilience at the Centre is motivated by recognition that sometimes change is "sudden, disorganizing and turbulent [as] reflected in climate impacts, earth system science challenges and vulnerable regions" (Stockholm Resilience Centre 2007). In a time of global warming, in particular, "Evidence points to a situation where periods of such abrupt change are likely to increase in frequency and magnitude. This challenges the adaptive capacity of societies" (Stockholm Resilience Centre 2007).

In examining the regional or local case studies presented below, it is evident, as Smit and Wandel (2006: 289) point out, that: "Studies of adaptation to climate change have provided many insights but to date, have shown only moderate practical effect in reducing vulnerabilities of people to risks associated with climate change." In part this is true because cultural adjustments undertaken to deal with the pressing effects of climate change are rarely developed in response to climate change alone. Not only do societies face other ecological crises, but also they may be constrained in their actions by broader political-economic forces. While the notion of "capacity to adapt" (Yohe and Tol 2002) has been used to assess the internal features of a society facing climate change or other environmental challenges (Handmer *et al.* 1999; Turner *et al.* 2003; Wisner *et al.* 2004), and this has led to the development of tools for measuring societal vulnerability (Cutter *et al.* 2009), internal features alone are not all that are in play. Also of considerable importance are the ways a community or region is impacted by broad political and economic forces and the use of power in intergroup social relations (e.g., neoliberal policies and pressured restructuring to enhance market dominance and foreign economic penetration). In this regard, Smit and Wandel stress that climate change adaptations often are not discrete, standalone, climate-focused initiatives, but are part and parcel of efforts to change broader economic-social-political structures that are seen as encumbering communities and increasing their vulnerability. Indeed, they note, "vulnerability reduction appears to be most effective if undertaken in combination with other strategies and plans at various levels" (Smit and Wandel 2006: 289).

Case studies

In order to illustrate how anthropologists seek to integrate various theoretical perspectives in their analyses of climate changed-related phenomena, and the ways in which they use anthropological and other concepts in their analyses of climate change-related social issues, we present a series of case studies based primarily on anthropological work on the following topics: (1) climate change and peoples living in Arctic and sub-Arctic regions; (2) climate change and peoples living on low-lying islands in the South Pacific; (3) climate change and the inhabitants of Bangladesh; (4) climate change and peoples living in high mountainous areas; (5) climate change and peoples living in dry, arid places; (6) climate change and the indigenous US Southwest; (7) climate change in developed societies; and (8) the conflicted relations of climate scientists and climate denialists. As is evident, while the first seven of these case studies focus on peoples living in particular environmental contexts, the last one focuses on quite different issues that climate-oriented anthropologists have begun addressing in their work.

Admittedly, our case studies in large measure, although not entirely, coincide with Orlove et al.'s (2014: 251) observation that Arctic and low-lying islands receive a "great deal of attention as sites of climate change impacts," with "mountains and deserts figuring "less prominently in discussions of climate change." Ironically, all of these places are marginal sites with relatively small populations. Thus, it is important that anthropologists give more consideration to the impact of climate change on people living in more populated places, particularly cities. Bearing this thought in mind, we have included a case study on responses to climate change in developed societies.

Case study 1: climate change and peoples in Arctic and sub-Arctic regions

The impact of climate change on the lifeways and settlement patterns of indigenous peoples in Arctic regions has been the subject of intense study. As anthropologist Julie Cruikshank (2001, 2007) has shown, narratives of climate change and the ways it affects indigenous people has a long history in anthropology. Most of this research has been guided by either the cultural interpretive perspective or the cultural ecological perspective, or a combination of the two.

Exemplary is the work of Timothy B. Leduc (2007, 2010), who completed a PhD in Environmental Studies at York University in Toronto, and worked for a number of years in northern indigenous communities in Canada. In his research, Leduc posits indigenous knowledge about the environment as a legitimate source that complements conventional science. For example, he notes that the Inuit people of Canada view Sila, the spirit of the air, as a force that is related to weather. When the Inuit speak of Sila's actions, they in essence are referring to "cultural and spiritual dimensions that interpret climate change as the world's ethical response to improper human actions" (Leduc 2007: 242). This combined spiritual/ethical orientation is very different, Leduc (2011) emphasizes, than the one informing the actions of the Canadian government, which:

> embody a set of powerful Western cultural assumptions and economic prac-
> tices that are connected both to the history of colonialism and Canada's poor
> climate response. In other words, climate change is secondarily a function of
> greenhouse gases and primarily related to a long historic Western approach to
> environment and Indigenous cultures that informs our current unsustainable
> fossil fuel use.

Indeed, a theme found in the Canadian discourse on climate change reflects the "winners and losers" paradigm discussed further below, with emphasis often being on Canada as a winner or beneficiary of improved conditions in a warming world. More broadly, the government orientation in Canada (and other places that might see themselves as benefiting from climate change) reflects a pattern Naomi Klein (2007) has called "disaster capitalism," a term she uses to label the treatment of disasters and crises as productive market opportunities. In this view, the capitalist world system, which "requires constant growth, while bucking almost all serious attempts at environmental regulation, generates a steady stream of disasters all on its own, whether military, ecological or financial" (Klein 2007: 426). These disasters are not viewed as threats to the system, but rather as critical occasions for deregulation, privatization, and profit-making. For example, oil companies have come to see the melting of Arctic sea ice (and all that it threatens to unleash for the indigenous peoples and animals of the region) as a tremendous opportunity for oil exploration. Dreams of extensive new oil profits have been sparked by reports from the US Geological Survey that the Arctic may contain as much as 14 percent of the world's untapped oil reserves (Baily 2007). From Leduc's (2011) viewpoint, however, "the logic of a climatically prosperous Canada is fundamentally consistent with those values and beliefs that have historically fuelled today's northern warming and global changes." While Western "cultural and religious understandings are intertwined with maladaptive political and economic tendencies," he believes that the under-standings of indigenous peoples "can offer us wisdom and inspiration for making the significant changes required for becoming a sustainable and just global society" (Leduc 2011).

In the climate change literature, the Arctic often is portrayed as the "canary in the coalmine." For example, climate scientists have noted that winters in southern Alaska have been 2–3°C (3.6–5.4°F) warmer than they were 30 years ago. Indigenous Arctic peoples will, as noted, have to cope with the loss of sea ice and its impact on traditional hunting and fishing activities, changing migration routes of animals, coastal erosion due to wave action on ice-free coasts, loss of permafrost, and changes in the abundance of traditional food sources on land and in water. The Inupiat village of Shishmaref, for example, consisting of some 600 residents on Sarichef Island in northwest Alaska, finds itself besieged by a rising sea and increasingly violent storms (Lynas 2004: 45–51). According to anthropologist Anthony Oliver-Smith (2010:

178), Shishmaref is "as emblematic in the popular press of the impacts of global climate change and sea level rise as Tuvalu," an island nation discussed below. One aspect of climate change experienced by the people of Shishmaref is the melting of the tundra beneath their feet and beneath their homes. One result has been house collapse and the sliding of coastal homes into the ocean. Despite such drastic circumstances, most residents of Shishmaref do not wish to become climate refugees by relocating to the regional hubs of Nome or Kotzebue or to the cities of Fairbanks or Anchorage, although in reality at least some of them have moved to these places for employment opportunities (Marino and Lazrus 2015: 346).

In the report of the Arctic Climate Impact Assessment, anthropologist Mark Nuttall *et al.* (2004) examine the ways various indigenous arctic communities have been adapting to climate change. They present case studies of the Inuvialuit community of Sachs Harbor in the Canadian Western Arctic, the Canadian Inuit in Nunavut (which means "our land" in Inuktitut, and is the northernmost territory of Canada), the Yamal Nenets of northwestern Siberia, and the indigenous peoples of the Russian North. In the case of Sachs Harbor on Banks Island, the team found that climate change has resulted in less sea ice during the summer, making the water rougher; more rain in summer and autumn, making travel difficult; unpredictable sea ice conditions during the colder months, making both travel and hunting hazardous; and greater infestations of mosquitoes during the summer months (Nuttall *et al.* 2004). These conditions have resulted in more restricted access to seals, which have served traditionally as important sources of food, clothing and trade. According to the report:

> One major impact of climate on the local perception is the issue of loss of predictability. Land-based livelihoods in the Arctic depend on people's ability to predict the weather . . . read the ice . . . judge the snow conditions . . . and predict animal movements and distributions. A hunter who cannot predict the weather or read the ice would be limited in mobility; one who cannot decide what to hunt and where cannot bring back much food.
>
> *Nuttall* et al. *2004: 670*

Additionally, living in the Arctic environment and acquiring and consuming traditional foods forms a foundation of the cultural identities of Arctic peoples. Hence, threats to the economic aspects of life in the region are equally threats to people's sense of meaning, purpose, and stability. Loss of these contributes to breakdowns in social resiliency and enhanced vulnerability, as discussed in Chapter 1.

In the short run, Arctic hunters respond to climate change by altering their hunting patterns to accommodate changes to ice, tundra vegetation, and the distribution of terrestrial and marine animals. This response is based on a cultural attribute borne of long experience in a never static Arctic environment, namely "adaptive flexibility." As contrasted with the notion of the "rigidity trap" discussed above, this term, reflecting a built-in form of resilience, refers to the incorporation of diverse subsistence strategies, geographic mobility, shifting settlement patterns, and food storage technologies as means of coping with the shifting challenges of Arctic life. Thus, maintaining a flexible arrangement in Inuit settlement patterns and demographic organization "ensured both the availability and production of food and acted as regulatory social mechanisms which were able to respond to environmental change" (Nuttall *et al.* 2004: 650). The existence of this capacity notwithstanding, the Arctic Climate Impact Assessment report stresses that:

> while indigenous peoples have generally adapted well to past climate change, the scale, nature, and extent of current and projected climate change brings a very different sense of uncertainty, presenting different kinds of risks and threats to their livelihoods and cultures.
>
> *Nuttall* et al. *2004: 650*

This is an important feature of climate change. While past challenges faced by indigenous communities certainly suggest the types of responses they are likely to adopt as the effects of a warming planet take hold, the scale and multifaceted nature of contemporary climate change and its co-occurrence and interaction with other anthropogenic ecocrisis threatens to overwhelm even the most time-tested of indigenous adaptive skill sets.

Thus, Kirsten Hastrup (2009a: 245) of the University of Copenhagen reports that hunters in and around the vicinity of Qaanaaq (a settlement of some 600 people created when the United States expanded its airbase at Thule and forcibly relocated indigenous peoples) in northern Greenland are possibly "facing the demise of their age-old way of life, all the while catching more polar bears than before, as these leave the ice-floes for firmer grounds." The people of Qaanaaq report that there is less ice than previously, that the ice thickens later and breaks up earlier, and that it is thinner and marked by more and larger holes, and furthermore travel by dog sled has become more difficult than in the past (Hastrup 2009a). People in northern Greenland also report that the climate has become rainier and snowier and that the earlier break-up of the ice restricts travel between settlements in their district (Hastrup 2009a). Despite their creativity, flexibility, and resilience, Hastrup (2009a: 270) observes that the "well-known safety net fitted to the Arctic hunters' environment—their mobility and their feel for nature—is becoming increasingly threadbare."

Inuit people, of course, no longer live traditional ways of life, but rather have lifeways that reflect a blending of traditional and introduced elements. Anthropologist Anne Henshaw (2009: 155) observes that traditionally mobility plays a big role in how the Inuit experience and respond to their environment. However, the creation of sedentary villages and towns due to their incorporation in the larger world system has created certain vulnerabilities, as is evidenced by their reliance on "fossil fuels for heat and transportation" (Henshaw 2009: 157). The Inuit in Nunavut have been expressing their concerns about the impact of climate change on their communities and are working with non-government organizations, including the

Inuit Circumpolar and the Inuit Tapiriit Kanatami, to draw attention to their plight (Henshaw 2009: 159). Conversely, other Inuit in the territory are "actively pursuing economic opportunities that can result from a warmer, more ice-free environment" (Henshaw 2009: 159). The Nunavut territorial government and local communities have been supporting the development of a military training center as part of Canada's efforts to assert its sovereignty over Arctic waters with more patrol boats and reserve troops in response to the retreat of the Arctic polar ice cap (Henshaw 2009: 160). While recognizing the paradoxical situation taking place among the Inuit in Nunavut, Henshaw (2009: 162) asserts that, as anthropologists, "we thrive in such complexity and are in a unique position to use our anthropological lens to carry out the kinds of in-depth and compassionate investigations an issue of this magnitude deserves."

Elsewhere in the Arctic, Elizabeth Madrino and Peter Schweitzer (2009) conducted research in five communities in northwest Alaska in which they documented how the Inupiag people perceive the impact of climate change at the local level. They report:

> some Inupiaq people find hunting more dangerous and more difficult with thinning sheet ice in the winter . . . traditional water sources are threatened by increasing and northward-moving beaver populations. Local experts report a previously unknown problem with beetles and other insects infecting and killing trees on the Seward Peninsula.
>
> *Madrino and Schweitzer 2009: 211*

Visitors, ranging from scientists to media representatives and politicians, serve as a source of information about global climate change, but the local people tend to frame their perceptions of the local environment in terms of specific changes, such as the drying up of tundra ponds (Madrino and Schweitzer 2009: 213–214). Madrino and Schweitzer (2009) caution that anthropologists, in framing their questions in terms of *climate change* per se, may miss detailed accounts based upon local knowledge. In other words, they need to identify other aspects of environmental changes that indigenous people perceive as well. The relationships of climate and the physical environment are complex, and it is important for anthropologists studying climate change to maintain a broad perspective on perceived changes of various sorts in indigenous communities. Nicole Herman-Mercer *et al.* (2011) have examined the local knowledge of climate change among hunters and elders in the villages of St. Mary's and Pitka's Point in the Lower Yukon River Basin of Alaska. All of the informants interviewed by this research team agreed that ice on the rivers in the region has become thinner in recent years, a development that impacts the ability to travel on frozen rivers via snow mobiles or sled dogs (Herman-Mercer *et al.* 2011: 248). Herman-Mercer *et al.* (2011: 249–51) maintain that observations made by their informants are in parallel "with those reported in the scientific literature," and that "Indigenous knowledge and scientific research must work in concert to further understand specific climate change impacts in specific locations in order to develop appropriate adaptation strategies"—a recommendation made by a number of anthropologists and others studying indigenous experience of climate change in various environments.

Notably, Shannon McNeeley and Orville Huntington (2007), who worked with other climate change researchers in May 2003 and again in January 2004 in the Koyukon Athabascan village of Huslia, found that while residents acknowledge that climate change has been adversely impacting their community, like other peoples in the Arctic, they too are locked into a fossil fuel-driven economy:

> [Alaska Natives] use fossil fuels to heat and light their homes, to cook, and to travel by boats, snow machines and all-terrain vehicles to pursue their traditional subsistence activities. Without a viable alternative to cheap fossil fuels they cannot get to the fish and game they depend on. They are also dependent on the oil industry for the revenue it generates and returns to them through the dividend checks, jobs created, and state-sponsored services. Thus, local measures to reduce greenhouse gas emissions are not currently a focal point in the native discourse on climate change.
>
> *McNeeley and Huntington 2007: 145*

Indeed, a significant portion of the Alaskan economy within which both Native and non-Native Alaskans are embedded is tied up with the drilling and shipping of oil, a fossil fuel which is one of the main sources of greenhouse gas emissions. As this discussion suggests, while anthropologists traditionally have sided with indigenous peoples in their struggles against government or corporate land grabs, deforestation or other resource extraction efforts, environmental pollution and dumping, and other issues and contestations, and rightly so, it is easy to idealize indigenous peoples as natural stewards of the environment who live in a far greater balance with their physical surroundings than do societies organized around market economies. While there is some truth to this, there also is a history of land misuse, overhunting, and species extinctions in indigenous societies that suggests caution in overly romanticized portrayals of them (e.g., Keeley 2003).

This point notwithstanding, it is certainly the case that some Arctic/sub-Arctic peoples, such as those affiliated with the Inuit Circumpolar Conference and the Gwich'in Council, are grappling directly with the contemporary climate change problem. Inuit activist and Nobel Prize nominee Sheila Watt-Cloutier (2007) argued in her presentation to the Inter-American Commission on Human Rights of the Organization of American States that, for indigenous communities, being protected from the effects of anthropogenic climate change constitutes a human rights issue. In light of the model introduced in Chapter 1, the issue clearly is raised about the vulnerability of indigenous people in the Arctic in a time of global warming. Frank Sejersen (2009) addresses this issue, arguing that the marginal status of indigenous people in the Arctic vis-à-vis external political and economic forces makes them particularly vulnerable to climate change. He states:

> Marginal and vulnerable peoples are already struggling with existing societal and economic problems and thus their potentials to cope with climate change have to be seen in a larger framework. Therefore, the solutions to reducing their vulnerability are extremely complex and involve issues related to societal transformations only distantly related to what we normally consider relevant and necessary for climate change adaptation.
>
> *Sejersen 2009: 221*

The socioeconomic conditions faced by indigenous people in the Arctic that are paramount in their daily lives are access to meaningful employment, health care, and education, as well as issues of cultural identity as a marginalized ethnic minority group within their respective nation-states. Further, Sejersen asserts that while there are only some 400,000 indigenous people in the Arctic, and while they constitute less than 2 percent of the world's indigenous population, their experience of coping with climate change may serve as a template for action not only for "other indigenous peoples but for marginalized and vulnerable groups worldwide" (Sejersen 2009: 222).

In contrast to the Arctic Council, which seeks to represent indigenous people at the grassroots levels in terms of climate change issues, some indigenous people may find themselves embedded in government structures that support development efforts that contribute to increased greenhouse gas emissions and thus climate change. Greenland's government, for example, has requested that Greenland be allowed to increase its CO_2 emissions by 1,500 percent in order to sustain a program of rapid industrialization (Sejersen 2009: 235). Indeed, in terms of the Arctic, Nuttall (2009: 293) argues that the "various ways climate change is perceived, and how urgent or otherwise climate change is felt to be, depend on how individuals or communities are positioned." He asserts that climate change may be beneficial for certain sectors of the Greenland economy, such as the fishing industry (Nuttall 2009: 300). Indeed, Emmerson (2010: 315–316) asserts that for Greenland fishermen, "a warming Arctic climate could bring benefits—fish are heading north." Indeed, fisheries contribute 93 percent of Greenland's exports (Delaney 2016). Alyne E. Delaney (2016) conducted fieldwork in the Greenlandic town of Upernavik (population 1,129) and four outlying communities. She found that, to date, climate change has not had a significant impact on coastland Greenland halibut fishermen as they have been able to adjust where they fish, although sometimes under more difficult and dangerous conditions. The 2012 Coastal Greenland Halibut Management Plan was altered in 2014 to allow the opening of quota-free fishing zones, a policy which prompted fishermen to shift their operations from quota-restricted areas to new free-zone areas. For the foreseeable future, Delaney concludes that the Upernavik case study indicates that any inability to adapt successfully to the impact of climate change may be more a result of neoliberal policies than climate change per se.

Due to the retreating ice cap in Greenland, various mining companies are hoping to gain easier access to various minerals, such as molybdenum, lead, zinc, diamonds, and even uranium, which presently cannot be mined due to legal restrictions

(Emmerson 2010: 296). The Greenland Bureau of Minerals and Petroleum envisions seven mines opening in coming years, which would result in some 15,000 jobs in a country with approximately 56,000 permanent residents at the present time. According to Nuttall (2009: 297), with the melting of the inland ice, a "new Greenland is emerging"—one that some Greenlanders reportedly see as a positive development that will allow their country to "become a modern nation."

As noted earlier, from a critical anthropological perspective, we question the type of "winners and losers" paradigm implied in Nuttall's conclusions, one that even the Intergovernmental Panel on Climate Change has adopted in places in its various reports. Such an interpretation completely defies the holism that anthropologists seek to achieve in recognizing the web-like nature of the global human–environment interface. Further the "winners and losers" paradigm ignores the multidimensional turmoil model of climate change introduced in Chapter 1 that results in local improvements in one domain (e.g., length of the crop-growing season) that are counterbalanced by other, more damaging climate-related changes in other domains (e.g., the spread of infectious vector-borne diseases among humans and animals or pest species among plants). Additionally, the paradigm fails to consider the occurrence of multiple interacting anthropogenic ecocrises known, as indicated in Chapter 1, as pluralea interactions. Even beyond entwined ecocrises are other kinds of adverse interactions involving climate change that tend not to find their way into "winners and losers" assessments. While, as noted, climate change is contributing to the spread in the ranges of both vector-borne and water-borne diseases, this diffusion is occurring at a time when the overuse and misuse of antibiotic drugs are contributing to the development of antibiotic resistance among various pathogens. In her first annual report, Dame Sally Davies, the UK Government's Chief Medical Officer, noted that:

> Antimicrobial resistance is a ticking time-bomb not only for the UK but also for the world. We need to work with everyone to ensure the apocalyptic scenario of widespread antimicrobial resistance does not become a reality. This threat is arguably as important as climate change for the world.
>
> *Davies 2013: 16*

Even so, Davies does not state that it is a fact that the effects of climate change and microbial resistance are not fully independent impacts on human well-being. Not only does climate change contribute to the dispersal of infectious agents, it can damage and destroy health service infrastructures. In an age of global warming, in other words, as infectious diseases are spreading to new populations, our pharmaceutical capacity to respond to deadly infections is collapsing and, in areas hardest hit by the effects of climate turmoil, the infrastructure to respond to infectious epidemics may be crippled by extreme weather events.

In our assessment, the "winners and losers" paradigm constitutes a blatant illustration of the weaknesses of neoclassical microeconomics or neoliberal discourse. While it is generally recognized that people in much of sub-Saharan Africa and small island nations will be among the losers on a heating planet, various mainstream economists and businesspeople assert that communities in what are generally low-density populated areas, such as much of Canada, Siberia, Tasmania, and New Zealand, will be among the winners in terms of longer growing seasons, such as for vineyards, and increasingly habitable lands. The problematic nature of this type of "winners and losers" perspective is reflected in the remarks of no less than Robert W. Coreil, the chairperson of the Arctic Climate Assessment, to the US Senate Committee on Commerce, Science, and Transportation on November 16, 2004:

> Climate change is . . . projected to result in major impacts inside the Arctic, some of which are already underway. Whether a particular impact is perceived as negative or positive depends on one's interests. For example, the reduction in the sea is very likely to have devastating consequences for polar bears, ice-dependent seals, and local people for whom these animals are a primary food resource. On the other hand, reduced sea ice is likely to increase marine access to the region's resources, expanding opportunities for shipping and possibly for offshore oil extraction (although operations could be hampered initially by increasing movement of ice in some areas).
>
> *Coreil 2004: 3*

While Coreil recognizes that reduced sea ice with increased shipping and resource extraction could damage the environment and marine life, and thus adversely affect indigenous Arctic peoples and their cultures, he fails to note that oil extraction would ultimately contribute to even more CO_2 in the atmosphere, to say nothing of the kinds of damaging oil spills we have seen in recent years. Needless to say, Coreil does not even come close to recognizing the climate science warning that, if left unchecked beyond 2100, global capitalism could very possibly contribute to massive health, food, and safety crises around the world on a tragic scale multiple times what we are already seeing in contemporary climate change-caused heat waves, flooding, droughts and crop loss, displacement, and the spread of infectious diseases. Moreover, in a globalized world, disaster in one place has trenchant impacts in many places as societies become destabilized. As writer Kurt Cobb (2006) notes: "To imagine that global warming is a game with 'winners' and 'losers' may be the surest way to make losers of us all." Certainly, in the case of Greenland, emerging plans for increased oil drilling, mining and other mineral extraction, and expanded fishing efforts, if driven by the conventional productivist ethic of "more is better, faster is best," are not likely in the long run to be a "winning scenario."

Ann McElroy has spent a long career conducting fieldwork among the Inuit in the eastern Canadian Arctic. As part of a larger examination of cultural and ecological change in the Arctic, she interviewed Inuit elders between 1999 and 2006 in Iquluit, Pangnirtung, Qikiqtarjuaq, and Cape Dorset (Kinngait) on Baffin Island (McElroy 2013). Her interviews revealed that though the elders and other Inuit were aware of the impact of climate change on their natural habitat, they had more immediate concerns, such as food security, maintenance of sharing networks, the right to harvest traditional foods, the degree of access to country food, threats to sustainability of traditional Arctic foods, access to adequate income and health care, psychic injuries from past and present traumas, issues around their identity as residents of the Nunavut Territory, and skepticism about government regulations based on scientific studies. Historically, the Inuit have adapted to climatic fluctuations in their natural environment over the course of thousands of years and have created a miniscule carbon footprint compared with most other North American populations to the south of them. However, relying upon:

> behavioral flexibility intrinsic to traditional culture, Inuit are combining traditional ecological knowledge with modern technology, including GPS systems, personal locator beacons, satellite phones, and immersion suits to train youth in land skills, geared toward assessing risks of changing snow cover, ice formation, and weather patterns.
>
> *McElroy 2013: 167*

The polar bear stranded on ice floes has become the "canary in the bird cage" in terms of the impact of climate change on the Arctic region. Churchill, Manitoba, a small town on the edge of the Canadian Arctic, has been daubed the "Polar Bear Capital of the World" because thousands of tourists visit it each autumn just before the bears head off for their hunting season. Once the tourist season is over, however, most local people lose interest in the topic of climate change and get on with a slower-paced life, which includes being able to cross the local iced-over river. Nevertheless, as Claudia Grill (2015: 113) observes:

> Despite many Churchillians rejecting anthropogenic causes of climate change and disclaiming its significance for them, the concept makes its way north every fall and cannot be overlooked. For 6–8 weeks of the year it takes over and challenges patterns of interpretation.

Unfortunately, to date virtually all anthropological studies of climate change issues in the Arctic have been restricted to cultural ecological and cultural perspectives, which, while providing valuable insights, fail to make or downplay global–local or macro–micro linkages between indigenous Arctic communities and the larger capitalist world system. Geographer Emilie S. Cameron (2012: 104), however, points the way for a critical anthropology of climate change in the Arctic and elsewhere when she argues that a "substantive reckoning with colonial, postcolonial, and decolonizing histories, practices, and ideas is necessary . . . to move the field forward." A critical anthropology of climate change in the Arctic ultimately needs to recognize that powerful economic and political interests are pushing for economic development of the Arctic, regardless of their consequences for indigenous peoples in the region. Peter Jull, for example, a Canadian political scientist, observes that dramatic climatic changes impacting the Arctic sea ice and Greenland glaciers:

have spawned an explosion of interest and activity related to Arctic shipping, whether through the High Arctic islands (Lancaster Sound and the Northwest Passage) or even across the open Arctic Ocean near the North Pole. The Northeast Passage, around Norway and across the top of Russia to the Far East, is also in play, as the Russians have much more experience in Arctic shipping.

Jull 2009–2010: 45

Overall, it is clear that change is coming rapidly to the Arctic, all of the features and consequences of which cannot yet be seen. Without question, the Arctic is feeling climate change earlier and more intensely than other regions of the planet—an issue of mounting concern to indigenous peoples and other residents.

Case study 2: low-lying islands in the South Pacific

Various island nations, particularly in the South Pacific and Indian Ocean, are in danger of oceanic inundation. These include Tuvalu (pop. 10,544), Kiribati (pop. 78,000), the Marshall Islands (pop. 58,000), Tokelau, a dependent territory of New Zealand (pop. 2,000), and the Maldives (pop. 269,000). In the case of the principal islands in Tuvalu in the South Pacific and the Maldives in the Indian Ocean, the main islands are "less than four metres above mean sea level and much of the area is less than two metres" (Whyte 2008: 184).

Anthony Oliver-Smith (2009) notes that climate change will result in increases in forced migration for certain populations, such as peoples living on low-lying islands and coastal area. The Carteret Islands, for example, a ring of six atolls 80km off of the coast of Papua New Guinea, are expected to slip below sea level in the near future. One of the atolls, known as Huene, has been split by the rising sea into three parts. Tidal surges have left debris of branches and coconut tree stumps sticking up through the water. The 3,000 residents of the atolls began a phased evacuation to Papua New Guinea in 2005, and as a result have been called the first refugees of climate change. Efforts to keep the sea at bay through the building of a sea wall and the planting of mangroves failed, leading to a continued pattern of storm surges, washing over the island and pulling homes and trees into the ocean, drowning vegetable gardens in saltwater, and contaminating drinking water. At the experiential level, the impact of these changes can be seen in the case of Selina Netoi, who lives on one of the surviving parts of Huene atoll with her husband and disabled son, and one other family member. Reports Selina: "We survive on coconut milk and fish. . . . We have one meal a day. If the sea is too rough to fish or it's too windy to climb the coconut trees, we have nothing to eat." She laments that Huene is her home, and that:

> it will be difficult to leave but we must. . . . We're not safe here anymore. When the King Tide comes, water floods our home. If there is a cyclone or a tsunami, we'll be swept away. We're just waiting to [go to] allocated

land on Bougainville [New Guinea]. The irony is that I left Bougainville during the conflict there in the 1990s. I was a war refugee and now I'll be a climate one.

quoted in Caritas Internationalis 2012

More than any other South Pacific Island nation, Tuvalu, a former British colony known as the Gilbert and Ellice Islands that gained independence in 1978, has captured worldwide attention with respect to the dangers of rising sea levels. This remote country situated roughly midway between Hawaii and Australia derives its name from the words for "Cluster of Eight" in the local language (because one of the nine islands that comprise this tiny state was uninhabited at the time of European contact). The bits of land that make up Tuvalu are spread across 676km of sea and constitute a total in landmass of a mere 26km^2. Roughly 80 percent of Tuvaluans over age 15 engage in farming and fishing, with the remainder of the labor force working in waged jobs either in the public or private sector in the capital city of Funafuti (Ralston *et al.* 2004). In addition to marine life, the population traditionally consumed taro, coconuts, pandanus fruit, and bananas. Climate change is not a future event for Tuvaluans, who have been experiencing the erosion of their beaches, damaging tidal surges, the intrusion of saltwater into cultivate areas, and the destruction of natural breakwaters, such as coral reefs. Despite such grim realities, Heather Lazrus (2009: 244), in the course of her fieldwork in Funafuti and elsewhere in Tuvalu, felt "overwhelmed by people's energy and vitality" in response to repeated devastating storms. Indeed, at various levels of their society, Tuvaluans have served as exemplars of agency in the face of incredible adversity due to global climate change to which they have, for all practical purposes, not contributed in any significant way. In 2005, at the 58th Session of the United Nations General Assembly, Prime Minister Saufatu Sopoanga of Tuvalu declared that his people:

live in constant fear of the adverse impacts of climate change. For a coral atoll nation, sea level rise and more severe weather events loom as a growing threat to our entire population. The threat is real and serious, and is [no different than] a slow and insidious form of terrorism against us.

Sopoanga 2003

In the words of David Stanley (2007), "as ocean levels continue to rise, the entire population of Tuvalu may have to evacuate, third world victims of first world affluence." In the mean time, as Oliver-Smith (2010: 176) observes: "Tuvaluans recognize the possibility of permanent migration due to sea level rise in the future, but their current strategy is to develop locally based responses and adaptations rather than wholesale migration." Conversely, many residents from Nanumea, the northernmost atoll of Tuvalu and home to about 600 people, work on international ships and in the capital of Funafuti or even in Fiji, Australia, and New Zealand (Marino and Lazrus 2015: 346).

The ways in which people might adapt to climate change vary. Adopting a cultural interpretive perspective, Cecilie Rubow (2009), of the Department of

Anthropology, University of Copenhagen, examines religious responses to climate change in the South Pacific, particularly the Cook Islands, a region that that has experienced increased intensity and frequency of cyclones, other storms, and flooding of low-lying areas in recent years. She observes:

> During a fieldwork in the Cook Islands, primarily studying the burial tradi-tions in the Cook Islands Christian Church, I . . . witnessed the linking of people's immoral actions such as taking a swim just outside the church on Sunday mornings to the enhanced cyclonic activities. However, I learned that this was only one voice among many others, not only in a community with many different attitudes towards the church and Christianity, but also in the individual speaker, having more than one position to think, act, and speak from.
>
> *Rubow 2009: 106*

Although, at the governmental level, the Cook Islands have participated in var-ious international and political commissions and organizations, such as the South Pacific Regional Environmental Programme, seeking to address climate change, many Cook Islanders, most of whom adhere to one variant or other of Christianity, seek to comprehend and respond to climate change through theological means.

Peter Rudiak-Gould (2010) has done the most extensive anthropological work to date on climate change in low-lying islands in the South Pacific, in his case the Marshall Islands, an archipelago of coral atolls with an average elevation of just over 2m, and a height of not greater than 9.75m above sea level. The Marshall Islands consist of 1,225 islets totaling 180km^2 spread out over 1,942,490km^2 of ocean. One small island in the Marshalls has already sunk below sea level, leaving little doubt about the direction of future events. Rudiak-Gould conducted 146 interviews with Marshall Islanders, including 18 interviews with government officials and other leaders in Majuro, the capital city. He maintains that recent social changes such as foreign influences and the cash economy are perceived by the Marshallese as threats to three indigenous values: authenticity, conviviality, and subsistence (Rudiak-Gould 2010). The Marshallese fear the loss of their land will inevitably result in the demise of their culture and their ability to interact with each other in traditional ways. Rudiak-Gould (2010: 70) identifies two principal popular Marshallese strategies for interpreting climate change:

> the first is to dismiss or ignore the idea, which I term climate change dis-avowal. The second is to incorporate it into pre-existing beliefs, which becomes climate change pessimism. When I say that there are two preexisting beliefs, I do not mean that some percentage of Marshall Islanders employ the first one and another percentage employ the second one. I mean that both strategies are available, with some people adhering closely to one, some people to the other, and many individuals employing one or the other in different contexts.

The reasons for denial include: (1) a sense that local environmental changes have been minor; (2) a sense that the climate is essentially constant and benign; (3) a reluctance to make predictions about future weather; (4) acceptance of climate denial on the part of Christian ministers; (5) discrepancies between scientific and local knowledge of the world; (6) a distrust of scientists; (7) denial or refusal to discuss a disturbing phenomenon; and (8) belief in supernatural intervention (Rudiak-Gould 2010: 74–81). Reasons for pessimism include: (1) a pre-existing belief that the good life is declining; (2) a sense of disempowerment; (3) media alarmism; and (4) the ironic hope that some other country will rescue them from the ravages of climate change (Rudiak-Gould 2010: 86–88).

In Rudiak-Gould's experience, Marshall Islanders' understanding of climate change includes an awareness of scientific assessments of the situation. However:

> This scientific information is supplemented by firsthand observation of burgeoning local impacts (increasing sea levels, erosion, droughts, and temperatures) as well as Biblical exegesis: for example, some islanders say that the prediction of nationwide inundation is false because God promised in the book of Genesis never to flood the earth again, while others believe that climate change is true because climatic chaos is predicted in the book of Revelation.
>
> *Rudiak-Gould 2012a: 5*

While disavowal and pessimism are the most common strategies that Marshall Islanders utilize in seeking to comprehend climate change, a few resort to "activism." For example, the nation's leader President Kessai stated:

> Even if God is causing this [climate change], God also gave us our capacity to reflect and do something about it. God also gave people intelligence so that they can know what they need to do. I believe in these things . . . God helps those who help themselves. So you know what they need to do. I believe in these things . . . God helps those who help themselves. So you know you got to do what you can do first and that will help.
>
> *quoted in Rudiak-Gould 2010: 98*

As the people of the Marshall Islands look at their changing environment through a complex cultural lens that melds traditional beliefs and knowledge, Western-introduced biblical exegesis, and concepts derived from even more recent exposure to climate science, they see various omens that their land faces a grave crisis. Yet they reject the idea of resettlement, based on a belief in historic cycles of world improvement and decline. Ultimately, the Marshall Islanders tend to blame themselves for climate change based on their recognized loss of traditional cultural elements and the adoption of Western patterns (Rudiak-Gould 2013).

Holly M. Barker affirms that at least certain sectors of Marshall Island society have adopted a pro-active stance on climate change. She reports:

In the Marshall Islands the government and business community are examining local opportunities to help mitigate the impacts of climate change, including dredging policy, waste management, coastal construction, and community outreach and education. Island leaders are vocal; they want their perspectives on climate change heard and are demanding that the world come to terms with the thousands of years of island history and culture that the behavior of the industrialized countries now imperils.

Barker 2011: 429

Representatives from many of the various other low-lying South Pacific Islands have embraced collectively a pro-active approach to climate change. In August 2002, government leaders from 16 Pacific island nations held the 33rd Pacific Islands Forum in Suva, Fiji, at which they expressed their shared strong concerns about the extreme hardships climate change was inflicting on their peoples. Participants issued a communiqué to the developed nations responsible for most greenhouse gas emissions to begin addressing the global effects of climate change.

Despite documenting these kinds of efforts, Rudiak-Gould (2011: 9) asserts that anthropologists "as yet lack a well-developed understanding of how societies receive, interpret, understand, and utilize" the "scientific discourse of global anthropogenic climate change." Based upon his research in the Marshall Islands, he calls upon anthropologists to become more involved in climate change reception studies because their discipline "brings valuable skills to the job: a keen appreciation of the intersection of the local and the global, and long experience in studying the incorporation of foreign institutions and ideas in local society" (Rudiak-Gould 2011: 12). Rudiak-Gould (2012b), again drawing upon his experiences in the Marshall Islands, argues that public knowledge about climate change requires translation of climate science on the part of specialist bodies, such as the IPCC, to ordinary people and from scientific terminology to the vernacular. However, this is a formidable task in that most indigenous languages lack separate terms for weather and climate. Even in Western societies, people often conflate climate and weather, or may attribute an isolated weather event, such as a cold spell or a heat wave, to climate change. Rudiak-Gould acknowledges that climate change communicators can be assisted in their efforts by anthropologists, linguists, and other scholars sensitive to local meanings. Nonetheless:

mistranslation is often inevitable, [as] the options are limited and the reasons are deep rather than superficial: to translate English "climate" or "weather" faithfully would entail the introduction into these nature–culture conflating societies of an entirely new concept, one which excludes "social" phenomena—a radically foreignizing, "abusive" translation strategy, unlikely to resonate with locals.

Rudiak-Gould 2012b: 52

Beyond its impact on residents, climate change is adversely affecting the tourist industries on many of the South Pacific islands by destroying coral reefs, damaging beaches, creating increasingly uncomfortably high night-time temperatures, and taxing the availability of freshwater. Ironically, as Becken (2005: 381) observes: "there is increasing awareness that tourism is an important contributor to climate change through its consumption of fossil fuels and resulting gas emissions."

Because, in a sense, they are captured populations, climate change is having multiple adverse impacts on the peoples living on low-lying islands, as well as other fauna and flora found on such islands. Indeed, these islands constitute natural laboratories in which indigenous ways of life are both conceptually and behaviorally confronting climate change ahead of many populations of the world. How they respond to climate change, and how the world responds to their plight, holds lessons for broader patterns in the human/climate interface. Thus, as Heather Lazrus (2012: 293) observes:

> Migration as a response to climate change impacts is a critical issue at the heart of much climate discourse and debate within and concerning island communities: Will islands become inhabitable as a result of the effects of climate change? Where and when will people go? How will relocation be financed? Who should make relocation decisions? How will the cadre of citizenship rights be configured for people relocated across national borders? How will cultural continuity and integrity be impacted?

Failure to respond to the needs of the peoples of low-lying islands suggests that we face a bleak future as the human toll of global warming mounts. Conversely, a global focus on cases like low-lying island populations before conditions become untenable could help put in place a pattern of collective social responsibility in responding to climate change.

Case study 3: climate change and the inhabitants of Bangladesh

Bangladesh, a densely populated country of some 150 million people, is often mentioned in the climate change discourse as being under immediate threat from rising sea level. Apart from some city-states, it is the most densely populated country in the world. Most of its inhabitants reside in the delta formed by the Ganges, Brahmaputra, and Meghna rivers. Indeed, about 90 percent of Bangladesh is a flood plain. It is situated between the Indian Ocean and the Himalaya Mountains, a location which "gives the country its monsoons, vital for agriculture, but also exposes it to periodic catastrophic disasters, which include tropical cyclones, storm surges and floods, bringing loss of life on a massive scale" (Whyte 2008: 188). Storm surges that strike coastal Bangladesh generally move inland, resulting in colossal flooding:

> Among the most devastating human impacts in recent history were recorded in 1970 when some 300,000–500,000 Bangladeshis died in the south of the country as a result of coastal flooding. In 1991 another 140,000 died after

a cyclone hit the Bengal coast, and in November 2007 cyclone cycle SIDR resulted in a further 3,700 deaths. In addition, sea level rise is estimated to have risen by 20 cm over the twentieth century, while there are predictions that a further sea level rise of 45 cm may result in the loss of 10.9% of Bangladesh's land area if adequate protective measures are not created.

Findlay and Geddes 2011: 146

In addition to the inundation of people's homes and communities, rising sea levels endanger large expanses of rich agricultural land, the source of income for about 85 percent of Bangladesh's population. In Bangladesh, according to Saleemul Huq and Mizan R. Khan (2006: 186), "almost two-thirds of the labor force—about 38 million people—is engaged in agriculture, and this is the sector likely to be hit the hardest by the impacts of climate change, particularly in the coastal zone" of the country.

One of the sources of climate change risk in Bangladesh is through saltwater intrusion into drinking water sources in coastal regions. Factors contributing to the development of salinity include tidal flooding during the wet season, direct inundation with brackish water during storms, and through upward lateral movement of saline ground water. Salinity levels have also made it impossible to farm on affected lands. Due to saltwater intrusion, people are struggling to grow enough food, or to produce enough surplus that can be sold for other necessities like clothing. Loss of homes, inability to pay school fees, and increases in health problems (e.g., gynecological problems associated with using saline water during menstruation) are other burdens caused by water salinization. Ashiqur Rahman (2010) has studied this process ethnographically in Harinagar, a coastal village in the Satkhira district of Bangladesh, to assess how people are attempting to respond to this significant challenge from the environment. The impact of salinization is evident in the experience of one family:

> Global Warming has a taste in this village. It is the taste of salt. Only a few years ago, water from the local pond was fresh and sweet on Samit Biswas's tongue. It quenched his family's thirst and cleansed their bodies.
>
> But drinking a cupful now leaves a briny flavor in his mouth. Tiny white crystals sprout on Biswas's skin after he bathes and in his clothes after his wife washes them. . . . If sea levels continue to rise at their present rate, by the time Biswas, 35, retires from his job as a teacher, the only home he has known will be swamped, overrun by the ocean with the force of an unstoppable army. That, in turn, will trigger another kind of flood: millions of displaced residents desperate for a place to live.
>
> *Chu 2007*

For the people of Harinagar, salinity means "undrinkable," but the word also holds connotations of hunger, joblessness, and the consequences that accompany these conditions. As one villager told Rahman (2009: 38) "We have neither present nor future and it was salinity that ruined us."

In response to salinization, villagers in Harinagar began shrimp farming, crabbing, oyster- and other mollusk-gathering activities, and small-scale fishing. While shrimp farming has proved lucrative for wealthy individuals, poorer former rice paddy farmers may be forced to allow shrimp farms owned by the elite on their land. Crabbing also has failed to provide an adequate alternative livelihood to many failing paddy farmers. However, it did provide sufficient funds to allow short-term survival. At the time of Rahman's research, oyster and other shellfish collection was a relatively new economic activity, which people were viewing as "something being better than nothing." Additionally, many people were forced to migrate to cities in Bangladesh or to India to try to find work in ever more crowded urban landscapes. Others borrowed money and fell deeper into debt, losing their land in the process. While people struggle to eke out a livelihood, for many, "Salt water carries hunger, joblessness and misery" (Rahman 2009: 62).

Even without the growing impact of climate change, Bangladesh, as noted, is often subjected to violent storms, including at least one major cyclone every year. Climate change, however, appears to be increasing the frequency and intensity of such storms as well as the extent of their damaging impacts on local communities throughout the country. Bangladesh is one of the poorest countries in the world, which adds to its vulnerability in the face of the ravages of climate change. More than half of the population subsists on less than $1 a day (Oliver-Smith 2010: 172).

Anthropologist Timothy Finan (2009: 179) has applied the concepts of adaptation, vulnerability, and resilience in his examination of beels in southwest Bangladesh; these are "small depressions located at various distances from a coastline which are connected to the complex hydrology of a region through canals and minor rivers." Beels vary in size depending upon the season, and are used in boro rice cultivation during the wet months and as pasture for livestock during the dry months. During the monsoon season, when the beels fill up with water, they serve as a public fishing resource for nearby communities. Furthermore, a prawn export industry based on the beels has appeared over the course of the past two decades or so. According to Finan (2009: 179–180):

> The value of prawn exports in Bangladesh is now estimated at $350 million, behind only garments and remittances as the major sources of foreign exchange. . . . There are now over 100,000 golda [local term for fresh water prawn] producers, and many more households benefit from provisioning inputs to this system, particularly from the supply of post-larvae and labor.

Unfortunately, the possibility of sea level rise associated with climate change threatens the intricate system of boro rice cultivation and prawn production, in that it "will likely result in a much larger volume of saline water moving into the canals that feed the beel hydrology, contaminating water resources and eroding gher [earthen walls] embankments" (Finan 2009: 181). The Bangladesh government has responded to previous catastrophes by building some 2,500 concrete shelters high above pilings, installing warning systems, organizing rescue teams, and implementing evacuation plans (Pilkey and Young 2009: 135). While the government is considering building massive earthworks to stem the rise in sea level, such a development may not prove sufficient to save a complex hydrology system. Nevertheless, Finan (2009: 184) believes that the case of the beel system illustrates the role that anthropology can play in assessing the "distribution of local resource access, use and livelihood profiles," identifying "institutional relationships that link communities to broader systems," and facilitating the "process of local resource-management and problem solving." This is a fairly common approach in anthropological work on climate change, that is assessing responses to other environmental challenges and extrapolating how communities might react to the disruptions wrought by global warming.

As in other developed and developing countries, as Mozaharul Alam and Atiq Rahman (2008: 56) observe, in Bangladesh "a major agenda of the business group is expansion and promotion of their activities; the group has little interest in the social agenda." About 50 percent of the country's greenhouse gas emissions come from electricity generation and urea fertilizer production (Alam and Rahman 2008: 58). According to Alam and Rahman (2008: 59), carbon dioxide emissions increased dramatically in Bangladesh between 1990 and 2000 as a result of the following changes:

- Agriculture, fisheries, and forestry emissions increased from 680,000 to 1,830,000 tons.
- Commercial and institutional emissions increased from 239,000 to 274,000 tons.
- Residential emissions increased from 2,082,000 to 4,290,000 tons.
- Transport emissions increased from 1,892,000 to 4,760,000 tons.
- Manufacturing industries and construction emissions increased from 3,623,000 to 8,030,000 tons.
- Energy industry emissions increased from 4,763,000 to 13,145,000 tons.

Despite these dramatic increases, Bangladesh remains one of the lowest greenhouse gas emitters per capita in the world. While Bangladesh theoretically could contribute partially to climate change mitigation, as a poor peripheral country locked into the capitalist world system, its contribution would prove to be negligible at this stage of its economic development. The Ministry of Environment and Forests (MOEF) "has realized that adaptation is the utmost priority . . . because the main concern in Bangladesh is to reduce the adverse impacts of climate change and variability" (Alam and Rahman 2008: 61). At the national institutional level, the Bangladesh government is involved in a number of climate change adaptation schemes, including the National Adaptation Programme of Action, the Climate Change Strategy and Action Plan, the National Climate Change Trust Fund, and the multi-donor Climate Resilient Fund. The first of these, for example, is a multidimensional federal government strategy for reducing the impacts of climate change on various aspects of Bangladesh society, including plans to work with coastal communities on reforestation, developing systems of clean water distribution to combat increased salinity caused by sea level rise, and assessment of indigenous and other knowledge for eco-specific adaptive responses to climate change. Unfortunately, the 2010 International Corruptions Perceptions Index ranked Bangladesh 134th out of 178 countries—which, while an improvement compared to previous years, still indicates a critical challenge in moving from planned changes to actual, effective on-the-ground programs.

Based upon a survey of 278 households, three focus group discussions, and seven key informant interviews, Mahmud and Prowse (2012) found evidence of extensive corruption in pre- and post-disaster interventions in Khulna, the third largest city in the country, before and after Cyclone Aila in May 2009. Despite the existence of several climate adaptation schemes in Bangladesh, these researchers express concern that "without increasing integrity, hard-won funding will not increase the resilience of poor households and communities" (Mahmud and Prowse 2012: 941). Etienne Piguet (2008: 146) suggests that Bangladesh may constitute a rare example of a relatively large nation-state that may be reaching a point where environmental change would require large-scale emigration. Indeed, the Bangladeshi government has requested that the world community permit some 20 million of its inhabitants to resettle in other countries (Findlay and Geddes 2011: 150). This type of mass movement of people, fraught with multiple problems for refugees, is not likely to be well received by potential host countries because of existing patterns of "refugee fatigue" and concerns about their own existing economic challenges in a time of global warming. Indeed, both India to the north and west and Myanmar to the east are hostile to the prospect of being potentially flooded by climate refugees from Bangladesh. Fagan (2013: 164) reports:

> India is building a four-thousand kilometer fence to keep out migrants, cattle rustlers, and people seeking work. All of this is quite apart from the nuclear weaponry in the hands of both India and Pakistan, of which Bangladesh was, of course, formerly a part.

Case study 4: climate change and peoples living in high mountainous areas: the Andes, Himalayas, and Alps

Most mountainous areas have been experiencing accelerated patterns of climate change compared to lowland regions. An estimated 26 percent of the world's population reportedly lives in mountainous areas (Nogués-Bravero *et al.* 2007: 420). The special nature of mountain ecology not only impacts the people living on them or immediately below them, but also those living at considerable distances away in lowland areas that rely upon water from melting mountain glaciers and snowfall. Mountainous areas are important sources of hydroelectric power and sites of tourist activities, such as skiing, hiking, camping, and boating. But climate change is producing unstable patterns of hydroelectric generation and will increasingly adversely affect ski resorts, which unfortunately tend to be energy-intensive and ecologically destructive enterprises both in terms of the ski runs themselves and nearby, often luxury, accommodation (Scott *et al.* 2007).

Peru is often highlighted as one of the world's countries most vulnerable to climate change. It has about 70 percent of the world's tropical glaciers, providing most of the water for irrigation and consumption in the country's rural and urban areas (Paerregaard 2016: 250). Climate change scenarios forecast that in the next 15 years all of the glaciers below 5,500m elevation will have disappeared, a serious threat given that about 90 percent of Peru's inhabitants live in arid, semi-arid or sub-humid areas.

The magnitude and significance of glacier melt is revealed by new research on the margins of the Quelccaya ice cap in Peru showing that glacial ice that took at least 1,600 years to form has melted in just 25 years (Thompson *et al.* 2013). Rapid melting at Quelccaya in modern times has uncovered plants that were frozen in place when the glacier advanced thousands of years ago. Radiocarbon dating of those plants has provided scientists with an unusually precise method of determining the history of the ice sheet's margins. The melting of glaciers has had various adverse effects on human communities, including the formation of a large number of glacial lakes, as has occurred at Quelccaya, some of which constitute a risk from flooding for downstream inhabitants. Ben Orlove *et al.* (2008: 3) maintain that glaciers are illustrating the susceptibility of the planet to human activities. The rapid melting of glaciers in the Andes has forced people to grow their staple crops at even higher elevations, a practice that contributes to deforestation and soil erosion. The flight of highland or mountain people to cities often means that they have to cope with an atomistic existence in overcrowded and polluted slums or shanty towns and try to eke out a living at low-paying factory or low-status service jobs, or as street vendors in the informal economy. Particularly for Andean people, who are biologically adapted with their large hearts and low heart rates to the high-altitude *altiplano*, adjusting to life in coastal or lowland cities can be physiologically taxing. The health and social costs of crowding and urban poverty are no less stressful. In short, the changes being wrought by climate change to high-altitude areas are already significant, and will grow progressively more threatening over time.

Inge Bolin (2009) has examined glacial retreat in the high Andes, particularly in the provinces of Quispicanchis and Urubamba in the Cusco region of southeast Peru. The Andes, which stretch north to south for 7,250km, are the longest mountain chain in the world. Over the past two decades or so, the ice of the Peruvian Andes has been reduced by 20 percent (Bolin 2009: 230). Melting glaciers provide additional water over the short term, but they also result in rock falls, landslides, and floods. Eventually, however, diminishing snow masses contribute to the contraction and even disappearance of mountain lakes and creeks, which means less water for irrigating fields, drinking by both humans and animals, and generating hydroelectricity. Many Andean inhabitants are alarmed and feel confused by the retreating glaciers on their sacred mountains. According to Bolin (2009: 232):

Some indigenous people have wondered what they have done wrong to deserve the wrath of the gods who began to restrict the water that flows from their mountainsides. Although elders are often aware of the effects of El Nino that can cause havoc in the weather patterns, few know of the problems underlying the global climate change and of those responsible for causing this devastating process. . . . The slightest changes in the environment tell [the Quechua people] when something goes wrong. Thus, for example, the people living along the hillsides above the Vilcanota and Urubamba valleys observed already in the mid-1980s (and perhaps earlier) that important medicinal plants became increasingly hard to find, and where they persisted, their growth was stunted, usually because of water scarcity during at least part of the year.

As part of an effort to help the people in their field sites to adapt to the ravaging effects of climate change, Bolin *et al.* have incorporated indigenous Andean knowledge in establishing three priorities: (1) reconstructing ancient terraces and building new ones; (2) using conservation tillage; and (3) rejuvenating ancient irrigation systems. She asserts that: "Anthropologists working with indigenous and other place-based peoples have a critical role in the issue of climate change, working as research collaborators and mediators between the local and the global" (Bolin 2009: 236).

Elsewhere, Robert E. Rhoades *et al.* (2008) have explored local perceptions and social impacts of climate change as a result of glacial retreat on Cotacachi, the highest of the northernmost cluster of volcanic peaks in the Ecuadorian Andes. Indigenous Cotacacheños view this mountain as a mother on whose broad "skirt" they live. Rhoades *et al.* organized workshops with residents from several villages in order to ascertain their perceptions of the climate change and glacial retreat on Cotacachi. Whereas "Elderly people and those from more remote villages believed that [glacial retreat] was due to Mama Cotacachi's punishment . . . younger people with formal education and contacts pinpointed global climate change" (Rhoades *et al.* 2008: 221). Regardless of varying perceptions of climate change and glacier retreat, these events have been a source of disorientation for Cotacacheños because, in the past, Mama Cotacachi always supplied abundant water for subsistence and daily life. Rhoades *et al.* emphasize the need for collaborative research among various parties in comprehending what is happened to people who have historically relied on glacier melt-off. They assert: "Only with a strong interdisciplinary approach that involves the participation of the people directly affected can we hope to achieve solutions to what may become major disruptions of ancient cultures deeply rooted in glacier-fed mountain landscapes" (Rhoades *et al.* 2008: 225).

Karsten Paerregaard (2016) conducted ethnographic fieldwork periodically between 1986 and 2011 in Tapay, an Andean community dispersed at 2,200–5,400m elevation in the Colca Valley of Peru's southern highlands. Over the course of her fieldwork, the snow that falls and lies on surrounding mountains lasted for shorter time periods and resulted in less melt water. Some residents ascribed the rising temperatures in the region to the intrusion of modern lifestyles in Tapay and Peru's highly polluting mining industry. Some Tapay residents had even come to doubt the spiritual power of the mountain deities which had sustained their way of life in the past. Plans on the part of a Peruvian mining company to open gold extraction operations posed a further threat to the local availability of water.

Mattias Borg Rasmussen (2009) also examines the impact of climate change on peoples of the Peruvian Andes and focuses attention on the Declaration of Recuay in 2008. Drafted in the provincial capital of Recuay by representatives from surrounding communities, the five-page document addresses "the issue of global warming in the region and the vulnerability of the communities, [by] fiercely attacking the neo-liberal politics of the national government" (Rasmussen 2009: 198). In addition to climate change, ongoing expansion of mining in the Peruvian highlands will probably place massive pressure on limited water resources, creating a damaging pluralea interaction (Rasmussen 2009: 210). Rasmussen (2009: 212) argues that the Declaration of Recuay provides ethnographers with the challenge to identify the "resilient units on different scales, and to scrutinize how these different segments and levels of Peruvian society are related to each other both vertically and horizontally by tracking the watershed." Also of importance are factors like interacting climate change and the adverse effects of mining on disrupting community resiliency, resulting in increased vulnerability.

While the Declaration of Recuay identifies the complicity of Peruvian national elites in contributing to anthropologic climate change, Evo Morales, the president of Bolivia, a country situated in the Andean chain, convened the *World People's Conference on Climate Change and the Rights of Mother Earth* in Cochabamba in April 2010. Over 35,000 people from 142 countries attended the conference, at which Morales plainly asserted that "either capitalism dies or Mother Earth dies." The People's Agreement drafted at the conference called on the developed countries to take the lead in returning the planet's greenhouse gas levels (carbon dioxide) to 300ppm, thereby limiting the increase in the average global temperature to a maximum of 1°C (1.8°F). It further called for the creation of an International Climate and Environmental Justice Tribunal with the legal authority to judge and penalize states, industries, and people with regard to their contribution, either through commission or omission, to climate change.

The Himalayas, which are situated in Tibet, Nepal, and India, are iconic mountains for many people, including mountaineers who attempt to scale Mt. Everest (the highest peak in the world) and Sherpa guides who assist them in their treks and spiritual seekers who dispute the exile of the Dalai Lama from Tibet due to Chinese occupation, making it also a contested place. Their iconic status is being threatened due the melting glaciers and snows and resulting glacial lakes. Indigenous Tibetans regard the Himalayas as sacred mountains which reflect their well-being (Diemberger 2012).

Pasang Yangjee Sherpa is a native anthropologist who has examined four institutional climate change activities, and how her native people have been involved in them. Her research focused on the Pharak village of Lukla, which served as the base for the successful ascent of Everest by Tenzing Norgay Sherpa and Sir Edmund Hillary, a New Zealander, a feat which eventually prompted visits from more than 35,000 tourists annually. Needless to say, most of these tourists contribute to the generation of greenhouse gas emissions by flying to Nepal and leave an ecological footprint on the area, particularly Mt. Everest, which some of them attempt to scale.

Sherpa examines four different cases of institutions created between 2008 and 2011 for the Sherpas in the Everest region: (1) a workshop on "Adaptation to Climate Change and Increasing Resilience of Local People in Khumbu," (2) a Nepali cabinet meeting in Kalapatthar; (3) the Imja Tsho Action Event; and (4) and the Andean-Himalayan Glacial Lake Exchange and Collaboration Expedition. Ironically, some of these events generated more greenhouse emissions because some of the participants travelled long distances to attend them, including Sherpas living in other parts of the world. While the events highlighted the seriousness of the impact of climate change on the Himalayan region, their focus was primarily adaptation rather than mitigation. Finally, as Sherpa (2015: 21) observes: "Institutional activities have increased local receptivity to scientific climate change knowledge, but it has also increased fear of impending doom, and anger over the continuous discussion of climate change without concrete actions."

Vedwan and Rhoades (2001) examined the perceptions of apple farmers in the western Himalayas of India. Snowfall and rainfall data for the period from 1962 to 1996 indicate a climatic shift which local residents described in terms depicted in Table 5.1. Informants reported the climate as warming and "often remarked that the apple belt is moving up in the valley" (Vedwan and Rhoades 2001: 115). Furthermore:

> There is a widely held perception that the increasing incidence of pest and disease comprises a shift in disease ecology and that climate change has played a role. Canker, a disease that causes a tree to decay, has become more rampant.
>
> *Vedwan and Rhoades 2001: 115*

TABLE 5.1 Traditional calendar of the Kuilu Valley

Approximate period	Ideal pattern in the past (up to 1970)	Pattern in recent times
January 15–February 15	Cold with snowfall	Some rain and snow
March 15–April 15	Rain, snow rare	Some rain and snow
May 15–June 15	Hot	Dry
July 15–August 15	Rain	Hot and rainy
September 15–October 15	Clear	First half rainy and second dry
November 15–December 15	Snowfall	Same as ideal
December 15–January 15	Maximum cold with snow	Very little snow

Vedwan and Rhoades (2001: 117) believe that policy-makers need to consider local knowledge in arriving at decisions about climate change mitigation efforts, as local experience and on-the-ground observation over a long period can be valuable sources of insight about the actual nature of local changes.

Climate change and retreating glaciers are not only impacting people in developing high-altitude regions, such as the Andes and the Himalayas, but also in mountain areas in developed countries such as Switzerland and Austria, large parts of which are situated in the Alps. Sarah Strauss (2009: 167) notes that:

> Glaciers have historically been important to Alpine culture for many reasons: as reservoirs for drinking water and power generation, as raw materials for commerce (in the time before refrigeration), as tourist destinations, as visible markers of environmental change, and as repositories for lost souls.

She has conducted ethnographic research on water, weather, and climate in Leukerbad, located in the Dalatal, a side valley off the Rhone River valley in the Swiss canton of Wallis (or "Valasis" in French). The village is the site of thermal springs, freshwater springs, rivers, lakes, and glaciers, as well as a ski area. Seventy-five percent of the respondents in a survey she administered indicated that the local climate has become warmer and wetter than in previous decades (Strauss 2009: 170). Although the residents of Leukerbad rely upon climate models and scientific knowledge in efforts to assess their future, they do not find such information empowering. Strauss (2009: 172) reports:

> Most of the Leukerbadners I have spoken with over the years—whether overtly religious or not—feel that they can deal with whatever situation comes to pass. They have had a hard life before, and may well again, and if they have to leave their homes, moving to the urban or lower areas to find work—well, none of these things are really in their control, so there is no point to worrying about them. No matter if they believe that climate change is happening, that it is anthropogenic in origin, or that it will drastically affect their own and their children's lifestyle—there is still the feeling that nothing preventative can be done.

Leukerbadners exemplify yet another instance of people around the world, whether in developed or developing countries, who feel that climate change is beyond their immediate control. Some place their faith in strategic elites in the corporate and government sectors or in multilateral bodies such as the United Nations to remedy the situation. Other stalwart individuals feel that strategic elites are too wedded to "business as usual" and the core features of the reigning global economy to be able to effectively mitigate climate change, and have sought instead to work directly for a safe climate within the context of the climate movement that will be discussed in Chapter 6.

Case study 5: climate change and peoples living in dry places: sub-Saharan Africa and Australia

The growing pattern of severe drought in dry and arid regions, increasingly certain to be driven by climate change (although also affected by human land mismanagement and unequal distribution of water resources), is adversely affecting horticulturalists, pastoralists, and agriculturalists across the planet. Sub-Saharan Africa, a region comprised of nearly 50 sovereign states, is particularly at risk from the adverse agricultural effects of climate change. Over 600 million people live in sub-Saharan Africa, and the vast majority of them depend directly on the land and on food production for their sustenance. According to Lennart Bage, President of the International Fund for Agricultural Development: "Increasing crop failures and livestock deaths are already imposing high economic losses and undermine food security in parts of sub-Saharan Africa, and they will get far more severe as global warming continues" (quoted in Kenya Environment and Political News 2007). Reduced food supplies and resulting higher food prices have an immediate impact on landless workers as well: individuals and households that are never able to develop much in the way of savings to protect them during difficult times.

In the case of the African Sahel, the semi-arid ecozone between the Saharan desert to the north and the savannah country to the south, declining rainfall adversely impacted agricultural productivity by 1 percent per annum between 1970 and 2000 (Eggleton 2013: 77):

> And in parallel, desertification has increased. Although some improved farming practices have started to reverse the declining food production of the late 20th century, the region is still highly susceptible to drought. By early 2010, failure of the rains in the previous year had led to a 30 per cent drop in cereal production in Chad. Neighbouring Niger had its worst crops in two decades. According to the United Nations Children's Fund (UNICEF), in the Sahel 300,000 children under age five die each year. The drying of the Sahel is attributed to an increased Atlantic sea-surface temperature difference north and south of the equator, as well as warming of the Indian Ocean.
>
> *Eggleton 2013: 77–78*

One of the most egregious expressions of desertification in sub-Saharan Africa is the shrinkage of Lake Chad, which historically straddled Chad, Cameroon, Niger, and Nigeria. In the 1960s, the lake was 38,000km^2 in size and supported human, animal, and plant life in all four of its bordering countries (Aulakh 2013). Today, as a result of global warming and the steady southward expansion of the Sahara Desert, Lake Chad measures only 1,300km^2. It is far from certain that Lake Chad will survive the twenty-first century. The result has been increased mass migration, malnutrition, and social conflict.

The drying of Lake Chad has forced growing numbers of people into the vulnerable status of being climate refugees. Exemplary is the family of Halime

Djime. The family were pastoralists who were sustained by several dozen camels that provided meat and milk. But, as the areas where they herded their livestock began to dry, there was less and less vegetation to support the herd (York 2010). Selling his remaining camels, Halime's husband sought work in Libya and eastern Chad. But as conditions worsened, she lost touch with her husband and no longer knows where he is. Her daughter, Fatime, is severely undernourished and facing starvation. The region where Halime's family lives has become among the poorest and hungriest in world, with nearly one-quarter of children dying before their fifth birthday.

Robert K. Hitchcock (2009) examined the impact of climate change on the San people in the Kalahari Desert of Botswana in southern Africa. While his San informants expressed varying views on the nature of environmental and climatic changes in the Kalahari, they generally shared a concern about a significant decline in the water table (Hitchcock 2009: 253). According to Hitchcock (2009: 256): "A significant number of San informants said that they felt that their government and the international community should do more to reduce the effects of global and local climate change." Some San told Hitchcock that they would be among the big losers in a winners and losers scenario of environmental change (Hitchcock 2009: 257). One San woman shared with Hitchcock what might be seen as a social justice perspective on solving the climate change crisis:

> Global climate change, she said, was something that would be difficult to deal with, but if everyone worked together, the old and the young, San and non-San, Africa and the rest of the world, they could cope with the challenges they faced, drawing on both scientific and local knowledge about ways to deal with natural disasters, social conflict, and environmental variability.
>
> *Hitchcock 2009: 259*

Magistro and Lo provide a case study of the ways in which the Senegalese government has responded to three decades of reduced precipitation by building a series of dams to capture available water for agricultural purposes. They report that the dams constructed in the mid-1980s "now stabilize the seasonality of stream flow, enabling a double crop season of rice harvests on irrigation schemes during the year" (Magistro and Lo 2001: 141). Little *et al.* (2001) examined responses to the 1996/1997 drought and a flood induced by the 1997/1998 El Niño event among pastoralists in northern Kenya and southern Somalia. Of note, they caution against a tendency to attribute the occurrence of "macro-climatic events, such as floods and droughts" to "exaggerated claims of global climate change" (Little *et al.* 2001: 152). Instead, the authors argue that climate is only one of a series of risks that herders and communities face in pursuing their livelihood. Others may include macro-market conditions or political instability and conflict, although it should be noted that the latter may be related to climatic events as well. In the years since the publication of this study by Little *et al.*, global warming has continued in a pattern predicted by climate change models at rates unprecedented in recent human history. Although multiple factors challenge pastoralists in the region studied by these researchers, attributing particular local weather patterns to climate change has become increasingly common and increasingly defensible among climate scientists. In their study, Little *et al.* (2001: 158) found that while some herders experienced profound suffering from the two climatic events in question, others were able to adjust because they had "sufficient household labor and favorable access to unaffected pastures." As this case indicates, resiliency is a variable, one that is tied to control of resources. As Adger *et al.* (2003: 179) indicate, while:

> all societies are fundamentally adaptive and there are many situations in the past where societies have adapted to changes in climate and to similar risks . . . some sectors are more sensitive and some groups in society more vulnerable to the risks posed by climate change than others.

A question raised in the contemporary period concerns the sustainability of resiliency in the face of climate turmoil and pluralea interaction, the very conditions being faced in the Horn of Africa countries discussed by Little *et al.* Their work indicates that pre-existent vulnerability will help determine the adverse impacts of climate change. However, if conditions continue to worsen, even households and communities that initially proved their adaptability may be unable to cope.

Clemens Romankiewicz and Martin Doevenspeak (2015) have also conducted research as part of an interdisciplinary project in the West African Sahel, particularly Mali and Senegal. Historically, the region is one of the most mobile in the world, with climate change acting, as various studies have indicated, as one of the drivers of migration. Temperatures in the western Sahel have increased since the 1960s, manifested by a rising number of warm spells and a decrease in cold days. Interviews with village elders coincided with meteorological records that indicate rainfall in recent times is lower than prior to the 1970s, but higher than during the severe droughts of the 1970s and 1980s. Romankiewicz and Doevenspeak (2015: 96), based upon a multi-sited approach, argue that:

> it is important to develop a deeper understanding of local meanings of environmental change and migration in the context of multiple, social, political and economic processes of change in order to understand if, how and to what extent certain climate and vegetation trends play a role for what kind of migration.

People in the Linnguerre region of the western Sahel, migrate toward cities and even Europe in many instances for education and better employment and income opportunities.

Another place of concern in this case study is Australia, which is almost as large in area as the 48 contiguous US states, but overall is a much drier and harsher country. Generations of Australian schoolchildren have learnt this fact, reciting

Dorothea Mackellar's poem "My Country" with its well-known line "I love a sunburnt country." Although Australia is bordered by three oceans—the Indian, Pacific, and Southern—it is often described with good reason as the driest inhabited continent on the planet. Australia is the developed country most vulnerable to the direct impacts of climate change and also to indirect impact from neighbor countries that are stressed by climate change. Australia's susceptibility to the worst effects of climate change is heightened because it is affected more than any other continent by the Southern Oscillation: the swings between El Niño and La Niña which shape both temperatures and precipitation variability. El Niño reduces Australian rainfall for up to seven years, creating droughts and leading to intensified bushfires. By contrast, during La Niña, there is more rain, and even heavy rains and flooding. Climate change appears to have increased the intensity of the Southern Oscillation. Also, since the late twentieth century, the Indian Ocean Dipole, an irregular oscillation of sea surface temperatures, has resulted in a warming of the west and reduced spring rains in southwestern Australia (Hennessey et al. 2007: 509). The 2007 IPCC Report delineated some of the following impacts of climate change on Australia: warming of 0.4–0.7°C (0.72–1.26°F) since 1950, with more heat waves, fewer frosts, more rain in the northwest, less rain in the southeast, more intense droughts, and a sea level rise of about 70mm (Hennessey et al. 2007). For Australia as a whole, 2009 was the second hottest year since high-quality temperature records were initiated in 1910, and August 2009 was the warmest August on record, while 2005 was the hottest year, 1.09°C (1.96°F) hotter than the standard mean for the period 1961–1990 (Australian Bureau of Meteorology 2009; Lindenmayer 2007). In 2010, the Australian Bureau of Meteorology reported that the decade of 2001–2010, the hottest on record, was 0.52°C (0.94°F) above the average; and that Australia's climate had steadily warmed over the previous 60 years, with very few cool years occurring in the last three decades. Australia was then ravaged by one of the most severe La Niña events in recorded history, in late 2010 and early 2011, aggravated by record-high surface temperature, very likely related to climate change. The Commonwealth Scientific and Industrial Research Organisation (CSIRO) and the Australian Bureau of Meteorology 2010 *State of the Climate* report calculated that Australian average temperatures are projected to rise by 0.6–1.5°C (1.08–2.7°F) by 2030; and, if global greenhouse emissions continue at current levels, warming is projected to be in the range of 2.2–5.0°C (3.96–9°F) by 2070. Heating of this magnitude will indeed make Australia a sunburnt country.

Of all Australians, Indigenous Australians or Aboriginal people, particularly those residing in remote communities in central and western Australia, are the most vulnerable to increasing temperatures and other climatic changes. Donna Green (2009) conducted research on how climate change might affect remote indigenous Australian communities and how they plan to respond to it. She convened a workshop that assembled 30 Elders and Traditional Owners of the Land from across northern Australia and 30 researchers and scientists (Green 2009: 220). The group decided to prioritize the impact of climate change on Torres Strait Islander peoples who reside on islands situated between mainland Australia and Papua New Guinea.

The Islanders reported that in recent years, the King Tides seemed higher and more powerful. Furthermore:

> On several of the islands, coastal tracks were being washed away and long-established graveyards and houses inundated. In addition to the psychological distress caused by the flooding, their remoteness makes repairing this damage extremely expensive, and Islanders lack access to the necessary resources to engage consultants to conduct awareness assessments or to actually carry out maintenance work on the basic infrastructure.
>
> *Green 2009: 221*

The Islanders are also concerned about how water inundations might result in contamination of freshwater supplies or flood their landfill rubbish dumps. The 2007 IPCC Report indicated that about half of the 4,000 people living on the Torres Straits Islands may have to be eventually relocated due to the rising sea level and associated storm surges (Hennessey *et al.* 2007).

The *Sharing Knowledge* website operated by the Climate Change Research Centre at the University of New South Wales in Sydney "provides climate change projections for most regions in northern Australia where remote indigenous communities live . . . [and] serves as a clearinghouse for TEK (traditional environmental knowledge) on weather and climate" (Green 2009: 225). Noted on the website is recognition that: "At present, there is only limited understanding about what role, if any, climate plays in affecting the health of Indigenous Australians, their communities, their culture and their country." To overcome this gap in knowledge, the Centre is undertaking several studies analyzing 20 years of admissions data from major hospitals in northern and central Australia, and relating findings to climate data. The second study involves taking trips with Wik and Kugu Traditional Owners and Elders to their original homeland areas, to film them talking about what they remember about their traditional country, and how it has changed. Much of their country is now accessible only by boat or helicopter, and as a result, many people are not able to return to it on a regular basis.

Marcus Barber (2011b), an anthropologist who has worked for several years for the CSIRO, notes that the Garnaut Review on climate change commissioned by the Australian government predicts that without significant mitigation, Darwin, the capital of the Northern Territory, will have over 200 days each year above 35°C (95°F) by 2070. He spent a significant portion of his time while working at CSIRO travelling through remote northern Australia, speaking to Aboriginal people about issues of water and local environmental change. His Aboriginal informants increasingly referred to "climate change" and "global warming" without prompting, suggesting the diffusion of these climate science concepts to even remote areas of the planet. Barber (2011b) asserts that one challenge for anthropologists is "how to find appropriate paths in talking to people who may be far removed from the places where this account of the future is being generated, and indeed from where the majority of causal factors emerge." In another essay, Barber (2011a: 94–95) states:

> A number of Yolngu people with whom I spoke in 2008 had heard of climate change in some form, but the detail varied. The polar ice melting and the possibility of sea-level rise were known phenomena, but knowledge about the relationship of this to carbon dioxide emissions was not evident amongst the people with whom I spoke. . . . A number of people spoke of how the sorcerers and magic men of times past were able to manipulate storms and weather, although in contemporary conversations such knowledge is often prefaced with a disclaimer to the effect that they are aware that non-Indigenous people find these accounts difficult to accept.

Nevertheless, Indigenous Australians across Arnhem Land in the Northern Territory are becoming increasingly aware of anthropogenic climate change due to reports in the mass media, reports written by Indigenous rangers, and government environmental reports. As a result, the Yolngu now regard climate change as a major threat to their way of life.

This threat is growing among Indigenous Australians generally. In the words of Melanie Koolmatrie of the Ngarrindjeri Community, reflecting on the changes she has witnessed:

> We have always lived by the water. We are water people. We are water spirits. I only have one country and it is this country. If that goes, I have no other home. . . . It is very hurtful. Our land is sick. Something needs to be done. It needs to be done now.
>
> *Hero Project 2009*

Green *et al.* (2010) maintain that Australian Indigenous people have accumulated records of ecological knowledge, including climatic and weather observations, which potentially can fill gaps in the climate data on seasonal changes for tropical northern Australia. Indeed, the Australian Bureau of Meteorology operates an online Indigenous Weather Knowledge Project which makes three weather calendars available for Indigenous communities. Green *et al.* (2010: 351) maintain that "Indigenous knowledge may well be one of the keys in understanding how best to engage in culturally appropriate climate change adaptations for these communities."

Case study 6: the indigenous US Southwest

Historically, the US Southwest reflects a climate–society pattern described in Chapter 3, namely that as complex social systems, under growing pressure from a changing set of climate and environmental conditions, lose their resiliency and fall apart, lower-density population groups, organized into simpler social arrangements, may continue to survive in the shadow of the collapsed society. In the case of the contemporary Native American peoples of the Southwest, John Hack (1942: 76) reported:

> It is well known that throughout the Plateau Country numerous ruins and works of the agricultural Pueblo testify to the former presence of a large population in regions which can scarcely support a widely scattered and dispersed semi-nomadic populations of Navahos, Apaches and Paiutes.

As the effects of anthropogenic climate change have begun to take hold, the Southwest is one of the regions in the US that is being hit the hardest, presenting a significant threat to the indigenous peoples of the region.

There are over 70 federally recognized Indian tribes living in the arid Southwest, a region that averages less than 25.5cm of rainfall annually, making water a scarce resource. As Justice William Brennan wrote in a decision by the Supreme Court: "It is probable that no problem of the Southwest section of the nation is more critical than that of scarcity of water" (Brennan 1976). While similar to other indigenous peoples, Native Americans in the Southwest have contributed very little to the causes of global warming, for geographic and political economic reasons, especially involving issues of water availability, they stand to suffer disproportionately from the negative effects of global warming (Krakoff 2008).

Richard Seager, a climate scientist at Columbia University's Lamont-Doherty Earth Observatory, and a specialist on climate factors in the Southwestern US, sees the area as having entered into a period of "permanent drought" on a par with the Dust Bowl of the 1930s, given global warming patterns now underway (Seager *et al.* 2007). Drought in the Southwest has been "an on-and-off affair for two decades, but since around 1996 it has been more or less constant, and the past five years have seen several of the hottest average temperatures on record" (Institute for Tribal Environmental Professionals 2008). According to Seager, the Southwest is dry because, like other parts of the so-called subtropics to the north and south of the equatorial tropics, the atmospheric flow tends to move far more moisture out of the region than the amounts that storms bring into it. Now, with increasing concentrations of heat-trapping greenhouse gases, the planet's atmosphere will retain even more moisture as it warms. Evaporation from lakes and rivers is likely to increase, soil is expected to become more arid, and plants will shed more moisture directly to the atmosphere.

Joseph Romm (2011), a physicist who edits the blog *ClimateProgress.org*, notes that in the past such conditions would be called desertification, but realized that "Dustbowlification" is a more accurate and vivid label for what is happening. With 2 million people displaced, the Dust Bowl of the 1930s was probably the worst environmental disaster in US history until now. Existing computer simulation projections suggest that deadly Dust Bowl conditions could stretch from Kansas to California by the middle of the twenty-first century (Seager *et al.* 2007). Research by Margaret Hiza Redsteer on sand dunes on the Navajo Nation in Arizona and New Mexico, for example, has found temperatures and plant evapotranspiration rates are rising, blowing dust is increasing, sand dunes are growing, and wells are drying up (Institute for Tribal Environmental Professionals 2008).

Although trained as a geologist, Redsteer, who has lived in the Navajo Nation, began to record accounts of Navajo elders about their experiences of the changing climate. She reports:

> The elders often talk about the difference in grass, how tall, how thick, how much of it there used to be. Some people say when they were young and herding sheep they had to stay right with the herd. If they didn't the sheep would get lost in the grass. It's not like that now. . . . The elders' memories can give us information that the physical records can't. They give a much better picture of what the ecological changes have been. For example, people talk about how, in the winter, the snow was chest high on the horses. They talk about using particular streams for irrigation of crops, but many of those aren't even flowing now.
>
> *Venton 2012*

Redsteer is impressed with how well the oral history accounts she has collected match with available meteorological data. With over 100 interviews completed, she finds that people who live in the same area tend to be consistent about past environmental conditions. She also notes that the drying climate is already affecting the subsistence patterns of the Navajo:

> A lot of people have already moved away from having livestock. There is just no water for them; there is no feed. And to haul hay to the reservation all the time is really expensive. You're often making a poor living or losing money in the deal. People have some livestock now, just not very many, and mostly for ceremonial purposes.
>
> *Venton 2012*

Notably, Redsteer finds that the Navajo she interviews, like some other indigenous peoples that have been studied, blame themselves for the adverse environmental changes they are witnessing. The changes, they say, are the result of Navajo becoming Westernized, driving cars, participating in wage employment, not taking care of the land, and not maintaining traditional rituals.

Research by the National Wildlife Federation has concluded that overall in the US, it is Native American people who are currently the most impacted by climate change. The study, entitled *Facing the Storm: Indian Tribes, Climate-Induced Weather Extremes, and the Future for Indian Country* (Curry *et al.* 2011) paints a rather dire picture for many Indian populations in the Southwest. Native American vulnerability, the report notes, rests on several factors, including: (1) their generally subordinate position in the wider society; (2) poverty and high rates of unemployment; (3) physical and cultural dependence on the land (especially reservation populations); and (4) lack of resources for adequate preparedness for environmental disasters. The report cites recent examples of Apache forests threatened by fires, Hopi villages battling floods, and extreme snowstorms stranding thousands of Navajo.

One of the critical issues facing indigenous peoples in the American Southwest is the fact that even though their presence long preceded other populations that have moved to the region, they have not been granted seniority rights to water. The rapid Euro-American settlement of the area in the nineteenth and twentieth centuries and the need for water to develop the region outpaced the ability or the willingness of state authorities to confirm Indian water rights through adjudication. As a result, others have control of the water flow in the Southwest to the detriment of indigenous peoples during a time of growing drought. According to Nikke Alex, a Navajo environmental activist with the Navajo Green Jobs and the Black Mesa Water Coalition:

> It's only going to get worse, and we don't have a plan. . . . We're talking about carbon sequestration, natural gas and cap-and-trade as our solutions to our environmental problems. Those are not real solutions. . . . [In my hometown of Dilkon], [t]hey're talking about building a hospital. . . . We don't have enough water for a Laundromat. How are we going to build a hospital? We've always been able to adapt. . . . That's why this whole topic drives me so crazy. We should be leading, developing our own solutions instead of waiting for answers from the mainstream.
>
> *quoted in Yurth 2011*

One of the places where home-grown responses to climate change are occurring among Indian peoples in the Southwest is on the lands of the Mescalero Apache Tribe. The Mescalero Apache reservation is located in southern New Mexico on 187,370ha of ancestral land. This land, brought to national attention by the exploits of Geronimo in a resistance struggle against US domination, has begun to feel the impacts of anthropogenic climate change, including a slide toward warmer and drier weather, shorter winters, longer summers, increasing frequency of wildfires, and a shrinking of the mountain alpine ecosystem. Efforts on tribal land to address climate change have included removal of invasive tree species like Chinese elm to support watershed restoration while providing firewood for elder tribal members, thinning of biomass to control wildfires, replacement of old wood-burning heaters and stoves with energy-efficient woodstoves, construction of a solar-powered water pump to move water from a storage pond to the community garden and animal farm (which allows a reduction in off-reservation vehicular trips to grocery stores) and solar-powered lighting in the tribal hatchery, development of a recycling program for cardboard, plastics, white paper, and various metals, use of native, drought-tolerant plants for landscaping, and the investigation of establishing a wind turbine installation as a source of clean renewable energy (Montoya 2013).

Parallel developments have also been initiated at Jemez Pueblo, in Sandoval County, New Mexico. Given its location, and the availability of 310 sunny days a year on average, Jemez Pueblo is in the process of developing a 4MW solar power plant with almost 15,000 solar panels on 12ha of reservation land. The plant will not only supply the Pueblo with power, but will generate trial funding for other projects through the sale of energy to outside customers. Jemez Pueblo is also exploring the possibility of developing its geothermal capacity. In collaboration with Los Alamos National Laboratory and several universities, it is investigating underground geothermal water resources that could be used to power greenhouse agricultural operations, heating systems, and a commercial spa (Sommer 2011).

The *Native Communities and Climate Change* report (Hanna 2007) made several recommendations to Congress to lessen the adverse impacts of climate change on Native American populations that have relevance for climate-impacted indigenous peoples of the Southwest. The first of these concerns issues of participation and tribal input. Specifically, the report urges that Congress should convene congressional hearings to gather information from tribes before enacting climate change-related legislation that will affect indigenous peoples. Additionally, the report argues that before Congress expands the administrative capacity for responding to climate change, it should establish dependable channels of communication with Indian tribes and their representatives so that tribal nations can be involved in the process of formulating meaningful climate policy. Further, the report recommends that Congress generate the revenue needed to assist tribes to adapt to climate change impacts as well as mitigation efforts. Finally, the report stresses the importance of federal investment in the development of alternative energy capacity on tribal lands. Wind and solar capacity would appear to be potential sources of energy on Southwestern tribal lands. As noted in the next case study, however, all of the recommendations of the *Native Communities and Climate Change* report have been blocked by the organized efforts of climate change deniers.

Case study 7: responses to climate change in developed societies

In contrast to the United States and Australia—countries with a large number of climate skeptics—people in Scandinavian countries generally acknowledge the gravity of anthropogenic climate change. In the case of Sweden, the government, industry, and many citizens view a program of ecological modernization as the best strategy for mitigating climate change (Graham 2015). As nature lovers, many Swedes view themselves as "green" and environmentally aware. Based upon interviews and ethnography among residents in Hammarby Sjoestan, Mark Graham made a number of revealing observations:

- Some informants expressed a faith in technological solutions or believed that they are imminent.
- Many informants had difficulty distinguishing between the *Merkwelt*, the world that they perceive, and the *Wirkwelt*, the impact of their actions. They frequently conflated environmental concerns, such as resource depletion and recycling, with climate change.

- Whereas some informants became upset by the felling of a few trees in the city, particularly in their middle-class neighborhood, they did not raise objections to the felling of Swedish primordial forest.
- Most informants did not express concern about the impact of the culture of consumption on climate change.

While the Swedish government continues to express faith in the economic growth paradigm, the failure of international climate change negotiations and agreements and the reality of resource depletion has prompted some Swedes to "shift attention closer to home and to local initiatives, including the emergence of a Transition movement in Sweden inspired by developments abroad" (Graham 2015: 245).

Geoengineering is a strategy related to ecological modernization which has found popularity with business leaders (such as Bill Gates and Richard Branson), governments, and policy advisors, as other efforts to mitigate greenhouse gas emissions, such a climate regimes and agreements, have generally failed to have a profound impact. Anthropologist Jonathan Marshall (2015: 253) reports:

> Geoengineering and other imagined technology are promoted as stabilisers for established cultural/economic ordering systems, particularly so in Australia. While the Australian Governments' 2012 Energy White Paper does not mention SRM [solar radiation management], it uses Australian treasury modelling describing how Australia will reduce its carbon emissions that are largely based upon imagined technology.

A popular imagined or geoengineering technology in Australia is carbon capture and storage (CCS). The University of Melbourne houses the Peter Cook Centre for Carbon Capture and Storage Research, which has a partnership with the Cooperative Research Centre for Greenhouse Gas Technologies, Rio Tinto, and the Victorian Government Department of State Development, Business and Innovation (Baer and Gallois 2016: 9). In practice, the coal mining industry spends a miniscule proportion of its revenue on CCS research. CCS is still an unproven technology that will supposedly capture CO_2 and inject it into the ground, or even the ocean, or possibly store it in old oil reservoirs or coal mines. If ever achieved on a mass scale, it would probably increase the price of electricity generation and reduce energy efficiency, in that it would require additional energy. Furthermore, there may not be a sufficient number of leak-proof sites around the globe to store large amounts of ever-increasing carbon. Geoengineering, including CCS, as Marshall (2015: 260) astutely observes, "appears to preserve the free-market culture complex of habits, powers, and certainties (even though it may disrupt them), while currently suppressing creative alternatives and aiming to discredit shadow groups."

Case study 8: climate scientists and climate change denialists

At this point in the social history of climate perspectives, it would be accurate to say that the formation of public understanding and attitudes about climate change is to some degree a product of an intense clash between the views of almost all climate scientists and a set of individuals and organizations who either deny global warming is occurring or dispute the human role as a key driver of the process. As Crate and Nuttall (2009b: 398) note in the epilogue of their book: "Climate change science contributes to the process of consensus decision-making, informing what people come to think about what is 'real' about the world and how it is changing." However, science does not tend to reach the public directly, but is filtered through the media (and sometimes through governmental bodies), which identifies storylines, accentuates particular issues, and constructs a narrative, often relying on a presumed mandate to offer a range of perspectives. In his analysis of scientific communicability, anthropologist Charles Briggs (2011) emphasizes the social and political nature of knowledge circulation involving experts, media, and public audiences. For example, while climate scientists thoroughly review and integrate the ever-growing body of scientific literature that constitutes the state of climate science knowledge in IPCC reports, the 30-page summary of the regularly released report for policy-makers is negotiated with government representatives who have their own political agendas.

In terms of the general audiences, broad agreements among climate scientists often reach the public in muted or conflicted form, diminishing focus on the urgency of scientific findings or steering action to the individual level (e.g., shutting off lights, using more efficient light bulbs). For example, in *TED Talks*, a speaker series sponsored by the Sapling Foundation, a private non-profit foundation initiated by magazine publisher Chris Anderson, James Hansen (2012b), a leading NASA climate scientist, reported that the current increase in global warming is "equivalent to exploding 400,000 Hiroshima atomic bombs per day 365 days per year." While this understanding and the profound implications it has for climate turmoil might be expected to generate intense public outcry for immediate, extensive, and effective changes in business-as-usual activities, this has not been the case. In the words of sociologist Ulrich Beck (2010: 254):

> Why is there no storming of the Bastille because of the environmental destruction threatening mankind, why no Red October of ecology? Why have the most pressing issues of our time—climate change and ecological crisis—not been met with the same enthusiasm, energy, optimism, ideals and forward-looking democratic spirit as the past tragedies of poverty, tyranny and war?

In part, this has not occurred because there are ardent opponents—most commonly not climate scientists—who vigorously reject the findings and conclusions of climate scientists. The terms "climate change skeptic" and "climate change denier" have been used to label those who seek, evidence aside, to label climate change knowledge as a hoax and climate scientists as conspirators who desire only to benefit from climate change research funding (Anderegg, Prall, and Harold 2010; Anderegg, Prall, Harold, and Schneider 2010). Those who embrace these ideas tend to reflect a broad environmental skepticism that "encompasses several themes, but denial of the authenticity of environmental problems, particularly problems such as bio-diversity loss or climate change that threaten ecological sustainability, is its defining feature" (Jacques *et al.* 2008).

The key features of climate change denial are that (1) it is led by a coordinated movement (and hence is planned and organized rather than a polycentric grassroots initiative); (2) it seeks to defend a threatened ideology (e.g., the belief that capitalism is not only a productive economic system, but is characterized by a moral and beneficent agenda); (3) the funding and organizational origins of the movement are largely hidden; and (4) it seeks to sow confusion in the media and among policy-makers and in the general public (Antilla 2005; Boykoff and Boykoff 2004). Although a survey of 1,372 climate scientists conducted by the US National Academy of Sciences found that 97–98 percent of them accept the IPCC's con-tention that recent climate change is largely anthropogenic, reflecting an unusually high level of agreement among scientists, climate deniers have clung to a set of disinformation objectives and have continued to gain "great visibility in the media, particularly after the climate summit in Copenhagen" in 2009 (Wijkman and Rockström 2011: 87–88).

Another aspect of climate change denial discourse merits mention: here we refer to the strong tendency to posit the existence of colossal conspiracies and grand hoaxes perpetrated by those who express concern about global warming. In "exposing" such diabolical intrigues, deniers routinely employ ad hominem attacks and direct considerable scorn at the individuals they see as leaders of insidious campaigns of deception. As a result of her role in helping to bring together the 1975 conference titled *The Atmosphere: Endangered and Endangering*, discussed in Chapter 2, for example, anthropologist Margaret Mead came under fire from climate change denier Marjorie Mazel Hecht (2007), also known for her factually challenged assertion that there is no such thing as nuclear waste (Hecht 2004). The acerbic tone of Hecht's (2007: 64) criticism surfaces quickly in her haggard claim that Mead's book *Coming of Age in Samoa* (1943 [1928]) "was later found to be a fraud." Hecht (2007: 64) goes on to attack the conference Mead helped organize by saying it was where "virtually every scare scenario in today's climate hoax took root." Based on Mead's voiced concern about the growing size of the human population (which has gone from 4 billion when the conference was held to over 7 billion today), and as a result placing significant demands on Earth's resources, Hecht (2007: 64) dishonestly alleges that "Mead's population-control policy was firmly based in the post-Hitler eugenics movement." As for Mead's opening speech at the conference, Hecht (2007: 65) maintains that it was "a naked solicitation of lying formulations to justify an end to human scientific and industrial progress." In her ultimate condemnation, Hecht charges Mead, because of her public commentary on social issues, with playing a "central role" in the growing degeneration of Western society. In short, what Hecht seeks to do is to confirm the existence of a conspiracy by locating the purported birthplace of what she sees as a vast and threatening climate change hoax, even if all that can be pointed to is a well-documented public conference which, as is typical of scientific meetings, was characterized by considerable disagreement among participants.

Ultimately, the attack on climate change science and scientists, as Jacques (2012: 11) argues, is driven by the fact that:

> climate change science provides an imminent critique of industrial power, Western modernity, and the ideals of Western progress, just as the study of ecology was at first seen as a "subversive" force because, if it were taken seriously, it would challenge the central workings of "modern" society.

More precisely, taken seriously, the findings of climate and other physical and social sciences on the dangerous trends in greenhouse gas emissions, black carbon, climate feedback loops and thresholds, and the tumultuous effects of global warming challenge the sustainability of the reigning capitalist world system. Hence finding some way to refute climate science is driven by deep-seated ideological commitments.

The ideological center of the climate change denier movement consists of a set of politically conservative think tanks and public policy advocacy organizations, entities that tend to champion the virtues of a market economy and free enterprise (including neoliberalism internationally), private property rights, limitations on government size and action, and a strong and globally active military. With regard to environmental issues, these organizations attempt to cast doubt on the seriousness of environmental problems of all sorts, view environmental concerns voiced by scientists as consisting of "questionable science, over-stated science, poorly reported science, and unwarranted statements by scientists themselves" (Michaels 2004: 5), reject policies that are designed to improve or protect the environment, oppose enforcing corporate liability for environmental damages, and see environmental protection as threatening economic progress (Jacques *et al.* 2008). Consequently, in an interview carried out by anthropologist Peter Little (2011), climate scientist Richard Somerville notes that:

> in climate science we are fighting a serious professional and well-funded disinformation campaign. It is exactly analogous to the tobacco wars where the tobacco industry funded contrarian scientists to stir in doubt and sow confusion to convince the world that the science connecting tobacco and disease was not settled. In the global climate change issue, which you know is a highly politicized topic, of course there are scientific things that still have to be studied and researched and learned about, but there is, and has been for a long time, in the expert community, an enormous degree of consensus on the big picture, on the main facts.

Moreover, Somerville (in Little 2011) notes:

> instead of saying I oppose carbon taxes or I oppose international treaties restricting emissions or I oppose government interference with free markets

or I oppose regulation by the EPA [Environmental Protection Agency], such people will instead often choose to attack the science and the scientists. That is crystal clear. I think that is very regrettable. It is really very regrettable. Yet you see it every day. You see it in the media, you see it in Congress, and you see it in many other places.

Exemplary of this pattern of targeting the messenger have been the personal attacks experienced by climate scientist Benjamin Santer of the Lawrence Livermore Laboratory. Because of his contributions affirming the existence of a greenhouse effect, which contributed to his being awarded a MacArthur "genius grant," Santer was selected to be the high-profile lead author of a chapter of the 1995 IPCC report. Shortly after the issuance of the report, which said that the balance of scientific evidence points to a discernible human influence on global climate patterns, an energy industry-funded group launched a campaign to discredit Santer personally by falsely claiming that he had altered the IPCC's findings (as discussed further below). Shulman (2010), who interviewed him, reports that Santer explained that:

Nothing in my university training prepared me for what I faced in the aftermath of that report. . . . You are prepared as a scientist to defend your research. But I was not prepared to defend my personal integrity. I never imagined I'd have to do that.

Since then, Santer has continued to be singled out for personal attacks by climate change deniers. He commonly receives hate mail. His were among the emails that were hacked when climate change deniers, individuals Santer calls the "forces of unreason," broke into the computer system at East Anglia University in the UK and afterward attempted to misrepresent what they found (e.g., through false claims that they had uncovered evidence of efforts designed to suppress data that did not support a global warming perspective).

The conservative think tanks, policy institutes, coalitions—groups like the George Marshall Institute, the Oregon Institute of Science and Medicine, Science and Environmental Policy Project, and the Global Climate Coalition (Baer 2012)—that have been the source of most climate change contrarianism and hostility toward climate scientists have been able to establish themselves in the eyes of the media, and in the view of some policy-makers, as "independent experts and . . . are often preferred to representatives from universities and interest groups as a source of expert opinion" (Beder 2001: 129). Yet, as Allen (1992: 90) observes, conservative think tanks "are professional social movement organisations that have been sponsored by economic elites as a means of influencing public opinion and the agendas of political elites." In other words, the independent nature of such entities is open to question.

As part of her study of climate change deniers, Lahsen (1999; 2008b) examined how Fredrick Seitz orchestrated a campaign against the IPCC on the grounds, noted above, that it had allegedly made unjustified revisions in 1995 between the draft and the final version of Chapter 8 of the 1995 IPCC report, a chapter which assessed whether observed climate changes resulted from human activities (Lahsen 1999: 112). Seitz, who served as chairperson of the Marshall Institute (which, as indicated, is a conservative think tank located in Washington, DC), earned a PhD in physics from Princeton University, and wrote a seminal book on solid-state physics and material physics. He held a number of significant positions, including becoming in 1965 the first full-time President of the National Academy of Sciences. However, Seitz also assisted in directing the health research effort sponsored by R. J. Reynolds Industries, a tobacco corporation, that sought to "create scientific legitimacy for skepticism regarding evidence of adverse health effects of smoking" (Lahsen 2008a: 209). Seitz accused the IPCC in a 1996 letter to the *Wall Street Journal* titled "A Major Deception on Global Warming" of deleting any reference to skepticism on the issue of anthropogenic climate change from its Second Assessment report. As Lahsen (1999: 112) observes:

> Suggestive of his social concerns and values, Seitz feared that policymakers would act to reduce greenhouse-gas emissions based on the IPCC report, something that he assumed to have "an enormous impact on U.S. oil and gas prices" and an "almost certainly destructive impact on the economies of the world."

Notably, scientists like Seitz, many of whom are not actually climate scientists per se, have exerted great influence in the climate debate in the United States, "despite the fact that they constitute a group of less than ten" individuals (Lahsen 1999: 113). S. Fred Singer, a solar physicist (who is unrelated to Merrill Singer), would be included in this small group of contrarian scientists. Lahsen (1999: 125) reports:

> Concerned to disseminate his views, Singer, like other contrarians, has established ties with groups of the political and religious Right in U.S. society. Singer has received material support from a conservative religious group led by Reverend Sun Yung Moon [the Unification church] which since the early 1980s has worked to build organizations promoting far right-wing politics. He has become a key organizer for scientists skeptical of the theory of human-induced climate change, often orchestrating letter-writing and petition campaigns against remedial action on behalf of human-induced climate change.

In a later essay, Lahsen focused on the views and activities of three prominent American climate denialists, namely Fredrick Seitz, Robert Jastrow, and William Nierenberg. The trio have long been associated with the Marshall Institute (Lahsen 2008b). In 1998, Seitz played a key role in gathering over 17,000 signatures (many of which were later shown to be from non-existent individuals) in a petition urging the US government to reject the Kyoto Protocol. Robert Jastrow, who had served as a president of the Marshall Institute, earned a PhD in physics, with specialties in astronomy and astrophysics, from Columbia University, worked for a while at the

Institute of Advanced Study in Princeton, New Jersey, as well as for many years at NASA's Goddard Institute for Space Science, and also taught at Dartmouth College. William Nierenberg was affiliated with the Marshall Institute until his death in 2000. He earned a PhD in physics from Columbia University and worked on the Manhattan Project between 1942 and 1945. While working on his PhD, Nierenberg held numerous prestigious positions, including replacing Seitz as Science Advisor to NATO in 1960. He also served as director of the Scripps Institute of Oceanography in California. Lahsen (2008b: 210) observes:

> The Marshall Institute physicists enjoyed great privilege during the first several decades of their professional careers in terms of the status, influence, and funding. An important aspect of the U.S. postwar social contract with science was the presence of scientists as advisors in the inner circles of political decision-making. . . . The trio was part of a small group of nuclear scientists which dominated the science-government interface in the U.S. for most of the twentieth century.

However, in the 1970s the environmental and peace movements challenged nuclear technology on the grounds that it posed a threat to humanity and the planet. As a consequence, a split developed in the US scientific community between scientists with close ties to the military-industrial complex and those involved in impact sciences (such as the impact of human activities on the environment) and production sciences, which apply engineering, economics, physics, and chemistry in the production of an array of things. Lahsen (2008b: 210–211) comments:

> the Marshall Institute physicists maintain a level of faith in science and technology not shared by their opponents on the issues of nuclear technology and climate change. The Marshall Institute scientists are generally not receptive to the survival discourse—at least as applied to climate change and other new environmental problems. Their discourses generally reveal a pre-reflexive modernist ethos characterized by strong trust in science and technology as providers of solutions to problems, whether environmental, social, or economic, an understanding of science and progress that prevailed during the first half of the 20th century.

A final issue of concern with regard to climate change denial concerns its sources of funding. The lack of independence of opponents of climate change science is made clear by an examination of the funding sources that back climate change denial. Three in particular merit mention because of the scale of their contribution to climate change denial: ExxonMobil, the Koch brothers, and Donors Trust. The first of these, the major energy corporation ExxonMobil, is "the biggest player in the world's gas and oil business, [and] also one of the world's largest producers of global warming pollution" (Union of Concerned Scientists 2007: 4). As documented by the Union of Concerned Scientists, during the 1990s ExxonMobil began funding and coordinating a concerted campaign of climate change denial that has multiple parallels (and overlapping personnel) with the now thoroughly discredited campaign by the tobacco industry to deny the link between smoking and cancer. The ExxonMobil effort included the following components: first, the corporation bankrolled established groups like the American Enterprise Institute, the Competitive Enterprise Institute, and the Cato Institute to aggressively oppose mandatory regulatory action on global warming as well as other environmental standards. Second, ExxonMobil supported an intertwined network of lesser-known organizations (with overlapping memberships) that distribute global warming disinformation to the media and other outlets intended to generate climate uncertainty in the general public. Third, ExxonMobil used its considerable economic resources to support a small number of scientific spokespeople who deny global warming or the human role therein, and to recruit new scientific voices to the denial perspective. Fourth, ExxonMobil pushed to shift the public debate from a focus on mitigating greenhouse gas emissions to a discussion of the need for what it calls "sound science" based on the establishment of complete certainty before any ameliorative action is taken by society (based on a misconstrued notion of certainty in science). Finally, ExxonMobil has engaged in lobbying (and campaign contributions) targeted at politicians in an effort to gain favorable policies or block action on greenhouse gas regulation. Through these well-funded tactics, ExxonMobil helped to block public recognition of both the extent not only of scientific evidence showing the occurrence of anthropologic climate change but also of the cost consequences for human communities and other species of a warming planet.

In 2010, Greenpeace issued a report entitled *Koch Industries: Secretly Funding the Climate Denial Machine*, which identified Koch Industries, an oil corporation that is the second largest privately owned company in America (and also a company with a particularly bad environmental record), as a "kingpin of climate science denial and clean energy opposition" (Greenpeace 2010: 6). The report showed that, from 2005 to 2008, the Koch brothers, Charles and David, vastly outspent ExxonMobil in giving money to organizations fighting legislation related to climate change, funding a sizeable network of foundations, think tanks, and political front groups that deny global warming. The Koch brothers, the report and subsequent Greenpeace research shows, have contributed $67 million to climate change denial organizations since 1997.

The Kansas-based Koch Industries includes oil refineries in Alaska, Texas, and Minnesota, including control of at least 6,440km of pipeline. Additionally, Koch Industries owns Brawny paper towels, Dixie cups, Georgia-Pacific lumber, Stainmaster carpet, and Lycra (clothing), among other commodities. The combined fortune of the Koch brothers is estimated to be $35 billion, and in the United States is exceeded only by those of Bill Gates and Warren Buffett. In late 2000, the company was charged with covering up the illegal releases of 91 tons of the known carcinogen benzene from its refinery in Corpus Christi, Texas. Initially facing a 97-count indictment and potential fines of $350 million, Koch cut a deal with then-Attorney General John Ashcroft to drop all major charges in exchange for a guilty plea for falsifying documents, and a $20 million settlement. A number of the far-flung Koch-owned enterprises have repeatedly violated environmental and other laws in the United States as well as elsewhere in the world, and they have been fined hundreds of millions of dollars for some of their offenses, although the fines have been miniscule compared to Koch Industries' profits (Lewis *et al.* 2013). According to Environmental Protection Agency statistics, Koch Industries is a major source of CO_2 emissions. In 2011, the EPA's greenhouse gas-reporting database shows that the company's oil refineries emitted over 24 million tons of CO_2, an amount typically emitted by 5 million cars (Mayer 2013). Charles Lewis, the founder of the Center for Public Integrity, a non-partisan watchdog group, has said:

> The Kochs are on a whole different level. There's no one else who has spent this much money. The sheer dimension of it is what sets them apart. They have a pattern of lawbreaking, political manipulation, and obfuscation. I've been in Washington since Watergate, and I've never seen anything like it. They are the Standard Oil of our times.
>
> *quoted in Oil Watchdog 2012*

The footprint of the Koch brothers on energy and related issues in the United States is noticeably large. The Koch brothers-backed conservative political activist organization the American Legislative Exchange Council (ALEC), has taken a lead in efforts to repeal or weaken the renewable energy portfolio standards (RPS) in many of the states that have them (Bull 2013). An RPS is a regulation that requires that increased production of energy by an energy producer come from renewable sources, such as wind, solar, biomass, and geothermal. Additionally, in 2011 and 2012, Koch Industries Public Sector LLC, the lobbying arm of Koch Industries, advocated for the Energy Tax Prevention Act, which would have rolled back the Supreme Court's ruling that the Environmental Protection Agency did have the authority to regulate greenhouse gases. At hearings about the bill called by the House Energy and Commerce Committee, Margo Thorning, an economist with the Koch-funded American Council for Capital Formation, testified that the regulation of greenhouse gas emissions "makes little economic or environmental sense" (quoted in Lewis *et al.* 2013). Thorning is just one of many representatives from Koch-funded organizations who regularly testify before Congress on energy issues. Moreover, a two-year study by American University's Investigative Reporting Workshop reported that through the efforts of one of the conservative organizations the Koch brothers fund, Americans for Prosperity, they have succeeded in persuading numerous members of Congress, as part of a total of 411 public office holders, to sign a pledge to vote against any legislation relating to climate change unless it is accompanied by an equivalent amount of tax cuts. As most viable solutions to the problem of greenhouse gas emissions require costs to the polluters and the public (e.g., for anti-polluting retooling), the pledge in effect commits those who sign to it to vote against almost any meaningful bill designed to mitigate global warning. This effort is tied to the broader Koch effort to fund ultra-conservative Republican candidates for public office. Thus, of the 85 freshman Republican congressmen elected in 2010, almost 90 percent have signed the pledge (Mayer 2013). The result has been a nearly complete inability to pass climate change mitigation legislation in the United States.

Despite their focused efforts, it has now become clear that the Koch brothers are not, in fact, the biggest (nor the most hidden) financial backers of climate change denial. In investigative journalism work, the British newspaper the *Guardian* has revealed the existence of a secret funding route, called Donors Trust, for very conservative and very wealthy British citizens to funnel money (approximately $120 million thus far) to over 100 anti-climate-change think tanks in the United States. Journalist Suzanne Goldenberg (2013) indicates that the funds distributed between 2002 and 2010 helped to build and support a broad network of think tanks and media activist organizations focused on redefining "climate change from neutral scientific fact to a highly polarising 'wedge issue' for hardcore conservatives." The funds are targeted toward promoting organizations working to discredit climate science or block climate action. The actual donors have been kept secret, leading the *Guardian* to label their donations "dark money." As these three sources of climate change funding (among various others also engaged in a concerted effort to keep understanding of global warming uncertain and controversial) reveal, the stakes are high, underscoring all the more the degree of success of climate scientists in keeping the issue before the public, as well as the responsibility of anthropologists to help build a popularly accessible social science of climate change.

Overall, Lahsen (1999: 133–134) concludes that climate contrarians constitute yet one more example of a long American tradition of conspiracy theories which "amount to little more than rhetorical means by which to cast suspicion on scientific and political opponents."

Ironically, climate science has been challenged not only by a few conservative physicists but also, on other grounds, by generally politically progressive scientists in the developing world. In the late 1990s, Lahsen interviewed a prominent US climate science administrator in a federal agency in Washington, DC. This administrator played a key role in creating the Inter-American Institute (IAI), a Brazil-based international organization committed to fostering international scientific cooperation and communication in understanding "goal change phenomena and their socio-economic implications" (quoted in Lahsen 2007b: 179). Ironically, he learned to his dismay that his Latin American colleagues suspected that IAI "served to advance US geopolitical interests" (Lahsen 2007b: 179). This experience has created a sensitivity to the political and economic agendas driving US government-supported initiatives.

It should be noted that the IPCC, while not a US initiative per se, is a contradictory body in that, on the one hand, it brings together strong evidence that anthropogenic climate change constitutes a serious problem that needs to be addressed, but on the other hand, as Larry Lohmann (2006: 36) observes, it "has helped shape climate problems and solutions in such ways that make them more acceptable to powerful governments and corporations." One of the glaring shortcomings of the IPCC is the underrepresentation of authors from developing countries; the IPCC's Fourth Assessment Report was written by 393 authors from OECD countries and 198 from non-OECD countries. While OECD countries include some higher-level developing countries such as Mexico, overall the developed world has a higher proportional representation on the IPCC than does the developing world, as is indicated by the fact that "some developing countries . . . do not send delegates for meetings of the panel" due to a shortage of funds (Barnett and Campbell 2010: 61).

In a similar vein, based upon interviews in Brazil, Lahsen (2007b: 182) reports that "decision makers expressed suspicion that the GEF [the World Bank's Global Environmental Facility] directs science agendas in LDCs [less-developed countries] in ways that favor Northern donor countries' policy preferences while weakening the Brazilian government's control over national climate affairs." One Brazilian decision-maker expressed the need for a Brazilian contribution to climate modeling in making a satisfactory national impact assessment in order to avoid a scenario in which his country would have to rely on foreign climate models. Lahsen (2007b: 182) argues that "resource disparities reduce the effectiveness of international efforts to assess and combat human-induced climate change." Moreover, Lahsen (2004: 161) found that Brazilian climate scientists often distrust the IPCC and other international scientific institutions, which "they describe as dominated by Northern framings of the problems and therefore biased against the interpretations and interests of the South." Furthermore, some key persons affiliated with the Brazilian Ministry of External Relations suspect that the IPCC and the Large-Scale Biosphere project, an international scientific effort to assess how activities in the Amazon Basin influence climate change, tend to overestimate the amount of CO_2 emissions emanating from deforestation in that region (Lahsen 2004: 164). Despite its members' best intentions to mitigate climate change, the IPCC as a scientific and policy advisory body has not been able to effectively influence corporations or government bodies to seriously curtail the increase in greenhouse gas emissions associated with the capitalist treadmill of production and consumption. As Luke (2008: 142) observes:

> The growing number of scientific studies heighten awareness of climate change, yet it is rarely stemmed. The existing inequality of commodity production and consumption spills over into new inequalities in commodity by-production and consumer choicelessness, because technoscience is left only to scrupulously document additional biospheric losses. However, it cannot easily change how loss is incurred.

In a subsequent ethnographic study in Brazil, Lahsen (2009) examined sharp conflicts between Brazilian climate scientists and policy decision-makers over the question of whether or not the Amazon rainforest is a carbon sink that removes CO_2 from the atmosphere and hence helps to limit global warming. While Brazilian climate scientists, with an eye toward forest conservation, asserted the importance of the Amazon as a carbon sink, policy-makers with authority over the country's positions in international climate negotiations involving the Kyoto Protocol disputed this assertion, resulting in struggles over how the issue would be presented to the Brazilian people through the media. Lahsen sought to explore the nature of this conflict and the interpretations made by each side of the available climate science evidence. Reflected in this clash is the suspicion of policy-makers that science is a force through which wealthy countries maintain dominance over underdeveloped and developing nations. This perspective is buoyed by recognition that many of the climate scientists received their scientific education outside Brazil in wealthy nations and continue to have strong connections with foreign interests through participation in scientific organizations, conferences, and collaborations. This reaction, she argues, reflects a historic insular and centralized approach to decision-making in Brazil relative to climate change. As this case suggests, policy-maker attitudes about climate science may not be based on the quality of the evidence being presented, but by deep-rooted cultural patterns and politically influenced ideas about the scientific producers of climate change knowledge. Further, the study reveals some of "the limits of science and of its ability to engender change in political affairs" regarding climate change response (Lahsen 2009: 365).

Some climate scientists in developed countries, such as James Hansen in the United States, Hans Schellnhuber in Germany, and A. Barrie Pittock in Australia, project climate change scenarios that are more radical than those generally presented by the IPCC. For example, Martin Skrydstrup (2009: 340) attended a climate conference in March 2009 at the Bella Centre in Copenhagen at which Stefan Rahmstorf, a climate scientist at the Potsdam Institute for Climate Impact Research, asserted that the IPCC predicted sea level rises of 18–59cm over the next 1,000 years "only included the thermal expansion of the oceans and did not include the full effects of the melting glaciers and continental ice sheets" because of allegedly insufficient scientific evidence about them. Hans Schellnhuber, the founding director of the Potsdam Institute and the Chief Advisor to the German Government at the COP (Conference of Parties) 15 conference in Copenhagen, proved to be the most critical climate scientist at the assembly, as seen in his remarks about the dangers of climate change. He argued that the IPCC expectation of a 2°C (3.6°F) increase, accepted by many climate policy decision-makers, is a timid assessment of coming increases in temperature. Schellnhuber discussed "the imaginary of a five degree [increase] world in which we would release different tipping elements, such as the melting of the ice cap of Greenland and the melting of 'the Achilles heel of this planet: the Tibetan plateau'" (Skrydstrup 2009: 347). He suggested that the resettlement of "climate refugees should be allocated according to a global distributional justice [plan]," with the United States accepting 25 percent of the world's refugees (Skrydstrup 2009: 347). Needless to say, given the number of people projected to be displaced by global warming over the next several decades, it is not likely that the United States will soon be committed to this economically just but socially challenging arrangement.

While criticism of climate science or of the IPCC has come from both conservative and progressive perspectives, the two critiques are not equivalent. While the conservative, denier movement seeks to defame climate science and scientists to wreak public confusion and avoid the implementation of government policies that hinder profit-making from unregulated production, the progressive critique is targeted, at least in part, at the interpretation of climate research in ways that favor the interests of developed over developing nations. The latter perspective raises a difficult challenge: that of how to allow the development of poorer nations without contributing further to the greenhouse gas blanket principally created by already developed nations.

From an anthropological perspective, an issue of concern is the understanding of climate science as social practice. Anthropologist Werner Krauss (2009), for example, conducted multi-sited research on the Institute for Coastal Research in Germany which involved examining everyday routines at the Institute, including reconstruction of past climates, and Institute media responses to the Elbe River bursting its banks due to heavy rains in August 2002, which some commentators regarded to be Germany's first authentic climate disaster. He describes the activities on the part of the Institute's scientists as constituting a rather frenetic and dynamic world:

> The director of the Institute, Hans von Storch, is a renowned climate researcher, who has travelled around the world, representing the Institute and participating (and initiating) debates on the global level. The activities ranged from high-water management to the hockey stick debate, from policy advising and public information to the management of the Institute. Climate and coastal research is a nervous system full of interdisciplinary and transnational projects and a wide range of research topics. . . . Regularly, the research results of the Institute were published in the media, the director gave interviews and public speeches, and there was steady output of scientific articles and papers. Scientists are also avid bloggers, and publications in *Nature* or *Science* usually spill over into the blogsphere.
>
> *Krauss 2009: 151–152*

Von Storch has proven to be a controversial figure, in that he challenged the hockey stick curve model formulated by world-renowned climate scientist Michael Mann, based at Penn State University. In contrast to climate skeptics, Von Storch did not question the blade, which depicts a rapidly rising curve in recent decades, but rather objects to "what Mann and his colleagues had interpreted as the relative constancy of climate in the last thousand years" (Krauss 2009: 157). The climate science world is one filled with contingencies and highly politicized debates, not only among the researchers themselves, but including disagreements that spill over into the larger universe of climate politics around the world. Indeed, as the eminent philosopher of science Bruno Latour (2003: 32) observes, as the work of many climate scientists illustrates:

many simulations and complex models are being tried out on huge computers, but the real experiment is happening to us, through the action of each of us [albeit certainly the privileged few more than the impoverished many], with all the oceans, high atmosphere and even the Gulf Stream—as some oceanographers argue—participating.

In a related examination of climate scientists as social actors, Lahsen (2005a) conducted participant observation over a six-year period which entailed many informal and formal conversations with climate modelers. She found that climate modelers come from an array of disciplines, particularly atmospheric science, mathematics, and physics (Lahsen 2005a: 898). Climate modelers function in a highly privileged, specialized, and competitive environment:

> The resources required to run the increasingly complex climate models are so extensive and expensive that relatively few countries and institutions can afford them. Most of these countries (for example, England, Germany, and Japan) have chosen to focus efforts on a single national model. The USA, however, has numerous modeling efforts, with no single national model. Consequently, model groups compete against each other for access to research funds from national agencies such as the US National Science Foundation, the Environmental Protection Agency, the National Oceanic and Atmospheric Administration, and the Department of Energy.
>
> *Lahsen 2005a: 898*

Lahsen maintains that while climate models are impressive achievements, they nonetheless manifest significant limitations and uncertainties. She asserts that "climate modelers' psychological and social investments in models and the social worlds of which they are part can at times reduce their critical distance from their own creations" and they "are not always willing or able to recognize weaknesses in their own models" (Lahsen 2005a: 903). Because of the highly charged political implications of their findings on climate change, climate modelers have learned to be cautious in how they present them in public forums (Lahsen 2005a: 905).

Based upon further interviews, Lahsen (2013) has delineated the following categories of positions on the part of natural scientists on anthropogenic climate change (ACC):

- Mainstream scientists who question only parts, at the most, not the theory as a whole and who tend to work in official scientific institutions, write in peer-reviewed scientific journals, and hold liberal political values.
- Mainstream skeptics who moderately question the evidence for ACC or the theory as a whole, but also work at official scientific institutions, write in peer-reviewed scientific journals, and are politically liberal.
- Contrarians who strongly or categorically deny ACC theory only in some cases work at official scientific institutions, but tend to write in non-peer-review outlets, and are politically conservative.

Lahsen (2015: 227) goes on to identify three subgroups of mainstream scientists who query ACC: (1) research meteorologists, (2) empirical climatologists, "especially older scientists who at some point in their lives worked in weather prediction," and (3) weather forecasters.

While most anthropologists examining climate change tend to accept ACC, as we do, she makes the valid point that IPCC climate scientists and social scientists are operating in different cultural universes, in that, on the one hand, social science in IPCC reports "tends to be limited to adaptation, vulnerability, and economic studies, reducing such research to human responses to changes in natural environments," and, on the other hand, for the most part "social scientists are slow and uncoordinated in responding to calls for research on specially *cultural* dimensions shaping climate science" (Lahsen 2013: 736).

Like Lahsen, who examined a middle-of-the-road group of scientists on their views of climate change, Werner Krauss (2016) has done research on middle-of-the road climate scientists, although perhaps different than the scientists in Lahsen's group, who define themselves as "climate realists" or "climate pragmatists," setting themselves apart from mainstream climate scientists, whom they view as climate alarmists or climate catastrophists. One of these climate realists is Hans von Storch, based at the University of Hamburg, who laments a purportedly "increasing tendency in climate science to link each and every event to climate change" (Krauss 2016: 416). However, our own periodic encounters with climate and atmospheric scientists do not validate this assertion, although obviously within the climate science community, as both Lahsen and Krauss note, there exist different camps and rivalries, a reality that also applies to any discipline, including anthropology (also see O'Reilly 2015). While climate scientists come in different political stripes, with most of them being liberal rather either conservative or radical, "For all its cultural capital, the climate community is surely no match for the vested interests and the power of the status quo" (Uekötter 2015: 179).

Jerome Whitington has also raised questions about climate science from an anthropological perspective. His focus is on the cultural role of quantification in the making of climate science. As Whitington (2013b) observes: "One does not need to go far in the public discourse surrounding climate change to be inundated with the mystique of number." As an anthropologist, Whitington seeks to dig beneath the extensive climate science work embodied in graphs, charts, tables, formulas, and other number-based tools to the imaginative dimensions of carbon accounting. His goal is to comprehend why numbers hold such powerful sway over possibilities for thinking about change in climate science, especially in light of the fact that "real-world changes in many cases are outpacing the [computer] modeled scenarios" (Whitington 2013a). Some of the answer lies in what it is now possible to do with numbers of diverse sorts and origins given the computational prowess of contemporary computers. Model building, so critical to climate science, has surged ahead, becoming increasingly more sophisticated and convincing. Yet, as Whitington notes, in the history of climate science, hard numbers overlay an artistry of imagination that could as easily produce the seeds of science fiction. In the words of

Gramelsberger and Feichter (2011: 9), which Whitington cites, the "scientific concept of climate [is] a mathematical construct that cannot be experienced directly." So, too, the element of hope in climate science derives not from quantification, but elsewhere in the human imaginary. Concludes Whitington (2013b):

> If apocalypse closes time by announcing the end of the world, climate science and climate politics both are oriented toward open futures in which it is possible—indeed, perhaps necessary—to reimagine contemporary forms of human living at a planetary scale.

One challenge for climate scientists is moving from complex scientific models to ways of communicating that are meaningful to laypeople and policy-makers.

Conclusion

As the case studies presented in this chapter suggest, while the anthropology of climate change is a relatively new subdiscipline within anthropology, studies already suggest the examination of the interaction of peoples and climate in several geographic zones, especially those with early or particularly accelerated patterns of change and particularly vulnerable populations. Moreover, this body of research reflects particular theoretical perspectives within climate change anthropology and the blending of perspectives in addressing certain issues. Further, certain topics, like the social world of climate scientists and the nature of climate change denialism as a social occurrence, are garnering increasing anthropological interest. In these various studies, there is support for the model presented in Chapter 1 involving the onset of climate turmoil (with differing patterns in different regions of the planet), pluralea interactions (that both complicate and worsen climate change impacts), and the importance of examining vulnerability and the factors that contribute to it or fight against it in particular populations and population segments and wider regions around the world.

Discussion of the threats of climate change raises fundamental questions about human response, and, for anthropology, its role in responding to the dramatic changes that are building. Work in applied anthropology that is beginning to address this issue is the focus of Chapter 6.

6

APPLICATIONS OF ANTHROPOLOGICAL RESEARCH ON CLIMATE CHANGE

Toward application

At the theoretical level, numerous universities have environmental education programs that touch on climate change. Furthermore, some anthropology departments have programs in environmental or ecological anthropology, and some environmental institutes include anthropologists on their respective staffs. Proponents of the cultural, cultural ecological, and critical anthropological perspectives in the anthropology of climate change also tend to go beyond theory-building and acknowledge that their research has an applied component, both for specific groups or societies that constitute the focus of their research and for the future of humanity in general. With regard to environmental anthropology, Eleanor Shoreman-Ouimet and Helen Kopnina (2011: 7) observe that it "is not just becoming more involved with politics, but starting to become more political itself."

In terms of applied work, anthropologists have been working on climate change issues at two broad and quite distinct levels, namely in the formulation of climate policies and by becoming involved in climate action groups and the climate movement that supports social and economic changes in the interest of limiting global warming. In her list of issues that engaged anthropologists examine, Warren (2006: 213) includes "social justice, inequality, subaltern challenges to the status quo, globalization's impacts, and ethical positioning of our field research in situations of violent conflict." Ultimately, however, many of these issues are related to anthropogenic climate change. Additionally, many applied anthropologists work on environmental issues such as community perceptions of the environment, alternative environment-based subsistence strategies, culture and environmental resource management, environmental degradation in local contexts, and social roles in the identification and response to environmental change—types of work that position them to address the environmental impacts of climate change. More generally, at this point in the accumulation of changes that are occurring, it is evident that more anthropologists need to (and will) become involved as observers and engaged scholars in applied initiatives seeking to respond to climate change on the local, regional, national, and global scales. This requires that anthropologists in many instances be part of larger collective efforts to mitigate climate change, whether by working in relationship with international climate regimes, national and state or provincial governments, NGOs and environmental groups, concerned communities, or climate action and sustainability social movements.

Climate policy

Steve Rayner has been a pioneer in applied anthropological work focused on environmental and climate policy analysis since the early 1990s, publishing his first article on greenhouse gases in 1991. Rayner serves as Director of the Institute for Science, Innovation and Society in the School of Anthropology and Museum Ethnography at Oxford University, a center of research on contemporary and emerging issues involving social, scientific, and technological change. In his work, Rayner has tended to adopt what he terms a "cultural analysis" that recognizes the necessity for decision-makers to design policies which conform to the cultural realities of various societies or institutions (Rayner 1991). He observes that institutional cultures often cross-cut national boundaries and have the potential to "provide important opportunities for formulation and implementation of global environmental agreements" (Rayner 1991: 78). Rayner delineates three models of international decision-making: (1) the realist model; (2) the regime or polycentric model; and (3) the quasi-realist model. In the realist model, individual governments set their own policies depending on their own special interests, then the various governments "come together and generate an international consensus that is embodied in a treaty" and subsequently enacted by the various national governments (Rayner 1991: 79). The realist model informed the passage of the 1985 Vienna Convention for the Protection of the Ozone Layer. In the regime or polycentric model, decision-makers belong to competing interest groups, including national governments, NGOs, scientific and technical bodies, environmental groups, and corporations (Rayner 1991). This model guided creation of the Montreal Protocol for the Protection of the Ozone Layer in 1987. Rayner (1991: 81) maintains that the:

> polycentric regime model offers the possibility that international constituencies may reach consensus about how to deal with various aspects of a complex large-scale problem, such as climate change, without committing nation states to positions that may be viewed by powerful internal interests as being contrary to national self-interest.

Finally, the quasi-realist model re-inserts the priority of national cultures over institutional cultures, as exemplified by the Intergovernmental Panel on Climate

Change. In the IPCC, it is national governments, rather than the United Nations Environmental Program, the World Meteorological Organization, or NGOs that set the parameters for decision-making. Rayner (1991: 83) contends that the quasi-realist model "remains more open to direct participation of a variety of institutional cultures than was the case with the realist process of decision-making." He posits that culture functions as a "social control system" by which humans "impose some sort of order and coherence on stream of events" (Rayner 1991: 84).

In 1993, Rayner (1993a) edited a special journal issue on *National Case Studies of Institutional Capabilities to Implement Greenhouse Gas Emissions*. This special issue included studies of efforts to reduce greenhouse gas emissions in the United States, India, Indonesia, China, and the European Community. Rayner (1993a: 10–11) reports the implications of these cases, noting:

> In sum, the overall picture presented in all of these studies is that there is a dynamic relationship between centralized national programmes and the local decentralized initiatives through which informal institutions are becoming an increasingly critical factor in shaping and implementing environmental policy. While both national and local institutions are seeking creative policy instruments in addition to command and control regulation (fiscal, informational, and RD&D [research, development, and demonstration] mechanisms) wide variations in political culture do seem to exert a significant influence on the choice of policy instruments and how legitimate policy targets are defined.

In his analysis of CO_2 emissions reduction policy, Rayner (1993b: 12) observes that the United States up until the early 1990s had focused on forestry and energy as the primary components of its efforts to reduce greenhouse gas emissions. He notes that for the most part, "US political culture prefers to leave demand for goods, services, and activities up to individuals and businesses, and does not consider public policies (or tax laws) explicitly formulated to influence demand to be legitimate" (Rayner 1993b: 14). Rayner (1993b) identifies efforts to reduce greenhouse gas emissions in several areas of energy use: (1) electric utilities; (2) transportation; (3) manufacturing; and (4) residential and commercial locations. He identifies the US stance on three responses to global warming, namely prevention, adaptation, and sustainable development. Those who embrace a preventionist perspective favor alternative energy sources as well as regulation and taxation as strategies for reducing greenhouse gas emissions. Adaptionists favor market mechanisms of various sorts to reduce greenhouse gas emissions as well as adoption of clean coal technologies and increase in use of nuclear power. Finally, the advocates of sustainable development maintain that "it is possible to avoid global catastrophe by careful stewardship of the opportunities that nature provides for controlled growth" (Rayner 1993b: 24). He argues that the concept of sustainable development contains an inherent ambiguity "that allows adaptionist technological pessimists and preventionist technological optimists to persist in their respective world views without acknowledging the conflict that is inherent between them" (Rayner 1993b: 25). Thus, sustainable development implies the possibility of a complementarity between economic expansion and environmental sustainability—a proposition that certainly flies in the face of the critical anthropological understanding of the expansionist engine driving climate change.

While Rayner (1993b: 30) does not recommend any specific policies for reducing greenhouse gas emissions in the United States, he argues that efforts to reduce emissions pose an incredibly difficult challenge which entails a "momentous political task." Ironically and tragically, the task nearly two decades later does not appear to be any less monumental, hence progress in achieving sustainability has been imperceptibly slow. Perhaps recognition of this sad reality prompted Rayner to conclude 14 years later that:

> from the point of view of public policy implementation, adaptation may have some advantages over policies directed at reducing greenhouse emissions. Adaptation may be more immediately relevant to stakeholders than cutting emissions as it directly addresses people, objects, and landscapes that were known to them and valued by them in their daily lives.
>
> *Rayner 2007: 18*

Our concern, however, is that such a stance may inadvertently undermine serious efforts to reduce greenhouse emissions and thus ultimately diminish changes of effectively mitigating climate change. Indeed, increasingly there appears to be a shift toward emphasizing adaptation over mitigation at many levels around the world. Without question, some level of adaptation is absolutely fundamental because of the "commitment to warming" that is already established by the existing greenhouse effect based on greenhouse gases that have already been emitted and will remain in the atmosphere for some time to come. However, a turn away from mitigation will only result in the continued accumulation of greenhouse gases and ever more difficult conditions to which people and societies must adapt. As stressed in Chapter 1, there are limits to adaptive capacity, hence failure to mitigate ensures growing vulnerability and consequences.

As part of his applied focus, Rayner served on the US Department of Energy Multi-Laboratory Climate Change Committee that produced the book *Energy and Climate Change* (US Department of Energy 1990), a review of the role of fossil fuel use in the creation of climate change. He has been a co-author on a number of papers on climate policy (Prins and Rayner 2007; Prins *et al.* 2009). He has also testified before US Congressional Committees on US policy regarding global change research and UK Parliamentary Committees on climate policy, and was lead author of or a contributor to various reports to the US Congress on climate change policy and implementation. Rayner has continued to write on climate policy, including on the Kyoto Protocol and the Copenhagen conference, often in collaboration with others.

Shirley J. Fiske, an environmental and policy anthropologist at the University of Maryland, advocates that anthropologists should become actors in the climate policy process. As she comments:

Very early in my career I became convinced that anthropology has important insights to offer and roles to play across the range of policy stages and issues; and I have dedicated myself to engaging with and making those models accessible to a broader range of the public and academia.

Fiske 2012a

She observes that while anthropologists have been chronicling the impact of climate change on peoples around the world, they have been reluctant to enter into national climate policy decision-making (Fiske 2009: 278). However, she is convinced that given "that the debate has moved to implementing carbon controls and how that might work, there are opportunities to bring anthropologists' participation, collaboration in the field, and critical analyses to the specific programs and activities" that are being initiated (Fiske 2009: 278). Referring primarily to US climate policy and the debate around emissions trade schemes, Fiske (2009: 280) hopes:

that anthropologists will consider taking a closer look at the domestic policy debate—writing op-eds, contacting congressional members, organizing professional associations, and commenting or testifying on legislative provisions that clearly affect both national policy and various stakeholder groups or constituencies. I would expect that many of these provisions could be of interest to anthropologists because each raises questions surrounding access to and use of carbon auction public funds, distributional effects of carbon taxes, environmental justice concerns, and equity among stakeholder groups in implementing them.

She further suggests that anthropologists concerned about climate change form links with organizations, think tanks, and foundations, such as the Pew Center for Climate Change and Physicians for Social Responsibility, which are addressing climate change issues (Fiske 2009: 288). Fiske (2012b: 161) refers to the presence of practicing anthropologists within the United States civil service and World Bank who work on projects relevant to climate policy and:

[the] fact that there were more anthropologists participating in the UN COP [Conference of Parties] 15 meeting in Copenhagen in December of 2009, than have collectively participated in a UNFCCC [United Nations Framework Convention on Climate Change] event at any time in the past.

Critical anthropological input into climate policy may, however, be extremely difficult, given that, as Fiske herself observes, US congressional committees have tended to draw on parties that ultimately do not radically question the parameters of the existing global political economy (Fiske 2009). While we agree with Fiske that anthropologists should seek to enter high-level policy-making circles, such as the UNFCCC or hearings of the US Congress, they may find the various state/provincial and local governments, NGOs and grassroots organizations, particularly those functioning within the climate movement, to be more amenable to their input, an issue which we discuss in greater detail below. As a general rule, however, as Eisenberg (2011: 100) emphasizes, "policy actors at the state and local level are more accessible and responsive to local citizens [including local anthropologists] than are policy actors at the federal level."

More recently, Fiske (2016: 319) has highlighted the need to acknowledge climate skepticism as a significant force at the national level that "catalysed opposition to [US] climate legislation" as well as climate skepticism in many local settings as a barrier to climate action. The election of Donald Trump, an outspoken climate skeptic and a staunch supporter of coal mining and ally of the fossil fuels industry, in November 2016 to the Presidency even further highlights the grim reality that climate skepticism continues to function as a formidable hegemonic force in the most powerful and richest country in the world.

Following somewhat similar lines of decentralized initiative, Elinor Ostrom (2009), a Nobel Prize winner and signatory of the Stockholm Memorandum at the Third Nobel Laureate Symposium on Global Sustainability, proposed a *polycentric approach* be adopted in efforts to mitigate climate change. This is a strategy that was developed in the interdisciplinary Workshop in Political Theory and Policy Analysis at Indiana University, founded by Ostrom and her husband. Based on field studies—an unusual methodology for an economist—of the on-the-ground ways people in various parts of the world collaborate and organize themselves to manage common resources like forests or fisheries and avoid resource depletion and ecosystem collapse, without government involvement, she came to recognize the multi-stranded nature of human–ecosystem interaction. As a result, she was cautious about singular magic bullet "solutions" for complex environmental crises and top-down governmental approaches to such problems. In the final paper she published before her death in 2012, Ostrom discounted the soundness of relying on single international agreements, arguing:

> We cannot rely on singular global policies to solve the problem of managing our common resources: the oceans, atmosphere, forests, waterways, and rich diversity of life that combine to create the right conditions for life, including seven billion humans, to thrive.

There is a need, instead, for grassroots diversity in green policy-making— a position that harmonizes with the views of many anthropologists. Thus, in examining efforts to mitigate climate change, she stressed the importance of polycentric initiatives which collectively have a potential to make a difference:

> the benefits from reduced greenhouse gas emissions are not just global in scope. The benefits are distributed across scales—from the household to the globe. Thus, because units smaller than the globe have sought to reduce emissions, at least some marginal reduction of greenhouse gas emissions is

likely to result from projects undertaken at multiple scales while waiting for global policies to evolve. Doing nothing simply means increasing the level of greenhouse gases, emitted at an ever greater rise. While not yet the amount of reductions that climate scientists estimate is needed to avert calamity, reduction levels do appear to be growing in at least some parts of the world, which may provide examples to other regions of what can be done and what these actions cost.

Ostrom 2009: 28

In other more explicitly applied anthropological work, Ilan Kelman and Jennifer J. West (2009) conducted a review of studies and projects on climate change in Small Island Developing States (SIDS). Based on this experience, they caution: "climate change is only one change-related challenge and opportunity affecting SIDS. Any information on climate change attempts to address vulnerability and adaptation to climate change needs to be considered within the context of multiple stressors" (Kelman and West 2009: 9).

This advisory underlines the importance of the pluralea interaction model. In the case of small island nations, for example, overfishing of the oceans by developed countries is interacting with climate change (including ocean acidification, sea level rise, and more frequent intense storm surges) to make life on low-lying islands less tenable.

P. J. Puntenney (2009: 313) maintains that solving environmental problems, including ones related to climate change, will require collaboration among diverse interests, including groups that are in competition with each other. She argues that anthropologists potentially can play a key role in arriving at climate change solutions in that, in contrast to simply thinking globally and acting locally:

[The] cultural anthropologist's context is more often "Think Locally, Act Globally." Wherein, the sciences focused on the human experience contribute their insights in forms meaningful to and useable by decision-makers regarding dynamic systems, with sustainability foremost in mind.

Puntenney 2009: 318

In 2009 and 2010, David McDermott Hughes (2013: 572) conducted ethnographic research with the "national intelligentsia of climate change" in Trinidad-Tobago, a small Caribbean island nation which holds the contradictory status of having initiated the Alliance of Small Island States (AOSIS) in the early 1990s and, due to its heavy involvement in the hydrocarbon industry, having a per capita emissions level three times higher than any other AOSIS country. Bahrain, a petro state with a 1990 per capita emissions level twice that of Trinidad-Tobago, opted not to join AOSIS. Hughes maintains that Trinidad-Tobago has assumed a compartment that he terms the "victim slot," which as a developing country exonerates its high emissions level. Like many other island nations, Trinidad-Tobago faces the threat of rising sea levels. While Hughes's informants all accepted the findings of climate science, he found that:

> the national climate change intelligentsia situated Trinidad in a multiplex victim slot. In considering their landmass, in performing at diplomatic fora, and in planning for hazards, these experts represented their nation and their institutions as innocent. A generous pardon, it reached all the way to the country's gas rigs and petroleum refinery.
>
> *Hughes 2013: 578*

Climate change mitigation will ultimately require agreement by the vast majority of countries in the world, particularly those that are the largest emitters of greenhouse gases. All climate regimes ranging from the Kyoto Protocol, the COP Paris Agreement of 2015, the EU Emissions Trading Scheme, and a multiplicity of national, state/provincial, and city regimes face serious implementation and accountability problems. Climate change conferences and climate regimes repeatedly recommend or set targets for reducing greenhouse gas emissions. Unfortunately, as Kiely (2007: 148) observes, conventional climate regimes "are too easily guilty of ignoring the uneven development of international capitalism, and therefore the unequal context in which rights, values, ethics, and international institutions operate." Obviously, any effort to create a radical global climate governance process will ultimately have to come from below.

Working with communities

As we have seen in some of the case studies in Chapter 5, anthropologists have been working on climate change issues with local communities, including indigenous ones in regions such as the Arctic, the Andes, and the South Pacific. Susan A. Crate (2011b: 415), who has been conducting research for years on the impact of climate change among the Viliui Sakha, agro-pastoralist horse and cattle breeders in nor-theastern Siberia, facilitated a community sustainability project from 2003 to 2006 which in its final year focused on "elder observations of climate change and its impact on lives and livelihood, thoughts about causality, and visions for the future." All of the elders in the study indicated that climate change would make subsistence activities, social life, and health worse for their communities. Drawing upon her experiences with the Viliui Sakha, Crate (2011b: 422) convincingly argues that anthropologists "must work rigorously, side by side with communities on local scales, to address this immense threat to culture and human rights." Indeed, various anthropologists are already engaged in working with communities on climate change issues in different parts of the world.

Pokrant and Stocker (2009) focus on the contribution of anthropology to climate change adaptation responses in coastal Western Australia and Bangladesh. They assert that climate change:

provides anthropologists with an opportunity to play an important role singly and in collaboration with others in integrating [an] impersonal knowledge of climate into the life-worlds of ordinary people and equip[ing] communities with skills, practices, guides and other enabling mechanisms to deal with the impacts of CC-induced hazards.

Pokrant and Stocker 2009: 181

They refer to an interdisciplinary government-funded project called "Enabling Science Uptake in Australia's Coastal Zone" that seeks to bring together social scientists, natural and environmental science, business, policy-makers and local communities in an effort to create cultures of resilience in coastal communities (Pokrant and Stocker 2009: 187). Slowing efforts to build resilience is a phenomenon that has been referred to as "the science–policy divide," which labels obstacles to the practical uptake of new scientific knowledge and tensions between scientific, managerial, and community knowledge. One pattern that has been described is that as decision-makers move towards policy decisions, the level of active science input declines (Stocker *et al.* 2010). This pattern is noteworthy because it means that decision-makers may, in the final process of policy formation, be more influenced by special interest lobbyists (such as former office holders hired by energy companies) than prevailing scientific knowledge. Recognition of this pattern is one of the factors that has led climate scientists to redouble their efforts to communicate with policy-makers and the public, as described in Chapter 5.

In Bangladesh, anthropologists also have been collaborating with local governments, NGOs, development practitioners, and other researchers in an effort to "make development planning more climate-change resilient" (Pokrant and Stocker 2009: 188). For Pokrant, this has involved a collaborative program of research to link local understandings of climate change to regional, national, and international scales through more deliberative forms of participation, information sharing, collective mobilization, cooperation with national planning bodies, and representation at international fora (Pokrant and Stocker 2009: 188–189).

Pamela McElwee (2015) has examined the impact of REDD+ (Reducing Emissions from Deforestation and Degradation) in Vietnam. REDD+ is an UN-linked program that came out of the Bali Conference of the Parties in 2009 in which households and governments are given payments and other types of compensations that equal or exceed what these parties could theoretically earn by cutting down trees. REDD+ theoretically would serve as a carbon sequestration scheme. Based upon her research in Vietnam, McElwee (2015: 97) argues that REDD+ projects in that country "have not been designed to deal with two major equity issues that have long plagued the forest sector: uneven land tenure and the lack of participatory role for local people, especially ethnic minorities." Based upon his research on REDD+ projects in Amazonia, David Rojas (2016: 22) concludes that, at least in that setting, they were not developed in order to challenge the socio-political arrangements, but to be "compatible with dynamic assemblages of migrant populations, land, forests, machinery, seeds, cattle, and wealth." REDD+ permits corporations to claim that they are committed to environmental sustainability while continuing to generate greenhouse gas emissions which they offset by supporting forest conservation projects in various parts of the world. Aside from the issue of displacement of indigenous and peasant populations, REDD+ as a purported climate mitigation strategy faces the difficulty of measuring the amount of CO_2 sequestered in the process of allowing trees to stand or planting new ones. Given the numerous problems with REDD and REDD+, it is not surprising that they have encountered widespread opposition from indigenous organizations and environmental groups around the world.

In contrast to a countries with a lot of rainfall and forest cover, Jessica Barnes (2015) has examined the possible implications of climate change-driven shortage of water flow in the Nile River in Egypt, a country that is also in danger from rising temperatures and sea levels. She asserts that it is crucial to acknowledge the political ramifications of potential water shortages, not only for the future of Egyptian agriculture, but also Egyptian cities and industries.

Elsewhere, Jennifer Hirsch et al. have been part of applied ethnographic research at the Field Museum's Division of Environment, Culture, and Conservation to identify the perceptions of climate change held by members of various neighborhoods in Chicago (Hirsch et al. 2011). In their research, Hirsch et al. focus on two contrasting neighborhoods, South Chicago and North Kenwood/Oakland (NKO). South Chicago is a racially and ethnically diverse area which is 62 percent African American, 33.4 percent Latino, and 5.6 percent white, and is made up primarily of working-class people (Hirsch et al. 2011: 271). In contrast, NKO is nearly 97 percent African American, but highly stratified along class lines. Residents of the two neighborhoods hold starkly different perceptions about climate change:

> in South Chicago and on the Southeast Side there is significant interest in the concepts of climate change, global warming, and "going green" that relates to the area's long interconnected history with the natural environment. This recognition is directly tied to historical memory of the impact of mills on local air and water quality, as well as current struggles with open space, landfills impacting the region, and coal piles releasing pollutants into the area. In contrast, for residents of NKO, climate change tends to be a more abstract and distant concern that is not recognized as an immediate threat to the environment in the Chicago region.
>
> *Hirsch* et al. *2011: 275*

While residents of South Chicago often feel that they bear individual responsibility for environmental and climatic problems, NKO residents tend to feel that their role in contributing to these problems is inconsequential compared to the contribution of corporations and the US government, and that solving the climate change problem is outside their control. Despite finding starkly contrasting perceptions, Hirsch et al. (2011) have sought to identify local concerns that could be addressed through climate action work around five strategies: improved energy efficiency in buildings, support of the use of clean and renewable energy, improved transportation options, waste reduction, and enhancing adaptation. They maintain that their most important contribution has been the development of the Energy Action Network, a pilot program launched in late November 2009 that seeks to work with Chicagoans to "expand heating assistance and reduce energy use through utility subsidies, weatherization, and housing retrofits" (Hirsch *et al*. 2011: 291). Hirsch *et al*. (2011: 294) feel that city policy-makers have been receptive to their anthropological work, which they assert "provides opportunities for developing broader participatory models for democratic processes and policy development in climate action."

Merrill Singer (2011a) has suggested the possibility of anthropology becoming a "sustainability science" using as an example the work of the Northeast Climate Change Action Research and Education (NCARE) initiative which was organized to call attention to and explore present and possible future climate change impacts on Hartford, Connecticut. As a critical medical anthropologist, he began collaborating with colleagues in various disciplines, including chemistry, ecology, marine science, economics, and education, at the University of Connecticut, and was pleased to discover "their openness to anthropological perspectives about the special risks of global warming for populations already suffering the multiple burdens of structure violence" (Singer 2011a: 5). The NCARE initiative emerged to "use knowledge gained through working with community-based organizations to jointly produce interactive learning modules on climate change, impacts and adaptation" (Singer 2011a: 10). The primary challenge it faced was in attracting funding support in a time of shrinking research dollars, an obstacle of increasing seriousness in generating new knowledge in the anthropology of climate change and beyond.

Gregory V. Button and Kristina Peterson (2009) conducted a participatory research project with the community of Grand Bayou in Louisiana in which they collaborated with physical scientists in an effort to assess the local knowledge of residents with respect to the impact of climate change, tropical storms, and hurricanes upon their lives. Ethnically, Grand Bayou is a mixed community consisting of people of Native American, French, Spanish, and African ancestry. The community was adversely affected by Hurricane Katrina in 2005 and ignored by Federal Emergency Management Agency (FEMA) officials for four months following this devastating event. Participatory research commenced in Grand Bayou in January 2003, and has resulted in interaction between community members and numerous outside groups, including the Corps of Engineers, the National Hazards Workshop, the National Academies of Science, Oxfam America, the National Council of Churches, the National Science Foundation, NOAA Coastal Services Center, and the Louisiana Department of Natural Resources (Button and Peterson 2009). Button and Peterson (2009: 335) maintain that Grand Bayou "residents believe, and the scientists on this project agree, that it is much more efficient in terms of timing and research costs for experts to seek local knowledge before than during the implementation of new research projects."

Noor Johnson (2016) discusses the challenges of gaining entrée into conducting a survey in Clyde River, a predominantly Inuit community of some 1,000 residents in northeast Baffin Island, and in Iqaluit, the capital of Nunavut Territory in Canada. While the research committee of the Ittaq Heritage and Research Center of Clyde River in Inuktitut queried the necessity of his proposed project "based on the fact that a considerable amount of work on climate change had already been done in the community," ultimately the committee approved his project, which proposed investigating "what frameworks, understandings, and actions on climate change had developed in the community through these earlier projects" (Johnson 2016: 399). Johnson maintains that social scientific, including anthropological, research needs to give greater attention to bureaucratic networks and publications to which local communities are linked through national governments and global institutions of various sorts.

The challenges involved in incorporating climate change awareness into universities have been examined by Peggy Bartlett and Benjamin Stewart (2009). They see this as an issue of curriculum reform, but also in terms of the introduction of sustainable practices in campus operations and new building design. At their home institution, namely Emory University, they introduced a series of climate change dinners for faculty and both graduate and undergraduate students which sought to "build a supportive group environment, share factual information and diverse perspectives on climate change, and then, through small group discussions, to encourage the leap to imagine a different Emory, a different Georgia, or different national policies" (Bartlett and Stewart 2009: 362). Bartlett and Stewart maintain that any effort to instill climate change and sustainability awareness on campus must be embedded in knowledge of attitudes and social life at the university.

The challenges of confronting climate change and sustainability on the university campus are evident at the University of Connecticut, where Merrill Singer is a tenured faculty member. The university, which has received substantial state financial support, has demonstrated a strong commitment to sustainability by becoming one of only a small number of universities across the United States to develop a plan for environmentally sustainable development. A component of this guideline involves the incorporation of LEED (Leadership in Energy and Design) standards in university capital improvement projects. The LEED standards were developed by the United States Green Building Council in late 2000, and include a Green Building Rating System for guiding the construction of sustainable buildings (e.g., in terms of water savings, energy efficiency, materials selection, and indoor environmental quality). The University of Connecticut also uses STARS (Sustainability Tracking Assessment and Reporting System), an approach developed by the Association for the Advancement of Sustainability in Higher Education. The STARS system is a reporting format used by groups like the Sierra Club and the Princeton Review to establish standards for campus sustainability rankings. In recognition of such efforts, in 2012 the University of Connecticut was ranked number one in the world in the University of Indonesia Green Metric World University Ranking program. In this assessment, universities are judged based on a number of criteria, including green statistics, energy and climate change, waste management, water usage, transportation, and education. Despite this accomplishment, the university is becoming increasingly embroiled in a controversy over water accessibility. While the university has invested millions of dollars in water conservation, it still must look elsewhere in the state for additional water if it is to continue to grow, which is a central university objective (e.g., a $170 million technology park is in development). As a result, the University of Connecticut is attempting to tap reservoirs in the Farmington River watershed. Residents living in the watershed area have protested the university's plans, knowing well that in 2005, after one of the driest summers on record, the university pumped a river near campus dry. The competition for water in Connecticut, as elsewhere, is complicated by the vagaries created by climate change and the growing inability to be certain how much precipitation there will be, and when. While thus far the Northeast has been comparatively wet, in drier zones like the US Southwest and in Australia, the water vulnerability has been growing.

In response, Australian universities have also embarked upon a large-scale program of achieving environmental sustainability on their campuses. Many Australian universities employ a "green scorecard' to highlight their efforts to be environmentally sustainable.

Nineteen of the 38 Australian universities are signatories to the international Talloires Declaration initiated in October 1990 by 22 presidents, rectors, and vice-chancellors of universities as part of an effort by their institutions to confront environmental degradation. Since October 2010, 427 universities from 52 countries have signed the declaration. While Australian universities have exhibited some progress toward a policy of *greenshift*, in reality adherence to this policy is uneven and inconsistent. As Rafferty and O'Dwyer (2010: 22) observe, there is a "residual—sometimes yawning—greengap between sustainability rhetoric and the active implementation, integration and embedding of sustainable systems across all dimensions of university operations." Based on case studies in terms of environmental sustainability practices at six Australian universities, namely the Australian National University, Charles Sturt University, Griffith University, La Trobe University, Macquarie University, and the University of Sydney, they conclude:

> We contend that Australian universities generally are being shaped by global and community concerns: they are responding to rather than defining and leading the debate. While the sustainability strategies and planning methods employed by institutions are overly engaging with community concerns, the tenor and language of discussion and reportage marks a deep complicity with the dominant discourses and global market forces. The rationalist synthesis of the forces and voices of managerial accountability, EfS [Education for Sustainability] and mainstream politics provides an illusion of order and security in the face of the perceived radical threat of global climate change.
>
> *Rafferty and O'Dwyer 2010: 34*

Baer's participation and observations as the National Tertiary Education Union representative on the University Sustainability Forum and later the University

Sustainability Advocates Forum at the University of Melbourne since late 2010 confirm Rafferty and O'Dwyer's observations of greenshift practices at other Australian universities. For example, despite much discussion of turning off lights, except for safety lights, around campus during off-hours, lights on remain on in many buildings at night in offices, classrooms, and meeting rooms. Installation of light sensors has been a slow process. Another example of unsustainability is the practice of various food vendors in the student union using plastic plates, cups, and utensils. When Baer spoke with a representative of the student union management about the unsustainable practices of one of the vendors, the representative asserted that the union would be unable to alter the practice under the existing contract with this vendor for the duration of its existing contract. Despite the launching of a University Sustainability Charter in late 2015 and a Sustainability Plan, the University of Melbourne has resisted calls on the part of a largely student-led campaign, Fossil Free Melbourne University, to divest itself from undisclosed amounts of investments in fossil fuels (Baer and Gallois 2016).

Anja Nicole Stuckenberger (2009) discusses another approach to increase university awareness of the impact of climate change on human societies, namely the *Thin Ice: Inuit Traditions within a Changing Environment* exhibition at Dartmouth College Hood Museum of Art. This exhibit, which Stuckenberger curated, examines historic and contemporary perceptions of the environment and climate change. In addition to some 3,000 artifacts relating to art and material culture of peoples in Greenland, Alaska, Canada, and other regions of the circumpolar North, the exhibition includes a video program titled *Eyewitnesses to Change: Inuit Observations on Climate Change*. According to Stuckenberger (2009: 390):

> As *Thin Ice* shows, the curation and exhibiting of the cultural dimensions of climate change is not intended as mere display for an uncritical public gaze. It is one crucial way that anthropologists, in partnership with people experiencing the immediate effects of climate change, can take anthropological action and engage, communicate and educate in an effective, creative and powerful way.

Last, but not least, universities, despite their corporatization, still remain significant loci for critical pedagogy on a wide variety of issues, including climate change, a topic that both of us have emphasized in our teaching of various courses both in the United States and Australia. However, the critical pedagogy of climate change also can be practiced in a multiplicity of settings outside of the academy. As Chris Hebdon *et al.* (2016: 389) assert:

> Critical pedagogy represents an oppositional strain compared with mainstream pedagogies, preferring being situated over imperial knowledge and rejecting the idea that while the expert speaks the student should be mute. Importantly, it helps one realize that there are many existing traditions of communication in which people with different skills work together: apprenticeship,

cooperation, reciprocal work, town–hall-style democracy, community media, and other forms of mutual learning in which difference can be made more productive.

Climate action groups and movements

Ultimately, as discussed more fully in Chapter 7, it is our contention that addressing climate change in a responsible manner will entail nothing short of what John Bellamy Foster (2010) terms an "ecological revolution"—one that will over the long run lead to a new world system based upon social equity and justice, democratic processes, and environmental sustainability. In that corporations and most governments have not been acting in a responsible manner in terms of serious climate change mitigation, despite considerable rhetoric to the contrary, much of the collective effort will have to be spurred by anti-systemic movements, including a burgeoning international climate movement which is quite variable in terms of addressing social justice or equity issues (Baer and Singer 2009; Baer 2011). As Kent (2009: 145) so aptly argues: "Successful social movements need to jointly build on individuals' choice and freewill in order to respond to climate change, as well as deliver the means for linking up personal with societal level action."

The climate movement, both internationally and nationally, is a broad and disparate phenomenon that in part draws from earlier movements, particularly the environmental movement, but also the anti-corporate globalization movement (Dietz and Garrelts 2014). Many climate action groups in North America, Europe, and Australia tend to focus on ecological modernization as their primary climate change mitigation strategy, thus either ignoring or downplaying social justice issues. The international climate movement appears to have started in 1989 with the formation of Climate Action Network (CAN), which by mid-2008 had grown into an alliance of some 430 NGOs (Camilleri and Falk 2010: 309). The climate movement both at the international level and within specific countries is quite fragmented, with some of its segments trying to work within the parameters of global capitalism, and others, such as Friends of the Earth, Rising Tide, and various socialist and anarchist groups, challenging it head-on. According to sociologist Manuel Castells (2009: 325): "The internet has played an increasingly important role in the global movement to prevent global warming." Used as a tool of inter-group communication, information dissemination and activist recruitment, public education, organizing and strategy building, fund-raising, and public protest (e.g., through sponsored email writing campaigns to politicians or other recipients), the internet has facilitated the creation of a loosely interlinked network of climate activist organizations and individuals worldwide.

One segment of the climate movement, exemplified by the International Rising Tide Network, emphasizes a "leave it in the ground" approach that seeks to halt the mining and shipping of coal (Cooke 2010). Climate camps directed at coal mines, coal ports, and coal-fired power plants have occurred in the United States,

Canada, France, Belgium, the Netherlands, Denmark, Ireland, the Ukraine, Australia, New Zealand, and India. Some climate action groups have targeted bio-fuel operations around the world. Bill McKibben, a well-known and vocal American environmentalist, and others formed 350.org (based on an understanding that 350 parts per million CO_2 in the atmosphere is the safe limit for humanity) as an effort to create a global climate movement. In reality, many environmental NGOs, such as Greenpeace, Friends of the Earth, Oxfam, and Christian Aid, already have become part of a quite disparate climate movement with many, often quite contrastive, sectors.

One sector of this movement is Mobilization for Climate Justice (MCJ), which is a North American-based network of organizations and individuals that espouse non-violent direct action and public education in order to counteract climate change (Tokar 2009). Another sector involves indigenous communities focused on addressing the effects of climate change they are already experiencing. Many indigenous groups operate under the umbrella of the Indigenous Environment Network (www.ienearth.org/) to communicate local indigenous knowledge about climate change (Johansen 2006: 280).

Additionally, some evangelical Christians in the United States have become part of the climate movement. Richard Cizik, a National Association of Evangelicals lobbyist, adopted a stance that he terms "creation care" around 2002. Linking with other Christian groups with an environmental concern, this led in 1993 to the formation of the Evangelical Environmental Network, "a ministry dedicated to the care of God's creation" that views biblical faith as essential to the solution of ecological problems like environmental toxins and climate change.

Efforts have also been under way as well by the Women's Earth and Climate Caucus to develop a Global Women's Earth and Climate Action Movement. As emphasized by Wangari Maathai (2010), founder of the Green Belt Movement and a 2004 Nobel Peace Prize laureate:

> Women are living on the frontlines of climate change, and are ready to be active partners in dealing with climate change. . . . If the international community is serious about addressing climate change, it must recognize women as a fundamental part of the climate solution.

Through personal, advocacy, training, and project-based approaches, the Women's Earth and Climate Caucus seeks to speed progress toward reducing carbon emissions and creating sustainable lifestyles. Central to the goals of the group is ensuring that women are seated at climate decision-making tables, especially women from developing countries and indigenous women. Exemplary of their efforts in 2013 as part of fossil fuel resistance efforts, the Caucus coordinated the Women of the Land Delegates' meeting with the US Environmental Protection Agency to discuss the environmental threats posed by the controversial Keystone XL Pipeline for frontline indigenous communities and women farmers/ranchers in Texas. The EPA sub-sequently issued a harsh review of the State Department's pro-pipeline environmental impact assessment (Banerjee 2013).

As this description of just a few of the various components of the climate movement suggests, it embraces considerable diversity and includes groups that, beyond a shared concern about environmental degradation and climate change, may have little in common.

The climate movement down under

To date, it appears that the only place where anthropologists have conducted ethnographic research on the climate movement is Australia. At least three Australian anthropologists, including Hans Baer, who actually holds both American and American citizenships, have explored various aspects of the Australian climate movement. The other two anthropologists who have examined the Australian climate movement are Linda Connor, based at the University of Sydney, and Jonathan Marshall, based at the University of Technology, Sydney.

In early 2008, Baer began to conduct observations and became involved in the emerging climate movement in Australia while attending the *Climate Movement Convergence* conference at Northcote High School in Melbourne on February 9, 2008. While most speakers and workshop organizers at the conference proposed strategies of adaptation and mitigation that clearly sought to address climate change within the parameters of "green capitalism," such as writing letters to and lobbying politicians and business leaders, Baer found that many conferees were committed to mass action and moving beyond "business as usual." A highlight of the conference was the launching of a report titled *Climate Code Red: The Case for a Sustainability Emergency*, authored by David Spratt and Philip Sutton (2008a), long-time social activists, and sponsored by Friends of the Earth. Spratt and Sutton (2008b) expanded their report into a book, which became a household item in the Australian climate movement, but also received attention beyond Australia's shores.

Baer's involvement with the climate movement continued with attendance at the first Climate Action Summit in 2009. Over 500 registered attendees from a wide diversity of groups attended the summit, which passed a resolution demanding that Australia participate in an international effort to reduce global levels of carbon dioxide to 300ppm no later than 2020, that Australia's CO_2 emissions should be reduced by at least 60 percent by 2020 and 90 percent by 2030 (from 1990 levels), and that the government enact a policy of 100 percent renewable energy by 2020 and establish a moratorium on all new coal- and gas-fired power plants immediately, revolutionize energy efficiency, promote mass transportation, foster agricultural biological resistance, and implement a moratorium on native forest logging. During the second half of 2009, Baer conducted extensive participant observation on the Australian climate movement at numerous climate action events in Victoria, South Australia, and New South Wales. For example, in September he attended the "Switch off Hazelwood, Switch off Coal" rally at the Hazelwood coal-fired power plant in the La Trobe Valley of southeastern Victoria. Environment Victoria reports that Hazelwood is Australia "dirtiest" power plant, responsible for 16 million tons of carbon dioxide each year, the single largest source of emissions in Australia (3 percent of Australia's and 15 percent of Victoria's). Some 500 protestors, about half of whom had spent the previous night camping nearby, gathered for the rally. International Power, a British-owned company, had erected a temporary fence at the outer edge of the parking lot, thus keeping the vast majority of the protestors out. Not to be deterred, 22 protestors managed to climb the fence, but were arrested before they could reach the main gate. Other protestors who tried to scale the fence were pushed back repeatedly by mounted police officers who charged them with their horses.

In late September 2009, Baer attended the Port Augusta Climate Camp on the edge of the Flinders Ranges in South Australia, about 60km from the rally site near two Port Augusta coal-fired power plants. About 2km from the site of the protest were two large prison buses parked at the edge of a petrol station. A driver explained that law enforcement authorities expected a large contingent of protestors at the rally the next day, and the buses were to hold any protestors who were deemed to be too unruly in their actions. The female driver also explained that the buses had been brought in from New South Wales because no such buses existed in South Australia, a much less populated state. Around 50 protestors assembled at the rally site, demanding closure of the power stations and their replacement with renewable energy-generating installations. Authorities designated the power stations a "protected area" for the duration of the climate camp. The protestors marched 2km into the "protected area" to a temporary fence and were met by around 70 police, including 12 on horseback. An unspecified number of police officers were positioned at other locations. For such a small group of protestors, the precautions the authorities had taken constituted a profound example of state-sanctioned overkill. The police permitted eight individuals to ride in a van to the main gate to deliver a Community Decommission Order and 350 flowers symbolizing the target of reducing atmospheric CO_2 to 350ppm.

The Australian climate movement consists of two broad layers. The first of these functions primarily within mainstream civil society, though occasionally in parliaments and local councils, and includes the Southern Cross Climate Coalition, NGOs, state-based nature conservation societies, and labor unions. The other layer acts primarily at the grassroots level. Baer found that the climate movement in Australia was divided on whether or not virtually any type of emissions trading scheme (ETS), including the Gillard government's proposed Carbon Price Mechanism (CPM), would be better than none at all. While some climate activists recognize and accept the shortcomings of ETSs, they proposed that the movement should support the CPM in order to get a carbon tax and then campaign against it rolling over into an ETS three years after its implementation. Whereas the Australian Council of Trade Unions joined the Greens in supporting the CPM, many grassroots climate activists opposed it as a market mechanism that would prove to be a distraction.

As a broad, nationally based initiative, the Australian climate movement fell into a lull of sorts after the passage of the CPM, which went into effect in July 2012. Nevertheless, many Australian climate activists continue to be involved in specific campaigns, such as the promotion of renewable energy sources, the Lock the Gate or anti-coal-seam-gas exploration campaign, and the leave coal in the ground campaign spearheaded by Greenpeace and endorsed by Greens leader Christine Milne. Beyond Zero Emissions and other groups in the climate movement have expressed concern that the Gillard and Rudd governments under the leadership of the Australian Labor Party have not been highly committed to renewable sources of energy, but have been proposing a shift from coal power to natural gas power. Elsewhere in Australia, Linda Connor and her colleagues have examined the climate movement as part of a larger research project that commenced in 2008, examining the impact that climate change has had on sociocultural life in communities in the Hunter Valley of New South Wales. In her contribution to a special issue of the *Journal of Australian Political Economy*, she asserts:

> Anthropology can critically analyse the effects, anthropogenic causes and actions taken in relation to anthropogenic climate change by contributing to interdisciplinary and applied research and by undertaking ethnographic analysis of specific localities and groups involved in the changes that are occurring or are anticipated to occur.
>
> *Connor 2010/2011: 248*

Connor's project with her colleagues entailed a longitudinal survey of residents' attitudes about and practices responding to climate change, and ethnographic research of climate action groups in three areas, namely the upper Hunter Valley, Lake Macquarie, and the city of Newcastle (Connor 2010/2011). They found:

> At the end of 2008, 30–60% of respondents in the three areas were observing a higher frequency of weather conditions that are considered core climate change indicators — heat, drought, more intense bush fires and storm/flood severity. When asked about loss of native plants and animals/ fish, there was a strikingly similar pattern of answers in the three areas, with 30–40% of respondents observing species loss. However, a significantly larger proportion of Upper Hunter people observed mature trees dying (55% vs. 30%). The majority of survey respondents (55–75%) witnessed change in seasonal patterns and the usual rhythms of nature, while about 27% of Lake Macquarie residents noted sea level rises along sea or lake shores.
>
> *Connor 2010/11: 257–258*

However, some respondents did not view these events as necessarily a result of anthropogenic climate change. Of the 567 (out of a total of 1,162) survey respondents who made optional comments at the end of the survey, 102, or 18 percent, of them invoked "'natural cycles' or 'natural cyclical change' to explain shifts in weather patterns or to argue against the idea of anthropogenic changes" (Connor 2010/ 2011: 258). Indeed, the percentage of both Australians as a whole and residents in the Hunter Valley who expressed concern about anthropogenic climate change had diminished between 2006 and 2009, in part due to growing concern about possible adverse economic impacts resulting from the global financial crisis and the growing influence of climate skepticism and the airing of such views in various guises in the mass media. Connor (2010/11: 254) maintains that "celebrity skeptics" can be viewed in Gramscian parlance as exemplars of "organic intellectuals of the corporate capitalist class" who have been able to influence the thinking of a significant portion of the Australian populace.

Despite inroads made by climate deniers among some Hunter Valley residents, Connor (2010/2011: 262–263) found that other residents have mobilized around various environmental problems:

> most notable are threats to land (as a source of identity Indigenous and non-Indigenous), property values and livelihood, and health (especially the health and welfare of children). Examples of recent issues that have created local protests, action groups and organizational alliances include the Southlakes Communities against the Mine (SCAM) opposition to the Centennial Coal Company's Awaba coal mine open cut extensions on the grounds of air pollution, children's health and environmental damage: the protests against the Anvil/Mangoolda mine in Wybong . . . ongoing resident coalitions to fight cumulative air pollution, water source destruction and adverse health effects from intensive coal mining in the Singleton/Camberwell area . . . and the Hunter Thoroughbred Breeders Association campaign for a moratorium on new mining and coal seam gas development in the Hunter Valley.

While not of all of these groups are part of the Australian climate movement, their concern with the impact of coal and coal seam gas mining certainly intersects with the concerns of the more explicitly climate action groups.

Between 1984 and 2011 Australia constituted the leading exporter of coal in the world, and Newcastle, at the terminus of the Hunter Valley, is reportedly the world's largest black coal exporting site. Connor *et al.* examined the formation in 2000 of the Anvil Hill Project Watch Association (AHPWA) on the part of Wybong residents who were concerned about the damage that the planned Anvil Hill mine would have on local flora and fauna (Connor *et al.* 2009: 494). The AHPWA became a member of the Anvil Hill Alliance (AHA) which emerged in 2006 when the New South Wales government approved development of the mine. Greenpeace and Rising Tide became involved in the campaign to stop the Anvil Hill mine by October 2005. The AHPWA found itself opposed by diverse "pro-mining civil society groups" which included "mining industry associations and unions representing mine and energy workers and coal exporters, all with shifting positions and alliances" (Connor *et al.* 2009: 503). The Construction, Forestry, Mining and Energy Union came to constitute a middle group between the Anvil Hill Alliance and the pro-mining civil society group in that, while in coalition with the coal producers and the New South Wales Minerals Association, it embarked an advertising campaign claiming that "climate change threatened miners' jobs and calling for the

Kyoto Protocol to be ratified; for a 60% emissions reduction target by 2050; and for more investment in 'clean coal technology'" (Connor et al. 2009: 504). According to Connor et al. (2009: 508), the climate movement has evolved into a "transformative discourse" in the Upper Hunter Valley, in that it challenges existing modes of energy utilization and consumerist lifestyles.

Connor (2012) also conducted ethnographic research on several climate action groups in the Hunter Valley, namely Transition Towns (Coal Point and Newcastle), Climate Action (Newcastle and Lake Macquarie), and Rising Tide Australia. Transition Town Newcastle and Transition Town Coal Point are part of an international Transition Town movement which has emerged as a segment of the climate movement, in that its adherents are seeking to have local neighborhoods transition into climate-friendly communities that meet the challenges of climate change. It seeks to move away from globalized distribution systems to localized ones in order to rejuvenate local economies. In large part, the Transition Town movement has been a phenomenon of the developed world, with its initiatives presently based primarily in the Anglophile countries, particularly the United Kingdom, but also the United States, Canada, Australia, and New Zealand (Hopkins 2010: 447). Climate Action Newcastle and Climate Action Lake Macquarie are local climate action groups which exist in great abundance throughout much of Australia (Burgmann and Baer 2012).

Connor and her research assistants as part of their Hunter Valley project interviewed 32 religious and spirituality adherents between 2008 and 2013 (Connor 2016: 178–190). While some of their interviewees were members of various religious groups, some characterized themselves as "spiritual" rather than religious. Views on the causes of climate change varied widely among their interviewees, which included "moral critiques of contemporary society" in each instance, and "moral degeneration in human's relationship to nature/the Earth" in many instances (Connor 2016: 178). Several of their interviewees were Pentecostals, and Ray, one of them, "viewed climate change as due to the will of God, scripturally preordained as an end time precursor" (Connor 2016: 188). Conversely, Vince, a Seventh Day Adventist, while being a creationist, "did not know whether climate change had anything to do with end of time events," but favored a "science-based discourse of the 'tipping point' over a religious explanation" (Connor 2016: 189).

Over the course of the past few years, a concerted anti-coal campaign called Stop Adani, which has the support of numerous environmental NGOs and the Green Party, has formed around the plans by the Indian conglomerate Adani to open a mega-mine in the coal-rich Galilee Basin of Queensland (Krien 2017). Unfortunately, the project has been given the go-ahead by both the Coalition federal government and the Queensland ALP government, with Bill Shorten, the leader of the ALP opposition in the federal parliament, giving his approval so long as Adani purportedly observes certain environmental standards. The coal mine, "if built would be the largest export coal mine in Australia: forty million tonnes of low-grade thermal coal would be shipped through the Great Barrier Reef via a proposed new port at Abbott Point, near Bowen" (Hepburn 2017: 12).

Jonathan Marshall (2012) has focused his work on the social imaginations of participants in the Australian climate movement than on the activities of the various groups involved in the movement per se. He notes:

> Climate movements are motivated by imaginings of the future, grouped by shared imaginings and by imagining themselves as joined. They work against imagined groups of others (who they rarely encounter in groups), and they imagine the consequences of their actions.
>
> *Marshall 2012: 266*

Three Australian scholars have written a study of activists who have participated in climate camps in Australia which was released as a book in October 2013. They are Stuart Rosewarne, a political economist at the University of Sydney; James Goodman, a political economist at the University of Technology, Sydney; and Rebecca Pearse, a postgraduate political science researcher at the University of New South Wales. Their book examines links with climate action campaigns in several locales (Rosewarne *et al.* 2013).

Climate activists often sense that mitigating climate change is a formidable goal, but generally feel compelled to act, in what ultimately prove to be disparate ways, to achieve a safe climate both in Australia and elsewhere. The disparate nature of the Australian climate movement, even at the grassroots level, raises certain questions about the social scientific portrayal of new social movements (NSMs). For example, Keith Faulks (1999: 88) maintains that:

> the novelty of NSMs can be seen in their disillusionment with the statist politics of the socialist left and the neo-liberal right, and their explicit rejection of the state as a tool that can be utilised to create social justice and ensure democratic accountability.

In the case of the Australian climate movement, many climate activists adhere to the notion that they can persuade politicians and even corporate elites to reform the political economy in such a way as to prevent dangerous climate change. Aside from the socialist groups and some groups such as Friends of the Earth and Rising Tide, the Australian climate movement by and large has expressed a muted critique of global capitalism and has tended to de-emphasize social and climate justice issues. This is quite in contrast to various other climate action groups around the world, particularly in developing countries, many of which might be more aptly termed *climate justice groups* than simply *climate action groups*.

The election of a climate denialist to the US presidency: a time for American anthropologists to become climate activists

In December 2016, Trump appointed Oklahoma Attorney General Scott Pruitt as Director of the Environmental Protection Agency. Pruitt is not only a climate denialist, but has been a staunch opponent of the EPA, as evidenced by suing it over carbon pollution regulations. Furthermore, Trump nominated ExxonMobil CEO Rex Tillerson as his Secretary of State and other billionaires and generals for cabinet positions, thus "effectively establishing the United States as a petro-oligarchy" (Helvarg 2017: 22). He has pledged to complete the Dakota Access Pipeline which Native Americans and their allies have been attempting to block.

In keeping with the spirit of the AAA Statement on Humanity and Climate Change, we urge anthropologists to become involved in the climate movement in the United States and other countries. On April 22, 2017, thousands of people participated in cities around the world in the March for Science, and also the Climate March the following week, expressing support for policies and actions based upon scientific principles. The Board of Directors of the Association of College & Research Libraries division of the American Library Association voted to partner with the March for Science and urged its members to attend rallies in various cities, including Chicago and Washington, DC, where reportedly 40,000 marched; in New York, where reportedly 20,000 marched, and in Philadelphia, where reportedly 10,000 marched (Enis 2017: 26). Project ARCC (Archivists Responding to Climate Change) formed on Earth Day 2015, "aiming to protect archival collections from the impact of climate change; reduce the profession's carbon and ecological footprint; elevate relevant collections to improve public awareness and understanding of climate change" (Enis 2017: 26). We urge the AAA to form a new task force to address the implications of the Trump presidency in terms of exacerbating the global climate change crisis.

Climate justice

To a large extent, the climate movement constitutes a subgenre of the environmental movement, although in both its international and national manifestations, it exhibits three tendencies: (1) a green social democratic one that calls for ecological modernization and the regulation of capitalism; (2) an anti-capitalist and radical one which believes that, ultimately, capitalism must be transcended to achieve a safe climate and livable environment; and (3) an in-between one that recognizes climate justice issues, but is not explicitly anti-capitalist. Whereas groups that belong to the first tendency generally do not give a great deal of attention to social justice issues, those that belong to the latter two tendencies do.

Many climate groups in North America, Europe, and Australia tend to focus upon ecological modernization, emphasizing in particular renewable sources of energy, energy efficiency, and improved public transport. In the process of emphasizing techno-fixes as a primary strategy for achieving climate change mitigation, they often either ignore or downplay social justice issues. Many environmental NGOs have become part of the climate movement, which includes many other types of groups, including socialist and anarchist ones and student environmental collectives. Conversely, some environmental groups that have become involved in the climate movement, such as the World Wide Fund for Nature, the Environmental

Defense Fund, and the Sierra Club, reportedly have strong corporate connections (Bond 2010: 24).

In contrast to the large climate movement, the climate justice movement emerged in 2000 at the Climate Justice Summit, which convened outside the Sixth Conference of the Parties in The Hague and posited that "the causes of climate change are the production and consumption patterns in industrialised countries." The Indian Climate Justice Forum (2002: 1) declared at the Climate Justice Summit in October 2002 in New Delhi that "climate change is a human rights issue" and rejected the "market-based principles that guide the current negotiations to solve the climate crisis." The Durban Group for Climate Justice emerged out of a seminar in South Africa in October 2004 that was convened by the Dag Hammarskjoeld Foundation in collaboration with various civil society organizations. Progressive religious groups also have become part of the climate justice movement. At the UNFCCC conference in Montreal in December 2005, the World Council of Churches released a statement, titled "A Spiritual Declaration on Climate Change," that asserted: "We commit ourselves to help reduce the threat of climate change through actions in our own lives, pressure on governments and industries, and standing in solidarity with those most affected by climate change." Other organizations involved in the international climate justice movement include Carbon Trade Watch (a project of the Transnational Institute), the World Rainforest Movement, and the Greenhouse Development Rights Network. Various indigenous groups also have become involved in the climate justice movement. One of these is the Inuit Circumpolar Council, which was established in 1977 in Barrow, Alaska, as a body that represents Inuit people from Greenland, Canada, and Alaska (Stern 2010: 175).

Climate activists from various groups mobilized for meetings held in conjunction with the UN climate change conferences in Poznan, Poland (COP 14) in December 2008 and Copenhagen (COP 15) in December 2009, as well as the 2009 World Social Forum in Belem, Brazil (Peterman and Langelle 2010). Out of this process, Climate Justice Action emerged as the principal organizing network for demonstrations at COP 15. Various Danish organizations formulated the People's Summit Klimaforum09, which featured workshops, debates, discussions, and artwork on the need for an alternative world system. Via Campesina, an organization with some 80 affiliates around the world, this was part of the call for action at the Copenhagen conference, and argued that the UNFCCC "has failed to radically question the current models of consumption and production based on the illusion of continuous growth" (quoted in Tokar 2009: 7).

An estimated 50,000–100,000 people demonstrated on December 12, 2009 on the streets of Copenhagen on an International Day of Action. Some 900 people reportedly were arrested (Peterman and Langelle 2010). In the aftermath of the Copenhagen conference, Climate Justice Now! called for "system change, not climate change" (quoted in Peterman and Langelle 2010: 6). Reflecting the theme of climate justice, Evo Morales, the President of Bolivia, convened the *World People's*

Conference on Climate Change and the Rights of Mother Earth in Cochabama in April 2010, which we discussed in case study 4 in the previous chapter.

Christine Frank (2009), coordinator of the Climate Crisis Coalition of the Twin Cities, Minneapolis, criticizes much of the environmental movement as being too soft on capitalism. She calls for an "uncompromising environmental movement led by working people in alliance with other oppressed groups," one that is imbued with "ecosocialist principles that go beyond the maintenance of capitalism and its suicidal and genocidal policies, and instead advances a zero-growth, zero-waste, steady-state, democratically planned socialist economy that puts planetary and human needs before profits" (Frank 2009: 43). Two broad tendencies were represented in the New York City rally on September 21, 2014, two days after the UN COP meeting there: (1) the supporters of green capitalism who view climate markets as being essential to mitigating greenhouse gas emissions, and (2) the defenders of life-affirming solar communing who "seek an end to capitalist relations (meaning the demise of corporate value chains)" and an elaboration of "commoners' value chains (better described as a web or matrix)" (Giacomini and Turner 2015: 30).

Conclusion

The application of anthropology to addressing real-world problems dates to early in the twentieth century, but notably advanced in the 1940s with the emergence in the United States of the Society for Applied Anthropology and other applied societies in other nations in subsequent years, in part as a result of anthropologist involvement in various kinds of practical work related to the war effort during World War II. While tensions remain between applied and general academic anthropology (Rylko-Bauer *et al.* 2006), practice across a wide range of issues, including environmental concerns, is well established. The application of the anthropology of climate change is in its infancy, and is still struggling to have an impact on climate-related policies and practices around the world. As indicated by the words of various anthropologists quoted in this book, frequent statements have been made about the strengths anthropology brings to the study of and response to climate change as a dual social and environmental issue. From the viewpoint of the critical anthropology of climate change, issues of social justice and the possibility of sustainability within the existing global economy are of fundamental importance. While this perspective has found a home in sectors of the broader climate social movement, its ability to gain acceptance and find translation in concrete applied initiatives may be critical to effective responses to the climate turmoil, pluralea interaction, and enhanced community vulnerability/precarity drama unfolding before us on Earth.

7

WHAT OTHER SOCIAL SCIENTISTS ARE SAYING ABOUT CLIMATE CHANGE

Across many disciplines

Climate change, including the anthropogenic etiology of our radically changed biosphere, is a topic that is inherently multidisciplinary and interdisciplinary because there are so many scholarly fields involved in studying aspects of this phenomenon, none of which can alone fully reveal its full nature. In the physical or natural sciences, this includes climate science, atmospheric science, meteorology, geology, and even engineering, among other scientific disciplines. In terms of the social and behavioral sciences, in addition to archaeology (as a subfield of anthropology) and anthropology more generally, as we have noted in previous chapters, sociology, political science, human geography, and psychology touch upon it. Finally, the humanities that address climate change include history, philosophy, English language or literature, and even religious studies and theology. Moreover, there are interdisciplinary areas, such as Earth sciences, environmental studies, development studies, and public policy, that concern themselves with climate change. Beyond these fields, various journalists, such as George Monbiot (2006), Fred Pearce (2006, 2007) and Mark Lynas (2004, 2007), have written popular books and multiple articles on climate change-related topics. Thus, the examination of climate change can, as indicated, be said to be an inherently multidisciplinary arena, with contributions from many directions, but, in addition, it is interdisciplinary in that collaborations of various sorts across disciplinary lines have added significantly to the field. In this regard, we find ourselves very much in agreement with Kirsten Hastrup's contention about the importance of an interdisciplinary approach to examining climate change:

> Anthropologists have addressed local implications of climate change all over the world and contributed to the discussion of the perceived turning

points between ordinary weather variability and permanent climate change. For all the merits of local ethnography, anthropological studies of climate change of this kind need to cultivate a comprehensive interest in the inter-penetration of local and global climate issues and of different registers of knowledge. This would link up anthropology with recent developments in other social sciences such as sociology, political science, economics, and science and technology studies.

Hastrup 2012a: 2

We feel very comfortable with an interdisciplinary approach to climate change because this has been our *modus operandi* over the course of our respective academic careers. Although Hans Baer taught primarily in sociology and anthropology departments in his regular positions and anthropology departments in his visiting positions in the past, since coming to the University of Melbourne he has taught in the Development Studies Program, which has been located in several different schools over time. Baer also taught in the Centre of Health Society in the School of Population Health at the University of Melbourne between 2006 and 2011. Similarly, but in somewhat different ways, Merrill Singer's career has emphasized interdisciplinary collaboration. Thus, he has worked on several multidisciplinary research teams composed of anthropologists, psychologists, epidemiologists, social workers, and others involved in community-based studies of pressing health issues like AIDS, sexually transmitted disease, and hepatitis. As Singer (2009b: 381) has written, multidisciplinarity involves "successful collaboration that transcends not only defended disciplinary boundaries but inherent conceptual worlds and jargon-filled disciplinary languages, and, perhaps more challenging, our ability to see through the historic blinders imposed by disciplinary bias and discipline-centrism."

Attempting to summarize the work of sociologists, political scientists, and human geographers on climate change is a rather daunting endeavor. Fortunately, some of this work has been brought together in edited volumes that facilitate access to multiple authors within and across disciplines. Thus, sociologist Constance Lever-Tracy (2008), based at the University of Adelaide, has played a key role in fostering the sociology of climate change. In addition to authoring a short book titled *Confronting Climate Change* (Lever-Tracy 2011), she edited the *Routledge Handbook of Climate Change and Society* (Lever-Tracy 2010). Bronislaw Szerszynski and John Urry (2010), leading British sociologists, guest-edited a special issue of the journal *Theory, Society, and Culture* on climate change. Finally, political scientists John S. Dryzek, Richard B. Norgaard, and David Schlosberg edited *The Oxford Handbook of Climate Change and Society* (2011b). Unfortunately none of these anthologies have included contributions from anthropologists. To some degree, this may be because the full range of contemporary studies in anthropology is less well known to many of our colleagues in other disciplines than the kinds of work anthropologists traditionally have done with smaller-scale cultural groups in very local settings around the world.

In March 2012, the International Social Science Council released a report on *Transformative Cornerstones of Social Science Research for Global Change* which proposes the design of a "10-year research funding and coordination initiative for the social sciences on climate change and global environmental change" (Hackmann and St. Clair 2012: 2). The report states: "For social scientists . . . the message is clear: issues of climate change and global environmental change lie at the heart of the social sciences" (Hackmann and St. Clair 2012: 4). In terms of publications on climate change and global environmental change, the report contends that political science, sociology, anthropology, and psychology all lag behind fields such as environmental studies, economics, and geography. While this has been true for much of the last 25 years, a period during which the reality of global climate change was becoming indisputable among climate scientists, as we have suggested, anthropologists are now working on this issue in still limited but ever-growing numbers, in diverse roles, and in far-flung settings around the inhabited parts of the planet. In effect, this book is intended to recognize, support, and advance this still-emerging arena of work among anthropologists in light of the human origins of climate change and the urgency of its growing impact on human communities and life experiences.

The sociology of climate change

Concerns about limited disciplinary involvement in climate change work have not been confined to anthropology. Constance Lever-Tracy (2008) published an article in which she lamented the paucity of sociological literature, arguing that sociologists are suspicious of naturalistic explanations and skeptical about discourses concerned with the future. Others, writing in response to Lever-Tracy, have offered alternative explanations, including suggesting that:

> sociologists have been cautious due to the overly political nature of the debates thus far, due to methodological differences with the natural sciences, and because they have learned to be sensitive about locating the phenomenon in the longue durée [the long term].
>
> *Grundmann and Stehr 2010: 898*

Since the publication of these papers, however, the sociology of climate change has taken off, although it may not yet be as embedded in the core of the discipline as Lever-Tracy might desire.

Historically, there are reasons to suggest that J. Timmons Roberts, the Director of the Center for Environmental Studies at Brown University, may qualify as the father of the sociology of climate change, although he is probably not recognized as such. Along with various colleagues who employ a world systems theory approach, Roberts has been involved in tracking the position of countries in the capitalist world system and their carbon intensity and CO_2 emissions (Roberts and Grimes 1997). Roberts in collaboration with Bradley C. Parks (2007) authored *A Climate of Injustice*, which constitutes the first book in the sociology of climate change, although it is not often celebrated as such. These authors argue "that global warming is all about inequality, not only in who will suffer its effects most, but also who created the problem in the first place" (Roberts and Parks 2007: 135). Roberts and Parks (2007: 10) report that the richest 20 percent of the world's population creates over 60 percent of the greenhouse gas emissions.

A Climate of Injustice is essential reading for any social scientist embarking on the study of climate change, in that it covers a diversity of topics, including the harsh impact of climate disasters on people in developing societies, climate regimes, and the need for North–South environmental cooperation. Moreover, it recognizes that the topic of climate change has become so political not because the scientific facts are in dispute, but because there are those who most benefit and those who most suffer from the consequences of the fossil fuel-driven world economic system.

Seeking to advance the sociology of climate change, Joane Nagel *et al.* (2009) convened a *Workshop on Sociological Perspectives on Global Climate Change* at the National Science Foundation. The conference focused on critical issues in climate change and the role of sociologists in studying and responding to it, including addressing the causes of climate change, perspectives on its impacts, sociological approaches to mitigation and adaptation, and approaches for advancing research on the sociology of global warming. Among the recommendations for catalyzing sociology to examine climate change, the report issued as a product of the conference recommended capacity-building by "increasing the number of researchers in the sociological study of the environment," increasing the "presence of sociologists in climate change research and policy organizations," and facilitating "sociologists' access to climate change research and policy networks" (Nagel *et al.* 2009: 5). The report also recommends collaboration between sociology and other disciplines, including encouraging "sociologists to embrace multi-method frameworks" and increasing "support of research networks and collaborations with natural scientists and engineers" (Nagel *et al.* 2009: 5). Finally the report recommended several forms of "capacity building and infrastructure development," including developing an "interdisciplinary Social Environment Observatory Network" and creating a "training institute focused on the social dimensions of climate change" (Nagel *et al.* 2009: 5). While the report recommends that sociologists contribute to climate policy decision-making, it does not encourage them to work with local communities on climate change issues or within the climate movement—a striking omission given that many environmental sociologists are involved in such work.

More recently, sociologist Christian Parenti (2011) has highlighted the vulnerability of much of the global South to the worst effects of climate change. He observes:

> Between the Tropic of Capricorn and the Tropic of Cancer lies what I call the *Tropic of Chaos*, a belt of economically and politically battered post-colonial states girding the planet's mid-latitudes. In this band, around the tropics, climate change is beginning to hit hard. The societies in this belt are also heavily dependent on agriculture and fishing, thus very vulnerable to shifts in weather patterns. This region was also on the front lines of the

Cold War and of neoliberal economic restructuring. As a result, in this belt we find clustered most of the failed and semifailed states of the developing world.

Parenti 2011: 9

Parenti (2011) explores the role climate change is already playing in contemporary, resilience-shattering conflicts, disruptions, and social breakdowns. In what he calls the Tropic of Chaos countries, violent conflict over shrinking and more erratic resources (e.g., water and grazing land) is being driven by the catastrophic convergence of poverty and the turmoil of climate change.

Prominent British sociologist Anthony Giddens authored *The Politics of Climate Change* (2009, 2011). He contends that "global warming is a problem unlike any other, however, both because of its scale and because it is mainly about the future" (Giddens 2009: 2). In what Giddens immoderately terms the *Giddens paradox*, he states that:

> since the dangers posed by global warming aren't tangible, immediate or visible in the course of day-to-day life, however awesome they appear, many will sit on their hands and do nothing of a concrete nature about them. Yet waiting until they become visible and acute before being stirred to serious action will, by definition, be too late.

Giddens 2009: 2

While it is undeniable that barring sweeping mitigation, Giddens is correct in asserting that the worst and most tumultuous effects of climate change lie in the future, in fact it is becoming increasingly clear that when it comes to issues of climate change, the future began some time ago. By this, we mean that already climate change is having significant impacts on communities and lives around the world, as seen in intense and damaging flooding, life-threatening droughts, the spread of vector- and waterborne diseases, the rising level of conflict noted by Parenti, and other diverse expressions and consequences of a warming planet.

Another British sociologist, John Urry, has been at the forefront of the sociology of climate change. Writing against anthrocentricism in his book *Climate Change and Society*, he states:

> I embed society, and hence sociology, as a subject within the analyses of climate change, and more generally within a world of objects, technologies, machines and environments. A strong claim is made here that the social and the physical/material worlds are utterly intertwined and the dichotomy between the two is an ideological construct to be overcome (as much writing in the sociology of science and technology has long maintained).

Urry 2011:8

Urry further contends that a social science of climate change thus far has not been well developed, although we believe this observation is in the process of being altered.

To date, economic models of human behavior have dominated the climate change discourse in the academic and environmental policy worlds. This dominance is exemplified by the much-cited *Stern Review*. Nicholas Stern (2007), head of the UK Government Economic Service and a former chief economist at the World Bank, proposed a celebrated neoliberal strategy for addressing climate change. He asserted that the "risks from the worst impact of climate change" can be appreciably reduced if greenhouse gas levels in the atmosphere could be stabilized between 450 and 550ppm carbon dioxide equivalent (i.e., the conversion of all greenhouse gas emissions to an amount of carbon dioxide) (Stern 2007: xv). The Stern Review has been heavily attacked by climate change deniers on the oft-repeated grounds that the mitigation formulas need "to be based on solid science and economics before hundreds of billions of dollars per year are invested in abatements" (Mendelsohn 2006–2007). By contrast, our own perspective is that the emissions reduction targets in the Stern Review are too limited to control temperature increases below a safe level, that the degree of climate change damage is underestimated in the review, and that, as Foster *et al.* (2010) argue, proposing more extensive emissions cuts has been avoided because it was feared that serious reductions in emissions would destabilize capitalism.

Of note, Urry (2011: 15) faults Giddens's *The Politics of Climate Change* (2009) for being "not sufficiently sociological" because Giddens places "too much emphasis upon national policy and politics and not enough grounding of high and low carbon systems and practices within 'society'" (Urry 2011: 15). Ultimately, Urry seeks to develop a *post-carbon sociology* as well as a *post-carbon society* that transcends the carbonized nature of modernity. In contrast to a post-Fordist or post-modern sociology, he views a post-carbon sociology as a sociology that "emphasizes how modernity has consisted of an essentially carbonized modern world, but this carbon underpinning has been obscured by most social thought" (Urry 2011: 16). Urry (2011: 16) contends that earlier sociologies have been "carbon-blind, never interrogating the resource and energy bases of economic and social life." He defines a post-carbon society as one that has transcended the current reliance on fossil fuels and fossil fuel-driven technologies, such as cars dependent on the internal combustion engine.

Urry moreover contends that sociology should engage with and contribute to the new catastrophism in the social and scientific literatures as manifested in numerous popular books, such as Jared Diamond's *Collapse* (2005), as well as in films and novels. He calls for "post-carbon analyses of climate change, the peaking of oil supplies, population increases and the (in)security of food and water," a recognition that consumer culture entails the energy-intensive production of objects and that military institutions exert a high ecological footprint and produce high levels of CO_2 emissions (Urry 2011: 46). He also highlights the role of fast travel involving private automobiles and airplane flights for a wide variety of purposes, including business and professional travel, adventure, tourism (including medical tourism), visits to family members, and "military mobility of armies, tanks, helicopters, aircraft, rockets, spyplanes, satellites and so on," in the generation of greenhouse gas emissions (Urry 2011: 69). Urry (2011: 100) forcefully contends that "Climate change politics involves campaigning not for abundance or growing abundance now, so as to ensure reasonable abundance in the long term and in other parts of the globe." While much of what he contends is critical of actually existing capitalism, he does not call for the transcendence of the capitalist world system per se. Instead, Urry (2011: 118) advocates "resource capitalism" which relies upon ecological modernization, and recognizes that "there is a limited capability to supply resources and to absorb pollution." In other words, Urry rejects free market fundamentalism, but not the privatization of production, and advocates what might be called capitalism with a conscience. This leads to a discussion of the ability of so-called green capitalism to solve our entwined economic and environmental problems, a topic we address in the final chapter.

In his most recent book, Urry (2013) highlights the need for capitalism to move beyond its heavy reliance on oil, upon which it is dependent for food production and distribution, transportation, and multiple other purposes. He advocates "powering down" to a "low-carbon civil society" that would entail possessing fewer things, lessening energy use, redesigning buildings and dwelling units, emphasis on slow and local travel rather than fast and long-distance travel, formation of social ties close to home, and urban gardening. Urry (2013: 240) sees the development of such a society as a way to "deal with the double whammy of rising temperatures and falling supplies of oil which we cannot live with but will not be able to live without."

In 2015, the American Sociological Association Task Force on Sociology and Global Climate Change sponsored an anthology titled *Climate Change and Sociology* which highlights some of the specific concerns of the sociology of climate change (Dunlap and Brulle 2015). These include anthropogenic drivers of climate change, climate change mitigation strategies, civil society groups and social movements responding to climate change, and strategies for incorporating sociological studies into the larger body of climate change research. In his overview of the contribution made by sociologists associated with the American Sociological Association's Section on Political Economy of the World-System to the analysis of climate change, Jorgenson delineates the following four points:

- the broader environmental sociology community's contributions to an understanding of anthropogenic climate change;
- a grounding of the human causes, consequences, and solutions to climate change in structures of power and inequality;
- recognition of the existence of internal peripheries in the core and the semiperiphery along with recognition of the injustices associated with climate change in a world system dominated by core nations;
- "societies can achieve a high standard of living while consuming relatively moderate levels of fossil fuels" (Jorgenson 2015: 270–271).

Overall, in our reading we find that the following broad themes appear in the sociology of climate change literature: (1) climate change as a risk embedded in social processes; (2) the existence of a metabolic rift between capitalism and the planet; (3) the contribution of production and consumption to climate change; (4) the role of sociology in climate change mitigation strategies; and (5) the need for an ecological revolution, as elaborated below. Some other topics for sociologists looking at climate change include the impacts of population on climate change; public values, attitudes, beliefs, and knowledge about climate change; media framing of climate change; and adaptation to climate change (Zehr 2015).

Climate change as a risk

In the early 1980s, the anthropologist Mary Douglas and her political science colleague Aaron Wildavsky raised the question: Why has there been a rise in alarm about threats to life in a time of improving health and expanding life expectancy? They further ask:

> What are Americans afraid of? Nothing much except the food they eat, the water they drink, the air they breathe, the land they live on, and the energy they use. In the amazingly short space of fifteen to twenty years, confidence about the physical world has turned to doubt.
>
> *Douglas and Wildavsky 1982: 10*

In explaining the growth of perceived precarity in society, and its relationship to people's trust and certitude about the safety of the environment on which they depend, Douglas and Wildavsky adopted a decidedly constructivist stance: namely, they believe that each society culturally constructs its own visions of threat and danger. Citing the case of the Lele of the Democratic Republic of the Congo, among whom Douglas conducted fieldwork in the 1950s, they note that despite living in a place replete with life-threatening tropical infections, Lele health fears were focused primarily on being hit by a bolt of lightning, suffering barrenness, and coming down with bronchitis. As this example shows, they argue, it is not objective reality, but culturally shaped understandings that give rise to local perceptions and conceptions of risk in society. What is of note about this work, in addition to its opening up of the topic of risk in the social sciences, is the way many other anthropologists, steeped like Douglas in a deep appreciation of the significance of culture, reacted to this constructivist argument. While Douglas and Wildavsky's book was greeted positively by some, others raised sharp criticisms. Reviewers in anthropological journals criticized the reduction of risk to a cultural metaphor as a trivialization of people's direct perception of threats to their well-being in polluted air (e.g., rising rates of asthma), polluted land (e.g., local cancer rates in impacted areas), polluted water (e.g., loss of potable water sources), and the effects of climate change (e.g., rise in the frequency and impact of extreme weather). Moreover, Douglas and Wildavsky's view that everything we perceive is nothing but a cultural artifact both diminishes people's ability (and need) to have some degree of accuracy in their perceptions of the world and at the same time provides thick scholarly cover for massive corporate pollution, which is only of importance because people have come to think of it culturally as a risk. As Ian Hacking (1982) emphasizes in his review, sometimes the reader of Douglas and Wildavsky's book "has to cry out that some pollution is real." Indeed, if anything, it might be argued that massive public relations and disinformation campaigns, which are a kind of cultural construction, by industry have led to a contained recognition of the multiple chemical, atmospheric, and other threats to well-being that are spewing into the environment.

Moreover, what is suggested by this discussion is the growing experiential sense of facing a future fraught with uncertainty and a foreboding of vulnerability in society. As indicated in Chapter 1, it is expected that as the effects of climate change and pluralea interaction mount, people's experience of precarity also will climb and begin to take a toll of its own beyond that of the new risks being faced in the environment. Barring social efforts to build unity, support, and mitigation/ adaptation, the growing sense of risk may contribute to a loss of trust in social institutions, breakdowns in the functioning of needed social systems, and a resulting increase in vulnerability to an ever more adverse environment. For this reason, the issue of risk, how it is understood and used in social science writings about climate change, and its relationship to the contingency of human existence, is of critical importance.

In this regard, German sociologist Ulrich Beck has written numerous books on what he terms *risk society*. Beck (1992: 21) defines risk as "a systematic way of dealing with hazards and insecurities induced and introduced by modernization." He maintains that humans have experienced risks, threats, and insecurity throughout their existence on the planet. As contrasted with older forms of risk, modern risk tends to be invisible (e.g., toxins in the environment), is rooted in industrial over-production, and jeopardizes not just humans, but all forms of life on the planet. Modern societies have become the quintessential risk societies in which risk is identified, monitored, governed, and controlled by institutional structures, such as the police, the courts, departments of public health, the banks, the military, and the state. A risk society, in other words, is characterized by new organizational patterns of power and authority unseen in earlier eras. Risk society has taken on a global dimension in the form of world risk society as manifested in international conflict, terrorism, economic crises, and environmental hazards (Beck 2007). In the world risk society, the vigor of anthropocentric perspectives is sapped because while in the past industrial society was based on a presumed antithesis between nature and society, "At the end of the twentieth century nature is society and society is also 'nature.' Anyone who continues to speak of nature as non-society is speaking from a different century, which no longer captures our reality" (Beck 1992: 81). In no small part, this is because through the actions of human societies, nature everywhere as it is known by humankind has become a "highly synthetic product."

While in most of his earlier books Beck only touches fleetingly on climate change, in *World at Risk* (2007) he begins to draw more attention to a topic which has already posed risks for many people in the world and promises to do so increasingly in the future. He argues:

> Climate change, for example, is a product of successful industrialization which systematically disregards its consequences for nature and humanity. The global economy is growing too quickly, affluence is rising too sharply, which simply means that the greenhouse emissions of the industrial countries are steadily increasing.
>
> *Beck 2007: 8*

Unfortunately, nation-states have not been able or willing to engage in meaningful climate change mitigation strategies, thus throwing the responsibility for doing so to multinational institutions. Beck (2007: 102) argues that when it comes to climate protection, an "alliance of global economic actors must be forged, one of whose major goals is to commit the nations and governments who are anxious about their sovereignty to the new vision of multistate cooperation."

Elsewhere, Beck (2010) proposes eight theses for guiding the sociology of climate change:

Thesis 1—Sociology needs to be drawn into the discussion of climate change because climate politics has tended to be an expert and elitist discourse in which ordinary people tend to be neglected.

Thesis 2—In order for the term *environment* to be sociologically meaningful, it must encompass human action and society.

Thesis 3—Climate change entails social inequality and power.

Thesis 4—While climate change exacerbates social inequalities between the center and periphery, it also will adversely impact the wealthy and requires a *cosmopolitan imperative* in which humanity either cooperates or perishes.

Thesis 5—Risk politics demands regulation in order to transcend organized irresponsibility in the modern world.

Thesis 6—The media has the potential to present global risks, including climate change, which depict human suffering.

Thesis 7—An alternative modernity that confronts global ecological risks will have to entail a new vision of prosperity that transcends the present emphasis on economic growth and instead privileges *well-being*.

Thesis 8—*Cosmopolitanism* or widespread consciousness of the world constitutes a perspective that transcends national interests and has the potential to create a green modernity.

Ironically, Beck eschews any specific reference to global capitalism, but refers to it as *industrial modernity* or *Western modernity*, a common pattern of avoiding open dialogue and debate about capitalism in contemporary sheepish academic speak. Nevertheless, Beck (2010: 264), in stating the following, recognizes that the latter is in the process of running its course:

> I maintain that, in the light of climate change, the apparently independent and autonomous system of industrial modernization has begun a process of

self-dissolution and self-transformation. This radical turn marks the current phase in which modernization is becoming reflexive, which means: we have to open up to global dialogues and conflicts about redefining modernity. . . . It has to include multiple extra-European voices, experiences and expectations concerning the futures of modernity.

Of course, it is not only European voices or even those from other developed countries around the world, but the voices of Africa, Asia, Latin America, and the Pacific Islands that also must be part of the discussion of human futures. Indeed, Asia, which contains about 60 percent of the world's population, accounts for 85 percent of those killed and impacted by disasters events, including ones related to climate change, in 2011 (Islam and Lim 2015). In terms of the Arctic region, while generally not recognized by the Canadian mainstream media, the greatest risks emanating from climate change, particularly melting ice, fall upon indigenous peoples (Stoddart and Smith 2016).

As exemplified in the work of cultural sociologists Philip Smith and Nicholas Howe (2015), there is growing recognition of the risks associated with climate change, perhaps first most profoundly depicted in Al Gore's blockbuster film *An Inconvenient Truth* in 2006, a social drama that allowed Gore to remake himself from a failed politician to the most public visible climate activist, although a rather mainstream one, in the world (Baer 2015). They assert that climate change is not simply a scientific fact or a social and political dilemma—a "wicked problem," so to speak—but a social drama in everyday life. Ironically, even in a relatively conservative country like the United States, surveys indicate that the majority of Americans believe that climate change is happening and constitutes a risk that needs to be addressed. Surveys also reveal that most people who recognize that climate change is a problem "do surprisingly little to change lifestyles or engage in collective action" (Smith and Howe 2015: 68), a sobering reality that confronts climate activists around the world.

The metabolic rift between capitalism and the planet

Environmental sociologists John Bellamy Foster *et al.* (2010: 7) maintain that an ecological disruption—or, using the term these authors adapted from Marx, a metabolic rift—has developed, particularly under capitalism, which is "alienating us from the material-natural conditions of our existence and from succeeding generations." They point to the work of Johan Rockström and his colleagues at the Stockholm Resilience Centre which identified the following nine "planetary boundaries," alluded to in Chapter 1, that are essential to address in maintaining a global ecosystem in which humanity can survive and thrive safely: (1) climate change which is on the verge of reaching a tipping point; (2) ocean acidification, also on the verge of reaching a tipping point; (3) stratospheric ozone depletion, also close to a tipping point; (4) disruption of natural nitrogen and phosphorous cycles; (5) human pressure on global freshwater availability; (6) conversion of forests, wetlands, and other vegetation types to agricultural lands; (7) biodiversity loss; (8) atmospheric aerosol loading; and (9) toxic chemical pollution. Foster *et al.* (2010: 78) maintain that:

> The development of capitalism, whether through colonialism, imperialism, or market forces, expanded the metabolic rift to the global level, as distant regions across the oceans were brought into production to serve the interests of capitalists in core nations. While incorporating distant lands into the global economy—a form of geographical displacement—helped relieve some of the demands placed on agriculture production in core nations, it did not serve as remedy to the metabolic rift. The systematic expansion of production on a large scale subjected more of the natural world to the dictates of capital. The consequence of this, as Marx noted, is that "it disturbs the metabolic interaction between man and the earth."

Foster *et al.* (2010: 122) suggest that Marx's metabolic analysis can be extended to an examination of global climate change involving the linkage of three dimensions: (1) the impact of capitalism on the global carbon cycle; (2) the Jevons Paradox, in which technological improvements in energy efficiency lead unexpectedly not to decreased but to increased utilization of natural resources, and thereby contribute to environmental degradation; and (3) the impact of capitalism on the destruction of carbon sinks. While a large section of the international elite have come to recognize the seriousness of climate change, the solutions they propose under the guise of ecological modernization, green capitalism, and existing climate regimes are insufficient to contain catastrophic climate change. In the view of Foster *et al.* (2010), humanity needs to undergo nothing short of an ecological revolution, a notion that is discussed in greater detail below. Moreover, as is evident from the imperiled list of planetary boundaries, climate change is not happening in a vacuum, but is growing at a time of multiple other anthropogenic ecocrisis, some of which, like ocean acidification and stratospheric ozone depletion, are verging on their own respective tipping points. Yet, as we stressed in Chapter 1 in discussion of our pluralea interactions, the issue is not just the co-occurrence of ecological crises caused by various human actions; it is the mutual enhancement of these crises through interlinkage with each other that is a particularly potent component of the metabolic rift endangering humanity.

The contribution of production and consumption to climate change

Prominent sociologist Zygmunt Bauman (2005: 24–26) argues that modern societies have shifted from "producer societies," which engage people primarily as manufacturers of goods, to "consumer societies," which seduce people to focus their lives around acquiring an endless array of consumer items in order to alleviate their boredom. In reality, production and consumption have become intricately interrelated in all capitalist societies, particularly developed ones, but increasingly in developing societies as well. A version of this theme is also taken up by sociologist John Bellamy Foster, who discusses how global capitalism with its *treadmill of production*, a concept introduced in Chapter 4, has placed increasing stress on the planetary ecology.

Australian sociologist Ariel Salleh (2009: 27), in analyzing the ecological and climate crises, operates within a "gender aware eco-socialist" perspective that asserts that women, especially those of the global South, generally are not culpable for climate change in that "as 75 percent of the world's poor, they may have no electricity, few consumer goods, and little time or money to spend on energy-guzzling leisure pursuits." Even in developed nations, this pattern holds. Salleh points, for example, to a 2006 Swedish Ministry of Sustainable Development report showing "that class notwithstanding, men's ecological footprint in that nation is remarkably larger than women's" (Salleh 2008: 104). More broadly, she argues that "Global warming causes, effects, and solutions are 'sex/gendered'" (Salleh 2008: 103). Salleh includes in her critique the failure of environmental activists to develop gender literacy in recognizing gender differences in resource use and access.

In contrast to the smaller ecological footprint of women, sociologist John Urry (2010: 205) points to the city of Dubai in the United Arab Emirates as the icon of the culture of consumption. Initially spurred on by oil production, consumption in Dubai has taken on a life of its own that is "made possible by migrant contract labourers from Pakistan and India who are bound to a single employer and subject to totalitarian control." Dubai has sought, in Urry's words (2011: 73), to become a "luxury-consumer paradise." Thus, despite being in an arid land, Dubai is one of the highest users of water in the world. Moreover, the country has one of the highest per capita energy consumption rates in the world, with a heavily reliance on energy-consuming air conditioning (which enables the existence of an indoor ski resort, and gardens sustained by cold air blown from outdoor air conditioners). Land use patterns (e.g., island-building to increase high-priced waterfront housing and hotels) and dredging have further threatened the local environment. In short, as Urry (2011: 73) observes, "Dubai is a place of monumental excess" in a time of global warming.

The private motor vehicle constitutes the leading mode of transportation in the world, as discussed in Chapter 6. Kingsley Dennis, a Research Associate at Lancaster University, in collaboration with John Urry, co-authored *After the Car*, in which they argue that the days of current car use are numbered, in that it is a dysfunctional system in a time of accelerating climate change, a presumed peaking of oil, the increased digitization of most aspects of economic and social life, and ongoing population growth (Kingsley and Urry 2009). They report that in 2004, the "UK transport sector was responsible for around 27 per cent of total carbon dioxide emissions, most of this coming from road traffic" and that the "US Environmental Protection Agency estimated that 60 per cent of all US carbon dioxide emissions are emitted by motor vehicles" (Kingsley and Urry 2009: 10). Kingsley and Urry (2009: 33–34) assert that the "Fordist production and consumption system" transformed the automobile as a luxury item for the wealthy into a "commodity for the masses and especially for many families living in the American suburbs." The Fordist system in time spread to Canada, Europe, Australia, and New Zealand, and has made inroads into the developing world, as evidenced by traffic congestion in far-flung cities such as Mexico City, Bogota, São Paulo, Beijing, Shanghai, and Jakarta. In addition to being a major source of air pollution and carbon dioxide emissions, and thus a central component of the "high carbon society" (Kingsley and Urry 2009: 47), the car is literally a "death machine" that results in somewhere in the order of 1.2 million deaths and 20–50 million injuries annually (Kingsley and Urry 2009: 28). This compares with fewer than 1,500 deaths due to air transport crashes annually (Aircraft Crashes Record Office 2013). Furthermore, sociologist Ariel Salleh (2008) points out that energy use in the transport sector is mediated by gender. For instance, she cites a 2006 European Parliament-commissioned report that indicates that "men in EU states tend to make trips by car for a single purpose; and over longer distances than women do" (Salleh 2008: 105). Salleh (2008: 105) also notes that "Air travel between cities is predominantly used by men." These data affirm Salleh's larger argument, noted above, about the highly gendered nature of anthropogenic climate change.

Kingsley and Urry (2009) engage in a type of sociology of the future by delineating three possible post-car scenarios for 2050. In the first of these, what they term *post-oil localism*, they suggest that the car system will be partially replaced by a wide range of local forms of transport and mobility, including walking, cycling, and presumably energy-efficient public transit systems. The second scenario is a dystopian case of *regional war lordism* in which movement is "hard to achieve because of the breakdown of many of the long-term systems of mobility and communications" and is "dangerous if one leaves behind the safety of one's particular fortress" (Kingsley and Urry 2009: 160–161). Kingsley and Urry (2009: 161), in their third scenario, posit the possibility of the emergence *of digital networks of control*, which envisages a "fully functioning post-car system which transforms very many kinds of vehicles away from being separate and autonomous towards the automation of movement." The notion of digital networks of control would include collectively owned cars instead of private ones, in which small, light mobile pods would be accessed by individuals when needed. In fact, some of these pods would be driverless. Furthermore, the "movement of vehicles would be electronically and physically integrated with other forms of mobility" (Kingsley and Urry 2009: 156).

Obviously, any effort to forecast the future in a world of increasing social disparities and environmental degradation, including climatic turmoil and a mounting mood of precarity, is fraught with monumental difficulties. Nevertheless, Kingsley and Urry (2009: 164) provide much food for thought in stating:

> Small decisions and disruptive innovations occurring now may be laying down a set of huge path-dependent patterns. These will have untold consequences for later generations, whose range of opportunities will be constrained as the peaking of oil and the consequences of climate change will have further speeded up. How the issue of personal mobility is dealt with will in part

determine whether and how people live their lives down the line, in small-scale localism, in a Hobbesian war of all against all, or in Orwellian systems of digital surveillance.

On a smaller scale, Stuart Sim (2009) argues that the climate crisis may require the phasing out of cheap package holidays and the scaling back of tourism, which he notes may adversely affect multiculturalism and the economies of various countries in Africa, the Caribbean, South America, and the Mediterranean. He observes, however, that the growing concern about the greenhouse gases emitted by airplanes and ships, both freight and cruise vessels, has prompted the proposal that humanity return to the era of sailing, which could entail the development of ships with giant "kite" sails (Sim 2009: 95).

Sociologist Constance Lever-Tracy (2011: 45) argues that while late capitalism has been based upon a treadmill of production and consumption, this has not always been the case, as exemplified by the World War II era, during which military production resulted in the "co-existence of full employment and reduced consumption" due to a government-imposed system of rationing and saving. Furthermore, following the war, the nuclear arms and space races pushed for the production of weapons, satellites, and other space devices that were not consumer items targeted at the general public. Lever-Tracy tends to be skeptical of the zero-growth paradigm to which eco-socialists, eco-anarchists, and even ecological economists such as Herman Daly and ecologists such as James Gustave Speth (2008) subscribe.

Climate change mitigation strategies

Sociologists vary widely in what they believe needs to be done to mitigate climate change. Giddens (2009) adopts a green social democratic stance in which he argues that the state will have to play a key role. He argues:

> There is no way of forcing states to sign up to international agreements: and even if they chose to do so, implementing whatever is agreed will largely be the responsibility of each individual state. Emissions trading markets can only work if the price of carbon is capped, and at a demanding level, a decision that has to be made and implemented politically. Technological advance will be vital to our chances of cutting greenhouse gas emissions, but support from the state will be necessary to get it off the ground.
>
> *Giddens 2009: 5*

Giddens (2009) delineates nine tasks states must undertake in dealing with climate change:

1. the introduction of long-term policies or planning on the part of corporations, civil society, and individual citizens;
2. the management of climate change and energy risks in the context of other social risks;

3. the promotion of political and economic convergence required for the achievement of a low-carbon economy;
4. the implementation of the "polluter pays" principle into market relations;
5. countering corporate interests which seek to stop climate change mitigation;
6. making climate change a top political agenda;
7. the development of appropriate economic and fiscal measures for shifting towards a low-carbon economy, such as subsidies for new energy-efficient technologies;
8. the preparation of needed climate adaptation measures; and
9. the integration of local, regional, national, and international climate change policies.

While Giddens (2009: 92) expresses skepticism about the viability of carbon markets, he argues that "there is a great deal that can be done to introduce full cost pricing, and therefore to allow market forces to become centered upon promoting environmental benefits." Furthermore, while he is cautious about manipulative corporate green-washing public relations tactics designed to make a company appear more environmentally friendly than its practices actually are, Giddens is clearly an advocate of green capitalism, in that he believes that government regulations can force corporations to engage in environmentally sustainable and climate-safe practices, and credits some of them with "transforming their attitudes just as radically as are states" (Giddens 2009: 122). Giddens (2009: 130), in fact, believes that humanity stands on the verge of a *third industrial revolution* which holds out the promise of a "global economy where millions of people produce renewable energy and share it with others through national and international power grids—as happens today with information." He contends that governments can play an important role in encouraging environmentally sustainable technological innovation, and views the creation of green jobs as a stepping stone in developing a low-carbon economy. Giddens (2009: 150) also advocates carbon taxes situated "as near to the point of production as possible, in order to apply to all relevant aspects of manufacturing processes." Conversely, while not being outright opposed to carbon trading markets or emissions trading schemes, he views them as being at an experimental stage and is uncertain whether "they can be introduced on an international, let alone global level" (Giddens 2009: 201).

Giddens's enthusiasm about the "third industrial revolution," modeled on the alleged information-sharing patterns of the internet, seems not be based on a realistic assessment of what has occurred with the internet in recent years, namely a corporate restructuring involving a move from the open flow of information to controlled and increasingly cost-based access to information, information steering, and advertisement flooding. In other words, his assessment seems not to take into account the power of corporations to occupy and control new areas of economic or energy development, including national and international power grids.

In contrast to Giddens, sociologist Charles Derber (2010: 1) proposes a more radical approach to climate change mitigation in his assertion that climate change "is so intertwined with our crisis-riddled economy that solutions to global warming cannot happen without rapid systemic changes in our capitalist order." In the case of the United States, he views the US presidency as having the potential to pave the way for systemic changes needed on Wall Street and in energy firms, specifically, and more generally the corporate system to address the climate crisis vis-à-vis the "90 Percent Solution," which includes the following policies:

- a requirement that each federal department create an emergency plan to cut emissions in its sector by 90 percent by 2050;
- the creation of a green financial system entailing regulation, public ownership, and "trust-busting" on Wall Street and the entire financial sector;
- the implementation of a clean energy foundation for the economy entailing regulation, public ownership, and financial incentives in the energy sector forcing a rapid shift from oil and coal to cleaner energy sources;
- the reconstitution of corporate charters in order to ensure an environmentally sustainable, full-employment productive system.

The president could achieve implementation of the above policies by exerting his constitutional authority to keep Congress in session until it passes legislation facilitating these changes. However much they may appeal to sentiments about having a bully pulpit presidency, we believe that Derber's proposal to keep Congress in session until needed legislation is passed is highly unrealistic. This could only happen if there was an enormous and sustained groundswell of popular support—in the streets—demanding that Congress act. As stated by Derber, realpolitik suggests that the president could not pull this off based solely on strong willpower.

As a temporary and more radical measure, Derber (2010: 130) proposes that the US federal government assume 51 percent ownership of the oil and coal companies. He advocates a paradigm shift from the growth paradigm inherent in a capitalist system to a society emphasizing quality of life. While Derber focuses on the changes needed to create a socially just and environmentally sustainable American society, he acknowledges that addressing climate change effectively will require an international effort, one that challenges the hegemony of corporate globalization. He proposes a systemic plan of green globalization and a global New Deal that entails five general policies: the regulation and slowing down of global capital; the fostering of governmental intervention; the globalization of the commons; the creation of green and socially just trade agreements; and the implementation of global campaign finance reform (Derber 2010: 181). Derber (2010: 183) maintains that global capitalism seeks to turn all natural resources, including water, land, and air, into commodities, and that green globalization would entail "rebuilding a global commons and ensuring that the biosphere is protected from predatory profit-seeking." He views *glocalism* as a key component of green globalization, under which as much production as possible is shifted from the global level to the local level. While glocalism is not pure localism, it emphasizes "local economies wherever possible, reserving global production for only those areas where local production cannot work" (Derber 2010: 185).

In Derber's (2010: 185) assessment:

> Green climate regime change will shift the balance back toward the local, because localism builds community, is economically beneficial in many sectors, and will become increasingly cost-efficient as the price of oil and other energy inevitably rises. The local is also good medicine for global warming in many sectors.

While Derber would like to see governments implement radical reforms that would contribute to green globalization and a safe climate, he stresses that social movements of various sorts, but particularly the social justice and environmental movements, have a key role to play in these developments. In reality, it seems that these movements will have to play *the* role, not simply a key role, but this would only be possible if they become truly mass movements. Only international mass movements are capable of controlling and rolling back the hegemony of corporate globalization.

Derber (2010: 203) argues that:

> Movements often must endure for decades or centuries to succeed, but when an existential systemic crisis such as global warming requires immediate emergency action only social movements can act with the blazing pace necessary, because they operate outside the system and refuse to be slowed or chained by the rules.

Derber (2010: 205) believes that in order to address the climate crisis, social movements must face the existential reality of climate change, struggle for regime change within nation-states and internationally, allow labor to take the lead, integrate personal and systemic changes, and both cooperate with heads of state and push them to take more radical stances on systemic problems. He maintains that the "labor movement has begun to advocate strongly for green economic solutions to the current crisis, as well as to remake the economy and ensure full employment for the long term" (Derber 2010: 209). Many environmentalists may be reluctant to put labor in a position of leadership because many labor union leaders are committed to providing their members with a high material standard of living with little thought of the environmental consequences associated with it.

Christopher Wright, an organizational sociologist, and Daniel Nyberg have written an illuminating book titled *Climate Change, Capitalism, and Corporations*, a truly impressive feat given that they are professors at the University of Sydney Business School and the Newcastle Business School respectively (Wright and Nyberg 2015). Although the UNFCCC, governments, politicians, and climate scientists tend to be publicly visible in the climate change mitigation discourse, private corporations tend to be less so, although increasingly so as more and more the findings of climate science have become normalized. In light of this reality, whereas corporations often were part and parcel of climate denialism, such as was the case for the Global Climate Coalition, more and more corporations have come to assert that they are striving to achieve environmental sustainability and reduce greenhouse gas emissions in their business practices.

Wright and Nyberg (2015) interviewed representatives from five corporations, to unravel the basic premises of corporate environmentalism: (1) a leading energy producer that was supplementing fossil fuel generation with renewable energy sources; (2) a major financial services company that was factoring a "price on carbon" into its lending policies to corporate clients; (3) a large insurance company that was measuring financial risks incurred by extreme weather events; (4) an international manufacturing company that was repositioning itself as a "green" firm producing more efficient equipment and renewable energy technologies; and (5) a media company that has embraced an eco-efficiency campaign to become "carbon neutral."

Based upon their interviews with sustainability managers and consultants at these corporations, they identified three dominant identities: (1) the rational manager, (2) the green change agent, and (3) the committed activist. The rational manager emphasizes improved energy efficiency and reduced costs as environmentally sustainable practices, and believes that engaging with climate change presents new business opportunities. The green change agent is personally committed to addressing environmental sustainability and the climate crisis within his or her corporation, but sometimes encounters internal opposition to proposed changes. The committed activist tends to operate outside the corporation and is involved with community environmental and climate action groups, but may experience disillusionment in trying to implement environmentally sustainable practices within the corporation. Wright and Nyberg maintain that corporate environmentalism tends to build on the notion of ecological modernization that stresses the ability to come up with technological innovations that are environmentally sustainable. Many corporate managers view carbon pricing and eco-efficiency as "win–win" scenarios for both their firms and the environment, and view themselves as "corporate citizens" who are promoting "sustainable businesses." Some corporations seek to pursue climate change mitigation policies by forming linkages with selected environmental NGOs, progressive think tanks, and even with sectors of academia.

Calls for an ecological revolution

John Bellamy Foster (2009) presents an even more radical approach than Derber in his proposed strategy for mitigating climate change. He identifies two types of ecological revolutions: eco-industrial revolution and eco-social revolution. The first of these entails the adoption of technological innovations or ecological modernization that include improved energy efficiency and the adopting of renewable sources of energy, an approach that has been hailed by a number of corporations and governments, particularly in Northern Europe, and most segments of environmental and climate movements. The second of these, which Foster (2009: 12–13) favors:

> draws on alternative technologies when necessary, but emphasizes the need to transform the human relation to nature and the constitution of society at its roots within the existing social relations of production. This can be

accomplished only through a process of sustainable human development. This means moving decisively in the direction of egalitarian and communal forms of production, distribution, exchange, and consumption, and thus breaking with the logic of the dominant social order. . . . Such changes involve a civilizational shift based on a revolution in culture, as well as economy and society.

Foster (2009: 33) adopts the late Hugo Chavez's notion of the *elementary triangle of socialism* as part of a *socialism for the twenty-first century*, which would entail "(1) social ownership; (2) social production organized by workers; and (3) satisfaction of communal needs." However, this elementary triangle of socialism, he maintains, needs to be coupled with the *elementary triangle of ecology*, based on "(1) social use, not ownership, of nature; (2) rational regulation by the associated producers of the metabolism between human beings and nature; and (3) the [sustainable] satisfaction of human needs" in the present and the future (Foster 2009: 33). Foster maintains that the Soviet Union, albeit created on the basis of socialist-oriented revolution, failed to achieve an eco-social revolution because of its mechanistic emphasis on production at the expense of workers' democracy. Moreover, the Soviet Union did not embrace the second of the elements of the elementary triangle of ecology, as indicated by its poor track record in environmental protection. Foster (2009: 34) firmly maintains that "Socialism is ecological, ecologism is socialist or neither can truly exist."

While recognizing that climate change poses the most profound immediate threat to human survival, Foster admits that the task of making a shift from capitalism to socialism is extremely difficult in terms of both theory and social action. While he does not lay out even a loose blueprint for such a transition, he does observe that:

> It follows that there is little real prospect for the needed global ecological revolution, unless these attempts to revolutionize social relations in the struggle for a just and sustainable society, now emerging in the periphery, are somehow mirrored in movements for ecological and social revolution in the advanced capitalist world.
>
> *Foster 2009: 276*

Even this approach is limited, in the view of Ariel Salleh. In an interview conducted by Gerry Canavan *et al.* (2010), Salleh argues that Foster, as well as Paul Burkett, another well-known eco-Marxist, fails to recognize that:

> [although] the end of capital is a necessary condition for sustainability, it is not a sufficient one. For capitalism itself is a modern version of patriarchal social relations, and so a parallel political devolution is called for. In other words, the ties between hegemonic masculinity and the diminishment of nature and of women still have to be unraveled. So far, neither Foster nor Burkett carry their work to this level, which means that their political

remedy for the emancipation of nature may be self-defeating in the end. Sex-gender silence is prevalent across the social sciences, among political economists, environmental ethicists, and so on.

quoted in Canavan et al. *2010: 187–188*

Christina Ergas and Richard York (2012) conducted a statistical, cross-national analysis in which they found that CO_2 emissions per capita tend to be lower where women have higher political status when GDP per capita, urbanization, industrialization, militarization, world-system position, foreign direct investment, age of dependency ratio, and level of democracy are controlled as variables. They conclude that efforts to engage in climate change mitigation can be coupled with those to increase women's status, as these may be mutually reinforcing social changes. These researchers and Salleh, among others, affirm that climate change and its study are not gender-neutral. While the effects of climate change tend to magnify existing gender inequalities (e.g., in terms of relative vulnerability), mitigation efforts often overlook the fact that women may be effective agents of change in responding to the assaults of climate turmoil (Dankelman 2010). Women may be "fiercely determined" in this regard because, as keepers of their families and households, their "struggles and . . . determination are [their] only respite" (Negi *et al.* 2010: 72). Understanding these aspects of the role of gender in social scientific study of climate change remains underdeveloped. Thus, they remain a vital arena of needed research not only in sociology, but cross-culturally in the anthropology of climate change.

Various criminologists, who tend to sit at the intersection of sociology and political science or politics, have adopted a peacemaking perspective on climate change which is ecocentric and committed to social justice. While not specifically calling for the eradication of global capitalism per se, McClanahan and Brisman (2015: 424), as proponents of the peacemaking perspective, call for "transformations that turn from violent conflict," which has contributed to climate change, and "suggest waging peace on climate change by waging peace on earth."

Community responses to climate change

Like anthropologists, various sociologists have conducted research on how diverse communities or peoples have been responding to climate change. Kari Marie Norgaard (2011), for example, conducted ethnographic research in Bygdaby (a pseudonym pronounced "big-DAH-bee"), a town of some 10,000–14,000 people situated in a mountainous region of western Norway. Her study took place in the autumn of 2000 and the winter of 2001, when the community experienced unusually warm weather. In contrast to the kinds of climate skepticism one might encounter in the United States and Australia, Norgaard met very few climate skeptics in Bygdaby. Despite this, she found the vast majority of her informants were not taking action on climate change, particularly collective action, despite the fact that the community residents were highly aware of their environment and thus in "a special position to notice climate change and to have their identity affected by it" (Norgaard 2011: 20). Despite a high level of political activism in Bygdaby, Norgaard (2011: 43) notes that "climate change was never discussed in any of the meetings that I attended in any of the city council or specific Labor Party strategy meetings or even in the meetings of the municipal subgroup on culture and environment." Informants tended to view climate change as more of a national or international issue that could not be addressed at the community level in any significant way. On the whole, community residents tended to feel helpless and powerless in the face of climate change, the effects of which they were experiencing first hand. Although Norway is a more progressive country on social welfare issues than either the United States or Australia, it is very much a part of the global North in that it has become the largest oil producer in Europe, the world's fifth largest oil exporter, and derives one-third of its national revenue from oil. Norgaard (2011: 70) reports that the "people I spoke with in Bygdaby played a critical role in legitimizing the status quo by not talking about global warming even in the face of late winter snow and a lake that never froze." She asserts that citizens of developed countries who do not respond to the reality of climate change benefit from their denial economically as well as by "avoiding the emotional and psychological entanglement and conflicts that may arise from knowing that one is doing the 'wrong thing'" (Norgaard 2011: 72). Such short-term benefits, of course, can produce long-term costs, but these might not yet be visible to the people of Bygdaby at this point in the ongoing escalation of global warming effects.

Norgaard's study reveals some of the complexities in the conceptual link between perceived environmental change and the emergence of precarity as lived experience. When the costs of a changing environment are not too high, and the uncertainties of how best to respond are too great, it appears that it is possible to adhere to a status quo as if nothing had happened. This underlines the importance of events that sufficiently upset everyday routines such that confidence in the dependability of the environment and of established social life begins to weaken.

In another study, sociologist Christine Shearer (2011) detailed how the residents of Kivalina, a village of some 400 people, situated about 120 miles north of the Arctic Circle in northwest Alaska, who still retain a largely foraging lifestyle and first observed the erosion of their island in the 1950s, have responded to climate change-related events. They voted to relocate in 1992 as a result of climate/environment changes, selected a new site in 1998, but quickly discovered that no government agency existed that could assist them with their proposed relocation. The community has thus far had little success with its relocation efforts, despite the fact that they find themselves in increasing danger. In February 2008, Kivalina, along with various indigenous rights and environmental justice organizations, filed a suit against 24 oil, electricity, and coal companies for contributing to the village's erosion through their role in contributing to greenhouse gas emissions and climate change and systematically fostering climate change denial. The village asked the fossil fuel industry to pay for its relocation costs, estimated at $100 million–400 million. Following highly complicated and drawn-out legal wrangling, Kivalina's claim was dismissed, thus requiring Kivalina residents to seek "other means to protect themselves and their homeland" (Shearer 2011: 124). Unfortunately, class action suits are generally very difficult, and often very expensive within the context of the US legal system.

In a similar vein to Hans Baer and Linda Connor's examination of the climate movement, particularly in the Australian context, a few sociologists have also studied this movement as a response to the climate crisis. In his book *Communication Power*, Manuel Castells (2009: 303–338) has a section titled "Warming Up to Global Warming: The Environmental Movement and the New Culture of Nature." He observes: "The alliance between scientists, environmentalists, and opinion leaders that ultimately put global warming on the public agenda cannot be understood without situating it within the context of the environmental movement, one of the decisive social movements of our time." Castells maintains that a wide array of environmental organizations and activists around the world have found common cause in their concern about climate change. He describes how climate action groups in the United Kingdom and the United States, as well as international groups such as Friends of the Earth, the World Wide Fund for Nature, and Greenpeace, have utilized the internet and public events to disseminate their message.

Parks and Roberts (2010) also make some brief but important observations about the climate movement in addressing climate justice issues. They state:

> the work of a new generation of bridge-builders and insider-outsider networks—that are bringing together "development" NGOs like Oxfam and ActionAid and "environment" NGOs like Friends of the Earth, WWF and Greenpeace—deserves greater scholarly attention. The work of the Climate Action Network, the new Climate Justice Now network and Third World network, for example, could prove instrumental in developing "hybrid justice" approaches that could break North–South impasse. Norm entrepreneurs, such as EcoEquity, are also beginning to forge links with civil society actors in the global South and pioneer new approaches to "global climate justice" that could bridge the gap between mitigation and the need for huge amounts of adaptation financing.
>
> *Parks and Roberts 2010: 153*

Parks and Roberts maintain that the climate justice movement has an uphill struggle in that many of its actors are opposed to emissions trading schemes, along with Climate Development Mechanism and Reducing Emissions from Deforestation and Degradation programs, and favor carbon taxes on the polluters and compensation for the victims of climate change when most climate regimes at international, regional, and national levels have accepted the emissions trading scheme process and market mechanisms as axiomatic.

The political science of climate change

Two political scientists have edited anthologies on climate change that include chapters written primarily by political scientists or political theorists, albeit not exclusively. The first one is *Political Theory and Global Climate Change*, edited by Steve Vanderheiden (2008), and the second is *The Oxford Handbook of Climate Change and Society*, co-edited by John S. Dryzek and his colleagues (Dryzek *et al.* 2011b), the latter of which we mentioned earlier. The first volume consists of eight chapters all written by political scientists, except for one, and is organized around two themes: (1) justice and ethics, and (2) nature and society. In the book, Leigh Raymond explores five arguments for the allocation of the *global atmospheric commons*; Stephen Gardiner, a philosopher, examines the ethical implications of climate change; Steve Vanderheiden reviews three environmental rights to be considered in the design of a global climate regime, namely the rights to develop, expend a minimum level of per capita greenhouse emissions simply to survive, and to achieve climate stability; and Martin Adamian applies insights from critical legal studies to climate change politics and policy. The essays in Part I of the book vary, from the generally conventional approaches of Vanderheiden and Gardiner, who propose that climate justice can be achieved within the parameters of global capitalism, to the more critical perspectives which question the notion that equity in terms of greenhouse gases allocated to individuals or countries can be achieved within those parameters.

In Part II, Amy Lauren Lovecraft provides a social-ecological analysis of the impact of climate change on the Arctic ecosystem; Timothy Luke critically explores the social construction of the notions of *global warming* and *global cooling*; George A. Gonzalez provides a neo-Marxian analysis of the impact of urban sprawl and fossil fuel combustion on climate change; and Peter F. Cannavo examines climate change-induced displacement in the aftermath of Hurricane Katrina. All of the essays in Part II examine the societal–nature nexus, but from different perspectives, ranging from a normative one exhibited in Lovecraft's essay, which views values as shaping the political decision-making process, to Gonzalez's perspective, which is congruent with our critical anthropological approach to climate change.

Although *The Oxford Handbook of Climate Change and Society* includes contributions from scholars from a diversity of disciplines, including sociology, geography, environmental sciences, development studies, physics, energy studies, science and technology studies, economics, communications, business, and climate science, at least 20 out of the 69 contributors appear to be political scientists. The absence of anthropologists from this collection, as well as from *Political Theory and Global Climate Change*, strikes us as noteworthy. As indicated, we suspect that this exclusion may have been due to in part to the common presumption on the part of political scientists, as well as many sociologists, that the main purview of anthropological research is indigenous societies and peasant communities. We have both encountered surprise on the part of colleagues in other disciplines that we are engaged in research on climate change. At any rate, the encyclopedic *Oxford Handbook of Climate Change* consists of 12 parts: (1) an introduction by the editors; (2) the challenge of climate change; (3) scientific, societal, and public opinion stances on climate change; (4) the social impacts of climate change; (5) the security implications of climate change; (6) climate justice; (7) the response of various publics and movements to climate change;

(8) government responses to climate change; (9) climate policies; (10) corporate responses to climate change and green consumption as a problematic climate change mitigation strategy; (11) global climate governance; and (12) efforts to achieve legitimate climate governance in the wake of the Copenhagen conference and the notion of resilience in the face of runaway climate change. In seeking to validate their effort to provide a multidisciplinary perspective on the relationship between climate change and society and how to solve the climate crisis induced by human activities, Dryzek *et al.* (2011a: 17) assert: "climate change presents perhaps the most profound and complex challenge to have confronted human social, political and economic systems. It also presents one of the most profound challenges to the way we understand human responses."

Political scientist John Barry (2012) has authored an incisive book titled *The Politics of Actually Existing Unsustainability*, in which he examines various political agendas being proposed by assorted actors in their efforts to "flourish" in a "climate-changed, carbon-constrained world." Barry is by no means a neutral social scientist, as attested by his role as co-leader of the Green Party in Northern Ireland between 2003 and 2009. He argues that humanity is "facing inevitable ecological, resource, and socio-economic challenges and we are singularly unprepared for them" (Barry 2012: 25). In seeking a pathway to preparedness, he offers an alternative to the growth paradigm inherent in global capitalism and makes a case for *economic security* in which "quality of life and well-being (especially free time) become central objectives of macro-economic policy and the way we think about a sustainable economy" (Barry 2012: 25). He views the Transition Towns movement, a grassroots network of communities that have embraced the importance of building responsive capacity in the face of threats from climate and economic instability, an initiative that is particularly strong in the UK, as comprised of "resilience pioneers." However, this movement tends to be confined to Anglophone countries and has yet to show promise as a truly global response to climate change. Barry makes a case for what he terms *green civic republicanism* committed to democracy, cultural diversity, equality, respect for the non-human world, and environmental sustainability. He sees the *green republican state* as "regulating the market in order to protect the community from its corrosive effects, in order to enhance community resilience" in a world characterized by "carbon, climate, and resource limits and thresholds" (Barry 2012: 278). While many of Barry's proposals for a sustainable world are to be lauded, for the most part they are framed largely with the developed world in mind and resemble the call for a Green New Deal on the part of various parties, including Tim Jackson (2009: 7), the economics commissioner of Sustainable Development in the UK, who also questions the "underlying vision of prosperity built on continual growth." As green Keynesians of somewhat different sorts, both Barry and Jackson appear to assume that global capitalism can function as a non-growth system when history repeatedly has told us that, by its very nature, it must grow or die out, and, as we argue in this book, if it continues to grow as it has, it will die nonetheless, and take many humans and many other species with it.

Climate regimes

Climate regimes include governments (national, state or provincial, and local), international and regional bodies such as the United Nations Framework Convention on Climate Change and the European Union's Emissions Trading Scheme (EU ETS), business and industrial non-governmental organizations, and environmental non-governmental organizations. Much of the work of political scientists has focused on various aspects of climate regimes, particular the UNFCCC process and the EU ETS. Paul G. Harris (2000), an international relations specialist and Professor of Global and Environmental Studies at the Hong Kong Institute of Education, edited *Climate Change and American Foreign Policy*, a volume that contains contributions from other political scientists as well as scholars from various interdisciplinary fields such as international and environmental studies. His volume contains sections on critiquing US climate change policy, the politics of US climate change policy, and the relationship between international norms and US climate change policy. Harris has also edited *Global Warming and East Asia: The Domestic and International Politics of Climate Change* (2003), which includes chapters on climate politics and policy in China, Japan, the Philippines, Indonesia, and Southeast Asia. More recently, he has argued that climate change is a global problem that lies beyond the control of any one nation-state, and thus "cries out for a cosmopolitan response with new cosmopolitan institutions" (Harris 2011b: 650). In Harris's view, national borders should not constrain obligations to address climate change. It is broad human interest and well-being rather than the narrow political and economic interest of the nation-state that should be the grounds for establishing ethical behavior and environmental policy in a time of global warming. He also has argued for the importance of citizen action as an essential complement to state policy in response to climate change.

Harris edited *China's Responsibility for Climate Change* (2011a), an anthology that includes contributions from not only other political scientists, but also policy analysts, energy analysts, and geographers. Given that China has become the largest national source of greenhouse gas emissions in the world, he asserts that the "predominant emphasis on responsibility of developed countries for climate change will have to be overcome if the world is to take the extraordinary steps necessary to combat the problem aggressively in coming decades" (Harris 2011a: 1). The most critical essay in Harris's anthology was not written by a political scientist, but by a geographer, Olivia Bina, who asserts:

> Chinese leaders have an opportunity to show a different path, living up to the promise of an ecological civilization that is not simply a rehearsal of technocratic beliefs and efficiency-driven solutions. There is a need for radically different ways of thinking about the medium term—for long term is now a luxury of the past if the conclusions of climate scientists are to be taken at face value—and there is a need to experiment now with models that will have to be in place in a matter of decades, not centuries.
>
> *Bina 2011: 68*

In contrast to parliamentary democratic states, political scientist Miranda A. Schreurs (2011) delineates the parameters of the authoritarian climate regime that has emerged in China. It has embarked upon a large-scale program of promoting energy efficiency and renewable energy sources, as well as formulating a National Climate Change Action Plan in 2007. Schreurs (2011: 460) observes: "The Communist Party still prohibits party competition but it has allowed for a degree of open debate about environmental matters. Still, the challenges to transforming the economy in a low-carbon direction remain daunting. Implementation challenges abound."

The emissions challenges faced by China can also be seen with regard to the release of air pollution. While the capital of Beijing has grown and developed rapidly, and traffic jams are now occurring, the quality of the air in the city has grown so bad that people have begun migrating to other areas of the country with better air quality, although some of the places they are going to are also polluted, but just not as badly as the capital.

While power brokers and political pundits in the United States often express fear of the rising economic power of China, in reality it is facing the possibility of a environmental disaster, including one induced by climate change, given that with about one-fifth of the world's population, it is "endowed with a mere 11% of the world's primary energy supply, and an even more meager seven percent of its arable land and freshwater reserves" (Gulick 2011: 26). However, it is important to note that China is seeking to stave off the depletion of its own resources by acquiring resources elsewhere, such as oil from Iraq. Climate change is already contributing to the desertification of the country and diminished run-off from its mountains. Massive water schemes to divert water to desired areas and large cities have led to population displacements, pollution, and high cost.

Political scientists David Held *et al.* (2011) edited *The Governance of Climate Change*, which includes chapters written by both social scientists, such as sociologist Ulrich Beck, other political scientists, including ethicist Peter Singer, David King (the UK Government's Chief Scientific Advisor and Head of the Government Office of Science from October 2000 to 2007), and British Labour Party politicians David and Ed Miliband, the sons of the renowned British socialist Ralph Miliband. In the introduction to their anthology, the editors assert:

> This book explains why acting now in relation to climate change is scientifically rational, economically and ethically desirable. Yet it also highlights how extraordinarily difficult it is to produce a clear and coherent political and economic response in a world of divided communities and competing states.
>
> *Held* et al. *2011: 10*

Matthew Paterson, Professor of Political Science at the University of Ottawa and IPCC member, has been researching the political aspects of climate change since the late 1980s and has also authored a book, *Automobile Politics: Ecology and Cultural Political Economy* (2007), on car culture. He argues that the Kyoto Protocol, which came out of the UNFCCC's deliberations in the 1990s, laid the basis for carbon markets: "Once set up, carbon markets have rapidly proliferated, and have until recently been in a phase of very rapid expansion. As they have done so, the business-politics dynamic has become the most important one in driving forward their development" (Paterson 2011: 617).

However, it is important to note that the politics of climate change mitigation "goes much deeper than headline questions of much existing climate policy such as the use of a tax or trading scheme" and ultimately requires addressing the very nature of a capitalist world system characterized by a treadmill of production and consumption heavily reliant on fossil fuels and patterns of gross social inequality (Kuch 2015).

In his discussion of the automobile, Paterson (2007) stresses that by the early twentieth century, the car had already become central to the organization of modern capitalism as well as deeply embedded in the architecture of individual identities. Cars have become far more than transport; in addition they are now a coveted source of value and a culturally constructed domain of meaning. In light of climate change and the cultural centrality of cars, sustainability initiatives must find ways to radically reduce the impact of cars on the environment.

Critical political scientist Achim Brunnengräber (2006) maintains that the Kyoto Protocol (KP), as a multilateral international agreement, essentially constituted a capitalist-oriented form of regulation that catered to corporate and national government interests around the world, particularly those based in developed countries. The KP gained the support of most of the petroleum, natural gas, and coal companies which ultimately are responsible for most of the CO_2 emissions in the world. Brunnengräber (2006: 226) delineates the following three flaws of the KP and the UNFCCC process in general: (1) "its emphasis on economic instruments, which largely excludes alternative approaches to solving the problem, such as far-reaching structural change in energy production and use"; (2) a tendency to define the "problem in apparently 'objective' scientific terms"; and (3) a focus on the "international level of policy-making, even though at this level the consensus required for action is very weak, and allows for only very limited agreements." Further, argues Brunnengräber, self-regulation of emissions by governments and corporations will, within the framework of a skillfully maintained CO_2 bookkeeping balance sheet, show reductions, when in absolute terms no reduction at all has taken place. Carbon economics, in other words, has fallen into a well-worn groove in which those with the most power not only dictate favorable terms, but engage in sleight-of-hand manipulation of the rules. This pattern increases all the more the importance of independent analyses from across the disciplines, including anthropology.

Political scientist Peter Christoff (2010: 651) provides the following sobering assessment of the Copenhagen conference (COP 15) in 2009 to deliver a binding agreement to reduce greenhouse gas emissions:

> Current pledges under the Accord cannot deliver its 2°C [3.6°F] goal, but leave the world in peril of global warming of over 4°C [7.2°F] above

pre-industrial levels by 2100. The very limited window of opportunity for significant action to avoid catastrophic global warming may thus be missed.

COP 15 failed to produce a new treaty to replace the Kyoto Protocol with binding mechanisms to keep the global mean temperature rise below 2°C (3.6°F), a temperature target based on the 2007 IPCC report. The Copenhagen Accord, in effect, constituted a desperate effort to mask the failure of Copenhagen and was constructed during the last 24 hours of the conference by a small group of government leaders, including President Obama. Political scientist Karin Bäckstrand (2011: 681) observes:

> The Copenhagen Accord marked a new multi-polar global climate order where multilateral practices were marginalized and replaced by a non-transparent bargaining process between coalitions of willing states. It paved the way for decentralized climate governance architecture building on voluntary pledges rather than mandatory emissions cuts and timetables. While democratic intergovernmentalism recognizes the primacy of sovereignty, Copenhagen was a setback for efforts to increase the accountability and transparency of climate diplomacy.

In contrast to COP 15, many political pundits, and even at least some environmental NGOs, celebrated the Paris Agreement arrived at in late 2015 when the United States and China joined hands with virtually all other nations in agreeing to limit emissions within the parameters of a 2°C (3.6°F, even 1.5°C (2.7°F), world. However, given the fact that emissions targets that nations have voluntarily pledged to achieve would only achieve a 2.7–3.5°C (4.86–6.3°F) world and that the Paris Agreement still operates with the parameters of the existing global economy with its commitment to the growth paradigm, a larger number of both social scientists and climate activists are skeptical of the excitement expressed by UNFCCC delegates and politicians by the outcomes of the 2015 Paris meeting (Lyster 2017). In reality, the planned transition to a sustainable economy that shifts away from fossil fuels, particularly coal, and toward renewable energy sources will require a high degree of regulation at both the national and international levels, as well as addressing differential access to material resources around the world (Mulligan 2016; Newell 2016). Jonas van Vossole (2017) asserts that global climate governance continues to operate in a "chronic crisis mode," in that it has been unable to adequately address the global ecological and climate change crises. In the mean time, new capitalist enterprises have emerged that seek to "decarbonize" and develop a green economy "with minimal disruption to patterns of economic growth and the expansion of the global economy" (Van Vossole 2017: 11). Aside from the issue of how effective the EU Emissions Trading Scheme has been in reducing greenhouse gas emissions, the European Commission's climate change mitigation campaign views climate citizenship in terms of individual actions, such as turning heating down, turning off electrical devices, recycling, walking rather than driving, and engaging in green consumerism (Vihersalo 2017).

At the national level, climate regime politics tends to be shaped by lead states, which promote efforts to mitigate climate change, such as most European Union nations, and veto states, which seek to subvert or counteract efforts to mitigate climate change, such as the United States (a pattern continued across several presidents) and Australia under former Prime Minister Howard. Based upon a comparative study of 20 states which collectively account for 85 percent of greenhouse gas emissions, political scientists Peter Christoff and Robyn Eckersley maintain that finding a single factor or small number of factors explaining why certain countries are *climate leaders* and others *climate laggards* is a very difficult exercise. Despite significant differences in their respective parliamentary systems, both Germany and the United Kingdom have emerged as climate leaders:

> Germany's status as a leader arose at the beginning of the international climate negotiations whereas the UK emerged much later, in the mid-2000s. . . . Starting out as a leader early in climate negotiations has made it easier for Germany to remain a leader. But a delayed start did not stop the United Kingdom from moving into this space.
>
> *Christoff and Eckersley 2011: 444*

Political scientist Lisa Vanhala (2013: 447) maintains that the failure of international and national climate regimes to effectively provide solutions to climate change mitigation has resulted in courts in various countries emerging as the new "battlefields in climate fights." She provides a cross-national comparative analysis of climate change litigation efforts in three Anglophone countries, namely the United Kingdom, Canada, and Australia. Although environmentalists and climate activists often view litigation as an important means by which to circumvent the cumbersome processes involved in creating climate change mitigation legislation in these countries, Vanhala highlights that the former approach has also proven to be difficult. She observes:

> While there have been some significant court victories in terms of holding governments to account in regulating GHG [greenhouse gas] emissions, efforts to force major corporate emitters to reduce their emissions have been largely unsuccessful. The examples of tar sands litigation in Canada and coal mining cases in Australia are among the most worrying for environmental advocates because of the very high levels of emissions involved. As the political science literature on courts has long suggested, victories in court do not necessarily translate into changes on the ground.
>
> *Vanhala 2013: 461*

In a similar vein, international relations theorist John Vogler (2016: 174) cautions that "There is a danger that interstate action and the UNFCCC process will simply be seen as, at best, a minor distraction and, at worst, a dangerous irrelevance to genuine global climate governance." For better or worse, public concern about climate change tends to be shaped by "elite partisan" debates about its severity

(Carmichael and Brulle 2017). Furthermore, politicians' reliance on climate science tends to be highly selective, with little consideration of its abrupt or irreversible impacts (Willis 2017).

Guri Bang *et al.* (2015b) have edited an anthology that examines seven key actors in international climate cooperation, namely the United States, the EU, Japan, Russia, China, India, and Brazil. Combined, these actors account for nearly 70 percent of the world's total greenhouse emissions, with China and the US alone accounting for about 45 percent of the greenhouse gas emissions. In both China and Russia, decisions, including those on climate policy, are made at top levels and disseminated to lower levels of the political system, whereas the US, EU, and Brazil, have multiple veto players on climate policy, and Japan and India have a moderate number of veto players on climate policy (Bang *et al.* 2015a: 192). Societal demands for climate change mitigation efforts vary widely, being "low but with some active pushers" in the US; varying in the EU, although "higher in Western than in Eastern Europe;" "low–moderate" in Japan; "very low" in Russia; "moderate–high" in Brazil; "low but growing (due mainly to concern with local pollution)" in China; and "low" in India (Bang *et al.* 2015a: 199).

Green capitalism

Peter Newell, a development studies specialist, and Matthew Paterson, a political scientist, call for *green capitalism*, a concept discussed in Chapter 4, but recognize that it will not be easy to achieve as:

> the challenge of climate change means, in effect, either abandoning capitalism, or seeking to find a way for it to grow while gradually replacing coal, oil, and gas. Assuming the former is unlikely in the short term, the questions to be asked are, what can growth be based on? What are the energy sources to power a decarbonised economy? . . . What kind of climate capitalism do we want? Can it be made to serve desirable social, as well as environmental, ends?
>
> *Newell and Paterson 2010: 9*

Newell and Paterson delineate four possible scenarios for climate capitalism. The first of these they term a *climate capitalist utopia*, which will entail a rapid decarbonization of the global economy and "investment in renewable energy, energy efficiency and conservation, carbon capture and storage, advanced public transport and urban infrastructure reform," along with emissions trading (Newell and Paterson 2010: 162). The second scenario they call *stagnation*, where carbon markets fail and international efforts to set emissions targets collapse, resulting in a dystopian situation in which humanity seeks at best to "adapt to whatever climate change has to offer" (Newell and Paterson 2010: 168). Scenario three would be a *carbonized dystopia*, where a low-carbon global economy is achieved, but engages in a type of carbon colonialism in which "money pours into biofuels both in the North and the South, producing large mono-crop plantations with appalling working conditions, the destruction of biodiversity, and price rise of key food crops which place them beyond the reach of the poor" (Newell and Paterson 2010: 169–170). In addition, climate refugees will be denied access to less climate-ravaged countries or held in camps indefinitely (Newell and Paterson 2010: 172). Newell and Paterson (2010: 178) deem their fourth scenario, *climate Keynesian*, the most favorable, in that governments would regulate carbon markets and implement distributive mechanisms both within and between nation-states, and thus "create stable conditions for investment in carbon markets and in renewable energy, energy efficiency, and so on." Ultimately, they anticipate that over the course of the next 20–30 years, the mostly likely outcome will be "some messy mix" of their four scenarios, with "some areas of the world stagnating, others going ahead with a pure neoliberal version, while others still regulate the carbon economy even more stringently" (Newell and Paterson 2010: 178). Looked at from an anthropology of the present perspective—that is, in terms of what is the situation at the present moment—there is only a limited attempt to move toward either of Newell and Paterson's first or last categories. We are, however, witnessing money pouring into biofuels, the emergence of large biofuel mono-crop plantations with appalling working conditions, the destruction of biodiversity, and a rise in food prices moving beyond the reach of the poor. As well, there are various signs of dystopia that could result in peoples being pushed to adapt as best they can (or cannot) to whatever climate change has to offer.

Critical political scientific analyses of capitalism and climate change

Most political scientists who have grappled with climate change tend to more or less accept the parameters of existing climate regimes and green capitalism. In this section, we highlight the work of three political scientists whose observations parallel those of critical anthropologists and critical sociologists examining climate change-related issues. The late Australian political scientist Del Weston (2014) viewed climate change or global warming as one of an array of problems emanating from a capitalist political economy, and argued that alienation constituted a significant issue "both for understanding problems of global warming and a myriad of other ecological and social problems faced in a capitalist world." She viewed emissions trading schemes as by and large being ineffective, inefficient, and socially unjust climate change mitigation strategies that potentially could exacerbate the problem they are designed to remedy and thereby delay meaningful climate action (Weston 2014: 33). As a scholar who had conducted research in Africa, particularly South Africa, Weston (2014: 97) argued: "Africans have contributed least to global warming and yet are those who will suffer first and worst as a result." In addressing the "deep structural chasm that has developed in the metabolic relations between humans and between humans and nature as a result of the social relations of production inherent in the capitalist system," she called for constructing "new political, economic and cultural systems that are metabolically restorative, equitable, resilient, just, diverse and democratic" (Weston 2014: 197).

Ciplet *et al.* (2015: 24) delineate the following four perspectives in the analysis of international climate politics:

- a structural perspective which posits climate inaction as emanating from persisting unequal interstate relations, including political, economic, military, and ideological asymmetries;
- an institutional perspective which focuses upon international institutions for resolving environmental and climate conflicts;
- a market pragmatist perspective which seeks to mitigate climate change by reforming corporations through market mechanisms;
- an eco-socialist perspective which seeks to mobilize social movements and local communities to confront corporate power, particularly those of the fossil fuel industry, and offers alternative frameworks for organizing social life.

They also identify six future scenarios that humanity can adopt in confronting the ecological and climate crises:

Scenario 1—exclusive inaction in which negotiations over the ecological and climate crises have collapsed, resulting in the major countries grabbing for existing fossil fuels and water, the emergence of an increasing number of totalitarian regimes, and the possibility of a 6°C (10.8°F) world by 2100;

Scenario 2—exclusive action consisting of "minlateral" or "plurilateral" forums, such as the existing Asia-Pacific Partnership, and sectoral groupings, such as the G7, G20, and the Major Economics Forum, which seek mitigation and adaptation strategies on climate change;

Scenario 3—desperate techno-fixes, such as carbon and capture sequestration and geoengineering, that seek to mitigate climate change under a largely business-as-usual situation;

Scenario 4—shifting to "zero carbon energy" or renewable energy sources, such as solar, wind, and geothermal energy, thus making fossil fuel energy sources unnecessary and successfully containing climate change;

Scenario 5—"going local" in terms of addressing the ecological and climate crisis, a strategy adopted by a wide array of actors, ranging from eco-anarchists to local governments to international networks and social movements supporting community models that challenge powerful corporate interests;

Scenario 6—a global climate justice approach favored by the authors that calls for broad-based climate action at the national level and for a more democratic processes at the international level (Ciplet *et al.* 2015: 209–232).

Finally, Chatturvedi and Doyle (2015) maintain that the most graphic and compelling evidence for global warming is manifested at the three poles, namely the Arctic, the Himalayas, and Antarctica. While these areas are all characterized by small number of human inhabitants or visitors, the effects of global warming or climate change at them are having profound adverse impacts on peoples living in much more densely populated areas. Chatturvedi and Doyle (2015: x) assert that climate change is "not simply a matter of abrupt, unprecedented 'global' manifestation of anthropogenic assaults on nature, but also differentiated geographies of responsibility and accounting."

The human geography of climate change

Geography is a discipline in which the topic of climate has waxed and waned. Early on, Ellsworth Huntington (1922) developed a form of climatic determinism in which he asserted that climate influenced civilizations and cultures to the point that some were productive and innovative, and others were stagnant and backward. In time, geography distanced itself from the racist and ethnocentric implications of climatic determinism, to the point that many geographers, along with other social scientists, "shied away from talking to much about climate–society interactions" (Randalls 2017: 8). Geography appears to be more of a disparate discipline than do both sociology and political science, in that it is divided into physical geography and human or cultural geography. In some ways, it is similar to the four-field model of American anthropology which entails physical anthropology, archaeology, sociocultural anthropology, and anthropological linguistics. Physical geography is closely related to the Earth sciences because its practitioners concern themselves with topics such as resource management, erosion, hydrology, and climate variability. The concept of *landscape* cross-cuts physical and human geography, and unites both branches of geography with other disciplines or fields, such as geomorphology, paleobotany, ecology, archaeology, history, and sociocultural anthropology. Landscape entails human interaction and transformation of the natural environment through a wide array of activities, including food collection and production, construction of dwelling units or other types of buildings, and movement from one place to another for a variety of reasons. As Catherine Brace and Hilary Geoghegan (2010: 289) observe:

> landscape becomes a possible means with which to organize the immediate and the future, spatially and temporally intimate relations between people, flora, fauna, topography, environment and, crucially, weather. It is the subtle real and imagined, past, present and future changes in the configuration of land and weather that will become identified as the artefacts of climate change as much as the scientific artifacts of atmospheric CO_2, increases in mean temperature and the circulation of ocean currents.

Human geography is closely related to sociocultural anthropology, and there have been a few combined departments of geography and anthropology at some universities in the United States, such as the one at Louisiana State University, as well as various collaborative research initiatives. Human geography and environmental anthropology exhibit similar concerns in that both are interested in the human–environment nexus and often draw on similar theoretical perspectives, such as cultural ecology, political ecology, and post-structuralism (Robbins 2012). As geographers, Brace and Geoghegan (2010: 295) assert, in much the same vein as anthropologists who stress the need to document the local knowledge of various peoples about the environment and climate change, a "focus on familiar landscapes allows us to consider the nature of lay knowledges of climate and the ways it might change, accumulated and enacted outside the spaces, conventions, rigours and epistemology of science." Geographers also have commented on the impact of environmental and climate concerns on university departments. According to Christian A. Kull and Simon P. J. Batterbury (2013: 5–6):

> The new environmental studies programs [which began to first appear in the 1960s and 1970s] at many universities grew to compete with, but also to complement, geography departments. The programs were often structured not as academic departments, but as research institutes, postgraduate degrees, or interdisciplinary programs, allowing individual geographers to play a role. The cat was out of the bag and for students interested in pressing issues like population pressure on resources, rainforest loss, and sustainability, at most universities the first stop was not geography but environmental studies. Some geographers . . . embraced the new interdisciplinary units; others stuck to disciplinary tradition.

The diverse interest of both physical and human geographers is reflected in an anthology titled *Geography of Climate Change* edited by Richard Aspinall (2012), which consists of articles first published as a thematic special issue of *Annals of the Association of American Geographers*. In terms of the human geography of climate change, contributors authored chapters or articles on climate change adaptation in general, livelihood vulnerability due to climate change-induced glacial retreat in Peru, climate change adaptation in Andean ecosystems, local and scientific knowledge about the impact of climate change and drought on Jamaican agriculture, climate change adaptation in the United States–Mexico border region, climate change mitigation efforts in Seattle, carbon markets, the double exposure of the climate change and global financial crises in California's Central Valley, the challenge of climate change and capitalism for transdisciplinarity, contested sovereignty in the Arctic as a result of climate change, the impact of climate change on the whaling cycle among the Inupiat of Alaska, and benchmarking the war against global warming. This collection illustrates that—like anthropologists, sociologists, and political scientists—human geographers interested in climate change are working on a wide array of issues, many of which overlap with the issues of concern of the other social science disciplines. In his essay in the original collection, R. Balling (2000: 115) boldly asserts that "the entire global warming/greenhouse issue is perfectly suited to our discipline" because geographers are specialists in spatial analysis, echoing the somewhat similar claims of anthropologists on the grounds that climate change is both anthropogenic and portends enormous human consequences. However, Joel Wainwright (2012) contends that geography no longer has a clearly defined focus, such as spatial relations, human–environment relations, and geographical regions. He also maintains:

> As a discipline with scientists and nonscientists working side by side on a vast range of questions and problems, geography stands alone. With the possible exceptions of anthropology and psychology (and only then in certain instances), there are no disciplines where scientists and "humanists" have sustained shared curriculum and research for long periods.
>
> *Wainwright 2012: 273*

While much of what Wainwright asserts is correct, his distinction between "scientists" and "nonscientists" or "humanists" is somewhat simplistic. Most sociocultural anthropologists and virtually all sociologists and political scientists view themselves as social scientists, and certainly many departments of anthropology have sustained shared scientific and humanist components in their curricula, although they are not by any means always free of conflict and debate over these issues. A more valid distinction would be between "natural science" or "physical science" and "social science," although even this division (and the disciplinary-centric biases it contains) is open to debate. Many sociocultural anthropologists view themselves as having one foot in the social sciences and the other in the humanities (whereas probably most archaeologists and physical anthropologists view themselves as being "scientists," perhaps as mixed natural and social scientists).

While political scientists have tended to dominate the topic of climate governance, some geographers have entered into this domain (Bulkeley and Newell 2015). Harriet Bulkeley (2015: 3) seeks to go beyond merely looking at climate governance as entailing various actors and institutions by, following the work of Michel Foucault, "considering governance as the orchestration of distinct modes of power and seeks to explore the workings, politics and geographies of its operation."

In the remainder of this section, we focus on three topics which certain human geographers have been exploring, namely the impact of climate change on Pacific islands, the impact of climate change on cities, and climate justice, and then present a discussion of one of the ways anthropologists have been studying research on climate change by other disciplines.

The impact of climate change on Pacific islands

Geographers Jon Barnett and John Campbell (2010) have written a comprehensive overview of the impact of climate change on Pacific Island countries (PICs) or small island developing states (SIDS) and how the global community, including the UNFCCC and natural scientists, as well as South Pacific Islanders, both political leaders and ordinary people, are responding to climate change in terms of adaptational practices. Drawing upon Michel Foucault (1980), they assert that the "representation of climate change in SIDS is a discursive formation that limits understanding and action to address the interest of people living in islands" (Barnett and Campbell 2010: 1). Although natural science, including climate science, has greatly contributed to developing widespread awareness of the risks that climate change poses to SIDS, it has a tendency to marginalize local knowledge approaches to climate change. Pacific Island countries are extremely diverse in their size, topography, colonial histories, and national economies, which are, to a greater or lesser degree, integrated into the global economy, and are situated in three principal regions, Melanesia, Micronesia, and Polynesia. While New Zealand and Hawaii are generally considered to be part of Polynesia, the former is a highly developed independent nation closely linked economically to Australia, and the latter is the 50th state of the United States, despite its considerable distance (2,390 miles, or about the distance from Maine to Ireland) from the mainland. In contrast, all other Pacific Island states are part of the developing world. In this regard, like many other developing countries, they will suffer from the most severe effects of climate change, despite the fact that they have contributed little to the generation of greenhouse gas emissions. Total emissions from the 11 PICs, namely Cook Islands, Fiji, Kiribati, Nauru, Niue, Palau, Papua New Guinea, Samoa, Solomon Islands, Tonga, and Vanuatu, contribute roughly 0.04 percent to the global total. Barnett and Campbell (2010: 10) report:

> In terms of per capita emissions too, many of the 11 Pacific countries rank lowly, with Kiribati second from the bottom, while all the others (except for Palau and Nauru) are well into the bottom half. Palau is the 24th largest emitter, and Nauru the 29th. These countries have quite small populations but reasonably high levels of consumption.

Numerous international and regional bodies, including the IPCC, the Association of South Pacific Environmental Institutions Initiative (a consortium consisting of the Universities of Guam, Papua New Guinea, and Samoa, the regional University of South Pacific, and the South Pacific Applied Geoscience Commission), the Secretariat of the Pacific Regional Environment Programme Initiatives, and Start-Oceania, have been assessing the impact of climate change on PICs. Furthermore, numerous international, regional, and national programs have been created to assist PICs in adapting to climate change. In their analyses, Barnett and Campbell delineate five discourses or tropes of climate change vulnerability to which PICs have been subjected. The trope of "titanic states" depicts sinking islands at greatest immediate risk as a result of sea level rise. These islands are defenseless on their own, and can only be saved through the assistance of others, particularly through various schemes developed under the Kyoto Protocol. The "high tide trope" also refers to the inevitability of additional island states becoming partially submerged due to rising sea levels. The "dark clouds over Paradise trope" depicts a sinking idyllic world of happy South Sea Islanders who will need to find refuge abroad. The "coalmine canaries trope" portrays places such as Tuvalu as harbingers of the devastation that will be incurred in time elsewhere in the world. The final option, the "extinction and survival trope," communicates the disappearance of a way of life with no realistic chance of survival. From a perspective similar to Elinor Ostrom, discussed in Chapter 6, Barnett and Campbell lament that the vast majority of decisions about how Pacific Island countries will have to adapt to climate change are being orchestrated by donors and multilateral agencies. In contrast, the "exceptions—the knowledge of, and the community-based projects implemented by, people from within the region—are significant, but by and large unrecognized and ignored" (Barnett and Campbell 2010: 174). Barnett and Campbell recommend that funding be provided to communities in PICs which will enable them to assess the risks that climate change poses for them and to allow them to develop the capacity to adapt to climate change in order to preserve and enhance their distinctive ways of life.

Despite the fact that Tuvalu is often portrayed as on the front line of the impact of climate change in the South Pacific, Colette Mortreux and Jon Barnett (2009: 108), based upon 28 interviews with residents of Funafuti, the atoll that serves as the capital of the island nation, found that 19 of their respondents "planned to continue living in Funafuti indefinitely, with nine indicating that they wanted to leave Funafuti at some time in the future." Funafuti respondents who planned to remain on the island cited lifestyle and cultural identity as their primary reasons for not wishing to relocate. Nevertheless, Tuvaluans are experiencing the erosion of their beaches, damaging tidal surges, and the intrusion of saltwater into cultivated areas, a pattern that, as it worsens with increased global warming, may erode the resilience of these committed island dwellers. As their sense of precarity mounts, the historic cultural appeal of their homeland may begin to crumble. For those who have already fled outer islands for Funafuti, this erosion may already be in process.

Climate change in cities

The relationship between climate change and cities has come to receive a considerable amount of attention from a number of quarters and has been the focus of a growing number of publications (Rosenzweig *et al.* 2011; Stone 2012). Urban geographer Harriet Bulkeley has emerged as a leading authority on climate change and cities. She and Michele M. Betsill, a political scientist, co-authored *Cities and Climate Change: Urban Sustainability and Global Environmental Governance* (2003), in which they provide an overview of climate change politics at the global, national, and local levels. Bulkeley and Betsill (2003: 48–49) observe:

> Greenhouse gas emissions originate from processes which are embedded in specific places, and it is often argued that the local is the most appropriate political jurisdiction for bringing about any necessary reductions in these emissions . . . . It is in cities that humans produce and consume fossil fuels for manufacturing, electricity, transportation and household heating, accounting for 78 percent of global carbon dioxide emissions . . . . In addition, cities are places where the vast majority of waste is created and disposed of, and local governments have significant influence when it comes to developing recycling programmes and managing landfills.

In addition to examining the role of local climate governance, Bulkeley and Betsill present case studies of this process in six cities, namely Newcastle upon Tyne, Cambridge, and Leicester in the United Kingdom; Denver and Milwaukee in the United States; and Newcastle in New South Wales, Australia. What is missing from their book, however, is an examination of climate governance in the cities of developing countries, some of which now reach megacity proportions (i.e., having populations of more than 10 million people). In their assessment of the Cities for Climate Protection program in their case studies, Bulkeley and Betsill maintain that there does not have to be a conflict between the "simultaneous globalization and localization of the sustainability agenda," but maintain that their case studies "also make it clear that the trend toward multilevel governance requires a full and critical treatment of the possible inconsistencies and contradictions between the aims of sustainable environmental policy in different sectors, over different scales, and between different places" (Bulkeley and Betsill 2003: 193).

Bulkeley and Betsill (2013) subsequently revisited the issue of urban politics and explored the ways in which climate change is affecting urban governance agendas. In their recent article on Australia, they present a short case study of climate politics in Melbourne and the activities of the Northern Alliance for Greenhouse Action in the state of Victoria. Although once again their article focuses on urban climate politics in the developed world, they observe that "There is also evidence that alternative discourses supporting urban responses to climate change are emerging in cities in the Global South" and briefly describe the nature of these responses in the Khayelitsha area of Cape Town in South Africa (Bulkeley and Betsill 2013: 148).

In her most recent book, also titled *Cities and Climate Change*, Bulkeley (2013) provides a comprehensive overview of a topic which she has been researching for a decade. She observes: "Because of the history of economic development, cities can occupy locations that are regarded as particularly vulnerable to climate change" (Bulkeley 2013: 7).

Unlike her earlier work, where she tended to focus on the climate change–urban nexus in developed societies, Bulkeley examines this relationship in various cities in developing countries, including Mexico City, Quito in Bolivia, Cape Town in South Africa, Lagos in Nigeria, and Amman in Jordan. In addition to examining the sources of urban greenhouse gas emissions, Bulkeley (2013) analyzes urban climate governance and climate change mitigation and adaptation strategies in cities. Elsewhere, geographer Peter J. Marcotullio and his colleagues analyze greenhouse gas emissions in Asian cities. Despite the fact that greenhouse gas emissions have been rising in Asian cities, they stress "that emission per capita averages are lower than those at the national level" or their respective countries as a whole (Marcotullio *et al.* 2012: 944).

In all of these locations, cities have attracted the attention of natural and social scientists because they tend to be hotter than the surrounding less urban or non-urban areas. This warming, known as the heat island effect, is the result of:

- heat absorption by tall buildings, roads, sidewalks, roof tops, and parking lots;
- comparatively limited vegetation (which diminishes heat);
- tail-pipe emissions from vehicles that increase ground ozone levels.

These conditions pose significant health impacts from heat-related conditions (e.g., heat stroke) in cities, especially for the poor, those with pre-existing health conditions, the elderly, small children, and pregnant women. In doing so, they increase the vulnerability of already vulnerable populations, often individuals with the fewest resources and the least attention from government bodies. While preparation for increases in the frequency and duration of lethal urban heat waves are taking place in various cities around the world, planning bodies tend not to reflect the populations at most severe risk.

Climate justice

Like other social scientists, various human geographers have raised concerns about climate justice issues. These include three contributors to an anthology edited by W. Neil Adger *et al.* titled *Fairness in Adaptation to Climate Change* (2006). In the volume, geographer Kirstin Dow and two colleagues observe that climate justice entails issues of how climate change is:

> associated with other broad inequalities in wealth and well-being, dis-associations between those who will benefit from and those who will bear the burdens and damage associated with climate change, procedural justice issues as to how decisions have been made in structuring international approaches to access scientific issues and creating the institutions of the global climate change regime to address these problems.
>
> *Dow* et al. *2006: 79*

They delineate three categories of ethical consideration in choosing climate change adaptation strategies. In the first, *avoiding harm and reducing risks*, preference is given to strategies that seek to minimize harm rather than compensate for it after it has occurred. In terms of *reducing vulnerability*, preference is given to strategies that "increase the capacity of the most vulnerable to manage risks on their own" (Dow *et al.* 2006: 95). Finally, in terms of *supporting human rights and well-being*, preference is given to strategies that promote basic human rights and ensure improved living standards and respect self-determination.

While admitting that the unequal distribution of climate change impacts is a necessary step in recognizing climate justice issues, Geographers Robin Leichenko and Karen O'Brien (2006: 113) repeat the caution expressed in Chapter 5 that acceptance of the "winners and losers" binary risks "reifying biophysical inter-pretations of climate change vulnerability while downplaying the role of social and political factors in influencing differential vulnerability and shaping adaptive capacity." Moreover, in light of the nature of many of the proposals that have been made for addressing climate change impacts, Leichenko and O'Brien point out that strict emphasis on technological fixes may reinforce rather than reduce unequal economic and power relations between and within societies.

Jon Barnett (2006: 115) maintains that climate change policies may inadvertently result in "unfair outcomes by exacerbating, maintaining, or ignoring existing and future inequalities." He asserts that climate change poses a *double vulnerability* for many people when it is coupled with poverty. Barnett, like so many others, reiterates the oft-noted but nonetheless imperative message that those people who have contributed the least to climate change will suffer the most from it. Furthermore, violent conflict, which has so adversely impacted people in places such as Afghanistan, Angola, Burundi, the Democratic Republic of the Congo, Iraq, Somalia, and Sudan, "restricts people's access to human and social, economic, and natural capital, which are necessary to adapt to climate change" (Barnett 2006: 124). Barnett maintains that climate change probably does not pose a higher priority than do more immediate pressing issues such as food security and resettlement for people in post-conflict societies. He concludes by noting that "addressing the political economy of insecurity would require a whole range of activities that are not merely about the environment, nor even just about 'development,' but are, more broadly about peace and justice" (Barnett 2006: 129). Unfortunately, Barnett fails to ask how both peace and justice can be achieved within the parameters of global capitalism. Moreover, food security and refugee issues do not stand separate from climate change, but rather are tolls on humanity that will be increasingly magnified by climate change. It is for this reason that in this book we stress the importance of a pluralea interaction approach that recognizes that issues like war and climate change do not just overlap temporally, they are highly interactive, with climate change producing points of tension in social relationships (e.g., over access to food and water) and war being a significant source of greenhouse gas emissions. Indeed, as geographer David N. Livingstone (2015: 437) observes: "national security agencies and other interested parties now often regard conflict as the inevitable consequence of climate change."

Conclusion

We began this chapter by noting that the nature of climate change, in both its physical and its social dimensions, requires the contributions of multiple scholarly disciplines as well as other fields to understand the complexities, multiple systems, and interactions that constitute this domain. Moreover, as we have seen, the field benefits from collaborations and dialogues across disciplinary lines. We have described various expressions of the interdisciplinary process, such as the ways data on environmental system change from the physical sciences is being brought together and triangulated with ethnographic research on the environmental experiences of peoples living in particular environments. At the same time, while climate scientists might recognize the adverse trends suggested by their research, they may have limited experience working with communities to share their findings, leading them to collaborate with social scientists with experience in this activity.

In particular, this chapter has focused on the work of sociologists, political scientists, and human geographers on climate change. As anthropology finds itself seeking to come to terms with the world today, they need assistance from historians, sociologists, Earth and climate scientists, as well as representatives from numerous other disciplines, including psychology, philosophy, cultural and media studies (Eriksen 2016:4).

Evident in this review is the high degree of overlap and reinforcement of key points across disciplines. It is clear that to some degree, sociologists, political scientists, and human geographers as well as anthropologists think about the world in the same ways, but there are also areas of divergence and differences in emphasis (e.g., the level of social structural focus among sociologists, the focus on issues of governance and policy among political scientists, attention to spatial issues among human geographers, and the micro–macro holistic vision and emphasis on cultural patterning among anthropologists). Collaboration serves to bring strengths from the various disciplines to what is a monumental but undeniably vital task: understanding and effectively responding to climate change. At the same time, it raises challenges of disciplinary hierarchies, alternative jargons, discipline-centric bias, different desired publishing venues, and a host of other problems. In the end, the importance of the task at hand has pushed for expanded multidisciplinarity, although even to the degree that the disciplines have worked together, the powerful voices that seek to dispute the reality of climate change have thus far blocked the level of social response from coming anywhere near that required to avert the worst-case scenarios of climate change projections.

8

CONCLUSION

Toward a critical integrated social science of climate change

A pathway forward

In this concluding chapter, we describe a pathway toward the future of the critical anthropology of climate change within a broader interdisciplinary critical social science of climate change. While we believe that most of the theoretical perspectives in the social scientific study of climate change are useful in the elucidation of how political, economic, social, and cultural processes contribute to anthropogenic climate change, we privilege insights from critical approaches because they tend to address structural causes of our current environmental crisis and underline the need to make climate justice a central theme of efforts for change. D. Abbott and G. Wilson (2015) invoke an interdisciplinary approach to addressing climate change, one which draws upon both the natural sciences and the social sciences. In the case of the latter, they assert that:

> Whilst a social science analysis can also have its difficulties in representing climate change fully and there are several problems on choosing representative samples when representing lived experience, its strength lies in its ability to untangle individual and societal histories within complex power relationships.
>
> *Abbott and Wilson 2015: 79*

While we have made our perspective known throughout this book, we have not fully discussed why we embrace a critical perspective in the anthropology of climate change. We begin this chapter by addressing that issue.

The unlevel environmental playing field

As we examine the world in the first decades of the twenty-first century, we see that the well-being of human communities and the health of the environments they inhabit are significantly impacted by the use of power to enforce wealth disparity, social inequality, and structural injustice. The social worlds humans inhabit, in other words, do not unfold on level playing fields. Contemporary societies are divided by steep and, for those on the bottom, painful inequalities that are maintained through an array of structural mechanisms. As indicated by Eric Wolf (1974: 261), a critical task of anthropology is to "spell out the processes of power which created the present-day cultural systems and the linkages between them."

In terms of the global distribution of wealth, it is estimated that the richest 1 percent of people in the world control a third of the world's net financial assets. By adding the next wealthiest 1 percent to this upper echelon group, we find that control over the world's wealth by this tiny fraction of the world's population rises to about 50 percent. The addition of yet another few thin layers of the wealthy, to include the wealthiest 8.4 percent of people in the world, brings the share of wealth controlled by the super-rich to 86 percent. By contrast, the vast majority of people in the world, meaning approximately 5.98 billion people in a world with a total population of 7.12 billion, control under 20 percent of the world's wealth (Shirrocks and Davies 2013). Further, Institute of Development Studies (2013) analyses show that the "bottom billion" of poor people, or 72 percent of the world's poor, now live in middle-income countries, suggesting the widening gap between the wealthy countries and all other countries as well as vast internal inequalities within the nation-states of the world. Among the world's children, approximately 50 percent are living below the $2 per day international poverty line (Ortiz and Cummins 2011). At the top end of this very steep economic ladder are very rich children who lead, on average, far healthier, far more comfortable, and far longer lives in far cleaner environments than the bottom 50 percent of children in the world.

The severity of the contrasts seen in the lives of children is illustrated by the birth in 2013 of a son to the UK's Prince William and Kate, Duchess of Cambridge. The event was closely covered in great detail by global mass media. Outside St. Mary's Hospital where the baby was born, frenzied journalists and photographers gathered in large numbers despite a record heat wave that prompted health warnings from authorities. While the new baby will grow up in a royal environment of considerable wealth (*Forbes* magazine in 2010 estimated the royal family's wealth at $535 million), on the same day he was born approximately 700 babies in the UK were born to poor families. The life chances and life experiences of these children will be starkly different from those of the royal baby. Lifespans for poor children in Britain are several years shorter than the wealthy children, they are more likely to suffer infant death, and they generally suffer more chronic diseases later in life, including those influenced by global warming (Spencer 2006).

There is, in short, extreme inequality in the distribution of the world's wealth and all that tends to accompany it in terms of health, well-being, and quality of life. Social epidemiologist Nancy Krieger, who studies health inequity, indicates the dramatic consequences of this kind of extreme inequality:

> Social inequality kills. It deprives individuals and communities of a healthy start in life, increases their burden of disability and disease, and brings early

death. Poverty and discrimination, inadequate medical care, and violation of human rights all act as powerful social determinants of who lives and who dies, at what age, and with what degree of suffering.

Krieger 2005: 15

How can we understand the punishing level of inequality of wealth and associated social inequality that characterizes our contemporary human world? Systemic and persistent health and social disparities are everywhere linked to underlying inequalities in power and resources (Birn *et al.* 2009). As the Institute of Development Studies (2013) emphasizes: "Poverty is not only about 'poor' people but also about the social and economic inequalities that compound and reproduce poverty. Social structures and relationships between the poor and the non-poor, middle class and elites . . . are also key."

In other words, it is social and political inequality that fosters economic inequality, while it is economic inequality that provides the global elite with the resources to maintain and enforce their entrenched positions of power and opulent lifestyles.

One critical arena of the exercise of power, as we have seen throughout this book, concerns how the environment is differentially engaged by human communities and societies. In the case of global warming, as has been emphasized in the prior chapters, it is the wealthiest nations that generate most greenhouse gas and black carbon emissions, but it is the poorer nations, with fewer resources to respond, who are paying the heaviest price for global warming and climate turmoil (Baer and Singer 2009). The same can be said with reference to the steep income inequalities that exist within nations; in any nation, the elite benefit the most from greenhouse gas production (in the form of the commodities and other value) and the poor benefit the least, or more accurately, suffer most the consequences. These patterns apply as well to most of the other ecocrises addressed in Chapter 1 in our discussion of pluralea interactions. The environment in the era of the Anthropocene—or, perhaps more appropriately, the Capitalocene—is one characterized not only by the deep impress of the human footprint, but by the unequal prints made by the expensive tailored shoes of the super-rich and smaller traces of the poorly shod or unshod feet of the poor and super-poor. From the growing extent of the greenhouse blanket that is retaining solar energy close to the planet, causing it to heat up, to the extensive oil spills (546 million gallons over the last five decades) by the Anglo-Dutch oil giant Shell in the Niger Delta of Nigeria, to the list of the top corporate air polluters in the world (Bayer Group, Textron, General Electric, Precision Castparts, and Koch Industries), to the fact that ethnic minorities bear 69 percent of the toxic air risk from facilities owned by ExxonMobil although they constitute less than 40 percent of the US population (Political Economic Research Institute 2012), and beyond, the damages being done to Earth and its inhabitants reflect structures of power and inequality worldwide. There is, in short, a social production of catastrophe occurring, involving existing inequalities and environmental degradations that will "become considerably higher because of the multiplier effects of climate change" (McMichael 2013: 1,340), and it is driven both by the exercise of political power (including both military might and the hegemonic ability to strongly influence public discourse and thinking about issues) and by the nature of the global economy.

In Chapter 5, we discussed the super-rich Koch brothers and their Koch Foundation as dominant players in and funders of the orchestrated climate change denier campaign. Koch Industries, the very profitable corporate arm of family operations, illustrates the role of power in the making and largely unpunished release of greenhouse gases, other forms of environmental pollutants, and the harms these disruptions of Earth's ecosystems cause. Koch companies, a multi-billion-dollar array of energy, consumer product, fertilizer, ranching, and other manufacturing and service entities, can be found in almost 60 countries and employ about 60,000 people. On its website, Koch Industries lists the multiple ways that it is transforming energy, communities, agriculture, nutrition, safety, travel, comfort, and daily life in the world. One of the companies owned by Koch Industries, for example, Georgia-Pacific (2013) maintains that it: "creates long-term value by using resources efficiently to provide innovative products and solutions that meet the needs of customers and society, while operating in a manner that is environmentally and socially responsible and economically sound."

The 6,000 people of Crossett, Arkansas, a poor minority community downriver from a Georgia-Pacific paper plant, have come to question the sincerity of such greenwashing statements and have a different view of how Koch Industries is transforming lives. Crossett has one of the highest rates of exposure to cancer-causing toxins in the United States. The Alpha Alternative School District in Crossett ranks in the top percentile nationally for exposure to probable human carcinogens, with the Georgia-Pacific plant listed as the polluter most responsible for the toxins (Zornick 2011).

The cinematic company Brave New Films produced an educational documentary on events in Crossett entitled *Koch Brothers Exposed*. In an interview with the *Huffington Post*, Robert Greenwood, the founder of Brave New Films, remarks:

> What we've been doing is finding personal stories so that people understand: This is what happens when money corrupts the political process. It's really as good an example as I think you're likely to find. You see it in Arkansas. The Koch brothers with their power and their money and their influence are literally causing people to lose their lives by taking away the protections that the laws and the EPA should offer.
>
> *Graves and Howard 2011*

The documentary also illustrates the ways that the Koch brothers seek to use their great wealth to sway the political process in their favor, through campaign donations, building alliances with conservative politicians, funding think tanks, organizing attacks on the regulatory mission of the EPA, and seeking to hold the line and roll back environmental protections. The pattern is one that has been characterized as "class war waged from the top down" (Moyers 2011).

Consequently, we contend that analyses of the causes of and solutions to climate change that fail to include examination of structures of power and social inequality do not provide adequate assessment of the nature of the problems at hand. Moreover, in the contemporary world and for the last several hundred years, structures of power and inequality have been recreated and reinforced by the reigning economic mode of production of capitalism. The nature of this global economic system—and its inherent emphasis on inequality built into capitalist class structuring, as well as its unyielding emphasis on economic expansion—merits examination in building an understanding of how we made our way into the crisis of climate change as well as how we might find our way out of this crisis. Central to this effort must be a focus on issues of justice as regards ethnic populations, women, and working classes internationally.

In this regard, anthropologist Alf Hornborg (2007: 1–2) observes that natural scientists and social scientists often talk past each other in examining the society–nature nexus:

> Working in parallel, and generally without much knowledge of one another, social and natural scientists have for several decades struggled to understand how the different parts of their respective domains fit together. One camp has discovered how human societies are globally interconnected in a shifting "world system" of trade, politics, and information flows. The other camp has developed an understanding of how ecosystems are connected in a common "Earth system" with planetary dynamics that affect all its constituent parts. . . . As we have become accustomed to thinking of our world as a single and coherent globe suspended in space, we more easily acknowledge that changes in the world system and changes in the Earth system may be recursively connected. The most concrete example of this change in thinking is probably our current concern over global warming. However, although an important one, climate change is only one of the ways in which the connections between global social and ecological processes are revealing themselves to us.

While climate scientists have done humanity a tremendous service by calling attention to the seriousness of climate change and many of the problems associated with it, the solutions they generally propose, both in terms of how humanity can "adapt" to and "mitigate" climate change, fail to fully come to grips with the harsh reality that climate change is ultimately a by-product of global capitalism with its emphasis on profit-making, ongoing economic expansion, and a treadmill of production and consumption that is heavily reliant on fossil fuels. In other words, global capitalism is the "elephant in the room" for the climate change debate.

As world systems theorists Peter Grimes and Jeffrey Kentor (2003: 261) assert, most climate scientists lack training in social scientific analysis that is essential in comprehending the "political, economic, and social forces" that drive climate change. A close reading of the 1991, 1996, 2001, 2007, and 2014 IPCC assessment reports bears this out. Also, it should be noted, the IPCC was set up by the UN, and it is consequently influenced by the political and economic agendas of member nations. In other words, IPCC reports are not solely responsive to scientific evidence, and as a result they tend to express issues in more muted forms and in a language that is acceptable, especially to powerful nations. This is not to say that science is distorted in IPCC reports, but rather that the language adopted in reports and what is included must meet more than scientific concerns.

To date, the climate change debate has been dominated by climate and other physical scientists as well as conventional economists, but, as we have seen in this book, anthropologists and other social scientists exhibiting various theoretical orientations have entered the climate change discourse over the course of the past 20 years or so with new questions and new perspectives. From a critical perspective, a central goal is a broadening of the discussion to include consideration of the ultimate socioeconomic causes of climate change, including the role of the capitalist mode of production.

Toward integrated understanding

Over the course of our efforts to develop a critical anthropology of climate change, we have made a concerted effort to acquaint ourselves with climate science by reading both focused scientific reports and broad overviews of this literature, including IPCC and many other reports, attending lectures, seminars, and workshops presented by climate scientists and other natural scientists, and conversing with them. Obviously, we are not seeking to become climate scientists and engage in physical research on natural systems, as we believe the social scientists have an important and distinct contribution to make to the climate change discourse. Conversely, climate scientists and other natural scientists are not generally in a good position to develop a detailed understanding of the way social systems operate, including in terms of how they contribute to climate change. We firmly believe that the effort to examine and respond to the adverse impacts of climate change on humanity and the environment has to be a multidisciplinary effort that entails collaboration between climate scientists, natural scientists, physical geographers, and environmental scientists, on the one hand, and social scientists, including anthropologists, archaeologists, sociologists, political scientists, and human geographers, on the other hand. Anthropologist and archaeologist Carole L. Crumley provides a rare example of a scholar who has managed to act as a disciplinary broker between the natural and social sciences. She reports: "I am trained in paleoclimatology, geomorphology, archeology, anthropology, ethnohistory, and classics; I have some familiarity with complex systems theory, ecology, history, and geography" (Crumley 2007: 16). This type of diverse range of skills no doubt facilitates work across disciplinary lines. Alternately, a wide range of skill availability can be achieved through multidisciplinary team research, an approach that requires communication and trust across traditional disciplinary divisions.

In April 2012, *Current Anthropology* published a "Forum on Anthropology in Public" which came out of an interdisciplinary discussion on climate histories at

Cambridge, UK in early 2011. The discussion sought to develop a network around the issue of communicating cultural knowledge of environmental and climate change (Diemberger *et al.* 2012). In her lead article, anthropologist Kirsten Hastrup (2012b: 227) focuses on the centrality of ice in Arctic life—it "impinges on the imagination, creates social dramas, and affords a wildlife from which the hunters live." In contrast, in their commentary, Hildegard Diemberger (Director of Tibetan Studies at the University of Cambridge) and Hans-F. Graf (a professor from environmental systems analysis) argue that local people believe that sacred mountains control the weather and serve as indicators of a moral climate as to whether or not they have abided by the dictates of the "lords of the land" in the case of the Tibetan plateau (Diemberger and Graf 2012: 234). Also commenting on local knowledge about climate change on the Tibetan Plateau, Jacqueline Hobbs (a PhD student in the Mongolia and Inner Asia Studies Unit at the University of Cambridge) and Jason Davis (a biologist) note that for the Chu khol ka nomads, the milkbird serves not only to mark the time when their female yaks begin to give milk, but with its decline, as a proxy for the increasing erratic nature of the world, with "'climate change' defined as both a political and natural threat to traditional lifestyles," and not only the moral decline of Amdo-Tibetans, but also the "possible extinction of humanity itself" (Hobbs and Davis 2012: 235). Maria Luisa Nodari (another PhD student in the Mongolia and Inner Asia Studies Unit at the University of Cambridge) and Giorgio Vassena (an academic in the Department of Civil, Architectural, Land and Environmental Engineering at the University of Brescia in Italy) observe:

> Glaciers are considered among the most sensitive indicators of climate change, but they are also social spaces and sites for human encounters among different people. . . . Rwenzori [a mountain in East Africa] has become a site of encounters between people who have different ways of perceiving its glaciers and who question its ice differently. Scientists search for data; mountaineers hope for the preservation of the integrity of their target; tourists admire tropical ice and snow; local people hope to preserve the integrity of their environment; and institutional representatives attempt to keep power by showing success in water preservation, environmental conservation, and economic development.
>
> *Nodari and Vassena 2012: 237*

They astutely note that the "new global geography of climate change is . . . vulnerable to fragmentation through misunderstandings across disciplinary boundaries, differing scientific cultures, and gaps between specialized knowledge and wider perceptions" (Nodari and Vassena 2012: 237). Without doubt, an effort to create an integrated interdisciplinary study of climate change uniting all sciences and relevant humanities is a formidable task, as too is the more modest effort to create an integrated social science of climate change.

Still, in fully coming to terms with climate change, Johan Rockström (2011: 25) maintains that what is needed is an "interdisciplinary science that focuses on solving problems" and seeks to "integrate social sciences, humanities and natural sciences." He asserts that in his work with two multidisciplinary research organizations—the Stockholm Environmental Institute and the Stockholm Resilience Centre—he has been lucky to find "economists, political scientists, political scientists, anthropologists, etc., who truly understand the complex dynamics of the biophysical systems of the Earth" (Rockström 2011: 25). While this indeed may be true, Hans Baer, in attending interdisciplinary seminars associated with the Melbourne Sustainable Society Institute at the University of Melbourne, often has had the impression that while the natural scientists, including climate scientists and engineers, recognize the importance of the social sciences in unraveling the complexities of the human–environment interface, they generally have a rather superficial understanding of the ways that political economic and social systems function. The reality is that natural scientists and mainstream economists tend to dominate much of the discourse on climate change, as is evidenced by the composition of the IPCC. Rockström (2011: 26–27) advocates moving beyond the "disciplinary status quo" characteristic of the sciences and universities and moving toward emphasis on "more integrated and problem-solving programmes." We could not agree more, but also maintain that climate change research needs to move beyond research centers and universities and collaborate with communities, particularly those which are being adversely impacted by climate change, as well as NGOs, progressive political parties, women's groups, and climate action groups that are pushing for effective climate change mitigation strategies informed by a strong sense of social and climate justice.

Echoing an older statement attributed to various individuals about wars and generals, Derber (2010: 3) maintains that climate change is "too important to be left to scientists, environmental groups, or any other specialized group," but needs to "become rapidly integrated into the social sciences and humanities courses of universities—as well as become a leading topic in churches, workplaces, and town halls across the country [United States] and the world." Yet, as Urry (2011: 3) argues, to date the social science of climate change remains a relatively undeveloped endeavor, "because of the dominance of economic models of human behavior in much of the academic and especially the environmental policy world."

What has become apparent to us in the process of reviewing not only the literature in the anthropology of climate change, but also sociological, political scientific, and human geographical perspectives on climate change, is that disciplinary boundaries are historic artifacts that in many ways are artificial and even may be irrelevant, despite the fact that each discipline brings certain unique insights to the table. Ultimately, it seems to us that what will be more important are theoretical perspectives which transcend disciplinary lines. In fact, many co-authored publications on climate change are written by people from various disciplines or interdisciplinary fields who happen to share more or less the same theoretical perspective. For example, Australian human geographers Lesley Head and Chris Gibson (2012: 699) emphasize that: "Anthropogenic climate change is a quintessential 'modern' problem. The fossil fuel-based economies of industrial capitalism, the key economic features of modernity, are the root cause of enhanced greenhouse gas emissions destabilizing global climate."

Such an observation harmonizes well with both the critical anthropology and the critical sociology of climate change, and surely there are critical political scientists who would agree with this observation as well. The same is true of the following comment by Joel Wainwright (2012: 275), a critical human geographer:

> The historical coincidence of the emergence of global capitalism with the transformation of our planet's atmosphere is no accident. Capitalism is at the heart of the challenge of confronting climate change, and any serious attempt to address global climate change must contend with global capitalism.

By contrast, Nicholas Stern and other conventional economists contend that market mechanisms, such as emissions trading schemes and carbon offsets, will solve the "diabolical problem" of climate change. Like many critical social scientists of various disciplines, however, we ask: "How can you expect the system that created the problem to solve the problem?" This question is especially relevant because the problem in this instance—climate change—was not caused by a peripheral feature of capitalism, one that can easily be expunged, but rather by the central engine of the system: the continual expansion of production and the promotion of continual growth in levels of consumption. This perspective unites various social scientists across disciplines, although it certainly is not the dominant perspective at this time.

In seeking to develop a critical anthropology of climate change, we have relied on the work of numerous scholars not only from anthropology, but from the other social sciences as well. Our approach to this work has been guided by an *integrated eco-social perspective* that is informed, as we note in Chapter 4, by three theoretical currents that have differing disciplinary origins: world systems theory, political ecology, and critical medical anthropology. Our integration of these three multi-disciplinary approaches suggests a theoretical framework that links: (1) structures of control and social disparity (as seen in the underlying social relations and processes driving capitalist production) to increasingly powerful forces of corporate globalization, human population growth, and urbanization; and, in turn, links these to (2) structures and processes in the production of greenhouse gases and resulting climate turmoil, as well as to environmental degradation and pluralea interactions more generally, resulting in significantly increased human vulnerability, suffering, sickness, and death. Further, our perspective on climate change is framed by an *engaged praxis orientation* that merges theory and social action around issues of equity and justice, participatory democracy, and environmental sustainability.

Imagining the future in the Anthropocene and the age of potential cataclysmic climate change

Historically, anthropologists have concerned themselves with human societies of the distant past—the domain of archaeology—and of the recent past or present—the domain of sociocultural anthropology. In contrast to the age of the Earth, the period that we humans have lived on this planet, roughly 5 million–6 million years, has been a blip in time. When we consider how long we have lived as farming and herding communities, some 10,000 years, or how long we have lived in state societies, some 6,000 years, marked by differential power relations and social stratification, our presence in such social arrangements is a tiny fraction even of the already brief timeline of our species. The IPCC and other scenario setters often speak of what the state of humanity on this planet may be like in 2050 or 2100, but generally not beyond. As Sheila Jasanoff (2010: 241) aptly observes: "Climate change invites humanity to play with time," including peering with the mind's eye into the future as we might imagine it will unfold. In a somewhat different but equally sobering vein, the Slovenian political philosopher Slavoj Žižek (2010: 332–333) argues:

> With the idea of humans as a species, the universality of humankind falls back into the particularity of an animal species: phenomena like global warming make us aware that, with all the universality of our theoretical activity, we are at a certain level just another living species on Earth. Our survival depends on certain natural parameters which we automatically take for granted. The lesson of global warming is that the freedom of humankind was possible only against the background of stable natural parameters of life on earth (temperature, the composition of the air, sufficient water and energy supplies, and so on): humans can "do what they like" only insofar as they remain marginal enough so as not to seriously perturb natural preconditions.

Over the past several decades, anthropologists and other social scientists often have alluded to a cavalcade of "posts": post-colonialism, post-industrialism, post-Fordism, post-socialism, post-modernism, post-structuralism, and post-feminism. Anthropologists and other social scientists might entertain the possibility of at least two other "posts," namely post-capitalism and post-climate change. To do so, we need to further develop a social science of the future. While, in the 1970s and 1980s, various anthropologists grappled with future scenarios for humanity, the demise of the Soviet bloc countries and the disillusionment with grand theory or meta-narratives under the guise of post-modernism appear to have predisposed a younger generation of anthropologists to steer away from seemingly grandiose projects of attaining a better world based on both social justice and environmental sustainability. Yet a revival of the anthropology of the future as well as a social science of the future, given an increasing awareness of the seriousness of anthropogenic climate change, strikes us as imperative (Marshall and Connor 2016).

This potential vision of a bleak future was voiced as well by James Lovelock, formulator of the Gaia theory referenced in Chapter 1. Asked by Shell oil company executives in 1965 what the world would be like in the year 2000, Lovelock did not provide fanciful descriptions of fusion-powered hovercraft, medical ability to reverse aging and cell deterioration, or other exciting technological breakthroughs;

rather, he dryly told them that the environment would be an ever more pressing problem that would seriously impact their business. In his book *The Revenge of Gaia*, Lovelock (2007) predicted that by 2020 extreme weather will become the new norm, causing global catastrophes, and that by 2040 much of Europe will be undergoing desertification while every coastal city in the world sinks below the rising oceans. Ultimately, he came to believe for a period that we already have passed the tipping point and climate turmoil is now unstoppable. Subsequently, he concluded that while climate change is happening, its worst effects will set in later than he had originally expected.

On a brighter side, John Bodley (2014), in the six editions of his book *Anthropology and Contemporary Human Problems*, has a concluding chapter on "The Future" in which he envisions a *sustainable planetary society*. Bodley's vision of a sustainable planetary society is consistent with what we, along with our colleague Ida Susser (Baer *et al.* 2013), refer to as *democratic eco-socialism* or what world systems theorists Terry Boswell and Christopher Chase-Dunn (2000) term *global democracy*.

In considering responses to the unsustainability of capitalism, the critical anthropology of climate change proposes the creation of a democratic eco-socialist world system as a form of what critical sociologist Erik Olin Wright (2010) terms a *real utopia*. Despite efforts in the Soviet Union, China, and numerous other post-revolutionary societies to create socialism, all of these efforts were powerfully hindered in achieving this ideal by complex historical and social structural conditions. Thus democratic eco-socialism still remains a vision, but one in this age of global warming that merits thoughtful consideration of the following dimensions or desired goals: (1) an economy oriented to meeting basic social needs, namely adequate food, clothing, shelter, and healthful conditions and resources; (2) a high degree of social equality and social fairness; (3) public ownership of productive forces; (4) representative and participatory democracy; and (5) environmental sustainability. Ultimately, the shift to democratic eco-socialism in any country would have to be part of a global process that no one can fully envision at the present time.

Obviously, the transition toward a democratic eco-socialist world system is not guaranteed, and will require a tedious, even convoluted, path. Nevertheless, while awaiting the "revolution," so to speak, progressive people can work on various transitional reforms. The critical anthropology of climate change proposes the following transitional reforms essential to implementing an ecological revolution and ultimately global democratic eco-socialism: (1) the creation of new left parties designed to capture the state; (2) the implementation of emissions taxes at the site of production that include efforts to protect low-income people; (3) public ownership in various ways of the means of production; (4) increasing social equality within nation-states and between nation-states and achieving a sustainable global population; (5) the implementation of socialist planning and workers' democracy; (6) meaningful work and shortening of the working week; (7) development of a steady-state economy; (8) the adoption of renewable energy sources, energy efficiency, and appropriate technology, and the creation of green jobs; (9) sustainable public transportation and travel; (10) sustainable food production and forestry; (11) resistance to the capitalist culture of consumption; (12) sustainable trade; and (13) sustainable settlement patterns and local communities (Baer 2018: 201–253). These transitional steps constitute a loose blueprint for shifting human societies or countries toward democratic eco-socialism and a safe climate, but it is important to note that both of these phenomena will entail a global effort, including the creation of a progressive climate governance regime.

Anti-systemic movements will have to play an instrumental role in bringing about the political will which will enable the world to shift to an alternative world system based upon social justice and environmental sustainability. Given the failure of established international and national climate regimes to date in adequately containing the climate crisis, efforts to create a global climate governance process will have to come from below. Ultimately, the climate justice movement will have to form strong alliances with other progressive social movements, perhaps in particular the anti-corporate globalization or global justice movement. Michael Hardt and Antonio Negri (2009: 94–95) suggest that "only movements from below" possess the "capacity to construct a consciousness of renewal and transformation"—one that "emerges from the working classes and multitudes that autonomously and creatively propose anti-modern and anticapitalist hopes and dreams."

Going from the present capitalist world system, which has generated and continues to generate anthropogenic climate change, to an alternative global political economy, however it is defined, will require much effort, and there are no guarantees that we will be able to create a more socially equitable and environmentally sustainable world. But do we really have any other meaningful choice than to change, or face the downward spiral and the destruction of much of humanity, loss of current biodiversity, and further environmental degradation? We do not believe that global capitalism has a serious potential to be either socially just or environmentally sustainable, and in light of that reality, humanity must move to something new and better, whatever we may call it. We are in basic agreement with Wallerstein (2007: 382) in his statement:

> I do not believe that our historical system is going to last much longer, for I consider it to be in a terminal structural crisis, a chaotic transition to some other system (or systems), a transition that will last at most twenty-five to fifty years. I therefore believe that it could be possible to overcome the self-destructive patterns of global environmental change into which the world has fallen and establish alternative patterns. I emphasize however my firm assessment that the outcome of this transition is inherently uncertain and unpredictable.

In conclusion, anthropologists and other social scientists can play a small but critical role in providing their analytical skills and insights to a much larger struggle to create a world in which we learn to live in harmony with one another and the planet, and in the process create a safe climate.

REFERENCES

Abbott, D. and G. Wilson. 2015. *The Lived Experience of Climate Change*. Basle, Switzerland: Springer International Publishing.

Adger, W. Neil, Saleemul Huq, Katrina Brown, Declan Conway, and Mile Hulme. 2003. Adaptation to climate change in the developing world. *Progress in Development Studies* 3(3): 179–195.

Adger, W. Neil, Jouni Paavola, Saleemul Huq, and M. J. Mace, Eds. 2006. *Fairness in Adaptation to Climate Change*. Cambridge, MA: MIT Press.

Agarwal, Anil and Sunita Narain. 1991. *Global Warming in an Unequal World*. New Delhi, India: Centre for Science and Environment.

Agrawal, Arun, Maria Lemos, Ben Orlove, and Jesse Ribot. 2012. Cool heads for a hot world—social sciences under a changing sky. *Global Environmental Change* 22(2): 329–331.

Aircraft Crashes Record Office. 2013. Number of yearly fatalities due to air transport crashes, 1918–2012. Online at: http://people.hofstra.edu/geotrans/eng/ch3en/conc3en/airfatalities.html. Accessed July 9, 2013.

Aitken, Donald. 2010. Global warming, rapid climate change, and renewable energy solutions for Gaia. In *Gaia in Turmoil: Climate Change, Biodepletion, and Earth's Ethics in an Age of Crisis*. Eileen Crist and Bruce Rinker, Eds. Pp. 125–150. Cambridge, MA: MIT Press.

Alam, Mozaharul and Atiq Rahman. 2008. Development and climate change policy-making process in Bangladesh. In *Climate Change in Asia: Perspectives on the Future Climate Regime*. Yasuko Kameyama, Agus P. Sari, Moekti H. Soejachmoen, and Norichika Kanie, Eds. Pp. 51–65. Tokyo, Japan: United Nations University Press.

Allen, Michael Patrick. 1992. Elite social movement organizations and the state: The rise of the conservative policy-planning network. *Research in Politics and Policy* 4: 87–109.

Ambrose, Stanley. 1998. Late Pleistocene human population bottlenecks, volcanic winter, and differentiation of modern humans. *Journal of Human Evolution* 34: 623–651.

American Anthropological Association. 2011. Anthropologists announce new task force on climate change. Press release, December 19. Washington, DC: American Anthropological Association.

American Anthropological Association. 2015. *AAA Statement on Humanity and Climate Change*. http://practicinganthropology.org/docs/01-29-15_AAA_CCS.pdf. Accessed December 19, 2017.

Anderegg, William, James Prall, and Jacob Harold. 2010. Reply to O'Neill and Boykoff: objective classification of climate experts. *Proceedings of the National Academy of Sciences* 107(39): E152.

Anderegg, William, James Prall, Jacob Harold, and Stephen Schneider. 2010. Expert credibility in climate change. *Proceedings of the National Academy of Sciences* 107(27): 12,107–12,109.

Anderson, David G., Kirk A. Maasch, and Daniel H. Sandweiss. 2007. Preface and acknowledgements. In *Climate Change and Cultural Dynamics: A Global Perspective in Mid-Holocene Transitions*. David G. Anderson, Kirk A. Maasch, and Daniel H. Sandweiss, Eds. Pp. xxi–xxii. Amsterdam, the Netherlands: Academic Press.

Antilla, Liisa. 2005. Climate of scepticism: U.S. newspaper coverage of the science of climate change. *Global Environmental Change* 15(4): 338–352.

Armelagos, George J. and Kristin N. Harper. 2010. Emerging infectious diseases, urbanization, and globalization in the time of global warming. In *The New Blackwell Companion to Medical Sociology*. William C. Cockerham, Ed. Pp. 291–311. Malden, MA: Wiley-Blackwell.

Aspinall, Richard, Ed. 2012. *Geography of Climate Change*. New York: Routledge.

Aulakh, Raveena. 2013. When the desert devours the lake. *The Star.com*. Online at: www.thestar.com/news/world/2013/04/06/when_the_desert_devours_the_lake.html. Accessed July 2, 2013.

Australian Bureau of Meteorology. 2009. Annual Australian Climate Statement 2009. Online at: www.bom.gov.au/announcements/media_releases/climate/change/20100105.shtml. Accessed July 23, 2013.

Bäckstrand, Karin. 2011. The democratic legitimacy of global governance after Copenhagen. In *Oxford Handbook of Climate Change and Society*. John S. Dryzek, Richard B. Norgaard, and David Scholosberg, Eds. Pp. 669–684. Oxford, UK: Oxford University Press.

Baer, Hans A. 2008. Global warming as a by-product of the capitalist treadmill of production and consumption: the need for an alternative global system. *Australian Journal of Anthropology* 19: 58–62.

Baer, Hans A. 2009. The environmental and health consequences of motor vehicles: a case study in capitalist technology and hegemony and grassroots responses to it. In *Killer Commodities: Public Health and the Corporate Production of Harm*. Merrill Singer and Hans A. Baer, Eds. Pp. 95–118. Walnut Creek, CA: AltaMira Press.

Baer, Hans A. 2011. The international climate justice movement: a comparison with the Australian climate movement. *Australian Journal of Anthropology* 22: 256–260.

Baer, Hans A. 2012. *Global Capitalism and Climate Change: The Need for an Alternative World System*. Lanham, MD: AltaMira Press.

Baer, Hans A. 2015. Al Gore and the Climate Reality Project down under: the up market of the climate movement. *Practicing Anthropology* 37(1): 10–14.

Baer, Hans A. 2018. *Democratic Eco-Socialism at a Real Utopia: Transitioning to an Alternative World System*. New York: Berghahn.

Baer, Hans A. and Arnaud Gallois. 2016. How committed are Australian universities to environmental sustainability? A perspective on and from the University of Melbourne. *Critical Sociology*. doi: 10.1177/0896920516680857.

Baer, Hans A. and Merrill Singer. 2009. *Global Warming and the Political Ecology of Health: Emerging Crises and Systemic Solutions*. Walnut Creek, CA: Left Coast Press.

Baer, Hans A., Merrill Singer, and Ida Susser. 1997. *Medical Anthropology and the World System: A Critical Perspective*. Westport, CT: Bergin & Garvey.

Baer, Hans A., Merrill Singer, and Ida Susser. 2003. *Medical Anthropology and the World System: A Critical Perspective* (2nd edition). Westport, CT: Praeger.

Baer, Hans A., Merrill Singer, and Ida Susser. 2013. *Medical Anthropology and the World System: A Critical Perspective* (3rd edition). Santa Barbara, CA: Praeger.

Baily, Alan. 2007. USGS: 25% Arctic oil, gas estimate a reporter's mistake. *Petroleum News* 12(42). Online at: www.petroleumnews.com/pntruncate/347702651.shtml. Accessed July 3, 2013.

Baker, Carolyn. 2013. Mutually assured well being: the continuity of community and individual resilience. Online at: http://carolynbaker.net/2013/02/08/mutually-assured-well-being-the-continuity-of-community-and-individual-resilience-by-carolyn-baker/. Accessed July 26, 2013.

Balling, R. 2000. The geographer's niche in the greenhouse millennium. *Annals of the Association of American Geographers* 90: 114–122.

Banerjee, Neela. 2013. EPA releases harsh review of Keystone XL environmental report. *Los Angeles Times*, April 22. Online at: http://articles.latimes.com/2013/apr/22/news/la-pn-epa-keystone-xl-environmental-report-20130422. Accessed July 20, 2013.

Bang, Guri, Arild Underdal, and Steinar Anderson. 2015a. Comparative analysis and conclusions. In *The Domestic Politics of Global Climate Change: Key Actors in International Climate Cooperation*. Guri Bang, Arild Underdal, and Steinar Anderson, Eds. Pp. 182–204. Cheltenham, UK: Edward Elgar Publishing.

Bang, Guri, Arild Underdal, and Steinar Anderson, Eds. 2015b. *The Domestic Politics of Global Climate Change: Key Actors in International Climate Cooperation*. Cheltenham, UK: Edward Elgar Publishing.

Barber, Marcus. 2011a. "Nothing ever changes": Historical ecology, causality and climate change in Arnhem Land, Australia. In *Ethnography and the Production of Anthropological Knowledge: Essays in Honour of Nicolas Peterson*. Yasmine Musharbash and Marcus Barber, Eds. Pp. 89–100. Canberra, Australia: ANU E Press.

Barber, Marcus. 2011b. *Talking about the weather: anthropology and climate change*. Paper presented at the *International Union of Anthropological and Ethnological Sciences/Australian Anthropological Society/Association of Social Anthropologists of Aotearoa New Zealand Joint Conference*, University of Western Australia, Perth, July 4–8.

Barker, Holly M. 2011. Snapshot: climate change and the small island experience. In *Life and Death Matters: Human Rights, Environment, and Social Justice* (2nd edition). Barbara Rose Johnston, Ed. Pp. 427–430. Walnut Creek, CA: Left Coast Press.

Barnes, Jessica. 2015. Scale and agency: climate change and the future of Egypt's water. In *Climate Cultures: Anthropological Perspectives on Climate Change*. Jessica Barnes and Michael R. Dove, Eds. Pp. 127–145. New Haven, CT: Yale University Press.

Barnes, Jessica and Michael R. Dove, Eds. 2015a. *Climate Cultures: Anthropological Perspectives on Climate Change*. 1–21. New Haven, CT: Yale University Press.

Barnes, Jessica and Michael R. Dove. 2015b. Introduction. In *Climate Cultures: Anthropological Perspectives on Climate Change*. Jessica Barnes and Michael R. Dove, Eds. Pp. 1–21. New Haven, CT: Yale University Press.

Barnes, Jessica and Michael R. Dove. 2015c. Preface. In *Climate Cultures: Anthropological Perspectives on Climate Change*. Jessica Barnes and Michael R. Dove, Eds. Pp. vii–viii. New Haven, CT: Yale University Press.

Barnes, Jessica, Michael Dove, Myanna Lahsen, Andrew Mathews, Pamela McElwee, Roderick McIntosh, Frances Moore, Jessica O'Reilly, Ben Orlove, Rajindra Puri, Harvey

Weiss, and Karina Yager. 2013. Contribution of anthropology to the study of climate change. *Nature Climate Change* 3: 541–544.

Barnett, Jon. 2006. Climate change, insecurity, and injustice. In *Fairness in Adaptation to Climate Change*. W. Neil Adger, Jouni Paavola, Saleemul Huq, and M. J. Mace, Eds. Pp. 115–129. Cambridge, MA: MIT Press.

Barnett, Jon and John Campbell. 2010. *Climate Change and Small Island States: Power, Knowledge and the South Pacific*. London: Earthscan.

Barry, John. 2012. *The Politics of Actually Existing Unsustainability: Human Flourishing in Carbon-Constrained World*. Oxford, UK: Oxford University Press.

Bartlett, Peggy F. and Benjamin Stewart. 2009. Shifting the university: faculty engagement and curriculum change. In *Anthropology and Climate Change: From Encounters to Actions*. Susan A. Crate and Mark Nuttall, Eds. Pp. 356–369. Walnut Creek, CA: Left Coast Press.

Bauman, Zygmunt. 2005. *Work, Consumerism and the New Poor*. Maidenhead, UK: Open University Press.

Bauman, Zygmunt. 2011. *Collateral Damage: Social Inequalities in a Global Age*. London: Polity.

BBC News. 2012. Jim Yong Kim takes top job at World Bank. Online at: www.bbc.co.uk/news/business-17757480. Accessed July 20, 2013.

Behringer, Wolfgang. 2010. *A Cultural History of Climate*. London: Polity.

Beck, Ulrich. 1992. *Risk Society: Toward a New Modernity*. London: SAGE Publications.

Beck, Ulrich. 2007. *World at Risk*. London: Polity.

Beck, Ulrich. 2010. Climate for change, or how to create a green modernity? *Theory, Culture & Society* 27(2–3): 254–266.

Becken, Susanne. 2005. Harmonising climate change adaptation and mitigation: the cause of tourist resorts in Fiji. *Global Environmental Change* 15: 381–393.

Beder, Sharon. 2001. Neoliberal think tanks and free market environmentalism. *Environmental Politics* 10(2): 128–133.

Beach, Timothy. 2016. Editorial: climate change and archaeology in Mesoamerica. *Global and Planetary Change* 138(20): 1–2.

Behringer, Wolfgang. 2010. *A Cultural History of Climate*. London: Polity.

Bina, Olivia. 2011. Responsibility for emissions and aspirations for development. In *China's Responsibility for Climate Change: Ethics, Fairness and Environmental Policy*. Paul G. Harris, Ed. Pp. 51–69. Bristol, UK: Policy Press.

Binford, Lewis R. 1968. Post-Pleistocene adaptations. In *New Perspectives in Archaeology*. S. R. Binford and L. R. Binford, Eds. Pp. 313–441. Chicago, IL: Aldine.

Birn, Anne-Emanuelle, Yogan Pillay, and Timothy H. Holtz. 2009. *Textbook of International Health: Global Health in a Dynamic World* (3rd edition). Oxford, UK: Oxford University Press.

Bocquet-Appel, Jean-Pierre and Alain Tuffreau. 2009. Technological responses of Neanderthals to macroclimatic variations (240,000–40,000 BP). *Human Biology* 81: 287–307.

Bodley, John. 2014. *Anthropology and Contemporary Human Problems*. Lanham, MD: AltaMira Press.

Bolin, Inge. 2009. The glaciers of the Andes are melting: indigenous and anthropological knowledge merge in restoring water sources. In *Anthropology and Climate Change*. Susan A. Crate and Mark Nuttall, Eds. Pp. 228–249. Walnut Creek, CA: Left Coast Press.

Bond, P. 2010. Maintaining momentum after Copenhagen's collapse: seal the deal or "Seattle" the deal? *Capitalism Nature Socialism* 21: 14–27.

Bond, T., S. Doherty, D. Fahey, P. Forster, T. Berntsen, and B. DeAngelo. 2013. Bounding the role of black carbon in the climate system: a scientific assessment. *Journal of Geophysical Research, Atmosphere* 118(11): 5,382–5,552.

Bostoen, Koen, Bernard Clist, Charles Doumenge, Rebecca Grollemund, Jean-Marie Hombert, Joseph Koni Muluwa, and Jean Maley. 2015. *Current Anthropology* 56: 354–384.

Boswell, Terry and Christopher Chase-Dunn. 2000. *The Spiral of Capitalism and Socialism.* Boulder, CO: Lynne Rienner.

Boykoff, Maxwell and Boykoff, Jules. 2004. Balance as bias: global warming and the US prestige press. *Global Environmental Change* 14(2): 125–136.

Brace, Catherine and Hilary Geoghegan. 2010. Human geographies of climate change: landscape, temporality, and lay knowledges. *Progress in Human Geography* 35: 284–302.

Brennan, William (Justice). 1976. *Colorado River Water Conservation District et al., Petitioners v. United States. Mary Akin et al., Petitioners, vs. United States.* 424 US 800. Nos. 74–940, 74–949.

Briggs, Charles. 2011. Biocommunicability. In *A Companion to Medical Anthropology.* Merrill Singer and Pamela Erickson, Eds., Pp. 460–476. Malden, MA. Wiley-Blackwell.

Brown, Kathryn S. 1999. Climate anthropology: taking global warming to the people. *Science* 283(5,407): 1,440–1,441.

Brown, Lester. 2011. Environmental and demographic forces that threaten state failure. *Earth Policy Institute.* Online at: www.earth-policy.org/book_bytes/2011/wotech7_ss1. Accessed February 2, 2013.

Brunnengräber, Achim. 2006. The political economy of the Kyoto Protocol. In *Coming to Terms with Nature.* Leo Panitch and Colin Leys, Eds. Pp. 213–230. London: Merlin Press.

Bulkeley, Harriet. 2013. *Cities and Climate Change.* London: Routledge.

Bulkeley, Harriet. 2015. *Accomplishing Climate Governance.* New York: Cambridge University Press.

Bulkeley, Harriet and Michele M. Betsill. 2003. *Cities and Climate Change: Urban Sustainability and Global Environmental Governance.* London: Routledge.

Bulkeley, Harriet and Michele M. Betsill. 2013. Revisiting the urban politics of climate change. *Environmental Politics* 22: 136–154.

Bulkeley, Harriet and Peter Newell. 2015. *Governing Climate Change.* Abingdon, UK: Taylor & Francis.

Bull, Pierce. 2013. Renewable energy vs. Koch Brothers and ALEC. *EcoNews.* Online at: https://www.ecowatch.com/renewable-energy-vs-koch-brothers-and-alec-1881726277.html. Accessed July 19, 2013.

Burgmann, Verity and Hans A. Baer. 2012. *Climate Politics and the Climate Movement in Australia.* Melbourne, Australia: Melbourne University Press.

Burke, Lauretta, Kathleen Reytar, Mark Spalding, and Allison Perry. 2012. *Reefs at Risk Revisited in the Coral Triangle.* Washington, DC: World Resources Institute.

Burroughs, William J. 2005. *Climate Change in Prehistory: The End of the Reign of Chaos.* Cambridge, UK: Cambridge University Press.

Button, Gregory V. and Kristina Peterson. 2009. Participatory action research community partnership with social and physical scientists. In *Anthropology and Culture.* Susan A. Crate and Mark Nuttall, Eds. Pp. 327–340. Walnut Creek, CA: Left Coast Press.

Butzer, Karl W. 2011. Geoarchaeology, climate change, sustainability: a Mediterranean perspective. In *Geoarchaeology, Climate Change, and Sustainability: Special Paper 476.* Antony G. Brown, Laura S. Basell, and Karl W. Butzer, Eds. Pp. 1–14. Boulder, CO: Geological Society of America.

Cameron, Emilie S. 2012. Securing indigenous politics: a critique of the vulnerability and adaptation approach to the human dimensions of climate change in the Canadian Arctic. *Global Environmental Change* 22: 103–114.

Camilleri, Joseph A. and Jim Falk. 2010. *Worlds in Transition: Evolving Governance across a Stressed Planet*. Cheltenham, UK: Edward Elgar.

Campbell, Alexia. 2017. Trump to Puerto Rico: your hurricane isn't a "real catastrophe" like Katrina. *Vox*. Online at: https://www.vox.com/2017/10/3/16411488/trump-remarks-puerto-rico. Accessed December 16, 2017.

Canavan, Gerry, Lisa Klarr, and Ryan Vu. 2010. Embodied materialism in action: an interview with Ariel Salleh. *Polygraph* 22: 183–199.

Caritas Internationalis. 2012. Paradise lost: rising seas threaten Pacific's Carteret Islands. *Caritas.org*. Online at: https://www.caritas.org/2012/11/paradise-lost-rising-seas-threaten-pacifics-carteret-islands. Accessed July 1, 2013.

Carmichael, Jason T. and Robert J. Brulle. 2017. Elite cues, media coverage, and public concern: an integrated path analysis of public opinion on climate change, 2001–2013. *Environmental Politics* 26: 232–252.

Cassidy, Rebecca. 2012. Lives with others: climate change and human-animals relations. *Annual Review of Anthropology* 41: 21–36.

Castells, Manuel. 2009. *Communication Power*. Oxford, UK: Oxford University Press.

Center for Global Development. 2007. World agriculture faces serious decline from global warming. Online at: www.cgdev.org/content/article/detail/14404/. Accessed March 3, 2013.

Center for Global Development. 2012. Pinpoint climate studies flag trouble for Mexico, CenAm farmers (Reuters). Online at: www.cgdev.org/content/article/detail/1426836/. Accessed March 3, 2013.

Chase, Arlen F. and Vernon Scarborough. 2014. Diversity, resiliency, and IHOPE-Maya: using the past to inform the present. *Archaeological Papers of the American Anthropological Association* 24: 1–10.

Chatturvedi, Sanjay and Timothy Doyle. 2015. *Climate of Terror: A Critical Geopolitics of Climate Change*. New York: Palgrave Macmillan.

Chew, Sing C. 2001. *World Ecological Degradation: Accumulation, Urbanization, and Deforestation—3000 B.C.–A.D. 2000*. Walnut Creek, CA: AltaMira Press.

Chew, Sing C. 2007. *The Recurring Dark Ages: Ecological Stress, Climate Changes, and System Transformation*. Lanham, MD: AltaMira Press.

Childe, V. Gordon. 1954 [orig. 1928]. *New Light on the Most Ancient East* (4th edition). London: Routledge & Kegan Paul.

Chomsky, Noam. 2013. Noam Chomsky: who owns the Earth? *Truthout*. Online at: www.truth-out.org/opinion/item/17402-who-owns-the-earth. Accessed July 5, 2013.

Christian, David. 2011. *Maps of Time: An Introduction to Big History*. Berkeley, CA: University of California Press.

Christoff, Peter. 2010. Cold extremes in Copenhagen: China and the United States at COP15. *Environmental Politics* 19: 637–656.

Christoff, Peter and Robyn Eckersley. 2011. Comparing state response. In *Oxford Handbook of Climate Change and Society*. John S. Dryzek, Richard B. Norgaard, and David Schlosberg, Eds. Pp. 432–448. Oxford, UK: Oxford University Press.

Chu, Henry. 2007. Where warming hits home. *Los Angeles Times*, February 21. Online at: http://articles.latimes.com/2007/feb/21/world/fg-warming21. Accessed July 12, 2013.

Ciplet, David, J. Timmons Roberts, and Mizan R. Khan. 2015. *The New Global Politics of Climate Change and Remaking of Environmental Inequality*. Cambridge, MA: MIT Press.

Cobb, Kurt. 2006. Will global warming create any winners? *Resource Insights*. Online at: http://resourceinsights.blogspot.com/2006/02/will-global-warming-create-any-winners.html. Accessed December 19, 2017.

Cole, John and Eric Wolf. 1974. *The Hidden Frontier: Ecology and Ethnicity in an Alpine Valley.* Berkeley, CA: University of California Press.

Connor, Linda H. 2010. Climate change and the challenge of immortality: faith, denial and intimations of eternity. *Anthropology and the Ends of Worlds.* Online at: https://anthroendsofworlds.files.wordpress.com/2011/04/connor-linda_final.pdf. Accessed May 3, 2013.

Connor, Linda H. 2010/2011. Anthropogenic climate change and cultural crisis: an anthropological perspective. *Journal of Australian Political Economy* 66: 247–267.

Connor, Linda H. 2012. Experimental publics: activist culture and political intelligibility of climate change action in the Hunter Valley, Southeast Australia. *Oceania* 82: 228–249.

Connor, Linda H. 2016. *Climate Change and the Anthropos: Planet, People, and Places.* London: Earthscan.

Connor, Linda H., Sonia Freeman, and Nick Higginbotham. 2009. Not just a coalmine: shifting grounds of community opposition to coal mining in southeastern Australia. *Ethnos* 7: 490–513.

Contreras, Daniel A., Ed. 2016. *The Archaeology of Human–Environment Interactions: Strategies for Investigating Anthropogenic Landscape, Dynamic Environments, and Climate Change in the Past.* London: Routledge.

Cooke, Sophie. 2010. Leave it in the ground—the growing global struggle against coal. In *Sparking a Worldwide Energy Revolution: Social Struggles in the Transition to a Post-Petrol World.* Kolya Abramsky, Ed. Pp. 424–438. Oakland, CA: AK Press.

Coreil, Robert W. 2004. Statement to the Committee on Commerce, Science, and Transportation, United States Senate, November 16. In *Arctic Climate Impact Assessment.* Carolyn Symon, Lelani Arris, and Bill Heal, Eds. Pp. 1–17. Cambridge, UK: Cambridge University Press.

Costanza, Robert, Lisa Graumlich, and Will Steffen. 2007. Sustainability or collapse: lessons from integrating the history of humans and the rest of nature. In *Sustainability or Collapse: An Integrated History and Future of People on Earth.* Robert Constanza, Lisa Graumlich, and Will Steffen, Eds. Pp. 3–18. Cambridge, MA: MI T Press.

Crate, Susan. 2008. Gone the bull of winter? Grappling with the cultural implications of and anthropology's role(s) in global climate change. *Current Anthropology* 49: 569–595.

Crate, Susan. 2009. Gone the bull of winter? Contemporary climate change's cultural implications in Northeastern Siberia, Russia. In *Anthropology and Climate Change.* Susan A. Crate and Mark Nuttall, Eds. Pp. 139–152. Walnut Creek, CA: Left Coast Press.

Crate, Susan. 2011a. Climate and culture: anthropology in the era of contemporary climate change. *Annual Review of Anthropology* 40: 175–194.

Crate, Susan. 2011b. Climate change, culture change, and human rights in northeastern Siberia. In *Life and Death Matters: Human Rights, Environment, and Social Justice* (2nd edition). Barbara Rose Johnston, Ed. Pp. 413–423. Walnut Creek, CA: Left Coast Press.

Crate, Susan and Mark Nuttall, Eds. 2009a. *Anthropology and Climate Change: From Encounters to Actions.* Walnut Creek, CA: Left Coast Press.

Crate, Susan and Mark Nuttall. 2009b. Epilogue: anthropology, science, and climate change policy. In *Anthropology and Climate Change.* Susan A. Crate and Mark Nuttall, Eds. Pp. 394–400. Walnut Creek, CA: Left Coast Press.

Crate, Susan and Mark Nuttall. 2009c. Introduction: anthropology and climate change. In *Anthropology and Climate Change.* Susan A. Crate and Mark Nuttall, Eds. Pp. 9–36. Walnut Creek, CA: Left Coast Press.

Crate, Susan A. and Mark Nuttall. 2016a. Introduction: anthropology and climate change. In *The Anthropology and Climate Change: From Actions to Transformations* (2nd edition). Susan A. Crate and Mark Nuttall, Eds. Pp. 11–34. New York: Routledge.

Crate, Susan A. and Mark Nuttall, Eds. 2016b. *The Anthropology of Climate Change: From Actions to Transformations* (2nd edition). New York: Routledge.

Crist, Eileen and Bruce Rinker, Eds. 2010. *Gaia in Turmoil: Climate Change, Biodepletion, and Earth Ethics in an Age of Crisis.* Cambridge, MA: MIT Press.

Cruikshank, Julie. 2001. Glaciers and climate change: perspectives from oral tradition. *Arctic* 54: 377–393.

Cruikshank, Julie. 2007. Melting glaciers and emerging histories in the Saint Elias Mountains. In *Indigenous Experience Today.* Marisol de la Cadena and Orin Starn, Eds. Pp. 355–378. Oxford, UK: Berg.

Crumley, Carole L., Ed. 1994. *Historical Ecology: Changing Knowledge and Changing Landscapes.* Santa Fe, NM: School of American Research Press.

Crumley, Carole L. 2007. Historical ecology: integrated thinking at multiple temporal scales. In *The World System and the Earth System: Global Socioenvironmental Change and Sustainability since the Neolithic.* Alf Hornborg and Carole Crumley, Eds. Pp. 1–11. Walnut Creek, CA: Left Coast Press.

Crutzen, Paul and Christian Schwägerl. 2011. Living in the Anthropocene: toward a new global ethos. *Yale Environment* 360. Online at: http://e360.yale.edu/feature/living_in_the_anthropocene_toward_a_new_global_ethos/2363/. Accessed April 3, 2013.

Crutzen, Paul and Eugene Stoermer. 2000. The Anthropocene. *Global Change Newsletter* 41: 17–18.

Curry, Renee, Charissa Eichman, Amanda Staudt, Garrit Voggesser, and Myra Wilensky. 2011. *Facing the Storm: Indian Tribes, Climate-Induced Weather Extremes, and the Future for Indian Country.* Washington, DC: National Wildlife Federation.

Cutter, Susan, Christopher Emrich, Jennifer Webb, and Daniel Morath. 2009. *Social Vulnerability to Climate Variability Hazards: A Review of the Literature.* Final Report to Oxfam America. Columbia, SC: University of South Carolina.

Dankelman, Irene, Ed. 2010. *Gender and Climate Change: An Introduction.* Washington, DC: Earthscan.

Davies, Dame Sally. 2013. *Chief Medical Officer's Summary. Annual Report of the Chief Medical Officer, Volume Two, Infections and the Rise of Antimicrobial Resistance.* London: Department of Health.

Dean, Jeffery. 2000. Complexity theory and sociocultural change in the American southwest. In *The Way the Wind Blows: Climate, History and Human Action.* Roderick McIntosh, Joseph Tainter, and Susan Keech McIntosh, Eds. Pp. 89–118. New York: Columbia University Press.

Dearing, John. 2007. Human–environment interactions: learning from the past. In *Sustainability or Collapse: An Integrated History and Future of People on Earth.* Robert Constanza, Lisa Graumlich, and Will Steffen, Eds. Pp. 19–38. Cambridge, MA: Massachusetts Institute of Technology.

De'ath, Glenn, Katharina Fabricius, Hugh Sweatman, and Marji Poutinen. 2012. The 27-year decline of coral cover on the Great Barrier Reef and its causes. *Proceedings of the National Academy of Sciences.* doi: 10.1073/pnas.1208909109.

Delaney, Alyne E. 2016. The neoliberal reorganization of the Greenlandic coastal Greenland halibut fishery in an era of climate and governance change. *Human Organization* 75: 193–203.

Dennis, Kingsley and John Urry. 2009. *After the Car.* London: Polity.

Derber, Charles. 2010. *Greed to Green: Solving Climate Change and Remaking the Economy.* Boulder, CO: Paradigm.

Diamond, Jared. 2005. *Collapse: How Societies Choose to Fail or Succeed.* New York: Penguin.

Diemberger, Hildegard. 2012. Deciding the future in the land of snow: Tibet as an arena for conflicting forms of knowledge and policy. In *The Social Life of Climate Change Models*. Kirsten Hastrup and Martin Skrydstrip, Eds. Pp. 100–127. Hoboken, NJ: Taylor & Francis.

Diemberger, Hildegard and Hans-F. Graf. 2012. Snow-mountains on the Tibetan Plateau: powerful proxies across different modalities of climate knowledge. *Current Anthropology* 53: 233–235.

Diemberger, Hildegard, Kirsten Hastrup, Simon Schaffer, Charles F. Kennel, David Sneath, Michael Bravo, Hans-F. Graf, Jacqueline Hobbs, Jason Davis, Maria Luisa Nodari, Giorgion Vassena, Richard Irvine, Christopher Evans, Marilyn Strathern, Mike Hulmer, Georg Kaser, and Barbara Bodenhorn. 2012. Communicating climate knowledge: proxies, processes, politics. *Current Anthropology* 53: 226–244.

Dietz, Matthias and Heiko Garrelts, Eds. 2014. *Routledge Handbook of the Climate Change Movement*. London: Routledge.

Dincauze, Dena Feran. 2000. *Environmental Archeology. Principles and Practice*. Cambridge, UK: Cambridge University Press.

Doran, Peter T. and Maggie Kendall Zimmerman. 2009. Examining the scientific consensus on climate change. *Eos* 90(3): 22–23.

Douglas, Mary and Aaron Wildavsky. 1982. *Risk and Culture: An Essay on the Selection of Environmental and Technological Dangers*. Berkeley, CA: University of California Press.

Douglas, Mary, Des Gasper, Steven Ney, and Michael Thompson. 1998. Human needs and wants. In *Human Choice and Climate Change: Volume One—the Societal Framework*. Steve Rayner and Elizabeth L. Malone, Eds. Pp. 195–263. Columbus, OH: Battelle Press.

Dove, Michael R., Ed. 2014. *The Anthropology of Climate Change: An Historical Reader*. Malden, MA: Wiley-Blackwell.

Dow, Kirstin, Roger E. Kasperson, and Maria Bohn. 2006. Exploring the social justice implications of adaptation and vulnerability. In *Fairness in Adaptation to Climate Change*. W. Neil Adger. Jouni Paavola, Saleemul Huq, and M. J. Mace, Eds. Pp. 79–129. Cambridge, MA: MIT Press.

Dryzek, John S., Richard B. Norgaard, and David Schlosberg. 2011a. Climate change and society: approaches and responses. In *Oxford Handbook of Climate Change and Society*. John S. Dryzek, Richard B. Norgaard, and David Schlosberg, Eds. Pp. 3–17. Oxford, UK: Oxford University Press.

Dryzek, John S., Richard B. Norgaard, and David Schlosberg. 2011b. *Oxford Handbook of Climate Change and Society*. Oxford, UK: Oxford University Press.

Dunlap, Riley E. and Robert J. Brulle, Eds. 2015. *Climate Change and Sociology: Sociological Perspectives*. American Sociological Association Task Force on Sociology and Global Climate Change. New York: Oxford University Press.

Edwards, Charlie. 2009. *Resilience Nation*. Demos. London: Magdalen House.

Eggleton, Tony. 2013. *A Short Introduction to Climate Change*. Cambridge, UK: Cambridge University Press.

Eisenberg, Merrill. 2011. Medical anthropology and public policy. In *A Companion to Medical Anthropology*. Merrill Singer and Pamela Erickson, Eds. Pp. 93–116. Malden, MA: Wiley-Blackwell.

Eisenstadt, Todd A. and Karleen Jones West. 2017. *Global Environmental Politics* 17: 40–58.

Elert, Emily and Lemonick, Michael. 2012. *Global Weirdness*. Grand Haven, MI: Brilliance Audio.

Elliott, Larry. 2013. World Bank chief: global poverty bigger challenge than action on HIV. *Guardian*, April 4. Online at: www.theguardian.com/business/2013/apr/04/worldbank-chief-poverty-hiv. Accessed July 14, 2013.

Emmerson, Charles. 2010. *The Future of the Arctic*. London: Bodley Head.

Enis, Matt. 2017. Library associations turn activist. *Library Journal*, June 1: 26–27.

Ergas, Christina and Richard York. 2012. Women's status and carbon dioxide emissions: a quantitative cross-national analysis. *Social Science Research* 41: 965–976.

Eriksen, Thomas Hylland. 2001. *Small Places, Large Issues: An Introduction to Social and Cultural Anthropology* (2nd edition). Sterling, VA: Pluto Press.

Eriksen, Thomas Hylland. 2016. *Overheating: An Anthropology of Accelerated Change*. London: Pluto Press.

Fagan, Brian. 1999. *Floods, Famines, and Emperors: El Niño and the Fate of Civilization*. Cambridge, UK: Cambridge University Press.

Fagan, Brian. 2000. *The Little Ice Age: How Climate Made History 1300–1850*. New York; Basic Books.

Fagan, Brian. 2009a. After the ice. In *How Climate Change Shaped the World*. Brian Fagan, Ed. Pp. 186–205. London: Thames & Hudson.

Fagan, Brian. 2009b. Introducing the Ice Ages. In *How Climate Change Shaped the World*. Brian Fagan, Ed. Pp. 6–15. London: Thames & Hudson.

Fagan, Brian. 2010. *Cro-Magnon: How the Ice Age Gave Birth to the First Modern Humans*. New York: Bloomsbury Press.

Fagan, Brian. 2011. *Elixir: A Human History of Water*. London: Bloomsbury.

Fagan, Brian. 2013. *The Attacking Ocean: The Past, Present and Future of Rising Sea Levels*. London: Bloomsbury.

Farley, John W. 2008. The scientific case for modern anthropogenic global warming. *Monthly Review* (July–August): 68–90.

Faulks, Keith. 1999. *Political Sociology: A Critical Introduction*. Edinburgh, UK: Edinburgh University Press.

Feng, Shuaizhang, Alan Krueger, and Michael Oppenheimer. 2010. Linkages among climate change, crop yields and Mexico–US cross-border migration. *PNAS*. Online at: http://www.pnas.org/content/107/32/14257.full. Accessed March 3, 2013.

Finan, Timothy. 2009. Storm warnings: the role of anthropology as adapting to sea-level rise in southwestern Bangladesh. In *Anthropology and Climate Change*. Susan A. Crate and Mark Nuttall, Eds. Pp. 175–185. Walnut Creek, CA: Left Coast Press.

Findlay, Allan and Alistair Geddes. 2011. Critical views on the relationship between climate change and migration: some insights from the experience of Bangladesh. In *Migration and Climate Change*. Etienne Piguet, Antoine Pecoud, and Paul De Guchteneire, Eds. Pp. 138–159. Cambridge, UK: Cambridge University Press.

Fischetti, Mark. 2012. Did climate change cause Hurricane Sandy? *Scientific American*, October 30. Online at: http://blogs.scientificamerican.com/observations/2012/10/30/did-climate-change-cause-hurricane-sandy/. Accessed March 3, 2013.

Fiske, Shirley J. 2009. Global change policymaking from inside the Beltway: engaging anthropology. In *Anthropology and Climate Change*. Susan A. Crate and Mark Nuttall, Eds. Pp. 277–291. Walnut Creek, CA: Left Coast Press.

Fiske, Shirley. 2012a. Faculty profile, Department of Anthropology, University of Maryland website. Online at: www.anth.umd.edu/facultyprofile/Fiske/Shirley. Accessed May 2, 2013.

Fiske, Shirley. 2012b. Global climate change from the bottom up. In *Applying Anthropology in the Global Village*. Christina Wasson, Mary Odell Butler, and Jacqueline Copeland-Carlston, Eds. Pp. 143–172. Walnut Creek, CA: Left Coast Press.

Fiske, Shirley. 2016. "Climate scepticism" inside the Beltway and across the Bay. In *Anthropology and Climate Change: From Actions to Transformations* (2nd edition). Susan A. Crate and Mark Nuttall, Eds. Pp. 319–335. New York: Routledge.

Fiske, Shirley., Susan A. Crate, Carole L. Crumley, Kathleen Galvin, Heather Lazrus, George Luber, Lisa Lucero, Anthony Oliver-Smith, Ben Orlove, Sarah Strauss, and Richard R. Wilk. 2014. *Changing the Atmosphere: Anthropology and Climate Change*. Final report of the AAA Global Climate Change Task Force. Arlington, VA: American Anthropological Association.

Ford, Anabel and Ronald Nigh. 2014. Climate change in the ancient Maya forest: resilience and adaptive management across millennia. In *Great Maya Droughts in Cultural Context: Case Studies in Resilience and Vulnerability*. Gyles Iannone, Ed. Pp. 87–106. Boulder, CO: University Press of Colorado.

Foster, John Bellamy. 1994. *The Vulnerable Planet: A Short Economic History of the Environment*. New York: Cornerstone Books.

Foster, John Bellamy. 2009. *The Ecological Revolution: Making Peace with the Planet*. New York: Monthly Review Press.

Foster, John Bellamy. 2010. Why ecological revolution? *Monthly Review*, January: 1–64.

Foster, John Bellamy, Brett Clark, and Richard York. 2010. *The Ecological Rift: Capitalism's War on the Earth*. New York: Monthly Review Press.

Foucault, Michel. 1980. *The Archeology of Knowledge*. London: Routledge.

Frank, Christine. 2009. The bankruptcy of capitalist solutions to the climate crisis. *Capitalism Nature Socialism* 20(2): 32–43.

Frej, Willa and Marina Fang. 2017. Trump downplays Puerto Rico's suffering, says it's not a 'real catastrophe like Katrina'. *Huffington Post*. October 4, http://www.huffingtonpost. ca/2017/10/03/trump-downplays-puerto-ricos-suffering-says-its-not-a-real-catastrophe-like-katrina_a_23231611/. Accessed March 1, 2018.

Fuentes, Miguel. 2016. The possibility of collapse from a marxist perspective: Marx, Luxemburg and Benjamin. Presentation at the conference on *Climate Change, Archaeology and History*, December 19–20, 2016, University College London, https://www.scribd. com/document/333824750/Climate-Change-Conference-Booklet. Accessed December 28, 2017.

Galvin, Kathleen A. 2007. Adding the human component to global environmental change research. *Anthropology Newsletter*, December: 11–12.

Garnaut, Ross. 2008. *Garnaut Climate Change Review: Final Report*. Cambridge, UK: Cambridge University Press.

Gates, Warren. 1967. The spread of Ibn Khaldûn's ideas on climate and culture. *Journal of the History of Ideas* 28(3): 415–422.

Georgia-Pacific. 2013. Sustainable practices. Online at: www.gp.com/sustainability. Accessed November 18, 2013.

Giacomini, Terran, and Terisa Turner. 2015. The 2014 People's Climate March and Flood Wall Street civil disobedience: making the transition to a post-fossil capitalist, commoning civilization. *Capitalism, Nature, Socialism* 26(2): 27–45.

Giddens, Anthony. 2009. *The Politics of Climate Change*. London: Polity.

Giddens, Anthony. 2011. *The Politics of Climate Change* (2nd edition). London: Polity.

Gill, Richardson Benedict. 2000. *The Great Maya Droughts: Water, Life, and Death*. Albuquerque, NM: University of New Mexico Press.

Goldenberg, Suzanne. 2013. How Donors Trust distributed millions to anti-climate groups. *Guardian*, February 12. Online at: www.guardian.co.uk/environment/2013/feb/14/ donors-trust-funding-climate-denial-networks. Accessed July 3, 2013.

Goodman, Alan, George Armelagos, and Jerome Rose. 1980. Enamel hypoplasias as indicators of stress in three prehistoric populations from Illinois. *Human Biology* 52: 515–528.

Graham, Mark. 2015. Official optimism in the face of an uncertain future: Swedish reactions to climate change threats. In *Environmental Change and the World's Futures: Ecologies,*

Ontologies and Mythologies. Jonathan Paul Marshall and Linda H. Connor, Eds. Pp. 233–246. London: Earthscan.

Gramelsberger, Gabriele, and Johann Feichter. 2011. Modelling the climate system: an overview. In *Climate Change and Policy: The Calculability of Climate Change and the Challenge of Uncertainty.* Gabriele Gramelsberger and Johann Feichter, Eds. Pp. 9–90. Berlin: Springer.

Graves, Lucia and Jordan Howard. 2011. Koch-owned Georgia-Pacific plant linked to high cancer rates, film alleges. *Huffington Post,* October 13. Online at: www.huffingtonpost. com/2011/10/12/arkansas-koch-industries-plant-high-rates-of-cancer_n_1007148. html. Accessed November 18, 2013.

Green, Donna. 2009. Opal waters, rising seas: how sociocultural inequality reduces resilience to climate change among Indigenous Australians. In *Anthropology and Climate Change: From Encounters to Action.* Susan A. Crate and Mark Nuttall, Eds. Pp. 218–227. Walnut Creek, CA: Left Coast Press.

Green, Donna, Jack Billy, and Alo Tapim. 2010. Indigenous Australians' knowledge of weather and climate. *Climatic Change* 100: 337–354.

Greenpeace. 2010. *Koch Industries: Secretly Funding the Climate Denial Machine.* Washington, DC: Greenpeace.

Greschke, Heike. 2015. The social facts of climate change: an ethnographic approach. In *Grounding Global Climate Change.* H. Greschke and J. Tischler, Eds. Pp. 121–138. Dordrecht, the Netherlands: Springer Science + Business Media.

Grill, Claudia. 2015. Animal belongings: human–non human interactions and climate change in the Canadian Arctic. In *Grounding Global Climate Change.* H. Greschke and J. Tischler, Eds. Pp. 101–117. Dordrecht, the Netherlands: Springer Science + Business Media.

Grimes, Peter and Jeffrey Kentor. 2003. Exporting the greenhouse: foreign capital and CO_2 emissions, 1980–1996. *Journal of World-Systems Research* 9(2): 261–275.

Grundmann, Reiner and Nico Stehr. 2010. Climate change: what role for sociology? A response to Constance Lever-Tracy. *Current Sociology* 58: 897–910.

Gulick, John. 2011. The long twentieth century and the barriers to China's hegemonic accession. *Journal of World Systems Research* 17(1): 4–38.

Gunderson, Lance and C. S. Holling, Eds. 2002. *Panarchy: Understanding Transformations in Human and Natural Systems.* Washington, DC: Island Press.

Hack, John. 1942. *The Changing Physical Environment of the Hopi Indians of Arizona: Report No. 1.* Cambridge, MA: Peabody Museum, Harvard University.

Hacking, Ian. 1982. Why are you so scared? *New York Review of Books* 34(14): 30–32 and 41.

Hackmann, Heide and Asuncion Lera St. Clair. 2012. *Transformative Cornerstones of Social Science Research for Global Change.* Paris, France: International Social Science Council.

Handmer, J., S. Dovers, and T. E. Downing. 1999. Societal vulnerability to climate change and variability. *Mitigation and Adaptation Strategies for Global Change* 4: 267–281.

Hanna, Jonathan. 2007. *Native Communities and Climate Change: Protecting Tribal Resources as Part of National Climate Policy.* Boulder, CO: Colorado University Law School.

Hansen, James. 2012a. Climate change is here—and worse than we thought. *Washington Post,* August 3. Online at: http://articles.washingtonpost.com/2012-08-03/opinions/35491435_ 1_climate-change-climate-model-normal-climate. Accessed March 3, 2013.

Hansen, James. 2012b. Why I must speak out about climate change. *TED, Ideas Worth Spreading,* February/March. Online at: www.ted.com/talks/james_hansen_why_i_must_ speak_out_about_climate_change.html. Accessed May 5, 2013.

Hardt, Michael and Antonio Negri. 2009. *Commonwealth.* Cambridge, MA: Harvard University Press.

Harris, Paul G., Ed. 2000. *Climate Change and American Foreign Policy*. New York: St. Martin's Press.

Harris, Paul G. 2003, Ed. *Global Warming and East Asia: The Domestic and International Politics of Climate Change*. London: Routledge.

Harris, Paul G., Ed. 2011a. *China's Responsibility for Climate Change: Ethics, Fairness and Environmental Policy*. Bristol: Policy Press.

Harris, Paul G. 2011b. Reconceptualizing global governance. In *Oxford Handbook of Climate Change and Society*. John S. Dryzek, Richard B. Norgaard, and David Schlosberg, Eds. Pp. 639–652. Oxford, UK: Oxford University Press.

Harvey, David. 1997. *Justice, Nature, and the Geography of Difference*. Malden, MA: Wiley-Blackwell.

Harvey, David. 2003. *The New Imperialism*. New York: Oxford.

Hassan, Ferri A. 1994. Nile floods and political disorder in early Egypt. In *Third Millennium BC Climate Change and Old World Collapse*. H. Nuzhet Dalfes, George Kukla, and Harvey Weiss, Eds. Pp. 1–23. Berlin, Germany: Springer.

Hassan, Ferri A. 2009. Human agency, climate change, and culture: an archeological perspective. In *Anthropology and Climate Change*. Susan A. Crate and Mark Nuttall, Eds. Pp. 39–69. Walnut Creek, CA: Left Coast Press.

Hastrup, Kirsten. 2009a. Arctic hunters: climate variability and social flexibility. In *The Question of Resilience: Social Responses to Climate Change*. Kirsten Hastrup, Ed. Pp. 245–270. Copenhagen, Denmark: Det Kongelige Danske Videnskabernes Selskab.

Hastrup, Kirsten, Ed. 2009b. *The Question of Resilience: Social Responses to Climate Change*. Copenhagen, Denmark: Det Kongelige Danske Videnskabernes Selskab.

Hastrup, Kirsten. 2009c. Waterworlds: framing the question of social relevance. In *The Question of Resilience: Social Responses to Climate Change*. Kirsten Hastrup, Ed. Pp. 11–30. Copenhagen, Denmark: Det Kongelige Danske Videnskabernes Selskab.

Hastrup, Kirsten. 2012a. Anticipating nature: the productive uncertainty of climate models. In *The Social Life of Climate Change Models*. Kirsten Hastrup and Martin Skrydstrup, Eds. Pp. 1–29. Abingdon, UK: Taylor & Francis.

Hastrup, Kirsten. 2012b. The icy breath: modalities of climate knowledge in the Arctic. *Current Anthropology* 53: 227–230.

Hastrup, Kirsten. 2015. Comparing climate worlds: theorising across ethnographic fields. In *Grounding Global Climate Change*. H. Greschke and J. Tischler, Ed. Pp. 139–154. Dordrecht, the Netherlands: Springer Science + Business Media.

Head, Lesley and Chris Gibson. 2012. Becoming differently modern: geographic contributions to a generative climate politics. *Progress in Human Geography* 36: 699–714.

Hebdon, Chris, Myles Lennon, Francis Ludlow, Amy Zhang, and Michael R. Dove. 2016. Pedagogy and climate change. In *Anthropology and Climate Change: From Action to Transformations* (2nd edition). Susan A. Crate and Mark Nuttall, Eds. Pp. 388–398. New York: Routledge.

Hecht, Marjorie Mazel. 2004. The myth of nuclear "waste." *Larouche PAC*. January 1. Online at: http://larouchepac.com/node/14724. Accessed July 21, 2013.

Hecht, Marjorie Mazel. 2007. Where the global warming hoax was born. *21st Century Science and Technology*, Fall: 64–68.

Held, David, Angus Hervey, and Marika Theoros, Eds. 2011. *The Governance of Climate Change: Science, Economics, Politics and Ethics*. London: Polity.

Helvarg, David. 2017. Defending the Earth from Donald Trump. *The Progressive*, February 1: 21–23.

Hennessey, K., B. Fitzharris, B. C. Bates, N. Harvey, S. M. Howden, I. Hughes, J. Salinger, and R. Warrick. 2007. Australia and New Zealand. In *Climate Change 2007: Impact, Adaptation and Vulnerability: Contribution of Working Group II to the Fourth Assessment Report of the Intergovernmental Panel on Climate Change.* Cambridge, UK: Cambridge University Press.

Henry, Donald O. 1989. *From Foraging to Agriculture: The Levant at the End of the Ice Age.* Philadelphia, PA: University of Pennsylvania Press.

Henshaw, Anne. 2009. Sea ice: the sociocultural dimensions of a melting environment in the Arctic. In *Anthropology and Climate Change.* Susan A. Crate and Mark Nuttall, Eds. Pp. 153–165. Walnut Creek, CA: Left Coast Press.

Hepburn, John. 2017. Opposing Adani. *Arena Magazine* 145: 11–13.

Herman-Mercer, Nicole, Paul F. Schuster, and Karonhiakt'tic Bryan Maracle. 2011. Indigenous observations of climate change in the Lower Yukon River Basin. *Human Organization* 70: 244–252.

Hero Project. 2009. *Nukkan Kungun Yunnan—Ngarrindjeri's Being Heard.* Online at: https://www.youtube.com/watch?v=rGIsv-dSs40. Accessed December 19, 2017.

Hetherington, Renee. 2012. *Living in a Dangerous Climate: Climate Change and Human Evolution.* Cambridge, UK: Cambridge University Press.

Hetherington, Renee and Robert G. B. Reid. 2010. *The Climate Connection: Climate Change and Modern Human Evolution.* Cambridge, UK: Cambridge University Press.

Hirsch, Jennifer, Sarah Van Deusen Phillips, Edward Labenski, Christine Dunford, and Troy Peters. 2011. Linking climate action to local knowledge and practice: a case study of diverse Chicago neighborhoods. In *Environmental Anthropology Today.* Helen Kopnina and Eleanor Shoreman-Ouimet, Eds. Pp. 267–296. New York: Routledge.

History.com. 1996. Margaret Mead speaks at first Earth Day. Online at: http://www.history.com/topics/holidays/earth-day-timeline/speeches/margaret-mead-speaks-at-first-earth-day. Accessed December 16, 2017.

Hitchcock, Robert K. 2009. From local to global: perceptions and realities of environmental change among Kalahari. In *Anthropology and Climate Change.* Susan A. Crate and Mark Nuttall, Eds. Pp. 250–261. Walnut Creek, CA: Left Coast Press.

Hobbs, Jacqueline and Jason Davis. 2012. The "milkbird" as proxy: anthropology meets biology on the Tibetan Plateau. *Current Anthropology* 53: 235–236.

Hoffecker, John. 2009. The human story. In *The Complete Ice Age: How Climate Change Shaped the World.* Brian Fagan, Ed. Pp. 92–141. London: Thames & Hudson.

Holmes, Seth and Heide Castañeda. 2016. Representing the "European refugee crisis" in Germany and beyond: "deservingness" and difference, life and death. *American Ethnologist* 43(1): 12–24.

Holmgren, Karen and Helena Oberg. 2007. Climate change in southern and eastern Africa during the past millennium and its implications for societal development. In *The World System and the Earth System: Global Socioenvironmental Change and Sustainability Since the Neolithic.* Alf Hornborg and Carole Crumley, Eds. Pp. 121–131. Walnut Creek, CA: Left Coast Press.

Hopkins, Rob. 2010. What can communities do? In *The Post Carbon Reader: Managing the 21st Century's Sustainability Crisis.* Richard Heinberg and Daniel Lerch, Eds. Pp. 442–451. Healdsburg, CA: Watershed Media.

Hornborg, Alf. 2007. Introduction: conceptualizing socioecological systems. In *The World System and the Earth System: Global Socioenvironmental Change and Sustainability since the Neolithic.* Alf Hornborg and Carole Crumley, Eds. Pp. 15–28. Walnut Creek, CA: Left Coast Press.

Hornborg, Alf. 2013. The fossil interlude: Euro-American power and the return of the physiocrats. In *Cultures of Energy: Power, Practices, Technologies.* Sarah Strauss, Stephanie Rupp, and Thomas Love, Eds. Pp. 41–59. Walnut Creek, CA: Left Coast Press.

Hubbert, M. King. 1956. Nuclear energy and the fossil fuels. Paper presented at the Spring Meeting of the Southern District Division of Production, American Petroleum Institute. Online at: www.hubbertpeak.com/hubbert/1956/1956.pdf. Accessed June 2, 2013.

Hughes, David McDermott. 2013. Climate change and the victim slot: from oil to innocence. *American Anthropologist* 115: 570–581.

Huntington, E. 1922. *Climate and Civilization*. New Haven, CT: Yale University Press.

Huq, Saleemul and Mizan R. Khan. 2006. Equity in National Adaptation Programs of Action (NAPAs): the case of Bangladesh. In *Fairness in Adaptation to Climate Change*. W. Neil Adger, Jouni Paavola, Saleemul Huq, and M. J. Mace, Eds. Pp. 181–200. Cambridge, MA: MIT Press.

Indian Climate Justice Forum. 2002. Delhi Climate Justice Declaration. *India Resource Centre*. Online at: www.indiaresource.org/issues/energycc/2003/delhicjdeclare.html. Accessed June 5, 2012.

Inglehart, Ronald. 1990. *Cultural Shift in Advanced Industrial Society*. Princeton, NJ: Princeton University Press.

Institute for Tribal Environmental Professionals. 2008. Navaho Nation: dune study offers clues to climate change impacts. Online at: https://tribalclimateguide.uoregon.edu/climate-planning/navajo-nation-dune-study-offers-clues-climate-change. Accessed December 19, 2017.

Institute of Development Studies. 2013. The new bottom billion. Online at: www.ids.ac.uk/project/the-new-bottom-billion. Accessed June 28, 2013.

International Food Policy Research Institute. 2009. *Climate Change, Agriculture, and Food Security: Impacts and Costs of Adaptation to 2050*. Washington, DC: International Food Policy Research Institute.

Islam, Md Saidul and Si Hui Lim. 2015. When "nature" strikes: a sociology of climate change and disaster vulnerabilities. *Nature and Culture* 10(1): 57–80.

Jackson, Tim. 2009. *Prosperity without Growth*. London: Earthscan.

Jacques, Peter. 2012. A general theory of climate denial. *Global Environmental Politics* 12(2): 9–17.

Jacques, Peter, Riley Dunlap, and Mark Freeman. 2008. The organization of denial: conservative think tanks and environmental scepticism. *Environmental Politics* 17(3): 349–385.

Jasanoff, Sheila. 2010. A new climate for society. *Theory, Culture & Society* 27(2–3): 233–253.

Johansen, Bruce E. 2006. *Global Warming in the 21st Century. Volume 2: Melting Ice and Warming Seas*. Westport, CT: Praeger.

Johnson, Noor. 2016. Bridging knowledge and action on climate change: institutions, translation, and anthropological engagement. In *Anthropology and Climate Change: From Actions to Transformations* (2nd edition). Susan A. Crate and Mark Nuttall, Eds. Pp. 399–412. New York: Routledge.

Jorgenson, Andrew K. 2015. Five points on sociology, PEWS and climate change. *Journal of World-System Research* 21(2): 269–275.

Jull, Peter. 2009–2010. Indigenous sovereignty in the Northwest Passage. *Arena Magazine* 103: 45.

Kahn, Brian H., X. Huang, G. L. Stephens, W. D. Collins, D. R. Feldman, H. Su, S. Wong and Q. Yue. 2016. ENSO regulation of far- and mid-infrared contributions to clear-sky OLR. *Geophysical Research Letters*. 24 August. Online at: http://onlinelibrary.wiley.com/doi/10.1002/2016GL070263/full. Accessed March 1, 2018.

Katznelson, Ira. 2005a. Welfare in Black and White. In *When Affirmative Action Was White: An Untold History of Racial Inequality in Twentieth-Century America*. New York: W. W. Norton.

Katznelson, Ira. 2005b. *When Affirmative Action Was White: An Untold History of Racial Inequality in Twentieth-Century America*. New York: W. W. Norton.

Kaur, Raminder. 2011. A "nuclear renaissance": climate change and the state of exception. *Australian Journal of Anthropology* 22: 273–277.

Keeley, J. E. 2003. American Indian influence on fire regimes in California's coastal ranges. *Journal of Biogeography* 29: 303–320.

Kellogg, William W. and Margaret Mead, Eds. 1980. *The Atmosphere: Endangered and Endangering*. Tunbridge Wells, UK: Castle House Publications.

Kelman, Ilan and Jennifer J. West. 2009. Climate change and small island developing states. *Ecological and Environmental Anthropology* 5(1): 1–16.

Kempton, Willett. 1991. Lay perspectives on global climate change. *Global Environmental Change* 1(3): 183–208.

Kempton, Willet, James S. Boster, and Jennifer A. Hartley. 1995. *Environmental Values in American Culture*. Cambridge, MA: MIT Press.

Kennedy, Donald. 2006. Preserving the conditions of life. In *Science Magazine's State of the Planet 2006–2007*. Donald Kennedy, Ed. Pp. 39–48. Washington, DC: Island Press.

Kennett, Douglas, Sebastian Breitenbach, Valorie Aquino, Yemand Asmerom, Jaime Awe, James Baldini, James Bartlein, Brenden Culleton, Clair Ebert, Christopher Jazwa, Martha Macri, Norbert Marwan, Victor Polyak, Keith Prufer, Harriet Ridley, Harald Sodemann, Bruce Winterhalder, and Gerald Haug. 2012. Development and disintegration of Maya political systems in response to climate change. *Science* 338(6,108): 788–791.

Kent, Jennifer. 2009. Individualized responsibility and climate change: "if climate protection becomes everybody's responsibility, does it end up being no-one's?" *Cosmopolitan Civil Society Journal* 1: 132–149.

Kenya Environment and Political News. 2007. African farmers need a financial umbrella says World Bank. Online at: http://kenvironews.wordpress.com/2007/10/29/african-farmers-need-a-financial-umbrella-says-world-bank/. Accessed July 3, 2012.

Kiely, Ray. 2007. *The New Political Economy of Development: Globalization, Imperialism, and Hegemony*. New York: Palgrave MacMillan.

Kim, Jim Yong. 2012. Foreword. In *4°: Turn Down the Heat—Why a 4°C Warmer World Must Be Avoided*. Pp. ix–x. Washington, DC: The World Bank.

Kim, Jim Yong. 2013a. Make climate change a priority. *Washington Post*, January 24. Online at: http://articles.washingtonpost.com/2013-01-24/opinions/36527558_1_global-carbon-dioxide-emissions-climate-change-climate-and-energy. Accessed July 15, 2013.

Kim, Jim Yong. 2013b. *World Bank President at G20 meeting: climate change represents real, present danger, Transcript of speech by World Bank President Jim Kim at G20 Meeting in Moscow*, World Bank, February 16.

Kim, Jim Yong, Joyce V. Millen, Alec Irwin, and John Gershman, Eds. 2000. *Dying for Growth: Global Inequality and the Health of the Poor*. Monroe, ME: Common Courage Press.

Klein, Naomi. 2007. *The Shock Doctrine: The Rise of Disaster Capitalism*. New York: Metropolitan Books.

Koensler, Alexander and Cristiana Papa. 2013. Introduction: beyond anthropocentrism, changing practices and the politics of "nature." *Journal of Political Ecology* 20: 286–294.

Kolbert, Elizabeth. 2011. Age of Man. *National Geographic*, March. Online at: http://ngm.nationalgeographic.com/2011/03/age-of-man/kolbert-text. Accessed March 5, 2013.

Kopnina, Helen and Eleanor Shoreman-Ouimet. 2017. An introduction to environmental anthropology. In *Routledge Handbook of Environmental Anthropology*. Helen Kopnina and Eleanor Shoreman-Ouimet, Eds. Pp. 3–9. London: Routledge.

Krakoff, Sarah. 2008. American Indians, climate change, and ethics for a warming world. *Denver University Law Review* 85(865): 1–33.

Krauss, Werner. 2009. Localized climate change: a multi-sited approach. In *Multi-Sited Ethnography: Theory, Praxis and Locality in Contemporary Research*. Mark-Anthony Falzon, Ed. Pp. 149–164. Farnham, UK: Ashgate.

Krauss, Werner. 2016. Escaping the double bind: from the management of uncertainty toward integrated climate research. In *Anthropology and Climate Change: From Action to Transformation*. Susan A. Crate and Mark Nuttall, Eds. Pp. 413–423. New York: Routledge.

Krieger, Nancy. 2005. *Health Disparities and the Body*. Boston, MA: Harvard School of Public Health.

Krien, Anna. 2017. Coal, coral and Australia's climate deadlock. *Quarterly Essay* 66: 1–116.

Kuch, Declan. 2015. *The Rise and Fall of Carbon Emissions Trading*. New York: Palgrave Macmillan.

Kull, Christian A. and Simon P. J. Batterbury. 2013. La géographie face aux défies environnementaux dans le monde Anglophone (Academic geography and environmental challenges in the Anglophone world). Unpublished paper.

Kuper, Rudolph and Stefan Kröpelin. 2006. Climate-controlled Holocene occupation in the Sahara: motor of Africa's evolution. *Science* 313(5,788): 803–807.

Lahsen, Myanna. 1999. The detection and attribution of conspiracies: the controversy over Chapter 8. In *Paranoia within Reason: A Casebook on Conspiracy as Explanation*. George E. Marcus, Ed. Pp. 111–136. Chicago, IL: University of Chicago Press.

Lahsen, Myanna. 2004. Transnational locals: Brazilian experiences of the climate regime. In *Earthly Politics: Local and Global in Environmental Governance*. Sheila Jasanoff and Larybeth Long Martello, Eds. Pp. 151–171. Cambridge, MA: MIT Press.

Lahsen, Myanna. 2005a. Seductive simulations? Uncertainty distribution around climate models. *Social Studies of Science* 35/6: 895–922.

Lahsen, Myanna. 2005b. Technocracy, democracy, and U.S. climate politics: the need for demarcations. *Science, Technology & Human Values* 30(1): 137–169.

Lahsen, Myanna. 2007a. Anthropology and the trouble of risk society. *Anthropology Newsletter*, December: 9–10.

Lahsen, Myanna. 2007b. Trust through participation? Problems of knowledge in climate decision making. In *The Social Construction of Climate Change: Power, Norms, and Discourses*. Mary E. Pettenger, Ed. Pp. 173–196. Aldershot, UK: Ashgate.

Lahsen, Myanna. 2008a. Commentary on "Gone the bull of winter? Grappling with the cultural implications of and anthropology's role(s) in global climate change" by Susan A. Crate. *Current Anthropology* 49: 587–588.

Lahsen, Myanna. 2008b. Experiences of modernity in the greenhouse: a cultural analysis of a physicist "trio" supporting the backlash against global warming. *Global Environmental Change* 18: 204–219.

Lahsen, Myanna. 2009. A science–policy interface in the global south: the politics of carbon sinks and science in Brazil. *Climate Change* 97: 339–372.

Lahsen, Myanna. 2013. Anatomy of dissent: a cultural analysis of climate scepticism. *American Behavioral Scientist* 57: 732–753.

Lahsen, Myanna. 2015. Digging deeper into the why: cultural dimensions of climate change scepticism among scientists. In *Climate Cultures: Anthropological Perspectives on Climate Change*. Jessica Barnes and Michael R. Dove, Eds. Pp. 221–248. New Haven, CT: Yale University Press.

Landler, Mark. 2017 Trump rates his hurricane relief: "Great." "Amazing." "Tremendous." *New York Times*. Online at: https://www.nytimes.com/2017/09/26/us/politics/trump-puerto-rico-hurricane.html. Accessed December 16, 2017.

Latour, Bruno. 2003. Atmosphère, atmosphère. In *Olafur Eliasson: The Weather Project*. Susan May, Ed. Pp. 29–41. London: Tate Publishing.

Lavell, Kristen. 2006. Hurricane Katrina: the race and class debate. *Monthly Review* 58(3): 52–66.

Lazrus, Heather. 2009. The government of vulnerability: climate change and agency in Tuvalu, South Pacific. In *Anthropology and Climate Change*. Susan A. Crate and Mark Nuttall, Eds. Pp. 240–249. Walnut Creek, CA: Left Coast Press.

Lazrus, Heather. 2012. Sea change: island communities and climate change. *Annual Review of Anthropology* 41: 285–301.

Leduc, Timothy B. 2007. Sila dialogues on climate change: Inuit wisdom for a cross-cultural interdisciplinarity. *Climatic Change* 85: 237–250.

Leduc, Timothy B. 2010. *Climate Culture Change: Inuit and Western Dialogues with a Warming North*. Ottawa, Canada: University of Ottawa Press.

Leduc, Timothy. 2011. Dialogue with the "Ecologist" review. *Climate, Culture, Change: Inuit and Western Dialogues with a Warming North*, February 24. Online at: http://climatecuturechange.wordpress.com/2011/02/24/dialogue-with-the-ecologist-review/. Accessed July 21, 2012.

Leichenko, Robin and Karen O'Brien. 2006. Is it appropriate to identify winners and losers? In *Fairness in Adaptation to Climate Change*. W. Neil Adger, Jouni Paavola, Saleemul Huq, and M. J. Mace, Eds. Pp. 97–114. Cambridge, MA: MIT Press.

Lever-Tracy, Constance. 2008. Global warming and sociology. *Current Sociology* 56: 445–466.

Lever-Tracy, Constance, Ed. 2010. *Routledge Handbook of Climate Change and Society*. London: Routledge.

Lever-Tracy, Constance. 2011. *Confronting Climate Change*. London: Routledge.

LeVine, Robert A. and Donald T. Campbell. 1972. *Ethnocentrism: Theories of Conflict, Ethnic Attitudes, and Group Behavior*. Oxford, UK: John Wiley & Sons.

Lewis, Charles, Eric Hombert, Alexia Campbell, and Lydia Beyoud. 2013. Koch millions spread through nonprofits, colleges. *Investigative Reporting Workshop, American University School of Communication*. Online at: http://investigativereportingworkshop.org/investigations/the_koch_club/story/Koch_millions_spread_influence_through_nonprofits/. Accessed July 19, 2013.

Lewis, Simon, Paulo Brando, Oliver Phillips, Geertje van der Heijden, and Daniel Nepstad. 2011. The 2010 Amazon Drought. *Science* 331(6,017): 554.

Lewis, Sophie and David Karoly. 2013. Anthropogenic contributions to Australia's record summer temperatures of 2013. *Geophysical Research Letters* 40(14): 3,705–3,709.

Lindenmayer, David. 2007. *On Borrowed Time: Australia's Environmental Crisis and What We Must Do about It*. Melbourne, Australia: CSIRO Publishing.

Lipset, David. 2011. The tides: masculinity and climate change in coastal Papua New Guinea. *Journal of the Royal Anthropological Institute* 17: 20–43.

Little, Peter. 2011. Speaking Truth to Power: Listening to a Seasoned Climate Scientist. Manuscript. Corvallis, OR: Department of Anthropology, Oregon State University.

Little, Peter D., Hussein Mahmoud, and D. Layne Coppock. 2001. When deserts flood: risk management and climatic processes among East African pastoralists. *Climate Research* 19: 149–159.

Livingstone, David N. 2015. The climate of war: violence, warfare, and climatic reductionism. *Wiley Interdisciplinary Reviews: Climate Change* 6: 437–444.

Lohmann, Larry. 2006. *Carbon Trading: A Critical Conversation on Climate Change, Privatization and Power*. Development Dialogue No. 28. Uppsala, Sweden: Dag Hammarskjoeld Centre.

Lora-Wainwright, Anna. 2013. The inadequate life: rural industrial pollution and lay epidemiology in China. *The China Quarterly* 214: 302–320. doi: 10.1017/S0305741013000349.

Lovelock, James. 2007. *The Revenge of Gaia: Earth's Climate Crisis and the Fate of Humanity.* New York: Basic Books.

Lovelock, James and Lynn Margulis. 1974. Atmospheric homeostasis by and for the biosphere: the Gaia hypothesis. *Tellus* A26(1–2): 2–10.

Lucero, Lisa J., Joel D. Gunn, and Vernon L. Scarborough. 2011. Climate change and classic Maya water management. *Water* 3: 479–494.

Luke, Tim. 2008. Climatologies as social critique: the social construction/creation of global warming, global dimming, and global cooling. In *Political Theory and Global Climate Change.* Steven Vanderheiden, Ed. Pp. 121–152. Cambridge, MA: MIT Press.

Lynas, Mark. 2004. *High Tide: The Truth about Our Climate Crisis.* New York: Picador.

Lynas, Mark. 2007. *Six Degrees: Our Future on a Hotter Planet.* London: Fourth Estate.

Lyster, Rosemary. 2017. Climate justice, adaptation and the Paris Agreement: a recipe for disasters? *Environmental Politics* 26: 438–458.

Maathai, Wangari. 2010. The world needs women to make progress on climate change. *Inter Press Service,* July 20. Online at: www.ipsnews.net/2010/12/the-world-needs-women-to-make-progress-on-climate-change. Accessed July 20, 2013.

Madrino, Elizabeth and Peter Schweitzer. 2009. Talking and not talking about climate change in northwestern Alaska. In *Anthropology and Climate Change.* Susan A. Crate and Nuttall. Eds. Pp. 209–217. Walnut Creek, CA: Left Coast Press.

Magistro, John and Medou Lo. 2001. Historical and human dimensions of climate variability and water resource constraint in the Senegal River Valley. *Climate Research* 19: 133–147.

Magistro, John and Carla Roncoli. 2001. Anthropological perspectives and policy implications of climate change research. *Climate Research* 19: 91–96.

Mahmoud, Hussein A. and Peter D. Little. 2000. Climatic shocks and pastoral risk management in northern Kenya. *Practicing Anthropology* 22(4): 11–14.

Mahmud, Tanvir and Martin Prowse. 2012. Corruption in cyclone preparedness and relief efforts in coastal Bangladesh: lessons for climate adaptation. *Global Environmental Change* 22: 933–943.

Marcotullio, Peter J., Andrea Sarzynski, Jochen Albrecht, and Niels Schulz. 2012. The geography of urban greenhouse gas emissions in Asia: a regional analysis. *Global Environmental Change* 22: 944–958.

Marino, Elizabeth and Heather Lazrus. 2015. Migration or forced displacement? The complex choices of climate change and disaster migrants in Shishmaref, Alaska and Nanumea, Tuvalu. *Human Organization* 74: 341–350.

Marshall, Jonathan. 2012. Climate change movements and psycho-social disorder. *Australian Journal of Anthropology* 22: 265–269.

Marshall, Jonathan Paul. 2015. Geoengineering, imagining and the problem cycle: a cultural complex in action. In *Environmental Change and the World's Futures: Ecologies, Ontologies and Mythologies.* Jonathan Paul Marshall and Linda H. Connor, Eds. Pp. 246–263. London: Earthscan.

Marshall, Jonathan Paul and Linda H. Connor, Eds. 2016. *Environmental Change and the World's Futures: Ecologies, Ontologies and Mythologies.* London: Earthscan.

Maslin, Mark. 2009. *Global Warming: A Very Short Introduction.* Oxford, UK: Oxford University Press.

Mayer, Jane. 2013. Koch pledge tied to congressional climate inaction. *The New Yorker,* July 1. Online at: www.newyorker.com/online/blogs/newsdesk/2013/07/the-kochs-and-the-action-on-global-warming.html. Accessed July 19, 2013.

McClanahan, Bill and Avi Brisman. 2015. Climate change and peacemaking criminology: ecophilosophy, peace and security in the "war on climate change." *Critical Criminology* 23: 417–431.

McCorriston, Joy and Frank Hole. 1991. The ecology of seasonal stress and the origins of agriculture in the Near East. *American Anthropologist* 93: 46–69.

McElroy, Ann. 2013. Sedna's children: Inuit elders' perceptions of climate change and security. In *Environmental Anthropology: Future Directions*. Helen Kopnina and Eleanor Shoreman-Ouimet, Eds. Pp. 145–171. London: Routledge.

McElroy, Ann and Patricia K. Townsend. 2009. *Medical Anthropology in Ecological Perspective* (5th edition). Boulder, CO: Westview Press.

McElwee, Pamela. 2015. From conservation and development to climate change: anthropological engagements with REDD+ in Vietnam. In *Climate Cultures: Anthropological Perspectives on Climate* Change. Jessica Barnes and Michael R. Dove, Eds. Pp. 82–104. New Haven, CT: Yale University Press.

McGovern, Thomas. 1994. Management for extinction in Norse Greenland. In *Historical Ecology: Cultural Knowledge and Changing Landscapes*. C. Crumley, Ed. Pp. 127–154. Santa Fe, NM: School of American Research Monograph.

McKibben, Bill. 2010. *Eaarth: Making a Life on a Tough New Planet*. New York: Henry Holt.

McMichael, Anthony. 2013. Globalization, climate change, and human Health. *New England Journal of Medicine* 368: 1,335–1,343.

McNeeley, Shannon and Orville Huntington. 2007. Postcards from the (not so) frozen North: talking about climate change in Alaska. In *Creating a Climate Change and Facilitating Social Change*. Susanne C. Moser and Lisa Dilling, Eds. Pp. 139–152. Cambridge, UK: Cambridge University Press.

Mead, Margaret. 1943 [orig. 1928]. *Coming of Age in Samoa: A Study of Adolescence and Sex in Primitive Societies*. Harmondsworth, UK: Penguin. (First published 1928. New York: William Morrow.)

Mead, Margaret. 1980. Preface. In *The Atmosphere: Endangered and Endangering*. William W. Kellogg and Margaret Mead, Eds. Pp. xvii–xxii. Tunbridge Wells, UK: Castle House Publications.

Meadows, D., D. L. Meadows, and J. Randers. 1992. *Beyond the Limits: Global Collapse or Sustainable Future*. London: Earthscan.

Meadows, D., J. Randers and D. L. Meadows. 2004. *Limits to Growth: The 30-year Update*. White River Junction, VT: Chelsea Green Publishing.

Meadows, D., D. L. Meadows, J. Randers, and W. Behrens. 1972. *The Limits to Growth: A Report for the Club of Rome Project on the Predicament of Mankind*. New York: Universe Books.

Mendelsohn, Robert. 2006–2007. A critique of the Stern Report. *Regulation*, Winter. Online at: www.cato.org/sites/cato.org/files/serials/files/regulation/2006/12/v29n4-5.pdf. Accessed June 23, 2012.

Michaels, Patrick. 2004. *Meltdown: The Predictable Distortion of Global Warming by Scientists*. Washington, DC: Cato Institute.

Milton, Kay. 1996. *Environmentalism and Cultural Theory: Exploring the Role of Anthropology in Environmental Discourse*. London: Routledge.

Milton, Kay. 2008. Climate change and culture theory: the need to understand ourselves. In *The Impact of Global Warming on the Environment and Human Societies*. PASI Research Paper No. 1. Hans A. Baer, Ed. Pp. 39–52. Melbourne, Australia: School of Philosophy, Anthropology, and Social Inquiry, University of Melbourne.

Minnegal, Monica and Peter D. Dwyer. 2008. Fire, flood, fish and the uncertainty paradox. *Australian Journal of Anthropology* 19: 77–81.

Mintz, Sidney W. 1985. *Sweetness and Power: The Place of Sugar in Modern History*. New York: Viking.

Monbiot, George. 2006. *Heat: How to Stop the Planet Burning*. Camberwell, Australia: Allen Lane.

Mongillo, John and Linda Zierdt-Warshaw, Eds. 2000. *Encyclopedia of Environmental Science*. Rochester, NY: University of Rochester Press.

Montoya, Michael. 2013. Mescalero Apache Tribe: innovative approaches to climate change adaptation. *Tribes and Climate Change*. Online at: https://nnigovernance.arizona.edu/mescalero-apache-tribe-innovative-approaches-climate-change-adaptation. Accessed July 19, 2013.

Moran, Emilio F. 2006. *People and Nature: An Introduction to Human Ecological Relations*. Malden, MA: Blackwell.

Moran, Emilio F. 2010. *Environmental Social Science: Human–Environment Interactions and Sustainability*. Malden, MA: Wiley-Blackwell.

Morgan, Gareth and John McCrystal. 2009. *Poles Apart: Beyond the Shouting and Who's Right about Climate Change?* Melbourne, Australia: Scribe.

Moritz, Max, Marc-André Parisien, Enric Batllori, Meg Krawchuk, Jeff Van Dorn, David Ganz, and Katharine Hayhoe. 2012. Climate change and disruptions to global fire activity. *Ecosphere* 3: 49.

Morris, Ian. 2011. *Why the West Rules—Rules for Now: The Patterns of History and What They Reveal about the Future*. London: Profile Books.

Mortreux, Colette and Jon Barnett. 2009. Climate change, migration and adaptation in Funafuti, Tuvalu. *Global Environmental Change* 19: 105–112.

Moyers, Bill. 2011. How Wall Street occupied America. *The Nation*. Online at: www.thenation.com/article/164349/how-wall-street-occupied-america. Accessed February 23, 2012.

Mulligan, Shane. 2016. Reassessing the crisis: ecology and liberal international relations. In *Energy, Capitalism and World Order: Towards a New Agenda in International Political Economy*. Tim Muzzo, Ed. Pp. 41–46. New York: Palgrave Macmillan.

Nader, Laura. 1972. Up the anthropologist—perspectives gained from studying up. In *Reinventing Anthropology*. Dell Hymes, Ed. Pp. 284–311. New York: Random House.

Nader, Laura. 2013. Afterword: maximizing anthropology. In *Cultures of Energy: Power, Practices, Technologies*. Sarah Strauss, Stephanie Rupp, and Tom Love, Eds. Pp. 317–323. Walnut Creek, CA: Left Coast Press.

Nagel, Joane, Thomas Dietz, and Jeffrey Broadbent. 2009. *Workshop on Sociological Perspective on Global Climate Change*. Arlington, VA: National Science Foundation.

Nebbia, Giorgio. 2012. The unsustainability of sustainability. *Capitalism Nature Socialism* 23(2): 95–107.

Negi, Biju, Reetu Sogani, and Vijay Pandey. 2010. Climate change and women's voices in India. In Dankelman, Irene, Ed. *Gender and Climate Change: An Introduction*. Pp. 72–75. Washington, DC: Earthscan.

Nelson, Donald R. and Timothy J. Finan. 2000. The emergence of a climate anthropology in northeast Brazil. *Practicing Anthropology* 22(4): 6–10.

Neubeck, Kenneth J., and Noel A. Cazenave. 2001. *Welfare Racism: Playing the Race Card against America's Poor*. New York: Routledge.

Newell, Peter. 2016. The political economy of (climate) change: low-carbon energy transitions under capitalism. In *Energy, Capitalism and World Order: Towards a New Agenda in International Political* Economy. Tim Di Muzzo, Ed. Pp. 127–142. New York: Palgrave Macmillan.

Newell, Peter and Matthew Paterson. 2010. *Climate Capitalism: Global Warming and the Transformation of the Global Economy*. Cambridge, UK: Cambridge University Press.

Nodari, Maria Luisa and Giorgio Vassena. 2012. The social life of climate change: weather data, glacial retreat, and mountaineering from the land of snow to the Rwenzori Mountains. *Current Anthropology* 53: 236–237.

Nogués-Bravero, D., M. B. Araújo, M. P. Errea, and J. P. Martinez-Ricaet. 2007. Exposure of global mountain systems to climate warming during the 21st century. *Global Environmental Change* 17: 420–428.

Noort, Robert van de. 2013. *Climate Change Archaeology: Building Resilience from Research in the World's Coastal Wetlands*. Oxford, UK: Oxford University Press.

Norgaard, Kari Marie. 2011. *Living in Denial: Climate Change, Emotions, and Every Day Life*. Cambridge, MA: MIT Press.

Noyes, P., M. McElwee, H. Miller, B. Clark, L. Van Tiem, K. Walcott, K. Erwin, and E. Levin. 2008. The toxicology of climate change: Environmental contaminants in a warming world. *Environment International* 35: 971–986.

Nuttall, Mark. 2009. Living in a world of movement: human resilience to environmental instability in Greenland. In *Anthropology and Climate Change*. Susan A. Crate and Mark Nuttall, Eds. Pp. 292–310. Walnut Creek, CA: Left Coast Press.

Nuttall, Mark, Fikret Berkes, Bruce Forbes, Gary Kofina, Tatiana Vlassova, and George Wenzel. 2004. Hunting, herding, fishing and gathering: indigenous people and renewable resources. In *Impacts of a Warming Arctic: Arctic Climate Impact Assessment*. Carolyn Symon, Lelani Arris, and Bill Heal, Eds. Pp. 649–690, Cambridge, UK: Cambridge University Press.

Nuzhet Dalfes, H., George Kukla, and Harvey Weiss, Eds. 1994. *Third Millennium BC Climate Change and Old World Collapse*. New York: Springer.

Officer, Charles and Jake Page. 2009. *When the Planet Rages: Natural Disasters, Global Warming, and the Future of the Earth*. Oxford, UK: Oxford University Press.

Oil Watchdog. 2012. Meet Koch Industries. Online at: www.consumerwatchdog.org/video/our-times-sq-ad-meet-koch-industries. Accessed November 18, 2013.

Oliver-Smith, Anthony. 2009. Climate change and population displacement: disasters and diasporas in the twenty-first century. In *Anthropology and Climate Change*. Susan A. Crate and Mark Nuttall, Eds. Pp. 116–136. Walnut Creek, CA: Left Coast Press.

Oliver-Smith, Anthony. 2010. Sea level rise, local vulnerability and involuntary migration. In *Migration and Climate Change*. Etienne Piguet, Atoine Pecoud, and Paul De Guchteneire, Eds. Pp. 160–187. Cambridge, UK: Cambridge University Press.

Ontario Lung Association. 2008. *The connections between climate change, air quality, and respiratory health*. Online at: www.lung.ca/protect-protegez/pollution-pollution/outdoor-exterior/climate-climatique_e.php. Accessed February 1, 2011.

O'Reilly, Jessica. 2015. Glacial dramas: typos, projections, and peer review in the Fourth Assessment of the Intergovernmental Panel on Climate Change. In *Climate Cultures: Anthropological Perspective on Climate Change*. Jessica Barnes and Michael R. Dove, Eds. Pp. 107–126. New Haven, CT: Yale University Press.

Orlove, Ben. 2003. How people name seasons. In *Weather, Climate, Culture*. Sarah Strauss and Ben Orlove, Eds. Pp. 121–137. Oxford, UK: Berg.

Orlove, Ben. 2005. Human adaptation to climate change: a review of three historical cases and some general perspectives. *Environmental Science & Policy* 8: 589–600.

Orlove, Ben and Steven C. Caton. 2009. Water as an object of anthropological inquiry. In *The Question of Resilience: Social Responses to Climate Change*. Kirsten Hastrup, Ed. Pp. 31–47. Copenhagen, Denmark: Det Kongelige Danske Videnskabernes Selskab.

Orlove, Ben and Merit Kabugo. 2005. Signs and sight in South Uganda: representing perception in ordinary conversation. *Ethnofoor* 18: 124–141.

Orlove, Ben, J. Chiang, and M. Cane. 2000. Forecasting Andes rainfall and crop yield from the influences of El Niño on Pleiades visibility. *Nature* 403: 68–71.

Orlove, Ben, J. Chiang, and M. Cane. 2002. Ethnoclimatology in the Andes: a cross-disciplinary study uncovers a scientific basis for the scheme Andean potato farmers traditionally use to predict the coming rains. *American Scientist* 90: 428–435.

Orlove, Ben, Ellen Wiegandt, and Brian H. Luckman. 2008. The place of glaciers in natural and cultural landscapes. In *Darkening Peaks: Glacier Retreat, Science, and Society*. Ben Orlove, Ellen Wiegandt, and Brian H. Luckman, Eds. Pp. 3–19. Berkeley, CA: University of California Press.

Orlove, Ben, Heather Lazrus, Grete K. Hovelsrud, and Alessandra Giannini. 2014. Recognition and responsibilities: on the origins and consequences of the uneven attention to climate change around the world. *Current Anthropology* 55: 249–275.

Orr, Yancey, J. Stephen Lansing, and Michael R. Dove. 2015. Environmental anthropology: systemic perspectives. *Annual Review of Anthropology* 44: 153–168.

Ortiz, Isabel and Matthew Cummins. 2011. *Global Inequality: Beyond the Bottom Billion*. UNICEF Social and Economic Policy Working Paper. New York: United Nations Children's Fund.

Ostrom, Elinor. 2009. *A Polycentric Approach for Coping with Climate Change*. Policy Research Working Paper 5,095. Washington, DC: World Bank, Development Economics, Office of the Senior Vice President and Chief Economist, October.

Ostrom, Elinor. 2012. Green from the grassroots. *Project Syndicate*. Online at: www.project-syndicate.org/commentary/green-from-the-grassroots. Accessed July 11, 2013.

Otterstrom, Sarah M. 2000. Variation in coping with El Niño droughts in northern Costa Rica. *Practicing Anthropology* 22(4): 15–18.

Paerregaard, Karsten. 2016. Making sense of climate change: global impacts, local responses, and anthropogenic dilemmas in the Peruvian Andes. In *Anthropology and Climate Change: From Actions to Transformations*. Susan A. Crate and Mark Nuttall, Eds. Pp. 250–260. New York: Routledge.

Parenti, Christian. 2011. *Tropic of Cancer: Climate Change and the New Geography of Violence*. New York: Nation Books.

Parks, Bradley and J. Timmons Roberts. 2010. Climate change, social theory and justice. *Theory, Culture & Society* 27(2–3): 134–166.

Paterson, Matthew. 2007. *Automobile Politics: Ecology and Cultural Political Economy*. Cambridge, UK: Cambridge University Press.

Paterson, Matthew. 2011. Selling carbon: from international climate regime to global carbon market. In *Oxford Handbook of Climate Change and Society*. John S. Dryzek, Richard B. Norgaard, and David Schlosberg, Eds. Pp. 611–624. Oxford, UK: Oxford University Press.

Pearce, Fred. 2006. *The Last Generation: How Nature Will Take Her Revenge for Climate Change*. London: Transworld Publishers.

Pearce, Fred. 2007. *With Speed and Violence: Why Scientists Fear Tipping Points in Climate Change*. Boston, MA: Free Press.

Peterman, A. and O. Langelle. 2010. What really happened in Copenhagen? *Zeta Magazine*, February 1. Online at: https://zcomm.org/zmagazine/what-really-happened-in-copenhagen-by-anne-petermann/. Accessed November 18, 2013.

Peterson, Nicole and Kenneth Broad. 2009. Climate and weather discourse in anthropology: from determinism to uncertain futures. In *Anthropology and Climate Change*. Susan A. Crate and Mark Nuttall, Eds. Pp. 70–86. Walnut Creek, CA: Left Coast Press.

Piguet, Etienne. 2008. *Climate Change and Forced Migration, New Issues in Refuge Research, No. 153*. Geneva, Switzerland: United Nations High Commission for Refugees.

Pilkey, Orrin H. and Rob Young. 2009. *The Rising Sea*. Washington, DC: Island Press.

Piven, Frances Fox and Richard A. Cloward. 1993. *Regulating the Poor: The Functions of Public Welfare*. New York: Vintage Books.

Pokrant, Bob and Laura Stocker. 2009. Anthropology, climate change and coastal planning. In *Environmental Anthropology Today*. Helen Kopnina and Eleanore Shoreman-Ouimet, Eds. Pp. 179–194. New York: Routledge.

Political Economic Research Institute. 2012. Toxic 100 air polluters. Online at: https://www.peri.umass.edu/index.php?option=com_content&view=article&id=74&Itemid=459/. Accessed November 18, 2013.

Popper, Karl. 2002. *The Logic of Scientific Discovery*. London: Routledge.

Potts, Richard. 1996. *Humanity's Descent: The Consequences of Ecological Instability*. New York: William Morrow.

Potts, Richard. 1998. Variability selection in hominid evolution. *Evolutionary Anthropology* 7(3): 81–96.

Potts, Richard. 2010. *What Does It Mean to Be Human?* New York: National Geographic.

Potts, Richard. 2012. Evolution and environmental change in early human prehistory. *Annual Review of Anthropology* 41: 151–167.

Prins, Gwyn and Steve Rayner. 2007. The Wrong Trousers: Radical Rethinking Climate Policy. Joint Discussion Paper of the James Martin Institute for Science and Civilization, University of Oxford and LSE.

Prins, Gwyn, Malcolm Cook, Christopher Green, Mike Hulme, Atte Korhola, Eija-Ritta Korhola, Roger Pielke, Jr., Steve Rayner, Akihiro Sawa, Daniel Sarewitz, Nico Stehr, and Hans von Storch. 2009. *How to Get Climate Policy Back on Course*. Institute for Science, Innovation and Society, University of Oxford. Online at: http://sciencepolicy.colorado.edu/admin/publication_files/resource-2731-2009.17.pdf. Accessed December 19, 2017.

Puntenney, P. J. 2009. Where managerial and scientific knowledge meet sociocultural systems: local realities, global responsibilities. In *Anthropology and Climate Change*. Susan A. Crate and Mark Nuttall, Eds. Pp. 311–326. Walnut Creek, CA: Left Coast Press.

Rafferty, J. M. and C. M. O'Dwyer. 2010. *The Functional Dynamics of Green Universities*. Melbourne, Australia: National Tertiary Education Union.

Rahman, Ashiqur. 2009. Salt Is Killing Us: Salinity and Livelihood in a Bangladesh Village. Masters thesis, Department of Anthropology, Lund University.

Rahman, Ashiqur. 2010. Local response to global climate change: a case of drinking water in a Bangladesh village. *International Journal of Climate Change* 2(1): 265–275.

Ralston, Holley, Britta Horstmann, and Carina Holl. 2004. *Climate Change Challenges Tuvalu*. Berlin, Germany: Germanwatch.

Randalls, Samuel. 2017. Contributions and perspectives from geography to the study of climate. *Wiley Interdisciplinary Reviews: Climate Change* 8: 1–16.

Rasmussen, Mattias Borg. 2009. Andean meltdown: comments on the "Declaration of Recuay." In *The Question of Resilience: Social Responses to Climate Change*. Kirsten Hastrup, Ed. Pp. 197–217. Copenhagen, Denmark: Det Kongelige Danske Videnskabernes Selskab.

Ray, Celeste. 2002. Cultural paradigms: an anthropological perspective on climate change. In *Global Climate Change*. Sharon L. Spray and Karen L. McGlothin, Eds. Pp. 81–100. Lanham, MD: Rowman & Littlefield.

Rayner, Steve. 1991. A cultural perspective on the structure and implementation of global environmental agreements. *Evaluation Review* 15: 75–102.

Rayner, Steve. 1993a. Introduction. Special issue: *National Case Studies of Institutional Capabilities to Implement Greenhouse Gases. Global Environmental Change* 3(1): 7–11.

Rayner, Steve. 1993b. Prospects for CO_2 emissions reduction policy in the USA. *Global Environmental Change* 3(1): 12–31.

Rayner, Steve. 2007. Creating a climate for change: the influence of Luther Gerlach on the development of critical thinking about climate change. In *Cultural Analysis and the Navigation of Complexity*. Lisa Kaye Brandt, Ed. Pp. 3–20. Lanham, MD: University Press of America.

Rayner, Steve and Elizabeth Malone, Eds. 1998a. *Human Choice and Climate Change: An International Assessment* (4 vols). Columbus, OH: Battelle Press.

Rayner, Steve and Elizabeth Malone. 1998b. Why study human choice and climate change. In *Human Choice and Climate Change, Volume One: The Societal Framework*. Steve Rayner and Elizabeth Malone, Eds. Pp. xiii–xlii. Columbus, OH: Battelle Press.

Redman, Charles L. 1999. *Human Impact on Environments*. Tucson, AZ: University of Arizona Press.

Redman, Charles L., Steven R. James, Paul R. Fish, and J. Daniel Rogers, Eds. 2007. *The Archaeology of Global Change: The Impact of Humans on Their Environment*. Washington, DC: Smithsonian Institution Press.

Redman, Charles, Carol L. Crumley, Fekri A. Hassan, Frank Hole, Joao Morais, Frank Riedel, Vernon L. Scarborough, Joseph A. Tainter, Peter Turchin, and Yoshinori Yasuda. 2007. Group report: millennial perspectives on the dynamic interaction of climate, people, and resources. In *Sustainability or Collapse? An Integrated History and Future of People on Earth*. Robert Costanza, Lisa J. Graumlich, and Will Steffen, Eds. Pp. 115–148. Cambridge, MA: MIT Press.

Rees, Martin. 2003. *Our Final Hour: A Scientist's Warning: How Terror, Error, and Environmental Disaster Threaten Humankind's Future in This Century—on Earth and Beyond*. New York: Basic Books.

Ren, C., G. Williams, K. Mengersen, L. Morawska, and S. Tong. 2008. Does temperature modify short-term effects of ozone on total mortality in 60 large eastern US communities? An assessment using the NMMAPS data. *Environment International* 34: 451–458.

Reuter, Thomas. 2010. Anthropological theory and the alleviation of anthropogenic climate change: understanding the cultural causes of systemic change resistance. World Anthropologies Network. *World Anthropology Network E-Journal* 5. Online at: www.academia.edu/11346248/ Anthropological_Theory_and_the_Alleviation_of_Anthropogenic_Climate_Change_ Understanding_the_Cultural_Causes_of_Systemic_Change_Resistance. Accessed June 12, 2013.

Rhoades, Robert, Xavier Zapata Rios, and Jenny Aragundy Ochoa. 2008. Mama Cotacachi: history, local perceptions, and social impacts of climate change and glacier retreat in Ecuadorian Andes. In *Darkening Peaks: Glacier Retreat, Science, and Society*. Ben Orlove, Ellen Wiegandt, and Brian H. Luckman, Eds. Pp. 216–225. Berkeley, CA: University of California Press.

Robbins, Paul. 2012. *Political Ecology* (2nd edition). Malden, MA: Wiley-Blackwell.

Roberts, J. Timmons and Peter E. Grimes. 1997. Carbon intensity and economic development 1962–91: a brief exploration of the Kunzets curve. *World Development* 25: 191–198.

Roberts, J. Timmons and Peter E. Grimes. 2002. World-system theory and the environment: toward a new synthesis. In *Sociological Theory and the Environment: Classical Foundations, Contemporary Insights*. Riley Dunlap, Fredrick Buttel, Peter Dickens, and August Gijswijt, Eds. Pp. 167–198. Lanham, MD: Rowman & Littlefield.

Roberts, J. Timmons and Bradley C. Parks. 2007. *A Climate of Injustice: Global Inequality, North-South Politics, and Climate Policy*. Cambridge, MA: MIT Press.

Rockström, Johan. 2011. Science's role and responsibility. In *Bankrupting Nature: Denying Our Planetary Boundaries*. Anders Wijkman and Johan Rockström. Pp. 19–35. London: Earthscan.

Rockström, J., W. Steffen, K. Noone, A. Persson, F. Chapin, E. Lambin, T. Lenton, M. Scheffer, C. Folke, H. Schellnhuber, B. Nykvist, C. De Wit, T. Hughes, S. van der Leeuw, H. Rodhe, S. Sörlin, K. Snyder, R. Costanza, M. Svedin, M. Falkenmark, L. Karlberg, R. Corell, V. Fabry, J. Hansen, B. Walker, D. Liverman, K. Richardson, P. Crutzen, and J. Foley. 2009. Planetary boundaries: exploring the safe operating space for humanity. *Ecology and Society* 14(2): 32.

Rojas, David. 2016. Climate politics in the Anthropocene and environmentalism beyond nature and culture in Brazilian Amazonia. *PoLAR: Political and Legal Review* 39(1): 16–32.

Romankiewicz, Clemens and Martin Doevenspeck. 2015. Climate and mobility in Western African Sahel: conceptualizing the local dimensions of the environment and migration nexus. In *Grounding Global Climate Change*. H. Greschke and J. Tischler, Eds. Pp. 79–100. Dordrecht, the Netherlands: Springer Science + Business Media.

Romm, Joseph. 2011. The next Dust Bowl. *Nature* 478: 450–451.

Roncoli, Carla and John Magistro. 2000. Global science, local practice: anthropological dimensions of climate variability. *Practicing Anthropology* 22(4): 2–5.

Roncoli, Carla, Todd Crane, and Ben Orlove. 2009. Fielding climate change in cultural anthropology. In *Anthropology and Climate Change*. Susan A. Crate and Mark Nuttall, Eds. Pp. 87–115. Walnut Creek, CA: Left Coast Press.

Rose, Deborah Bird. 2008. Love in the time of extinctions. *Australian Journal of Anthropology* 19: 81–84.

Rosenzweig, Cynthia, William D. Solecki, Stephen A. Hammer, and Shagun Mehrotra, Eds. 2011. *Climate Change and Cities: First Assessment Report of the Urban Climate Change Research Network*. Cambridge, UK: Cambridge University Press.

Rosewarne, Stuart, James Goodman, and Rebecca Pearse. 2013. *Climate Action Upsurge: The Ethnography of Climate Politics*. London: Routledge.

Rubow, Cecilie. 2009. Metaphysical aspects of resilience: South Pacific responses to climate change. In *The Question of Resilience: Social Responses to Climate Change*. Kirsten Hastrup, Ed. Pp. 88–113. Copenhagen, Denmark: Det Kongelige Danske Videnskabernes Selskab.

Ruddiman, William. 2005. *Plows, Plagues and Petroleum: How Humans Took Control of Climate*. Princeton, NJ: Princeton University Press.

Rudiak-Gould, Peter. 2010. *The Fallen Palm: Climate Change and Culture Change in the Marshall Islands*. Saarbrücken, Germany: VDM Verlag.

Rudiak-Gould, Peter. 2011. Climate change and anthropology: the importance of reception studies. *Anthropology Today* 27(2): 9–12.

Rudiak-Gould, Peter. 2012a. Progress, decline, and the public uptake of climate science. *Public Understanding of Science*, June 5. Online at: http://pus.sagepub.com.ezproxy.lib.uconn.edu/content/early/2012/06/03/0963662512444682.full.pdf+html (login required). Accessed November 18, 2013.

Rudiak-Gould, Peter. 2012b. Promiscuous corroboration and climate change translation: a case study from the Marshall Islands. *Global Environmental Change* 22: 46–64.

Rudiak-Gould, Peter. 2013. *Climate Change and Tradition in a Small Island State: The Rising Tide*. New York: Routledge.

Rylko-Bauer, Barbara, Merrill Singer, and John van Willigin. 2006. Reclaiming applied anthropology: its past, present, and future. *American Anthropologist* 108(1): 178–190.

Salleh, Ariel. 2008. Climate change—and the "other footprint." *Capitalism Nature Socialism* 13: 103–113.

Salleh, Ariel. 2009. Ecological debt: embodied debt. In *Eco-Sufficiency and Global Justice: Women Write Political Ecology*. Ariel Salleh, Ed. Pp. 1–40. London: Pluto Press.

Sandweiss, Daniel H. and Alice R. Kelley. 2012. Archaeological contributions to climate change research: The archaeological record as a paleoclimatic and paleoenvironmental archive. *Annual Review of Anthropology* 41: 371–391.

Sauer, Carl O. 1941. *Climate and Man: Yearbook of Agriculture.* Washington, DC: US Congress—House.

Scarborough, Vernon L. 2007. The rise and fall of the ancient Maya: a case study in political ecology. In *Sustainability or Collapse: An Integrated History and Future of People on Earth.* Robert Costanza, Lisa J. Graumlich, and Will Steffen, Eds. Pp. 51–59. Cambridge, MA: MIT Press.

Schreurs, Miranda A. 2011. Climate change politics in an authoritarian state: the ambivalent case of China. In *Oxford Handbook of Climate Change and Society.* John S. Dryzek, Richard B. Norgaard, and David Schlosberg, Eds. Pp. 449–463. Oxford, UK: Oxford University Press.

Scott, Daniel, Geoff McBoyle, and Alanna Minogue. 2007. Climate change and Quebec's ski industry. *Global Environmental Change* 17: 181–190.

Seager, Richard, Mingfang Ting, Isaac Held, Yochanan Kushnir, Jian Lu, Gabriel Vecchi, Huei-Ping Huang, Nili Harnik, Ants Leetmaa, Ngar-Cheung Lau, Cuihua Li, Jennifer Velez, and Naomi Naik. 2007. Model projections of an imminent transition to a more arid climate in southwestern North America. *Science* 316: 1,181–1,184.

Sejersen, Frank. 2009. Resilience, human agency and climate change adaptation strategies in the Arctic. In *The Question of Resilience: Social Responses to Climate Change.* Kirsten Hastrup, Ed. Pp. 218–243. Copenhagen, Denmark: Det Kongelige Danske Videnskabernes Selskab.

Shea, K., R. Truckner, R. Weber, and D. Peden. 2008. Climate change and allergenic disease. *Journal of Allergy and Clinical Immunology* 122(3): 443–453.

Shearer, Christine. 2011. *Kivalina: A Climate Change Story.* Chicago, IL: Haymarket Books.

Sherpa, Pasang Yangjee. 2015. Institutional climate change adaptation efforts among the Sherpas of the Mount Everest region, Nepal. In *Climate Change, Culture, and Economics: Anthropological Investigations.* Donald C. Wood, Ed. Pp. 3–23. Bingley, UK: Emerald.

Shirrocks, Anthony and Jim Davies. 2013. *Credit Suisse Global Wealth Report 2013.* Online at: http://thenextrecession.files.wordpress.com/2013/10/global-wealth-report.pdf. Accessed November 25, 2013.

Shoreman-Ouimet, Eleanor and Helen Kopnina. 2011. Introduction: environmental anthropology of yesterday and today. In *Environmental Anthropology Today.* Helen Kopnina and Eleanor Shoreman-Ouimet, Eds. Pp. 1–33. London: Routledge.

Shulman, Seth. 2010. Climate fingerprinter: profile: Benjamin Santer, Lawrence Livermore Laboratory. *Union of Concerned Scientists.* Online at: www.ucsusa.org/global_warming/science_and_impacts/science/climate-scientist-benjamin-santer.html. Accessed May 23, 2012.

Sim, Stuart. 2009. *The Carbon Footprint Wars: What Might Happen If We Retreat from Globalization?* Edinburgh, UK: Edinburgh University Press.

Singer, Merrill. 1995. Beyond the ivory tower: critical praxis in medical anthropology. *Medical Anthropology Quarterly* 8(1): 80–106.

Singer, Merrill. 1996. Farewell to adaptationism: unnatural selection and the politics of biology. *Medical Anthropology Quarterly* 10: 496–575.

Singer, Merrill. 2009a. Beyond global warming: interacting ecocrises and the critical anthropology of health. *Anthropology Quarterly* 82(3): 795–820.

Singer, Merrill. 2009b. Interdisciplinarity and collaboration in responding to HIV and AIDS in Africa: anthropological perspectives. *African Journal of AIDS Research* 8(4): 379–387.

Singer, Merrill. 2009c. *Introduction to Syndemics: A Systems Approach to Public and Community Health.* San Francisco, CA: Jossey-Bass.

Singer, Merrill. 2010a. Atmospheric and marine pluralea interactions and species extinction risks. *Journal of Cosmology* 8: 1,832–1,837.

Singer, Merrill. 2010b. Eco-nomics: are the planet-unfriendly features of capitalism barriers to sustainability? *Sustainability* 2(1): 127–144.

Singer, Merrill. 2010c. Ecosyndemics: global warming and the coming plagues of the 21st century. In *Plagues and Epidemics: Infected Spaces Past and Present*. Alan Swedlund and Ann Herring, Eds. Pp. 21–37. London: Berg.

Singer, Merrill. 2011a. Anthropology as a sustainability science. *Anthropology News*, April: 5 and 10.

Singer, Merrill. 2011b. Down cancer alley: the lived experience of health and environmental suffering in Louisiana's chemical corridor. *Medical Anthropology Quarterly* 25: 141–163.

Singer, Merrill. 2013. Respiratory health, sociology, and ecosyndemics in a time of global warming. *Health Sociology Review* 21(1): 98–111.

Singer, Merrill and Hans A. Baer. 2007. *Introducing Medical Anthropology: A Discipline in Action*. Walnut Creek, CA: AltaMira Press.

Singer, Merrill and Hans A. Baer, Eds. 2009. *Killer Commodities: Public Health and the Corporate Production of Harm*. Lanham, MD: AltaMira Press.

Singer, Merrill and G. Derrick Hodge. 2016. Ecobiopolitics in the making of Native American reservation health inequities. In *A Companion to the Anthropology of Environmental Health*. Merrill Singer, Ed. Pp 193–215. San Francisco, CA: Wiley-Blackwell.

Skrydstrup, Martin. 2009. Planetary resilience: codes, climates and cosmoscience in Copenhagen. In *The Question of Resilience: Social Responses to Climate Change*. Kirsten Hastrup, Ed. Pp. 336–359. Copenhagen, Denmark: Det Kongelige Danske Videnskabernes Selskab.

Smit, Barry and Johanna Wandel. 2006. Adaptation, adaptive capacity and vulnerability. *Global Environmental Change* 16: 282–292.

Smith, Philip and Nicolas Howe. 2015. *Climate Change as Social Drama: Global Warming in the Public Sphere*. Cambridge, UK: Cambridge University Press.

Sommer, Larissa. 2011. Pueblo of Jemez: leading the way to a renewable future. Online at: https://tribalclimateguide.uoregon.edu/climate-planning/pueblo-jemez-leading-way-renewable-future. Accessed July 19, 2013.

Sopoanga, Saufatu. 2003. Statement by The Honourable Saufatu Sopoanga OBE Prime Minister and Minister of Foreign Affairs of Tuvalu at the 58th United Nations General Assembly. Online at: www.un.org/webcast/ga/58/statements/tuvaeng030924.htm. Accessed November 15, 2013.

Spencer, Nick. 2006. *Health Consequences of Poverty for Children*. London: End Child Poverty.

Speth, James Gustave. 2008. *The Bridge at the Edge of the World: Capitalism, the Environment, and Crossing from Crisis to Sustainability*. New York: Oxford University Press.

Spratt, David and Philip Sutton. 2008a. *Climate Code Red: The Case for a Sustainability Emergency*. Melbourne, Australia: Friends of the Earth Australia.

Spratt, David and Philip Sutton. 2008b. *Climate Code Red: The Case for Emergency Action*. Melbourne, Australia: Scribe.

St. Peter, Anthony. 2010. *The Greatest Quotations of All-Time*. Bloomington, IN: Xlibris Corporation.

Stanley, David. 2007. *Tuvalu South Pacific Organizer*. Online at: www.southpacific.org/faq/tuv.html. Accessed August 23, 2008.

Stanley, Steven M. 1996. *Children of the Ice Age: How a Global Catastrophe Allowed Human to Evolve*. New York: Harmony Books.

Stern, Nicholas. 2007. *The Economics of Climate Change: The Stern Review*. Cambridge, UK: Cambridge University Press.

Stern, P. R. 2010. *Daily Life of the Inuit*. Santa Barbara, CA: Greenwood.

Steward, Julian. 1955. *Theory of Culture Change: The Methodology of Multilinear Evolution.* Urbana, IL: University of Illinois Press.

Stocker, Laura, Bob Pokrant, David Wood, Nick Harvey, Marcus Haward, Kevin O'Toole, and Tim Smith. 2010. Australian universities, government research and the application of climate knowledge in Australian coastal zone management. In *Universities and Climate Change: Introducing Climate Change to University Programmes.* Watler Fiho, Ed. Pp. 31–45. Hamburg, Germany: Springer.

Stockholm Resilience Centre. 2007. What is resilience? Online at: http://stockholmresilience. org/research/research-news/2015-02-19-what-is-resilience.html. Accessed December 19, 2017.

Stoddart, Mark C. J. and Jillian Smith. 2016. The endangered Arctic, the Arctic as resource frontier: Canadian news media narratives of climate change in the North. *Canadian Review of Sociology/Revue canadienne de sociologie* 53: 316–336.

Stone, Brian, Jr. 2012. *The City and the Coming Climate: Climate Change in the Places Where We Live.* Cambridge, UK: Cambridge University Press.

Strauss, Sarah. 2009. Global models, local risks: responding to climate change in the Swiss Alps. In *Anthropology and Culture Change.* Susan A. Crate and Mark Nuttall, Eds. Pp. 166–174. Walnut Creek, CA: Left Coast Press.

Strauss, Sarah and Ben Orlove, Eds. 2003. *Weather, Climate, Culture.* Oxford, UK: Berg.

Stringer, Chris. 2012. *Lone Survivors: How We Came to Be the Only Humans on Earth.* New York: Henry Holt.

Stuckenberger, A. Nicole. 2009. Anthropologists engaging in climate change education and outreach: creating *Thin Ice: Inuit Traditions within a Changing Environment.* In *Anthropology and Climate Change.* Susan A. Crate and Mark Nuttall, Eds. Pp. 380–393. Walnut Creek, CA: Left Coast Press.

Sutton, Mark Q. and E. N. Anderson. 2004. *Introduction to Cultural Ecology.* Walnut Creek, CA: AltaMira Press.

Szerszynski, Bronislaw and John Urry. 2010. Changing climates: introduction. *Theory, Culture & Society* 27(2–3): 1–8.

Tainter, Joseph A. 1988. *The Collapse of Complex Societies.* Cambridge, UK: Cambridge University Press.

Tainter, Joseph A. 2014. Collapse and sustainability: Rome, the Maya, and the modern world. *Archaeological Papers of the American Anthropological Association* 24: 201–214.

Tainter, Joseph A. and Carole L. Crumley. 2007. Climate, complexity, and problem solving in the Roman Empire. In *Sustainability or Collapse? An Integrated History and Future of People on Earth.* Robert Costanza, Lisa J. Graumlic, and Will Steffen, Eds. Pp. 61–75. Cambridge, MA: MIT Press.

Tattersall, Ian. 2012. *Masters of the Planet: The Search for Our Human Origins.* New York: Palgrave Macmillan.

Taylor, P. 1986. *Respect for Nature.* Princeton, NJ: Princeton University Press.

Thompson, J. Dana. 1980. Summary of the first day's discussion. In *The Atmosphere: Endangered and Endangering.* William W. Kellogg and Margaret Mead, Eds. Pp. 66–73. Tunbridge Wells, UK: Castle House Publications.

Thompson, L., E. Mosley-Thompson, M. Davis, V. Zagorodnov, I. Howat, and V. Mikhalenki. 2013. Annually resolved ice core records of tropical climate variability over the past 1800 years. *Science* 340(6,135): 945–950.

Thompson, William R. 2007. Climate, water, and political-economic crises in ancient Mesopotamia and Egypt. In *The World System and the Earth System: Global Socioenvironmental Change and Sustainability Since the Neolithic.* Alf Hornborg and Carole Crumbley, Eds. Pp. 162–179. Walnut Creek, CA: Left Coast Press.

Tilt, Bryan. 2010. *The Struggle for Sustainability in Rural China*. New York: Columbia University Press.

Tokar, B. 2009. Toward climate justice. *Zeta Magazine*, September. Online at: https://zcomm. org/zmagazine/toward-climate-justice-by-randall-amster/. Accessed October 15, 2012.

Toussaint, Sandy. 2008. Climate change, global warming and too much sorry business. *Australian Journal of Anthropology* 19: 84–88.

Townsend, Patricia K. 2011. The ecology of disease and health. In *A Companion to Medical Anthropology*. Merrill Singer and Pamela I. Erickson, Eds. Pp. 181–195. Malden, MA: Wiley-Blackwell.

Trigger, Brian G. 2006. *A History of Archaeological Thought* (2nd edition). Cambridge, UK: Cambridge University Press.

Trostle, James. 2010. Anthropology is missing: on the World Development Report 2010: Development and Climate Change. *Medical Anthropology* 29: 217–225.

Turner, B. L., Roger Kasperson, Pamela Matson, James McCarthy, Robert Corell, Lindsey Christensen, Noelle Eckley, Jeanne Kasperson, Amy Luers, Marybeth Martello, Colin Polsky, Alexander Pulsipher, and Andrew Schiller. 2003. A framework for vulnerability analysis in sustainability science. *Proceedings of the National Academy of Sciences* 100: 8,074–8,079.

Turner, Graham. 2008. *A Comparison of "The Limits to Growth" with Thirty Years of Reality*. Canberra, Australia: Commonwealth Scientific and Industrial Research Organisation (CSIRO).

Turner, Graham. 2014. *Is Global Collapse Imminent? An Updated Comparison of the Limits to Growth with Historical Data*. MSSI Research Paper No. 4. Melbourne, Australia: Melbourne Sustainable Society Institute, University of Melbourne.

Uekötter, Frank. 2015. You ain't seen nothing yet: a death-defying look at the future of the climate debate. In *Grounding Global Climate Change*. H. Greschke and J. Tischler, Eds. Pp. 175–181. Dordrecht, the Netherlands: Springer Science + Business Media.

Union of Concerned Scientists. 2007. *Smoke, Mirrors and Hot Air: How ExxonMobil Uses Big Tobacco's Tactics to Manufacture Uncertainty on Climate Science*. Cambridge, MA: Union of Concerned Scientists.

United Church of Christ's Committee on Racial Justice. 1987. *Toxic Wastes and Race in the United States*. Online at: http://d3n8a8pro7vhmx.cloudfront.net/unitedchurchofchrist/ legacy_url/13567/toxwrace87.pdf?1418439935. Accessed December 16, 2017.

Urry, John. 2010. Consuming the planet to excess. *Theory, Culture & Society* 27(2–3): 191–212.

Urry, John. 2011. *Climate Change and Society*. London and Malden, MA: Polity Press.

Urry, John. 2013. *Societies beyond Oil: Oil Dregs and Social Futures*. London: Zed Books.

US Department of Energy. 1990. *Energy and Climate Change: Report of the DOE Multi-Laboratory Climate Change Committee*. Chelsea, MI: Lewis Publishers.

Vanderheiden, Steve, Ed. 2008. *Political Theory and Global Climate Change*. Cambridge, MA: MIT Press.

Vanhala, Lisa. 2013. The comparative politics of courts and climate change. *Environmental Politics* 22: 447–474.

Vedwan, N. and R. Rhoades. 2001. Climate change in the Western Himalayas of India: a study of local perception and response. *Climate Research* 9: 109–117.

Venton, Danielle. 2012. Margaret Hiza Redsteer uses Navajo memories to track climate change. *High Country News*, April 4. Online at: www.hcn.org/articles/geologist-margaret-hiza-redsteer-tracks-climate-change-through-navajo-memories. Accessed February 2, 2013.

Vihersalo, Mirja. 2017. Climate citizenship in the European Union: environmental citizenship as an analytical concept. *Environmental Politics* 26: 343–360.

Vogler, John. 2016. *Climate Change in World Politics*. New York: Palgrave Macmillan.

Vossole, Jonas van. 2017. Global climate governance: a legitimation crisis. *Review* 35(1): 1–27.

Wagner, David. 2005. *The Poorhouse: America's Forgotten Institution*. Lanham, MD: Rowman & Littlefield.

Wainwright, Joel. 2012. Climate change, capitalism, and the challenge of transdisciplinarity. In *Geography of Climate Change*. Richard Aspinall, Ed. Pp. 270–278. London: Routledge.

Wallerstein, Immanuel. 2007. The ecology and the economy: what is rational? In *Rethinking Environmental History: World-System History and Global Environmental Change*. Alf Hornborg, J. R. McNeill, and Joan Martinez-Alier, Eds. Pp. 379–389. Lanham, MD: AltaMira Press.

Warren, Kay B. 2006. Perils and promises of engaged anthropology: historical transitions and ethnographic dilemmas. In *Engaged Observer: Anthropology, Advocacy and Activism*. Victoria Sanford and Asale Angel-Ajani, Eds. Pp. 213–220. New Brunswick, NJ: Rutgers University Press.

Watt-Cloutier, Sheila. 2007. Nobel Prize nominee testifies about global warming (testimony before the Inter-American Commission on Human Rights). Online at: http://earthjustice. org/news/press/2007/nobel-prize-nominee-testifies-about-global-warming. Accessed November 15, 2013.

Weller, Robert. 2006. *Discovering Nature: Globalization and Environmental Culture in China and Taiwan*. Cambridge, UK: Cambridge University Press.

Weston, Del. 2014. *The Political Economy of Global Warming: The Terminal Crisis*. London: Routledge.

Whitington, Jerome. 2013a. Fingerprint, bellwether, model event: anticipating climate change futures. *Limn* 3. Online at: http://limn.it/fingerprint-bellwether-model-event-anticipating-climate-change-futures/. Accessed July 10, 2013.

Whitington, Jerome. 2013b. Speculation, quantification, anthropogenesis. *Anthropology News* 54(7). Online at: http://onlinelibrary.wiley.com/doi/10.1111/j.1556-3502.2013.54703. x/. Accessed July 10, 2013.

Whyte, Ian. 2008. *World without End? Environmental Disaster and the Collapse of Empires*. London: I. B. Tauris.

Wijkman, Anders and Johan Rockström. 2011. *Bankrupting Nature: Denying our Planetary Boundaries*. London: Earthscan.

Wilk, Richard. 2009. Consuming ourselves to death: the anthropology of consumer culture and climate change. In *Anthropology and Climate Change*. Susan A. Crate and Mark Nuttall, Eds. Pp. 265–275. Walnut Creek, CA: Left Coast Press.

Wilkinson, Clive. 2008. *Status of Coral Reefs of the World*. Townsville, Australia: Global Coral Reef Monitoring Network.

Willen, Sarah. 2012. Special Issue Introduction: migration, "illegality," and health: mapping embodied vulnerability and debating health-related deservingness. *Social Science and Medicine* 74: 805–811.

Willen, Sarah. 2014. Lightning rods in the local moral economy: debating unauthorized migrants' deservingness in Israel. *International Migration* 53(3): 70–86.

Williams, Michael. 2003. *Deforesting the Earth: From Prehistory to Global Crisis*. Chicago, IL: University of Chicago Press.

Willis, Rebecca. 2017. Taming the climate? Corpus analysis of politicians' speech on climate change. *Environmental Politics* 26: 121–231.

Wisner, Ben, Piers Blaikie, Terry Cannon, and Ian Davis. 2004. *At Risk: Natural Hazards, People's Vulnerability, and Disasters*. London: Routledge.

Wolf, Eric. 1972. Ownership and political ecology. *Anthropological Quarterly* 45(3): 201–205.

Wolf, Eric. 1974. American anthropologists and American society. In *Reinventing Anthropology*. Dell Hymes, Ed. Pp. 251–263. New York: Vintage.

Wolf, Eric. 1982. *Europe and the People without History*. Berkeley, CA: University of California Press.

Wood, Bernard. 2005. *Human Evolution*. New York: Sterling.

World Bank. 2010. *World Development Report 2010: Development and Climate Change*. Washington, DC: World Bank.

Worth, Kenneth. 2010. *Peak Oil and the Second Great Depression (2010–2030): A Survival Guide for Investors and Savers after Peak Oil*. Parker, CO: Outskirts Press.

Wright, Christopher and Daniel Nyberg. 2015. *Climate Change, Capitalism, and Corporations: Processes of Creative Self-Destruction*. Cambridge, UK: Cambridge University Press.

Wright, Erik Olin. 2010. *Envisioning Real Utopias*. London: Verso.

Wright, Jeneva. 2016. Maritime archaeology and climate change: an invitation. *Journal of Maritime Archaeology* 11(3): 255–270.

Yarris, Kristin and Heide Castañeda. 2015. Special issue: discourses of displacement and deservingness: interrogating distinctions between "economic" and "forced" migration. *International Migration* 53(3): 64–69.

Yohe, Gary and Richard Tol. 2002. Indicators for social and economic coping capacity—moving toward a working definition of adaptive capacity. *Global Environmental Change* 12(1): 25–40.

York, Gregory. 2010. On the move in a warming world: the rise of climate refugees. *The Globe and Mail*, December 17. Online at: www.theglobeandmail.com/news/world/on-the-move-in-a-warming-world-the-rise-of-climate-refugees/article564941. Accessed July 13, 2013.

Yurth, Cindy. 2011. Study: tribes most impacted by climate change. *Navajo Times*, August 18. Online at: http://newamericamedia.org/2011/08/study-tribes-most-impacted-by-climate-change.php. Accessed March 30, 2013.

Zehr, Stephen. 2015. The sociology of global climate change. *Wiley Interdisciplinary Reviews: Climate Change* 6: 129–150.

Žižek, Slavoj. 2010. *Living in the Ends of Times*. London: Verso.

Zornick, George. 2011. The Kochs and cancer in a small town. *The Nation*. Online at: https://www.thenation.com/article/kochs-and-cancer-small-town/. Accessed December 16, 2017.

INDEX